The Infinite Retina

Spatial Computing, Augmented Reality, and how
a collision of new technologies are bringing about
the next tech revolution

Irena Cronin

Robert Scoble

BIRMINGHAM - MUMBAI

The Infinite Retina

Producer: Ben Renow-Clarke
Acquisition Editor – Peer Reviews: Suresh Jain
Content Development Editor: Dr. Ian Hough
Technical Editor: Gaurav Gavas
Project Editor: Radhika Atitkar
Proofreader: Safis Editing
Indexer: Dominic Shakeshaft
Presentation Designer: Sandip Tadge

First published: May 2020

Production reference: 1060520

Published by Packt Publishing Ltd.
Livery Place
35 Livery Street
Birmingham B3 2PB, UK.

ISBN 978-1-83882-404-4

www.packt.com

packt.com

Subscribe to our online digital library for full access to over 7,000 books and videos, as well as industry leading tools to help you plan your personal development and advance your career. For more information, please visit our website.

Why subscribe?

- Spend less time learning and more time coding with practical eBooks and Videos from more than 4,000 industry professionals

- Learn better with Skill Plans built especially for you

- Get a free eBook or video every month

- Fully searchable for easy access to vital information

- Copy and paste, print, and bookmark content

Did you know that Packt offers eBook versions of every book published, with PDF and ePub files available? You can upgrade to the eBook version at www.Packt.com and as a print book customer, you are entitled to a discount on the eBook copy. Get in touch with us at customercare@packtpub.com for more details.

At www.Packt.com, you can also read a collection of free technical articles, sign up for a range of free newsletters, and receive exclusive discounts and offers on Packt books and eBooks.

Foreword

When I was young, I told my dad that I'd rather own a computer than a home. Of course, that was back when a 4K Data General Nova cost more than a house in Silicon Valley.

Today, just a few decades later, we all carry a computer that is thousands of times more powerful than the computers of my childhood. Computers used to be huge, but today's tech is getting so small, we can wear them. The $250 Apple AirPods Pros have more compute power inside them than an iPhone 4 and certainly a lot more than that Data General computer that cost tens of thousands of dollars back in the 1970s.

People often ask me what I would engineer if I were starting out today. When I worked at HP we built calculators and huge laser printers. Currently, there's tons of research being done in Spatial Computing, which includes the hardware and software surrounding Robotics, Autonomous Vehicles, Augmented Reality, and Virtual Reality. All of these bring interesting engineering problems that would keep me interested for sure. I see the potential in all of them to bring computing to people in a way that is ubiquitous, more powerful, and far more personal.

Spatial Computing will move computing from something that sits on a desk, or that you hold in your hands, to something you move around with. There, you'll be joined by robots, virtual beings, and assistants. I'm optimistic that Spatial Computing will be used to serve us with a deeper understanding of ourselves, and give us wild new ways to experience the world and new ways to become more productive in businesses and classrooms.

Children soon will have "imagination machines" on their faces. That will be in contrast to the toys I grew up with. One of my favorites was a transistor radio, which had six transistors (a modern phone has billions of transistors, by comparison). That radio brought the world to me. Spatial Computing will open up new worlds to today's kids that simply didn't exist when I was growing up.

To me I'm excited by what the children of today will do with these technologies and hope they remember that life is about happiness. Smiling and laughing is good. Hearing music in new ways is good. Telling new jokes to each other is good. Spatial Computing can do all that and can bring new ways to learn, work together, and travel the world to boot.

What Irena Cronin and Robert Scoble have done in their book *The Infinite Retina* is provide readers with an accessible, useful and entertaining guide to all of the latest advances in Spatial Computing and how this new technology is influencing and priming the way forward for a host of new innovations that will affect how we live our lives, how we go to work, and how we communicate with each other for years to come.

– Steve Wozniak

Contributors

About the authors

Irena Cronin serves as CEO of Infinite Retina, which provides research and business strategy to help companies succeed in Spatial Computing. She was previously CEO of Transformation Group, which advised decision makers on business strategies related to Artificial Intelligence, Augmented and Virtual Reality, Machine Learning, Facial Recognition, Robotics, Autonomous Vehicles, and related disruptive technologies. Previous to this, she worked for several years as an equity research analyst and gained extensive experience of evaluating both public and private companies.

Cronin has a joint MBA/MA from the University of Southern California and an MS in Management and Systems from New York University. She graduated with a BA from the University of Pennsylvania with a major in Economics (summa cum laude). She has near-fluent proficiency in Mandarin, intermediate in Japanese, and beginner in Korean.

Robert Scoble is Chief Strategy Officer at Infinite Retina and works with companies that are implementing Spatial Computing technologies. He is a futurist and technology strategist and the author of three books about technology trends, being the first to report on technologies from autonomous vehicles to Siri. Previous positions include being a strategist at Microsoft, a futurist at Rackspace, and the producer and host of a video show about technology at Fast Company.

About the reviewer

Robert Crasco, futurist, thought leader, influencer, social media manager, and occasional developer and designer. His focus is on Spatial Computing (Virtual Reality, Augmented Reality, Mixed Reality, 360 Video, VR180, Volumetric Capture, and virtual worlds), Artificial Intelligence, Machine Learning, Robotics, 5G and technology's impact on society. He has a background in computer science and marketing and has worked for various tech companies, including AT&T, Ziplink, NewsCorp, and iBasis. He was a contributing author on *Convergence: How The World Will Be Painted With Data*. He has over a decade experience working with virtual worlds. He currently works with technology-focused individuals and brands on social media management, social amplification, social promotion, content curation, and content creation.

Table of Contents

Introduction

We live in a world that is today undergoing, or perhaps by the time you read this, has undergone, a shift due to the novel coronavirus disease, officially called COVID-19. COVID-19 has caused a change in our way of communicating and the way in which we conduct business, albeit, most everyone is still using two-dimensional visual communication apps, such as Zoom, versus three-dimensional visuals at this point and will be for the next few years. Following the outbreak in 2020, schools and universities were shut down for weeks, in some cases months (depending on the location), with classwork expected to be done online. Many venues closed and events were postponed or cancelled, from Disneyland, to conferences and music festivals, to baseball and all other live sports. Governments around the world ordered people to stay home. The world was not prepared for a pandemic like COVID-19.

As we stayed home for weeks, many of us discovered new ways to work, play, educate, entertain, and shop. We also saw new technology become more important, whether it be Artificial Intelligence being used to look at CAT scans, to look for the virus, or to create a vaccine, or new wearable computers used in China and elsewhere to diagnose people with the disease. Plus, having autonomous vehicles or robots preparing our food or delivering it seemed a lot smarter to us all of a sudden.

At home, music artists released performances for Virtual Reality (VR) headsets to keep fans entertained during the weeks when people had to stay home. New virtual events, some of which were being trialled in Virtual Reality, were announced to replace the physical conferences lost for the year. These are early signs of a set of new technologies that promise to deeply transform all of computing. We call this set of new technologies "Spatial Computing."

Spatial Computing – The New Paradigm

Spatial Computing comprises all software and hardware technologies that enable humans, virtual beings, or robots to move through real or virtual worlds, and includes Artificial Intelligence, Computer Vision, Augmented Reality (AR), VR, Sensor Technology, and Automated Vehicles.

Seven industry verticals will see transformational change due to Spatial Computing: Transportation; Technology, Media, and Telecommunications (TMT); Manufacturing; Retail; Healthcare; Finance; and Education.

These changes are what is driving strategy at many tech companies and the spending of billions of dollars of R&D investment. Already, products such as Microsoft's HoloLens AR headset have seen adoption in places from surgery rooms to military battlefields. Devices like this show this new computing paradigm, albeit in a package that's currently a little too bulky and expensive for more than a few of the hardiest early adopters. However, these early devices are what got us to be most excited by a future that will be here soon.

Our first experiences with HoloLens, and other devices like it, showed us such a fantastic world that we can predict that when this new world arrives in full, it will be far more important to human beings than the iPhone was.

We were shown virtual giant monsters crawling on skyscrapers by Metaio years ago near its Munich headquarters. As we stood in the snow, aiming a webcam tethered to a laptop at the building next door, the real building came alive thanks to radical new technology. What we saw at Metaio had a similar effect on Apple's CEO, Tim Cook. Soon, Apple had acquired Metaio and started down a path of developing Augmented Reality and including new sensors in its products, and the capabilities of this are just starting to be explored. Today's phones have cameras, processors, small 3D sensors, and connectivity far better than that early prototype had, and tomorrow's phones and, soon, the glasses we wear will make today's phones seem similarly quaint.

In Israel, we saw new autonomous drones flying over the headquarters of Airobotics. These drones were designed to have no human hands touching them. Robots even changed memory cards and batteries. New Spatial Computing technology enabled both to "see" each other and sense the world around us in new ways. The drones were designed to fly along oil pipelines looking for problems, and others could fly around facilities that needed to be watched. Flying along fences and around parking lots, their Artificial Intelligence could identify things that would present security or other risks. These drones fly day or night and never complain or call in sick.

Focusing on just the technology, though, would have us miss what really is going to happen to the world because of these technologies. Our cities and countryside will reconfigure due to automation in transportation and supply chains as robot tech drives our cars, trucks, and robots rolling down sidewalks delivering products. We'll spend more time in virtual worlds and metaverses. More of our interfaces, whether they are the knobs on our watches, cars, doors, and other devices, will increasingly be virtualized. In fact, many things that used to be physical may be virtualized, including stores and educational lessons from chemistry experiments to dissection labs.

Computing will be everywhere, always listening, always ready to talk back, and once we start wearing Spatial Computing glasses, visual computing will always be there ready to show us visualizations of everything from your new designs to human patterns in stores, on streets, and in factories and offices. Some call this "invisible computing" or "ambient computing," but to us, these systems that use your eyes, voice, hands, and even your body as a "controller" are part of Spatial Computing.

At the same time, all this new computing is joined by radically fast new wireless technology in the form of 5G. The promises of 5G are threefold. First, we'll have more than a gigabit of data if we have the highest bitrates, and even the lowest rates promise to give us more bandwidth than current LTE phones. Second, wireless will soon add almost no latency, which means that as soon as you do something, like throw a football in a virtual game, it'll happen, even if you have many players viewing the football in real time. Third, 5G supports many more devices per tower, which means you will be able to live stream even a Taylor Swift concert with tens of thousands of fans filling a stadium.

When you combine 5G with all the new things under the Spatial Computing umbrella, you get a big bang. All of a sudden, cars can work together, one sending detailed 3D imaging of streets instantly to others behind it. New kinds of virtual games will be possible in the streets, where hundreds of people can play virtual football games in parks and other places. Crazy new virtual shopping malls appear where virtual celebrities show you around, and you can imagine new products directly in a virtual scan of your home and in other places as well.

A range of new capabilities will appear over the next few years in devices you wear over your eyes. There will be very light ones that are optimized for utility, showing you navigation, notifications, reminding you where you have left things, or nagging you to do some exercise or meditation to keep on top of your physical and mental health. There also will be heavier devices that will be more optimized for everything from detailed design or architecture work to entertainment and video game work. We can even imagine owning several different kinds of Spatial Computing devices, along with some smart contact lenses, that will let us go out on a date night without looking like we have any computing devices on at all.

As the 2020s dawn, we have VR devices that cost a few hundred dollars that are great for games and a few other things, like corporate training. On the more expensive side of the scale, we have devices that can be used by car designers, or even as flight simulators to train airline pilots. The expensive ones, though, will soon look as out of date as one of the first cell phones does today. By 2025, the computing inside will shrink to a fraction of the size of today's devices and the screens inside will be much sharper and capable of presenting virtual and augmented worlds to us that far exceed what we can experience today.

It is this next wave of devices that will usher in the paradigm shift in computing and in human living that we are discussing here. Already these changes are benefiting many enterprises, raising productivity. Inside many warehouses, hundreds of thousands of robots scurry about, moving products from trucks to packages. These new warehouses have evolved over the past decade and enable retailers to keep up with floods of new online orders that, back in 2000, were only dreamt of in futuristic books like this one.

The productivity gains will spread to many jobs. At Cleveland Clinic, surgeons are already using similar technology that shows them digital views from ultrasound, CAT scans, and other sensors. Like the warehouse worker who sees a blue line on the floor telling her how to find the product she's looking for, in this case, when a surgeon navigates to the right place to cut out a cancerous tumor, it lights up like a missile guidance system and tells the surgeon they are in the right place.

Other systems help workers "phone a friend" with new remote assistance features. This can help companies that have expensive machinery, or other work forces, including surgeons, architects, and engineers, save money. At some plants, the savings will be substantial. It took us 30 minutes to simply walk across the Boeing floor where it builds airliners. Asking someone for advice virtually might save someone an hour of walking just to come over and see your problem in a plant like that.

New devices let these remote helpers see what you are dealing with, and they can often show you visually what to do. Imagine trying to remove an engine while holding a phone or tablet in your hand. These systems, because they use wearable glasses, can let workers use both of their hands while talking and showing the remote assistant what is happening. The savings in downtime can be extreme. Imagine a problem that is causing a shutdown in a line at Ford. Every minute it is down, Ford loses about $50,000.

Even for salespeople and managers, the cost savings add up. A flight from San Francisco to Los Angeles usually costs about $700, including airfare, hotel, a decent meal, and an Uber/taxi ride or two. Increasingly, these meetings will be replaced by ones held in Virtual Reality. Two headsets are $800. In just a couple of virtual meetings, the headsets pay for themselves. Social VR from Facebook, Spatial, Microsoft, and others are rapidly improving to make these virtual meetings almost as good as physical ones. The time and cost saved will add up to big numbers, and workers will be happier. Workforces will be less likely to pick up viruses from travelers, too, which will also add up to big savings for corporations and reduced risks.

More lives could be saved, too. Mercedes-Benz had an Augmented Reality system built to show first responders how to cut apart a wrecked car. The app showed where fuel and electrical lines were so that firefighters working to free an accident victim wouldn't start a fire or electrocute themselves. This isn't the only example we have of this technology helping first responders, either through better training or by giving them various assistance on scene. One such system helps police gather evidence and then be able to recreate crime scenes for juries that they can virtually walk around.

Here, we've given you a taste of just how much the world is about to get reconfigured because of Spatial Computing technologies. Let's dig into the details of the chapters ahead.

Exploring Technological Change

Spatial Computing's technological change is laid out in *Chapter 1, Prime Directive*. Mobile phones soon will give way to headsets and glasses that bring computing to every surface. What is driving all of this new technology? We have a need for complex technologies to keep us around on this planet longer and in a more satisfied and productive state. What will drive us to build or buy new headsets, sensors, and vehicles, along with the connected systems controlled by Artificial Intelligence? Augmentation is coming, and that can mean a lot of different things, which we will explore.

We look back in *Chapter 2, Four Paradigms and Six Technologies*, at the previous three foundations of personal computing and include the new Spatial Computing paradigm. The six technologies discussed are those that enable Spatial Computing to work: Optics and Displays, Wireless and Communications, Control Mechanisms (Voice and Hands), Sensors and Mapping, Compute Architectures (new kinds of Cloud Computing, for instance), and Artificial Intelligence (Decision Systems).

It all started with the personal computer of the late 1970s. That paradigm shift was followed by graphical user interfaces and networking in the 1980s and the mobile phone and other devices that started arriving in the 1990s, culminating with the iPhone in 2007. Then, we look forward to the next paradigm and why it will be so different and why so many more people will be able to get more out of Spatial Computing than the laptops, desktops, and smartphones that came before.

Human/machine interfaces are radically changing, and we visit the labs that brought us the mouse to understand the differences between how humans interfaced with computers with keyboard and mice to how we'll interface with cloud computing that is hyper-connected by using voice, eyes, hands, and other methods, including even wearing suits with sensors all along our bodies. It's amazing to see how far we've come from the Apple II days, where there were very few graphics, to Spatial Computing where cameras see the real world, decipher it, and decide how to drive a car around in it.

Transformation Is Coming

Because of this new technology, cities and even the countryside will change, autonomous vehicle pioneers tell us in *Chapter 3, Vision One – Transportation Automates*. Soon you will tell your glasses, "Hey, I need a ride," and you'll see your ride arrive. Sounds like Uber or Lyft, right? Look closer, there isn't a driver inside. Now think of the cost and the other advantages of that. Economists see that such a system could be a fraction of the cost, and could do many other things as well: "Hey car, can you go pick up my laundry and then dinner for our family?" The problem with such a world is that it is probable, many tell us, that we'll see much more traffic near cities as we use transportation to do new things, like pick up our laundry. This is why Elon Musk came up with the Boring Company to build tunnels under cities. We show some other solutions pioneers have come up with, including special roads for these vehicles and new kinds of flying vehicles that will whisk commuters into city centers, passing above all that new traffic.

Transportation soon will include more than just cars and trucks, too. Already, lots of companies are experimenting with new kinds of robots that will deliver products much more efficiently and, in a world where viruses are a new threat, without human hands touching them either. We talk with a company that is already rolling out such robots on college campuses and elsewhere.

Autonomous cars might look like they are rolling around the real world, but often they are developed by rolling them around inside a simulation. Simulations are how engineers are able to test out AI systems and come up with new ways to train the AIs. After all, you don't want to wreck 500 cars just to come up with how to handle someone running a red light, do you? If you walk around the simulations built by Nvidia and others, they look like real streets, with real-looking and acting traffic, pedestrians, and even rainwater and puddles after rain. This technology has many new uses other than training robots and autonomous vehicles, though. The technology inside is a radically different form of computing than was used to make Microsoft Windows for the past few decades, too.

Here, new AI systems fuse dozens of sensor and camera readings together and then look for patterns inside. Some of the cars rolling around Silicon Valley and other cities, like Phoenix, Arizona, have more than 20 cameras, along with half a dozen spinning laser sensors that see the world in very high-definition 3D.

Is that a stop sign or a yield sign? Humans are good at that kind of pattern recognition, but computers needed to evolve to do it, and we dig into how these systems work for autonomous cars and what else this kind of technology could be used for—maybe for playing new kinds of games or visiting new kinds of virtual amusement parks where virtual actors interact with you? How will such things be possible? Well, let's start with the huge amount of bandwidth that will soon appear as 5G rolls out and new devices show up on our faces and in our pockets to connect us to these new Spatial Computing systems. Yes, 5G can support these new kinds of games, but it also can tell cars behind you that there's a new hazard in the road that needs to be avoided.

New Vision

Games aren't the only things that better devices will bring. *Chapter 4, Vision Two – Virtual Worlds Appear*, provides details on Technology, Media, and Telecommunications, another of our seven industry verticals to be disrupted. We start out by detailing the different kinds of devices that are available to bring a spectrum of Spatial Computing capabilities to your face, from Virtual and Augmented Reality headsets to lightweight smart information glasses, and even contact lenses with displays so small that it will be very hard to tell that your friend is wearing one.

There are pretty profound trade-offs made as manufacturers bring devices to the market. VR headsets emphasize immersion, or the feeling you get when you see something beautiful wrapped all around you. Augmented Reality headsets focus on the virtual layer that they reveal on top of the real world. Often it's amazing and magical, albeit usually with less of that "I'm in a dark movie theater with a huge screen" feeling. Then there are a few other devices that focus mostly on being lightweight, bringing navigation and notification-style functionality. Our guide isn't designed to be comprehensive, but rather to you to understand the market choices that both businesses and consumers will have to soon make.

While cataloging the device categories, we also show some of the new entertainment capabilities that soon will come, which will be captured with new arrays of volumetric and light-field cameras. We visited several such studios and delivered you into a new entertainment world, one where you can walk around in, and interact with, objects and the virtual beings inside.

These new media and entertainment experiences are arriving with a bundle of novel technologies, from AR Clouds, which contain both 3D scans of the real world and tons of virtual things that could be placed on top, to complete metaverses where users can do everything from build new fun cities to play new kinds of games with their friends. In enterprises, they are already building a form of an AR Cloud, called a "Digital Twin," which is changing a lot about how employees are trained, work together, and manage new kinds of factories.

We have visited the world's top manufacturing plants, and in many of them, we see new kinds of work being done with lots of robots that didn't exist just a few years ago, with workers walking around wearing new devices on their faces helping them learn or perform various jobs. In *Chapter 5, Vision Three – Augmented Manufacturing*, you'll learn about how Spatial Computing is changing how factories are even designed. Increasingly, these factory floors are using robots. The robots are different than they used to be, too. The older ones used to be kept in cages designed to keep humans away. Those can still be found welding, or like in Ford's Detroit factory, putting windshields into trucks. Newer robots work outside cages and sometimes, can even touch humans. These types of robots are called "cobots" because they cohabit with humans and can greatly assist workers.

In the upcoming years, humans will both be trained to work with these new robots using new VR and AR technologies as well as train the robots themselves in new headsets with new user interfaces that let humans virtually control factory floors. As these new Spatial Computing technologies are increasingly used on factory floors, they bring new capabilities, from virtual interfaces to physical machines and new productivity enhancers. For instance, in many of these systems, workers can leave videos, 3D drawings, and other scans, and other notes for workers on the next shift to see. "Hey Joe, the cutting machine is starting to misbehave. I ordered a new motor for it so you can fix it when the line is down at 2 p.m."

Pervasive Change – Shopping, Healthcare, and Finance

The products that Joe makes will eventually be found in retail stores, many of which will be quite different than the ones that Sears ran decades ago. Walk into an Amazon Go store and look at the ceiling. You'll see hundreds of cameras and sensors aimed back at you, watching and categorizing every move you make. In the Go store, they charge you for the products you take without you having to talk to a checkout clerk or pull out a credit card, or really do anything other than walk out of the store. In *Chapter 6, Vision Four – Robot Consumers*, we detail these changes, along with others that make retail stores, even traditional ones, more efficient and better for both consumers and sales for producers, and useful new Augmented Reality technologies that make shopping at home much easier.

As we were finishing up this book, Apple announced a new iPad with a 3D sensor, and it demonstrated why people should buy one of these new iPads by showing off one of these futuristic shop-at-home experiences where the person holding the tablet could drop chairs and other items into their real home to see how they fit. The changes, though, don't stop at the shopping experience. Behind the scenes, these technologies are making things more efficient, helping logistics companies pick and pack products faster and getting them to stores faster and with fewer losses, and we detail how Spatial Computing is making a difference there.

Similar changes are underway in healthcare. They are so profound that Dr. Brennan Spiegel, Director of Health Research at Cedars-Sinai, says that we should expect a new kind of healthcare worker: "The Virtualist." This new kind of practitioner will perform several roles: help patients prevent disease, help doctors deliver a new form of healthcare, and help the nurses, doctors, and other staff perform their jobs more efficiently using new Spatial Computing technology. For instance, let's say you need surgery. Well, a new surgery team at Cleveland Clinic is already using Microsoft HoloLens 2 headsets to see inside you, thanks to images from scanners being visualized inside the surgeon's headgear. We discuss, in *Chapter 7, Vision Five – Virtual Healthcare*, how its system guides the surgeon to the right spot to cut out a patient's cancerous tumor.

That's just a tiny piece of what's happening in healthcare due to Spatial Computing technology. On another wing of the hospital, doctors are using VR to address mental illnesses and ailments from PTSD to dementia, with more applications on the way. At the University of Washington, they discovered it often is much better at treating pain than using opiates, which are much more dangerous, killing tens of thousands of Americans every year due to addiction. In other places, nurses noticed that patients going through tough procedures preceding childbirth felt a lot less pain, too, if they were watching a 360-video experience during the process. Other doctors even found ways to enhance athletes' perception. These brain tricks and virtual remedies have the capacity to significantly change healthcare. Pfizer's head of innovation told us that she views Augmented and Virtual Reality as the future of medicine.

How does all this work? Largely on data. New predictive systems will watch your health by having sensors look into your eyes, watch your vascular system, or blood streams, and sense other things, too, maybe to the point where they see that you are eating too much sugar or smoking too many cigarettes. One could even warn your doctor that you aren't taking your medicine or performing the exercises that she prescribed. Are we ready for new tough conversations with our doctors? Remember, in this future, maybe your doctor is a virtual being from whom you don't mind hearing the harsh truth. One of the studies we found showed that patients actually are much more honest about their mental health problems when talking with a virtual being, or in a chat that's run by Artificial Intelligence.

These AIs won't just be helping us keep our health on track, either. Similar systems might let us know about market changes that we need to pay attention to or, like banks already do when they notice that buying behavior is out of bounds, warn you about other things. The financial industry is generally a relatively conservative one, so adoption of Spatial Computing technologies there is contingent upon demonstrated and clear utility, and they must be additive to the bottom line. Currently, there is very little Spatial Computing that is being actively used there; however, the possibilities are very promising. In *Chapter 8, Vision Six – Virtual Trading and Banking*, we cover the future uses for Spatial Computing in the financial industry.

In this chapter, we review the functional areas where we think Spatial Computing will have its greatest impact, including 3D data visualization, virtual trading, ATM security and facial payment machines, and virtual branch functionality and customer service.

Someday soon, we may never go into a physical bank again due to these changes, but could the same happen with our schools? Already, teachers are using Augmented and Virtual Reality to teach all sorts of lessons, from chemistry experiments to math visualizations, to even virtual dissections of real-looking animals.

New Ways to Learn

COVID-19, though, showed us that sometimes we might need to rely completely on teaching virtually, and in *Chapter 9, Vision Seven – Real-Time Learning*, we talk with educators and others who are using technology aggressively to make learning more virtual. It isn't only for kids, either. Soon, because of automation, we'll need to retrain millions of adults around the world, and schools and universities are responding with new curricula, new learning programs for Virtual and Augmented Reality, and new support systems to enable even truck drivers to change careers. Speaking of careers, already at companies like Caterpillar, it is using Augmented Reality glasses to train workers to fix their expensive tractors in real time. Many new VR-based training systems are being developed, from simulators to help police learn how to deal with terrorist situations to ones that show quarterbacks how to perform better, to training at Walmart that shows retail workers how to manage stores better. Verizon even trained its retail store workers on what to do if they are being robbed using VR-based training. What if, though, the system could do even more, we asked, and predict what we might do next and assist us with that?

How can computers predict our next move? Well, truth be told, we are somewhat predictable. We buy groceries at the same store every week, visit the same gas stations, go to the same churches, schools, offices, movie theaters, laundries, and head home at pretty much the same time every evening.

Watching our friends, we can usually predict what they will order from menus or how they will complain when we try to get them off pattern. Ever try to take someone who prefers steak and potatoes to a sushi restaurant ? Can't we predict that they will have the same preferences tomorrow night? Yes, and so can computer algorithms, but Spatial Computing systems could soon know a lot more about us than even our best friends do, since they could watch every interaction, every product touched, every music song picked, and every movie watched. In *Chapter 10, The Always Predicted World*, we show how that data will be used in each of our seven disruptable industries to serve users in radically new ways.

Meeting the Pioneers

We predict that you will enjoy learning more about the seven people who are pushing Spatial Computing further in *Chapter 11, Spatial Computing World-Makers*. Instead of ratcheting through a list, we'd like to tell you why we picked the people here. One spends time in retail stores the world over and uses technology to help them become not only more profitable, but more customer-centric. Another developed Google's autonomous vehicle technology and has gone on to further build out a huge vision of the future of transportation. You'll meet one leader who, from their perch at Qualcomm, sees literally every new product coming before the rest of us do. Also on the list are a couple of investors, one East Coast, one West, who are pouring resources into entrepreneurs who are bringing us the future of virtual beings, robots and the AI that runs them. Finally, we have a doctor who is pushing the healthcare system forward into a world of Augmented and Virtual Reality and a successful innovator who builds companies that have immersiveness and VR at their core. We picked them out of the thousands that we've studied because they represent a guiding hand that will bring "superpowers" to us all.

Thinking Ahead

With these new superpower-like capabilities come responsibilities that the companies and organizations who create and use Spatial Computing owe to the people who use their technologies. New technologies bring with them new ways of doing things, and the more significant the change, the more unchartered and unknown are the ramifications that occur as a result of their use. In *Chapter 12, How Human?*, we provide a philosophical framework put forth by L.A. Paul of Yale University in her book, *Transformative Experience,* that explains why human beings tend to have cognitive issues with radical new technologies. We then discuss recent issues regarding privacy, security, identity, and ownership, and how they relate to Spatial Computing. Finally, we take up how Spatial Computing technologies can be utilized to bring about human social good.

Starting the Journey

We wrote *The Infinite Retina* for a wide audience of non-technical people, rather than for engineers. By the end of the book, you should understand the technologies, companies, and people who are changing computing from being something you do while sitting and facing a flat computer screen or while holding a phone, to computing that you could move through three-dimensionally. We focus on how Spatial Computing could be used by enterprises and effectively radically change the way human beings learn from information and visuals and understand their world. We very strongly believe that enterprise use of Spatial Computing will lead to massive consumer use, and we are excited to share our learning in this book with you.

Part I

Why Spatial Computing and Why Now?

The Significance of Spatial Computing

1

Prime Directive

A perfect storm of change will arrive during the 2020s. We predict that we will see computing switch from staring into a four-inch piece of glass in our hands to using devices on our face that bring computing to every surface. Along with that, we will see advances such as vehicles moving without humans in them for the first time. A fourth paradigm of the personal computing age is upon us, Spatial Computing, and it is one that truly makes personal computers even more personal.

With the coming of Spatial Computing and its two purest members, Virtual and Augmented Reality, we believe that businesses and human cooperation need to be aimed at one thing: working together to build complex technologies to keep us around on this planet longer and in a more satisfied and productive state, while paying attention to the effects that these technologies have on ourselves and the planet. Spatial Computing in the 2020s will see immense challenges, but great opportunities will be available for brands to use new technologies for combined social good. Just what is it about Spatial Computing that is making human beings crave it?

At stadiums around the world, they are getting ready for it. We visited a place in Las Vegas because of it. Hollywood is getting ready for it. We visited a huge studio in Manhattan Beach, California, to see it. Investors and entrepreneurs are getting ready for it. We visited several in Seattle, New York, Los Angeles, and Silicon Valley. Hospitals, shopping malls, hotels, cities, automotive companies, power companies, banks, and more are investing in it. Tens of billions of dollars are being invested in it by both big and small tech companies.

That "it," which is Spatial Computing, is computing that you, virtual beings, or robots can move around in. It includes all the software and technology needed to move around in a digital 3D world.

That is software and technology associated with AI, including Machine Learning and Natural Language Processing, Computer Vision, Augmented Reality, Virtual Reality, and all other apps that support the creation and maintenance of a digital 3D world. We see great strides that will be made in Spatial Computing uses for many industry verticals, including Technology, Media, and Telecommunications (TMT), Transportation, Manufacturing, Retail, Finance, Healthcare, and Education.

Before we dig into everything that's happening that caused us to write *The Infinite Retina*, let's back up and think about the Prime Directive that is driving billions of dollars in human effort into Spatial Computing. Why do human beings need robots delivering food and building things in factories, and why do we need Spatial Computing devices on our faces so that we can work, entertain ourselves, educate ourselves, and collaborate with each other in new ways?

What is the Prime Directive? Does it have something to do with why humans spend more and more on technology or tools every year? Are any new trends, like our changing understanding of climate change, causing this change? Does culture itself change in a major way because of the Prime Directive?

Photo credit: Robert Scoble. Attendees at the 2019 Game Developers Conference in San Francisco use a Magic Leap Spatial Computing headset.

What Makes Us Human?

Human beings are classified as Homo sapiens, which in Latin means "knowing man." Modern Homo sapiens are believed to have appeared a little over 300,000 years ago. The distinction between Homo sapiens and what came before has to do with the relatively sophisticated use of tools—tools that were used to survive more efficiently and with which humans gained control of their surroundings. Tools were also used by early humans to make art on cave walls and carve statuettes of female fertility goddesses. The tools served as augmenting devices—augmenting humans' chances of survival and also of expression.

With modern humans, this augmentation can take the form of education, which in turn is used to gain knowledge. With knowledge, our chances of survival should be better. In many ways, our Prime Directive is to know how to better survive and how to better express ourselves by willfully creating and using tools for those purposes. It is a dual directive, for it cannot be proven that one gives rise to the other, but rather both are mutually beneficial. And it is for both very practical and expressive reasons that tools have continued to be created from the time of early man to today. An example of a human being's ingenuity that traverses both the practical and the expressive are the iterative inventions of the writing "pen and paper" combination. This combination tool, which goes back millennia, started out with cave walls, some form of patchworked dried grasses, as well as stone, serving as the "paper" and natural dye and sturdy reed, as well as a stone or metal chisel, serving as the "pen." "Pen and paper" has been used to record both business and legal matters, as well as nonfictional and fictional narrative, and poetry, as well as visual art, such as paintings, when the "pen" is conceived as pigments. With the advent of the typewriter, there was even more of a separation between the practical and textually expressive and the visually expressive. A machine, the typewriter, was then replaced by the word processor and then the computer. And here we are these days utilizing our computers and their smaller counterparts—the smartphone. Computers did not only replace typewriters; they are also in the process of causing people to question the continued existence of physical books and newspapers, as well as movie theaters.

Our Prime Directive to know how to better survive and how to better express ourselves now has a new channel—Spatial Computing. With Spatial Computing, the uses of the technologies of Virtual Reality, Augmented Reality, and Artificial Intelligence eclipse those of the computer we know today. In the near future, we will no longer have to use a physical computer to do our work and browse the internet. And we will be able to do so much more with the three-dimensionality of Spatial Computing and speech recognition software. It turns out that our need to better express ourselves appears to include a need to experience a replicated reality.

Replicating of reality in the forms of paintings, fiction, and films, as well as other forms, has existed as long as human beings have had the need to express the conditions of both their individual and social existence in an effort to better understand themselves. Experiencing a replicated reality also turns out to be a very good way to achieve a new skill and to get knowledge in general. Spatial Computing is the next generation of imaging that is able to replicate reality, allowing the movement from two-dimensional imaging to three-dimensional. With three-dimensional imaging, the replication of reality is able to be more closely related to the reality it is trying to represent.

Human beings seem to get satisfaction out of presenting and experiencing narratives that have the appearance of being real. An example of this is a movie. It is difficult to say exactly why we get such pleasure out of viewing a "good" movie. Perhaps it is empathy, but the question still remains why empathizing with movie characters that appear to be real should make us feel good, much less entertained. With Spatial Computing, the visuals are even more true-to-life and we are able to move through them (Virtual Reality) or incorporate and manipulate non-real objects into our real world (Augmented Reality). Artificial Intelligence adds another layer to the existing reality by organizing previously unconnected data into meaningful systems that could then be utilized in Spatial Computing to feed our Prime Directive needs.

Photo credit: Robert Scoble. Here, you can see the slums and other residential buildings as seen from the Four Seasons luxury hotel in Mumbai, India. Billions of people live in similar accommodations around the world and they will experience the world far away soon in Spatial Computing devices.

Drivers and Benefits

The benefits of Spatial Computing play right into our Prime Directive of knowing how to better survive and how to better express ourselves through our creation and use of tools. Our need to have replicated three-dimensional worlds and objects in order to master our understanding and manner of expression is one that could be served by the software and technologies of Augmented Reality, Virtual Reality, and Artificial Intelligence.

Noted investor and Netscape founder Marc Andreessen has told markets he has a contrarian view to Silicon Valley's belief that Augmented Reality represents a better investment than Virtual Reality. He noted that it is a privileged view—that in Silicon Valley, residents have tons of beautiful places within an hour's drive, from beaches to vineyards. Most people in the world, he said, don't have those advantages.

Walk through neighborhoods, even middle-class ones, and you will see millions living in small homes in high rises. Telling them that they will want to wear computing devices while walking through a beautiful area won't be hard. Instead, Andreessen sees a world where people will wear headsets to visit the natural beauty well out of reach somewhere else in the world. Even in the United States, only about 20 percent own a passport, so asking them to visit historic sites in, say, Egypt or Israel, won't be possible for most. We can, instead, take them there with Spatial Computing.

However, unlike Andreessen, we don't view the question of whether Virtual Reality or Augmented Reality will be the "winner" between the two. We see that, by the mid-2020s, our Spatial Computing devices will let you float between putting virtual things on top of, or replacing things, in the real world.

Where we are going with this argument is that the hunger for these devices, services, technologies, and experiences that Spatial Computing affords will probably be far greater among the billions who can't afford a private jet to fly them to a Davos, Switzerland ski vacation, or even afford a Tesla for a weekend jaunt to Napa or Yosemite. That seems to be Andreessen's greater point; that the investment opportunity here is grand because it not only will improve the lives of billions, but may lead to us saving ourselves with new education and new approaches to living, including being able to take courses using Virtual Reality and "travel" to different locations in the world without having to jump on an airplane.

However, an argument could be made that human beings are social—our social natures have aided us greatly in our need to survive and thrive and that Spatial Computing is too isolating. With Spatial Computing, though, we could choose to experience and learn something solo or networked with others.

Spatial Computing on its own can serve as the medium to interface with ideas, locations, processes, people, and AI characters, or as Betaworks' John Borthwick likes to call them, synthetic characters. These synthetic characters will replace the Machine Learning text bots that are currently ubiquitous—in effect, putting a three-dimensional body to the words. The benefit of this is that we will feel like we are engaging with a real being that feeds our social natures.

Along these same lines, entertainment that utilizes Spatial Computing will make it even more true-to-life. Characters in these new kinds of narratives will be more real to us, allowing us to gain even more insights into the human condition. Spatial Computing is a major innovation; the latest in a long line of ideas and inventions aimed at improving the human condition. It makes our lives better, bringing knowledge to us faster and with less expense overall.

Potential Dangers

It could be said that with great knowledge comes great responsibility. There are several associated potential dangers that come with our use of Spatial Computing. Areas we will touch upon here include potential loss of personal control, dilution of the natural, and population segmentation.

In terms of potential loss of personal control, the major one that everyone has at the front of their minds because of Facebook's transgressions is the disappearance of privacy. Especially with Augmented Reality, unauthorized use of data and media by companies or authoritarian use by governments could potentially be a problem. Location and spending data, along with videos made with the knowledge of the viewer and recording speech when headsets/glasses are worn could present another wave of Google Glass-like uproar. However, we do not think this is going to happen since the uses of Augmented Reality have been lauded over the last few years and there also seems to be better advance acceptance of glasses-like headsets due to the public's understanding that privacy issues will be addressed by Augmented Reality hardware and software companies, along with much deeper utilities that today's technology affords. Companies will need to be especially clear as to what their data policies are and have appropriate opt-in policies to meet the expectations of the public. There is so much reward that could be received by providing data for Augmented Reality purposes—these rewards should be heralded while understanding that there are those that would prefer to not share their data.

Another potential loss of personal control is one of over-advertising. As Keiichi Matsuda's 2016 six-minute nightmare concept film "Hyper-Reality" portrayed, a world where Augmented Reality advertising is constantly overlaid over the real world is one that is unbearable.

Having an opt-in system should solve this, but it might still be an issue when there is a willful exchange of some kind of visual goods with advertising. Companies will probably push the advertising threshold with potential consumers to see how far they can go in this case.

Talking about extremes, this brings up the point of addiction that has come so naturally with the advent of the smartphone. And as with any other kind of addiction, it is certainly the case that personal loss comes attached with it. There are many cases of people who have died while taking selfies while in the throes of being distracted by their digital addictions. There is the possibility that a person walking around in a future blockbuster Augmented Reality game will walk into traffic or even off a cliff, so technical safeguards based in Computer Vision will definitely have to be built-in as an alert device.

Along with this kind of addiction comes dilution of the significance of the natural objects and environments of the world as they appear in reality. This is relevant with regard to both Augmented and Virtual Reality. Dystopian visions on this abound, ranging from people never wanting to be in the real world again, to the death of learning, to the abandonment of care about pollution and global warming. In Virtual Reality, a person could potentially hurt and even kill a digital character without having the full effect of what these actions would be like in real life. A worry might be that these actions via Augmented and Virtual Reality could become so common stance that the line between the imaginary and the real could become blurred to the extent that real people would then get hurt and killed. Industry oversight organizations might spring up to create ratings of Spatial Computing experiences that would rate the level of violent content so that viewings these experiences could be better managed and controlled. In this way, possible negative societal effects could be mitigated.

On the other side of this, the benefits of Spatial Computing will not be able to be shared by everyone on the planet due to economic reasons. Even in relatively well-off countries, there will be segments of the population that will not be able to afford Spatial Computing headsets or glasses. The result of this is that there will be great inequality with regard to information and productivity between the two groups. We believe that both laptop and desk computers, as well as tablets and phones, will be replaced by Spatial Computing headsets or glasses. Without Spatial Computing devices, both work and entertainment could prove to be difficult. Over time, we believe that the cost of Spatial Computing devices will come down due to technical efficiencies and product commoditization, so that much more of the world's population will be able to afford them.

There are many uses for Spatial Computing devices, which is a main theme of this book. We will now provide a backdrop for understanding why Spatial Computing will have the impact on the world we believe it will.

Understanding the Natural World

Sometimes, the storm of change comes as a real storm. Visit Half Moon Bay, California, which is a sleepy coast-side town near San Francisco and Silicon Valley, and you'll probably meet "Farmer John." That's John Muller, and he moved there in 1947 to open a small family-run farm that is still operating, mostly growing pumpkins. We met him a while back and he told us that when he started his farm, he had to guess the weather, mostly by "feel." Today, he told us his son relies on satellite imagery and AI models to know what tomorrow's weather will hold, rather than holding his finger to the wind and trying to guess if a storm is on the way. By knowing the weather, he can better hire people to plant or harvest, and that knowledge saves his family many dollars. Knowing a storm is coming a few days in advance can save much. Knowing that a heavy rainstorm that might flood fields is coming can save millions in seed cost, particularly in places like Kansas. Knowing a tornado will soon hit a neighborhood can save many lives.

Soon, Farmer John's family will be warned of changing weather with Augmented Reality glasses, and they will be able to see storms in 3D instead of watching Twitter accounts like many farmers around the world do today (we built a Twitter feed composed of meteorologists and scientists to watch our changing climate better at https://twitter.com/Scobleizer/lists/climate-and-weather1). The government and others have spent billions on this infrastructure. It is hardly the only expenditure humans have made to understand our changing environment.

In 2003, we had a discussion with Bill Hill, who was a computer scientist at Microsoft. He invented the font smoothing technology that we use on all of our devices now, and he told us how he invented the technique. He had an interest in animals, thanks to reading tons of books when he grew up in poverty in Scotland and learned to track them through forests and meadows by looking at their footprints, or other signals. While doing that, he realized that humans evolved over millions of years to do exactly what he was doing as a hobby. Those who survived had deep visual skills and generally could see tons of patterns, especially in the green grass or trees that our ancestors lived in. If you didn't, you were attacked and eaten by an animal who was camouflaged in those trees. So, those who couldn't see patterns, especially in the green foliage around us, had their DNA taken out of the gene pool. He used that knowledge to figure out that he could hide visual information in red color fringes that surround each letter on your screen. Get out a magnifying glass and look at fonts on Microsoft Windows and you'll see his work.

Today, we no longer need to worry about a lion hiding in the grass waiting to eat us, but we have new challenges that continue to push us toward developing new tools that can help us continue this great human experiment that we are all in.

The lions of today might be those in the capital markets that are pushing our companies to be more profitable. Or they might be a disability that is slowing down our ability to be our best. We think that's all important, but what did our ancestors do after they survived the day walking in the jungle trying to find food to feed their families? They gathered around fires to tell stories to each other after a day of hunting and gathering. We can see some of those stories even today as drawings on cave walls, where drawings show brave hunters facing down animals and dealing with the challenges of crossing mountains and streams. Today, we don't need to hunt to eat, but there are those who still want to do these things as sport, and what they are doing with technology demonstrates we are under a Prime Directive to build better tools and experiences, even to do something humans have done for many generations.

Let's look at another example of how people are utilizing technology in order to better understand their environment and augment their experiences. Vail Colorado resident Ryan Thousand, `https://www.linkedin.com/in/ryanthousand/`, is an IT administrator for a healthcare company, Vail Health. During the day and many evenings after work or on weekends, he is a passionate fly fisherman who loves catching fish, not to eat, but to capture for his Instagram channel to brag to his friends, before he releases them back into the stream for others to experience the same joy. He saw a need to track what kind of lures he was using as stream conditions changed, so now he's building 3D models of the streams he's fishing in. While wading in the water, he wears smart boots that measure water flow, temperature, and can capture other things. The data he is capturing using those and other tools is then captured on his phone and streamed to a database he's building, and also to the government, who is using the data from sportspeople to track environmental ecosystems.

His early attempts to build useful tools for fly fishermen brought him to Oakley's ski goggles, which had a tiny little monitor built into them. He is seeing a world, coming soon, where he can move away from having to view data through a tiny little monitor that gets in the way of the real beauty he is usually surrounded by, and instead transition to wearing a headset like Microsoft's HoloLens while fishing so that he can capture stream conditions on top of the actual stream. Soon, he sees, people will be wearing a set of Spatial Computing glasses, which will include a virtual guide that will not just show you potential fishing spots in rivers and lakes before you go on a fishing vacation, but will then help you learn how to properly cast a fly, and even tell you where to stand in the stream to have the best chance of catching a fish. Thousand's Prime Directive is to make fishing better and to help everyone who visits Vail learn more about the environment, which will help them save it for many future generations.

The changes, he told us, could change all human activity, even one as familiar as grabbing a fishing rod for a day of relaxation in a stream. That's due, in part, to things like new 3D sensors and new optics that will let us augment the real world with new kinds of digital displays.

Faster Wireless Leads to New Affordances

Watching hockey after the Spatial Computing storm hits will never be the same. John Bollen, https://www.linkedin.com/in/johnbollen/, seems to have a different Prime Directive. Not one of catching fish, but one of catching fans.

He is putting the finishing touches on the 5G infrastructure inside Las Vegas' T-Mobile Arena and has built hotel infrastructure for a few of Vegas' most modern hotels. If you check into a room at the Aria resort, you will see his work when you turn on the IoT-run lights in your room, but now he has a bigger project: to augment an entire stadium. He told us of 5G's advantages: more than a gigabit per second of bandwidth, which is about 200xLTE ("Long-Term Evolution" wireless broadband communication for mobile devices) with very little relative latency, about two milliseconds from your phone to an antenna, and that a stadium full of people holding phones or wearing glasses will be able to use to connect. That is what many of the first users of 5G are experiencing. The theoretical limits are far higher. If you've been in a packed stadium and weren't able to even send a text, you'll know what a big deal that is.

He is excited by this last advantage of 5G: that visitors to the stadium he's outfitting with 5G antennas will be able to all use their devices at the same time.

T-Mobile and other mobile carriers want to use Las Vegas to show off the advantages of using 5G. They have hired him and his team to hang those antennas and lace fiber optic cables above the hallways in the stadium. He dreams of a world where hockey fans will use Spatial Computing to see hockey in a whole new way: one where you can see the stats streaming off of your favorite player skating across the rink.

He also sees the cost advantages of augmenting concerts. To make the fan experience amazing, the teams he's working with often have to hang huge expensive screens. He dreams of a day when he can deliver virtual screens all over the concert venue without renting as many expensive, large, and heavy screens and paying crews to hang them in different configurations. That dream will take most of the 2020s to realize because he has to wait for enough fans to wear glasses to make that possible, but his short-term plans are no less ambitious.

Photo credit: Robert Scoble. John Bollen, left, gives a tour of the 5G infrastructure at Las Vegas' T-Mobile Arena to healthcare executives.

Soon, you will hold your phone in the air to see Augmented Reality holograms dance and perform along with the real performers on stage. Or, maybe they won't be real at all. In China, thousands of people have already attended concerts of holograms that were computer generated, singing and dancing and entertaining stadiums. He knows humans are changing their ideas of what entertainment itself is, and he and his new stadium are ready. There are new stories to be made. New stories that will put us in the game, or on stage at a concert.

What really is going on here is that soon, everyone in the stadium will be streaming data up to massive new clouds, particularly hockey players, who will be captured by new cameras that capture the game in volumetric detail, and the players will be wearing sensor packages that show coaches and fans all sorts in terms of biometric data, such as their current speed, and more. This Spatial Computing data will change not just hockey games, but will change how we run our businesses, how we shop for new things, and the games we play with each other.

Data, Data, Data Everywhere

Data clouds and data floods are coming to our factories and businesses, thanks in part to the 5G infrastructure that's being built. This will bring a storm of change and a need to see patterns in that data in a whole new way.

A few years ago, we visited the new Jameson Distillery near Cork, Ireland. At one point, we asked the chief engineer, who was proudly showing us around its new building and machines that makes the whiskey, "How many sensors are in this factory?"

"So many I don't even know the number." That was more than five years ago. Today, some warehouses and factories have tens of thousands of robots and hundreds of thousands of sensors. You won't find anything useful in the data that's streaming off by using Microsoft Excel; there's just too much data to look through grids of numbers.

Los Angeles-based Suzie Borders has a better idea. Turn those millions of numbers streaming off of sensors into something that humans can better make sense of; for example, a simple virtual light on top of a factory machine. She showed us what she meant by putting us inside various devices, including a Magic Leap Spatial Computing headset and a variety of Virtual Reality headsets, where she walked us around datasets. Datasets that don't look like datasets at all! They are more like a new kind of virtual interface to data that you can grab and manipulate.

Photo Credit: Robert Scoble. Suzie Borders, CEO/Founder of BadVR, sports her Magic Leap while showing us around a virtualized factory floor. Oh, while we were having Tea in San Francisco.

After getting a demo of a bunch of different ways to look at different businesses and different data (the data streaming off of a sensor is quite different and needs to be seen by humans differently, than, say, the transaction data coming off of its bank accounts or point of sale machines), we came away believing that an entirely new way of working will soon arrive: one that will demand using new kinds of Spatial Computing devices.

Yes, people will resist wearing glasses, but those who dive in will find they get the raises and kudos for seeing new ways to make companies more effective and efficient, and we are betting a lot of those new jobs will be using Suzie's software.

The upgrade from 2D technologies to Spatial Computing's 3D technologies has its roots in the analog to digital transformation that happened prior. It is important to understand some of the impetus behind the prior change and what significance it has for our shift.

The Impulse to Capture, Understand, and Share

Paradigm shifts, which come in storms of new technologies, maim big companies and create new stars. The iPhone marginalized both Eastman Kodak and Nokia. Both companies were dominant at one point, but new technology created new stars. The same will happen in the Spatial Computing decade, which is just beginning. The storm will be violent and swift but to understand why this is so, we need to go back to that earlier time.

Ansel Adams first visited Yosemite in 1916 when he was 12 years old, carrying a new camera he had been given as a gift. He was so stricken by the beauty he saw everywhere that he tried to capture it, with the intent of sharing it with friends and family back home. He was frustrated, his son Michael told us, that his photos didn't properly capture anything close to what he experienced in real life, and that drove him to spend the rest of his life trying to find ways to improve photography so that his photos would more closely match what he experienced.

That act has been followed by millions of visitors each year who stand in the spots where he captured Half Dome or El Capitan, but it is by visiting Adams' home in Carmel, California that you see the ties between photography of the past and where we are going next. In that home, you see the photography of the past. His darkroom still holds his dodging tools, enlarger, and the bottles of chemicals Adams used to develop, stop, and fix the silver halides that we all see in Adams' photography today. That was hardly the only technology Adams used in making his photographs, but it gives insight into Adams' creative process, which has been studied by many photographers even today.

In fact, that same creative process has been trained into many cameras' metering systems and, now, in modern phones from Huawei and Apple, has been taken further thanks to Computer Vision systems that make photos sharper, better exposed, and more colorful.

Photo credit: Robert Scoble. Michael Adams, Ansel Adams son, shows us Yosemite Valley and tells us how, and where, his dad took famous photos, with him in tow.

What we also learned is that Adams created much of Kodak's advertising, by using a tripod he invented that enabled him to take "wrap around" photography by shooting several images one next to the other. A phone's panoramic mode basically does the same thing, without needing a tripod with notches in it to properly align the images. A computer in your phone now does the work that Ansel used to do. What would Adams think about digital photography and the hordes of people taking photos on phones and other devices? Or AIs that "improve" photography by searching large databases and replacing things, like blurry overexposed moons with great-looking properly exposed ones, something that Huawei's latest phones do? Adams' son says that if Ansel were alive today, he would be right there along with other innovators: pushing the technology of photography even harder in an attempt to get closer to the natural world.

Why? He, and many environmentalists such as John Muir, played key roles in protecting Yosemite as a National Park, as well as getting many to visit the park through their work. Their idea was that if they could just show people the natural world better, they would be able to get people to travel to see it. If they could travel to see it, they might change their attitudes toward nature and change their polluting ways. This point of view is more needed today now that we can see man's impact on Earth is far deeper and more dangerous to our long-term survival than even Adams could see 100 years ago.

Who fills Ansel's shoes today? Or who will need new forms of images the way Kodak did to hang in Penn Station, New York, like it did with Ansel's photos? People like Ross Finman. He runs an Augmented Reality lab in San Francisco, California, for Niantic, the company who built Pokémon Go. We can see a world where games built on Niantic's platforms will change our behavior quite deeply. We saw thousands of people running across New York's Central Park just to catch a coveted rare Pokémon. This is a new behavior-change platform, and Finman and his team are the ones building the technology underneath it. Isn't behavior change what advertisers are paying for? Niantic's platforms understand the world better than most and were started by the team behind Google Earth, so they've been at this for quite some time.

His dad, Paul, and mom, Lorna, met at Stanford University where they both got PhDs. His was in electrical engineering, hers was in physics. Both are passionate about science and share a sizeable warehouse where Paul continues to develop new technologies. We visited this lab because it is where Ross developed his love of robotics (he later went onto Carnegie Mellon to study that very subject, and afterward started a company, Escher Reality, which was sold to Niantic. More on that in a bit). The first Niantic game to see his work was "Harry Potter: Wizards Unite," which shipped last year.

Outside of the lab in a huge field is an autonomous tractor moving around showing us that this isn't your ordinary Idaho farmer. This field is where Ross first developed his SLAM algorithms, which we now call the AR Cloud, and are the basis for how Augmented Reality works (and how that tractor navigates around the field). SLAM stands for "Simultaneous Location and Mapping" and builds a 3D map of the field, which a computer then can navigate around.

Augmented Reality glasses and Autonomous Vehicles, along with other robots, and virtual beings, all use SLAM to "see."

Photo credit: Robert Scoble. An autonomous tractor rolls around in a field surrounding Paul Finman's lab in Ceour d'Alene, Idaho. This field is where Ross Finman did his work building the Augmented Reality technology now being used in Niantic's Harry Potter game.

The SLAM/AR Cloud system that Finman is developing isn't directly connected to Ansel Adams' form of chemical-based photography, but there is a tie to both Adams' impulse to capture and share and Finman's. Ansel's work was analog. Finman's work is digital. Unlike earlier digital photographers, Finman's system captures the real world as a 3D copy instead of a 2D grid, which was closer to what Ansel did. Finman is the Ansel Adams of this new polygon-based age. His work will let us be in the photograph. Unlike Adams, though, we can use that data to train AIs that will keep us, or at least something that looks, moves, and sounds like us, around—potentially forever.

This process of understanding the real world, converting it into digital information, and then processing it into a form that can be transmitted and displayed (developers call it a mesh) is the basis of everything you will read about in this book.

Understanding the gap between the real world (we think of it as the analog world, because the photons, that is, light, that hits our eyes from, say, a sunset, or the audio that hits our ears, arrive as a smooth wave) and the digital one, which is quantized into streams of numbers, is key.

This is very different from the digital world that underpins Spatial Computing, which has been sliced and diced into polygons or quantized into streams of numbers playing on Spotify. You see it when you see virtual beings, like avatars, and there isn't enough resolution to properly "fool" your mind. The industry calls this "the uncanny valley" for the difference between our emotional response to seeing, say, a real human singer, and an artificial one.

Finman studies this uncanny valley, and in his work at Niantic he is working to more completely understand the real world, build systems that have deeper situational awareness, and then close the gap between how we sense the real world and how we perceive, and emotionally respond to, this new, digital, world.

The impulse, that Finman has to capture, understand, and share the world using new technology, is the same that Adams had with his camera, and that is what ties both of them into our prime directive to become better human beings.

Soon, Finman will bring us powers to capture, understand, and share our world that Adams probably would never have fathomed. Our children will be able to jump into family dinner, either remotely, or in the future go back in time to experience what it was like to have their mom serve them dinner. A new way of remembering your life and everything in it is on the way with Spatial Computing.

Soon, too, will analog experiences be relegated to special places like racetracks or rare vacations to beautiful places. Both things that increasingly you'll need to be wealthy to experience. The storm of change is about to see everything turn digital and that has deep implications for games, entertainment, and how we capture, understand, or share our own lives with others. Soon, we will be interacting with this virtual world, and the innovation teams are already gaining new skills to build new interfaces with this new world.

We won't be surprised if, in a few decades, Finman and other innovators like him are celebrated the way we celebrate Adams today as a true pioneer that pushed technology to its ultimate edge. We also won't be shocked if a few huge companies or product lines disappear over the next decade.

To understand more of the gap between this polygon-based digital age and the analog age of media that is coming to a close, we need to visit Neil Young's studio. He invited us in to listen to some of his music on a two-inch analog tape. He wanted to show us what we lost when we moved music from analog tape and vinyl records to listening on Spotify on our phones.

His audio engineer, John Nowland, played us "Harvest Moon" on that analog tape, and then we listened to it in digital form after that analog master was turned into slices. 600,000 of them a second, which is about 12x more than you will hear on a CD. So, pretty high resolution.

We could still hear a difference. "The closer you were to the analog, the more natural it felt," Nowland told us. "You lose the nuances and detail when you squash it down." That interview is at `https://youtu.be/Ta-RvERB6Ac`.

Photo credit: Rocky Barbanica. Robert Scoble meets with Neil Young's audio engineer, John Nowland, and listens to music in both analog and digital formats.

Dancing Into Different Worlds

The storm of change will mean that the nerds who used to build the computer software of old, by typing thousands of lines of code into a black box on a flat screen, might need to learn to dance.

Yeah, if you watch someone play in Virtual Reality you might think they are dancing, but that isn't what we are thinking about. There's a new type of computer science underway: one that uses choreography to train the AIs that control autonomous cars, robots, virtual beings, and even present humans in Augmented and Virtual Reality with interfaces that better serve us.

Machines can be cold. In the worst of cases, they can crush us on factory floors, or kill us in the streets, like a computer-controlled car developed by Uber did one unfortunate night in Arizona. In the best of cases, they can give us superpowers and make our lives easier, but even then they often can be made to better serve humans in a dance, of kinds.

Did you know there is an entire conference for research on these new ways of training machines called "Choreographic Interfaces?" We didn't either, until we were introduced to Catie Cuan, who is currently studying for a PhD at Stanford University on the topic. As she showed us around Stanford University's AI and robotics labs, where she is working on her studies, we discussed how innovation teams will soon be changed by her, and other people who are using techniques that humans use in dance choreography to train computers.

Photo credit: Robert Scoble. Catie Cuan, Stanford AI student, tells us about using dance choreography to train robots in the lobby of the Bill Gates building at Stanford University, which is the building where Google started.

What makes her unique among most of the computer scientists we've met? She's a former dancer. "Dance and choreography is all about moving with intention," she says, as pointing out that she spent more than two decades dancing and that she uses the knowledge she gained by studying how human bodies could be made to move in different ways, and then translates that training and knowledge to teaching robots and virtual beings to move.

Cuan is working for automobile companies who are developing autonomous cars, among others, as part of her studies (she did some of her schooling at the University of Illinois, which is where Tesla and PayPal started, among others). She told us that humans go through an intricate dance of sorts as they wave each other through intersections, for instance, and cars without human drivers can't communicate with humans on the street or in other cars that way, so they need to be trained both how to recognize human gestures, say, like a police officer standing in the middle of an intersection directing traffic, and communicate with humans their intention to move or stop, but do so in a pleasant, human way.

Now, as computing will be everywhere, we need new interfaces. Ones that respect us, understand us, warn us properly, all in a very human way. Building these new interfaces requires new kinds of innovation teams with, even, a dancer or two to help out. Why? Well, she says that she sees an optimistic future for human/ machine interactions, and what better way to make the machines more fun and engaging to be around? As this storm of change comes, though, it may frustrate many people who want things to stay the way they are, or who can't wrap their heads around the fact that they need to work with someone doing choreographic work. Many pioneers face similar resistance in their careers. We suggest that if you are feeling yourself resisting this change, you might need to be the one to change lest you, or your company, be left behind.

The Frustrated Pioneer

Doug Engelbart had a frustrated spirit when we first talked with him in 2005. If you search YouTube for "mother of all demos," you'll find the video of him demoing something that looked like the Macintosh. He guided a mouse cursor across the screen and showed off many new computing concepts that would dramatically change how we would view and use computing. The official title was "A research center for augmenting human intellect." Way back in 1968. Almost 20 years later, the Macintosh was born from many of the ideas he demonstrated in that demo. He later went on to win many awards and accolades, but he was particularly proud of the National Medal of Technology, United States' highest technology award, yet here, he was sharing his frustration that he wouldn't be around to help humans see what he told us would be his most important work: augmenting human beings. In other words, giving them the tools to make themselves better.

"Why are you frustrated?" we asked him. That led to a discussion of how Engelbart was kicked out of his own research lab back in the 1970s (which is the same lab, SRI International, then named Stanford Research Institute). This is the lab that brought us Siri, HDTV, and played key roles in many, many other things, including the internet itself). Some of his coworkers say that he was too focused on the future and not on getting revenue for the lab, but Engelbart answered "people don't understand what I'm saying." He explained that he was dreaming of a better future, where humans and machines would join together. In one trip, he pulled out a glove that would let people touch and type faster than on keyboards.

Photo credit: Robert Scoble. Robert Scoble's son, Patrick, talks with Douglas Engelbart and plays with the original mouse.

When asked why they didn't understand, he answered that for that, you have to go back to the context of the day. Back in the 1970s, before personal computers came along, computers were run by either data entry clerks or by PhDs and other highly trained people who wrote the code that ran them. When he told his coworkers and others that someday we'd have a supercomputer in our hands, he was laughed off as a crackpot.

He had always dreamed of a world decades away and talked with us about how computers would soon lead to different realities. As the inventor of the original mouse, he was always looking for ways for humans to use computers better than typing on a keyboard or stacking piles of punch cards into trays, which is what most computer users back in the 1960s were doing. Today, we all use the progeny of his work, and this pioneering spirit of dreaming of a better world, where humans would have better control of the technology they invented, continues to drive us to new and greater innovations.

His idea was that computing could go beyond merely performing calculations, and that it could be used to augment the capabilities of the human mind. Why was he frustrated? Because even as he was in the final phases of his life, he could see a world where people would see or sense computing all around them and be able to touch it, maybe with gloves, but hopefully, he told us, with sensors that could see the human hands, eyes, and maybe someday into their minds.

These are ideas that even today aren't largely used or popular. Virtual Reality has only sold a few million headsets at the time of writing this book. Most humans haven't had even an hour in one of those, and here this man is telling us about a world he saw way past Virtual Reality to one where computing was on every surface and where you could use your hands, eyes, voice, to control it! His thinking on this topic led him to develop what came to be known as Engelbart's Law: that computing was increasing at an exponential rate, so we would be able to exponentially increase our performance as well. We are seeing this become one of the key drivers behind the development of the technology we see about to disrupt seven industries, and probably more.

He saw a world where we would soon have technical capabilities beyond the imaginations of most people; for instance, cars that could drive themselves, or systems that would let us see a new digital layer making our understanding of the world far better than before. His ideas of augmenting human performance through technology changed all of our lives, and soon will bring us both new powers and a new understanding of what it means to be human, but to do that, he needed to wait for our machines to get new senses. We wonder if even Engelbart himself, though he usually was decades ahead of others in his thinking, could have imagined the 3D sensors that are now in our phones and cars. Could he imagine the databases and cultural changes that they are now bringing? Knowing how he thinks, he might resist some things for a few microseconds but then he'd smile, lose his frustration, and see that someone else is pushing the world toward his ideas. Let's meet one of these people now.

Breakthroughs in Sensors

David Hall had a building to fill. In the 1980s, the company he started, Velodyne, built subwoofers. Back in the day, they were the best subwoofers because they were the first to be digitally controlled. Audio fans lined up to get one, since they made your audio system dramatically better. But by around 2000, he realized that China had taken over manufacturing, so he sent his production to China since he couldn't get parts anymore to build them within the United States, as he told us in an interview here: `https://youtu.be/2SPnovjRSVM`.

Photo credit: Rocky Barbanica. Velodyne founder/CEO, David Hall, shows off his LIDARs and talks about his career as an inventor of everything from new kinds of subwoofers to self-leveling boats.

That left him with an empty building, so he started looking for new things to do. He heard of the DARPA Grand Challenge, a prize competition for American autonomous vehicles, funded by the Defense Advanced Research Projects Agency (DARPA), a prominent research organization of the US Department of Defense, and readied a vehicle to enter to attempt to win the $1 million prize. The military wanted to spur development of autonomous vehicles. Hall soon realized he didn't have the software engineers needed to win, because he was against teams of university students from schools like Stanford and Carnegie Mellon, but that showed him a new market: making sensors for the other teams. He had the engineers and production ability, thanks to his empty building, to do that, and so he started building LIDARs.

LIDAR, which stands for Light Detection and Ranging, is the spinning thing you see on top of autonomous cars often seen driving around San Francisco or Silicon Valley. Most of them are from Velodyne. Google's early cars used his LIDARs, which spun dozens of lasers many times a second. The cars used that data to build a 3D model of the world around the car. "If they have a spinning one, that's mine," he told us.

Invisible light from his spinning device bounces off the road, signs, other vehicles, and the rest of the world, or in the case of his boat, waves in the ocean. A computer inside measures how fast the light returns to the sensor and makes the 3D model of the world. Without these sensors, the car or robot can't see, so it can't navigate around the world. His new technology plays an important role in Spatial Computing because it gave computer scientists new data to train new kinds of systems. Google Maps, for instance, is better, its head of R&D, Peter Norvig, told us, because as it used Hall's LIDARs, it trained a system to gather data about street signs the car was passing.

"(Starting a LIDAR company) was over everyone's dead body," he said, because his company was so focused on making subwoofers. "I look for things that are electrical and mechanical." He convinced his team that they had a new market and a new thing to do, and now is an important player in the autonomous car space. He also used them to build a boat that won't make you sick (computers control hydraulic lifts to glide over waves).

In 2019, Google also used that data to turn on new Augmented Reality navigation features, where data from your phone's camera was used to compare with 3D models of the street built using data gathered from one of Hall's LIDARs. It is this impulse to build machines that can better see, and hence, make humans more powerful, that enabled these new features and for that, Hall is an American engineering star who is bringing us a whole new world. As we're about to see, this sort of development was not only happening in America, with sensors attached to a Spatial Computing device much smaller than an autonomous car.

Thousands of miles away, in Tel Aviv, Israel, was another innovator working on similar 3D mapping technology, and had a similar philosophy about how 3D sensors would soon play a key role in making human life better. That man is Aviad Maizels, and he started PrimeSense. PrimeSense was purchased by Apple and did much of the engineering on the sensor inside modern iPhones that see your face in 3D, which lets them unlock just by seeing your face, and soon will do much more.

Maizels told us back in 2013 that 3D sensors would soon be on everything. We met Maizels at the company's first suite at the Consumer Electronics Show in Las Vegas, where his company showed what 3D sensors could do—everything from seeing you buying cereal boxes to drawing on a standard desk with your finger. Today's Amazon stores demonstrate his vision was correct. In them, sensors watch you take products off the shelves and properly charge you with no registers or lines to wait in, saving you time and hassle.

It is worthwhile, though, to go back to that booth and take a look at how large PrimeSense's sensor was back then. In just a few years, it would shrink 20 times down to fit in the notch on current iPhones. Soon, it may disappear altogether since standard cameras now can build 3D models of the world, which has been proven by companies like recently acquired 6D.ai, which can do much more with a standard camera than even PrimeSense demonstrated in that suite back in 2013 in this video: https://youtu.be/4VtXvj4X0CE.

Even in autonomous cars, this argument between using standard cameras and 3D sensors is still playing out. Tesla's engineers told us that they are betting on cameras instead of the more expensive LIDARs that companies like Velodyne are producing.

If you visit Silicon Valley, you will see lots of autonomous cars from companies like Cruise, now owned by General Motors, Waymo, formerly of Google, and others, all using LIDAR to sense the world around the car, while Tesla is betting on cameras, along with a few cheaper sensors like radar and ultrasonic sensors.

Photo Credit: Robert Scoble. PrimeSense founder/CEO shows off the 3D sensor he and his team invented. This technology has now been sold to Apple, which shrunk it and included a similar sensor on the top of modern iPhones, where it senses your face to unlock your phone or do Augmented Reality "Animojis."

That is a tangential argument to the one that we are making. These innovators brought our machines new ways to see and because of that, we now have new ways to see ourselves and the world we live in, which will grant us superpowers, including ways to be remembered by future generations that only science fiction dreamed about before.

Driven to Improve

"Watch this," Elon Musk, CEO of Tesla, told us as he raced Jason Calacanis, driving a top-of-the-line Corvette through the streets of Santa Monica in the first street drag race done in a Tesla on February 18, 2008. Good thing the video hasn't survived, since speeds in excess of the speed limit were quickly reached and Calacanis was left in the dust (he soon became an early investor in, and owner of, his own Tesla). Elon was behind the wheel of serial model #1 of the first Roadster Tesla produced. What we learned on that ride has become a deep part of Tesla's story and gave us insights into Elon's philosophies early on. Yes, he was demonstrating the advantages of electronic motors. He bragged that a Tesla, with its high-torque electric motors, could accelerate faster from 0-60 mph than his million-dollar McLaren F1.

He bragged about something else, though, that stuck with us all these years: electric motors could be programmed never to slip, unlike most gas engines, which have to "wind up" 400+ parts to apply torque to the pavement. We got a look at this recently as the co-author, Robert Scoble, drove his Tesla Model 3 through the snow in Yosemite. It never slipped, even while going uphill in icy conditions.

Photo credit: Robert Scoble. Elon Musk, left, and Jason Calacanis check out the first Tesla only days after Elon got it off of the factory floor, before heading out for a street race where Elon demonstrated how much faster it was than Calacanis' new Corvette.

Today, Elon is bragging about Tesla's safety: every new Tesla comes with eight cameras, along with several other sensors, and he is adding new self-driving features every month to the fleet of hundreds of thousands on the road, thanks to an over-the-air update system that is way ahead of other automakers. In early 2019, he announced the production of a new kind of Machine Learning chip with 21 billion transistors on board; he says these will make Teslas the most advanced cars on the road and will make them much safer than those that only have a human to steer them.

It's called Autopilot, because as of 2019, a human is still needed to drive the car in city traffic and needs to be available in case other situations arise. It doesn't navigate around new potholes, for instance. That's a temporary step, though, as Elon has demonstrated full self-driving features where the car can drive without human intervention.

Industry observers like Brad Templeton, who worked on Google's autonomous vehicle program and who also owns a Tesla Model 3, say that Elon is too aggressive with his timeline and that it may take most of the 2020s to make it safe enough to remove humans from the equation completely.

Photo Credit: Robert Scoble. Some of Tesla's Autopilot/Full Self Driving Programming team hang out with Scoble's son at a Salinas Tesla Supercharger and talk about the future of autonomous cars.

What does this have to do with Spatial Computing and especially our Prime Directive? Everything. The techniques Tesla's engineers are developing (along with others like GM's Cruise, startups like Zoox, or the former Google team that now is starting a company called Waymo) are very similar to the techniques that Finman uses to enable a virtual Harry Potter to walk around the real world, and are similar to the techniques that Apple, Microsoft, Facebook, and others will use to guide users around the real world in Spatial Computing glasses that will soon come to the market.

Teslas are already saving their users' lives, as you can see on YouTube, as Teslas automatically stop or drive around potential accidents, even at high speeds. Don't discount the many hours given back to their owners as cars automatically drive in traffic during commutes. Those hours represent lives, too. Hours, er, lives, that can be used to do other things.

In *Chapter 3, Vision One – Transportation Automates*, we'll dig deeper into the other changes that soon will come as humans won't be needed for cars to move around as the Machine Learning/AI that runs the self-driving technology is put to work doing other things.

Things like going to an Amazon distribution center to pick up packages in a much more secure way than having a delivery person leaving them on your front porch, where they are easy to steal. Even in 2019, the computers in a Tesla also watch for people tampering with the car and can automatically record, say, someone breaking a window to steal something inside, and share that with owners via an app on mobile phones.

Hands-on Use

While Elon, and his teams, were working to make cars using Machine Learning to look at the road ahead, Andy Wilson was working in his lab inside Microsoft Research to come up with better technology tools, not for our roads, but for our hands.

Wilson was the first to show us how a computer could watch your hands for gestures. He demonstrated how a computer could see that you had pinched your thumb and finger together.

His first demo showed how you could "grab" a map in midair and zoom it and twist it. This gesture survives even more than a decade later on Microsoft's HoloLens.

Wilson has been trusted for decades by Microsoft. Back when Bill Gates was giving speeches, Wilson built the demos for showing off the most advanced technology. That earned him his own Augmented Reality lab. Once when we visited, he had a set of projectors and sensors hung from tresses overhead. He demonstrated how he could put computing on every part of your body, and even the room. "Here you go," he said, while dragging a virtual photo out of his pocket and handing it to us. It was the first time we had experienced Spatial Computing where we were "inside" the computer and it was interacting with us.

That research, along with others, came together to build the basis of HoloLens where, now, while wearing a $3,500 headset (instead of standing in a room with thousands of dollars of projectors and sensors), you can do the same thing. It's amazing to see how long it takes some things to get commercialized. We first started visiting Wilson's lab back in 2005, but there's a guy who has been working on this stuff for far longer: Tom Furness.

His work in the 1960s was as an airplane cockpit developer, and that's when he built new virtual interfaces that we think of today as Virtual Reality or Spatial Computing. Now, he is a professor at the University of Washington and founder of the Human Interface Technology Lab. That school did seminal work on studying how Virtual Reality could be used to cure pain. Its results, at http://vrpain.com, show that Virtual Reality, when used with burn victims, is better at removing pain than morphine is. Something we hope becomes more adopted as we try to keep people from being addicted to opiates.

Photo Credit: Robert Scoble. Tom Furness, right, and Robert Scoble hang out at Digital Raign's Reality Summit.

He told us that he and his students are developing Spatial Computing to engage, enlighten, and even entertain people in new ways. We include him here not just because he is seen as the grandfather of Virtual Reality, but because he is a great example of the pattern of how innovation frequently happens: first for military uses, later moving to consumer applications. Many of the industry's leaders follow this pattern and is why technology centers tend to cluster around strong military centers, whether in Tel Aviv, Silicon Valley, or in Las Vegas, where the military tests out new kinds of airplanes and continues Furness' early work today. We visited Nellis Airforce Base, where we met several pilots who fly F-35s. The pilots in them use a big, expensive, Augmented Reality headset. One of them said something that stuck: "I'll never lose to an F-16. Why? Because I can see you and you can't see me, and I can stop." The F-35 not only has those magic headsets, which let pilots see the airspace in great detail, but are designed to be stealthy against radar, so they can't be detected by other planes. They are equipped with engines that can direct the flow from the jets to literally stop in mid-air, which the F-16s can't do.

It isn't lost on us that recently there've been reports that newer F-35s get rid of the pilots altogether, and that the AI flying usually beats the pilots because the computers flying can perform maneuvers that humans just can't handle due to the forces involved.

Wars handled by machines is a controversial thing to be certain, and one we won't take sides on here, but that means fewer pilots coming home in a box due to accidents or being shot down, and the military sees that as just as good a thing as seeing fewer deaths on the road. No matter what way you look at these new technologies and their role, you can't deny that most of these technologies were first designed with a military use in mind.

Beginning

In this chapter, we have thrown a light on just a portion of the stories of innovators and the innovations that they are bringing to market, all of which we will all use by 2030, or most likely by 2025. We've given you an initial indication of how versatile and useful Spatial Computing is—for use by farmers to fly fisherman to businesspeople that use data analyses, to people who ride in Teslas and soon, autonomous vehicles. Technologies such as Machine Learning and 5G will further strengthen the reach of Spatial Computing.

We've been telling people we are just at the beginning of a new 50-year product cycle, which brings a new kind of personal computing that many have said will lead into the Singularity—a deep merging of humans with machines. Already in R&D labs, researchers are showing a new kind of computing coming where you will just "think" of doing something, like sending a message to a loved one, and a message will appear in mid-air and you'll send it just by thinking "send."

The road to Spatial Computing has been a very long one—one that humans have been on ever since they started making tools that could substantially improve their chances of survival and their quality of life. Where we stand now is in an iterative stage that will yield significant gains. It is as if we are back in 1976 and Wozniak and Jobs just showed us the prototypes of the Apple II. We are still seeing improvements to personal computers 40 years later; however, this new type of computing will be a major leap.

It appears that the closer a created Spatial Computing experience is to real life, the more satisfaction a viewer has from it—both from practical and entertainment perspectives. The utility makes sense given the tool nature of Spatial Computing. In which way and how far humans will take Spatial Computing is very much the reason for this book. We are approaching it from an enterprise perspective, focusing on the particulars of industry vertical use, although our discussion of particular technologies will make it clear that there is a massive potential for wide consumer use of Spatial Computing.

For the rest of this book, we will detail and discuss what we think will happen in Spatial Computing within the next five years, give some major indications of what could happen in 10, talk about what it could mean for humanity in 25 years—focusing on culture and society—and give some far-reaching comments on what we might see in 50 years' time. We will look at seven industries that are about to undergo massive changes and radical disruptions and to understand why, we'll dive into the technology driving this perfect storm of change and take a look at some of the changes coming to each of them.

2

Four Paradigms
and Six Technologies

Introduction

You aren't reading this book to learn about small new features of existing apps, but rather to more deeply understand what we are calling the "Fourth Paradigm" of personal computing—Spatial Computing.

This chapter will bring you up to date on the technology you need to know about to understand where Spatial Computing came from, where it's going, and why it's so fundamentally different than the desktops or mobile phones that came before, even though it is using a lot of technology invented for the machines of earlier paradigms. Spatial Computing is the fourth paradigm, and we see it as the most personal of all the personal computing paradigms yet to come. We will cover six technologies that enable Spatial Computing to work: Optics and Displays, Wireless and Communications, Control Mechanisms (Voice and Hands), Sensors and Mapping, Compute Architectures (new kinds of Cloud Computing, for instance), and Artificial Intelligence (Decision Systems).

The Four Paradigms

What do we mean by "paradigm"? The evolution of the user experience is the easiest way to understand this. The First Paradigm has to do with the beginning of personal computing and the interface being text-based. With the Second Paradigm, graphics and color capabilities were included.

Movement and mobility were added with the Third Paradigm in the form of mobile phones. With Spatial Computing, the Fourth Paradigm, computing escapes from small screens and can be all around us. We define Spatial Computing as computing that humans, virtual beings, or robots move through. It includes what others define as ambient computing, ubiquitous computing, or mixed reality. We see this age as also inclusive of things like autonomous vehicles, delivery robots, and the component technologies that support this new kind of computing, whether laser sensors, Augmented Reality, including Machine Learning and Computer Vision, or new kinds of displays that let people view and manipulate 3D-centric computing.

We will see seven industries that will be dramatically upended by the 3D thinking that Spatial Computing brings and will go into more detail on the impacts on those industries in further chapters. Soon, all businesses will need to think in 3D and this shift will be difficult for many. Why can we say that with confidence? Because the shift has started already.

The Oculus Quest, which shipped in May 2019, is an important product for one reason—it proves that a small computer can run an on-the-face spatial computer that brings fantastic visual worlds you can move around in and interact with. It is proving that the world of Spatial Computing has arrived with a device many can afford and is easy to use. It's based on a Qualcomm chipset that is already years old as you are reading this—all for $400, and with controllers that can move freely in space and control it all! Now that our bodies can move within a digital landscape, the Spatial Computing age, that is, "the Fourth Paradigm of Personal Computing," has arrived and will only expand as new devices arrive this year and the next. What we are seeing now are the Spatial Computing counterparts of products like the Apple II or the IBM PC of earlier paradigms.

The Quest isn't alone as evidence that a total shift is underway. Mobile phones now have 3D sensors on both sides of the phone, and brands are spending big bucks bringing Augmented Reality experiences to hundreds of millions of phones and seeing higher engagement and sales as a result.

Look at mobile phones and the popularity of Augmented Reality games like *Minecraft Earth* and Niantic's *Harry Potter: Wizards Unite* last summer. You play these while walking around the real world. A ton of new technologies are working in the background to make these 3D games possible.

How is this fourth paradigm of computing different? It is additive, including the technologies that came before it, even as it brings quantitatively different kinds of technology to our eyes and world. Spatial Computing promises to do what the previous three paradigms have failed to do: to map computing to humans in a deep way. Elon Musk says it will increase our bandwidth; what he means is that our computers will be able to communicate with each of us, and us with our technology, in a far more efficient way than we've ever done before. Paradigm one kicked it off by enabling us to converse with our own computer, one that was in our homes for the first time, through a keyboard. That brought a revolution, and the next paradigm promises a huge amount of change, but to understand the amplitude of that change, we should look back to the world that Steve Wozniak and Jobs brought us way back in 1977.

Paradigm One – The Arrival of the Personal Computer

The Apple II is as important as the Oculus Quest, even though most people alive have never used one. The Quest brought a new kind of Spatial Computing device to the market—one that mostly was biased toward Virtual Reality, where you can only see a virtual world while the real world is hidden from view. This $400 device was the first from Facebook's Oculus division that didn't require sensors to be placed around you, and didn't require a wire from the headset to a PC. It was all self-contained and it powered on instantly, which dramatically increased usage numbers.

Where the Quest let everyday people think about owning a VR headset for the first time, the Apple II acted in the same way for those back in the late 1970s, allowing people to own a personal computer for the first time! As the 1980s began, a lot of people, not just governments or big businesses, had access to computers. Four decades later, we are seeing the same trend with Spatial Computing.

The Apple II, and later the IBM PC, which ran Microsoft's DOS (for Disk Operating System), introduced the integrated circuit into a consumer-focused product and enabled an entire industry to be built up around it. By the end of the 1980s, literally every desk inside some corporations had a personal computer sitting on it, and the names of those who made them, such as Michael Dell, are still well-known today.

We expect that Spatial Computing will similarly lift previously unknown people up to wealth and household name status.

Photo credit: Robert Scoble. Steve Wozniak stands next to an Apple II at the Computer History Museum. He is the last person to have the design of an entire computer, from the processor to the memory to the display drivers, in his head. After this, teams took on the engineering of all those parts.

Speaking of Dell, he may not be the one that gets credit for starting the personal computing age, but only because he was able to make personal computing more accessible to the masses. He did this by licensing Microsoft's operating system and putting it in lower-cost machines, allowing companies like Dell to make many sales. We foresee that a similar pattern will probably play out. We expect Apple to enter the market in late 2020, but believe that its first products will be very controlling of privacy, tethered wirelessly to the iPhone, and much more expensive than, say, competitive products from Google and Facebook, not to mention those from the Chinese.

It is hard to see how early computers that could only display black and white computations on a screen could be relevant to Spatial Computing, but the concepts it introduced remain relevant even today, such as files, printing, saving, and others. The thing is that back in the beginning, there were no graphics; computers were way too big to hold (much less dream about putting in your pocket) and were much harder to use. Those of us who learned computing way back then remember having to look up commands in manuals to do something simple like print, and then you'd have to type those commands onto the screen.

Spatial Computing, or computing you can move through, is actually joined by much improved voice technology. Companies like Otter.ai are understanding our voices, and systems like Apple's Siri, Amazon's Alexa, Google's Assistant, and others are waiting for us to speak to them.

We imagine that, soon, you will be able to just say something like "Hey Siri, can you print out my report?" and it will be so. This new world of convenience that is being ushered in is, in our opinion, far preferable to the days of code and command lines that we saw during the first days of personal computing!

The first computers arrived with little excitement or fanfare. The first ones only had a few applications to choose from, a basic recipe database, and a couple of games. Plus, Apple founders Steve Wozniak and Steve Jobs were barely out of high school, and the first machines were popular mostly with engineers and technical people who had dreamed of owning their own personal computers. Those days remind us a lot of the current Virtual Reality market. At the time of writing this book, only a few million VR machines have sold. In its first year, only a few thousand Apple IIs had sold. It was held back because the machines were fairly expensive (in today's dollars, they cost more than $10,000) and because they were hard to use; the first people using them had to memorize lots of text commands to type in.

It's funny to hear complaints of "There's not enough to do on an Oculus Quest," which we heard frequently last summer. Hello, you can play basketball with your friends in Rec Room! Try going back to 1977, when the first ones basically didn't do anything and, worse, you had to load the handful of apps that were out back then from tape, a process that took minutes and frequently didn't work right at all. Wozniak told us his wife back then lost her entire thesis project on an Apple II, and even he couldn't figure out how to save it. Those problems aren't nearly as frequent in the days of automatic saving on cloud computing servers.

Why is the Apple II, along with its competitors and precursors, so important? What was really significant was that people like Dan Bricklin and Bob Frankston bought one. They were students at Harvard University and saw the potential in the machine to do new things. In their case, they saw how it could help businesspeople. You might already know the rest of the story; they invented the digital spreadsheet.

The app they developed, VisiCalc, changed businesses forever and became the reason many people bought Apple IIs. "VisiCalc took 20 hours of work per week for some people, turned it out in 15 minutes, and let them become much more creative," Bricklin says.

The Apple II ended up selling fewer than 6 million units. The Apple II, and its competitors that would soon come, such as the IBM PC, did something important, though—they provided the scale the industry needed to start shrinking the components, making them much faster, and reducing their cost, which is what computing would need to do to sell not just a few million machines, but billions— which it did in the next two paradigms.

Photo credit: Robert Scoble. Label on Tim Berners-Lee's NeXT computer on which he invented the World Wide Web while working at CERN. The NeXT operating system still survives in today's Macintosh and iOS, but is really the best example of concepts invented at Xerox Palo Alto Research Center in the early 1980s.

Paradigm Two – Graphical Interfaces and Thinking

In 1984, the launch of the Apple Macintosh computer brought us graphical computing. Instead of typing text commands to, say, print a document, you clicked an icon. That made computing much easier but also enabled the launch of a new series of desktop publishing apps. By the time Windows 95 arrived, finally bringing the idea to the mass market, the entire technology stack was built around graphics. This greatly increased the size of tech companies and led to profitable new lines of software for Microsoft and Adobe, setting the stage for Spatial Computing.

This graphical approach was much easier to use than learning to type in commands to copy files and print. Now, you could just click on a printer icon or a save icon. This increased accessibility brought many new users into computing. The thing to take away here is computing, with this, and each of the paradigm shifts that followed, made a massive move toward working more like humans do, and made handling computer tasks much easier. Spatial Computing will complete this move (Google's Tilt Brush in VR still uses many of the icons developed in this era to do things like choose brushes, or save/delete files).

It was a massive increase in the number of computer users (many stores had long lines of people waiting to buy Windows 95) that gave Microsoft, in particular, the resources to invest in R&D labs that led directly to the development of HoloLens 25 years after Windows 95's huge release.

Also, it took many graphic designers off of working on typesetting machines and brought them into computing, which accelerated with the popularity of the web, which also saw its debut on Windows 95 and Macintosh. When Tim O'Reilly and Dale Dougherty popularized the term Web 2.0 in 1994, even Bill Gates didn't understand how important having people interacting on web pages would be.

Weblogs were springing up by the millions and e-commerce sites like Amazon and eBay were early adopters of techniques that let parts of web pages change without being completely refreshed. Today, WordPress is used by about 20 percent of the web but back then, Gates and his lieutenant Steven Sinofsky didn't see the business value in Web 2.0, refusing to consider a purchase after the coauthor of this book, Robert Scoble, suggested such a thing when he worked as a strategist at Microsoft. He is now Chief Strategy Officer at Infinite Retina.

The web was starting to "come alive" and desktops and laptops were too with new video gaming technology. Nvidia, born in the 1990s, was now seeing rapid growth as computing got cheaper and better. Where a megabyte of RAM cost $450 in the late 1980s, by 2005, a gigabyte was running at $120 and while that was happening, internet speeds escaped the very slow modem age and were increasing to such speeds that new video services like YouTube and social networks, including LinkedIn, Twitter, and Facebook, were able to appear. Technology continues to get cheaper and smaller to this day. Today, 21 billion transistors fit into a chip the size of your fingernail (like the one that does self-driving in a Tesla) and memory now costs about $15 for 64-GB chips. It is this decrease in cost and increase in capabilities that is bringing us Spatial Computing.

This new user interface paradigm, while easier than typing text commands, still was difficult to use for many. More than one phone call to Microsoft's support lines demonstrated that many had difficulty figuring out how a mouse worked, and even dragging icons around the screen was daunting and scary to many. Those of us who grew up around computers saw it as easy, but many didn't. While the visual metaphors were there, the disconnect between moving your hand on a mouse on a desk while controlling a cursor on the screen meant that computers still didn't work the way we did. While most figured it out, computing had another problem—computing wasn't designed to fit in your hand or pockets, which is the vision that Douglas Engelbart, among other pioneers, had for all of us. Engelbart was the genius who, back in the late 1960s, showed the world the technology that it wouldn't get until the Macintosh arrived in 1984. Before he died, he told us he had an unfinished dream: of making computing even more personal, where you could communicate with computers with your hands and eyes. He predicted not only the move to mobile, but the move to truly Spatial Computing.

This brings us to Paradigm Three: Mobile.

Paradigm Three – Mobile

Humans aren't happy being tied to desks to do their work, and that enabled a new industry and a new paradigm of personal computing to arrive—one that brought computing off of desks and laps and into your hand. This paradigm shift enabled billions to get on the internet for the first time (we've seen very poor people in China and other places riding bikes while talking on their smartphones) and would be the platform that many new companies would build upon, thanks to new sensors, ubiquitous data networks, and new kinds of software that were designed for these devices we all now hold.

This third technology shift started in places like Toronto (RIM Blackberry) and Helsinki (Nokia). For years, these two companies, along with Palm, with its Treo, and a few others, started a new technology industry direction. They produced products that fit in your hand and didn't seem to be very powerful computers at the time. Mostly, they were aimed at helping you take a few notes (Treo) or make a call, while entertaining the ability to take a photo too (Nokia) or send a few text messages to coworkers (RIM's Blackberry). This turned into quite an important industry. Nokia alone, at its peak in 2000, accounted for four percent of its country's GDP and 70 percent of the Helsinki Stock Exchange market capital.

Photo credit: Robert Scoble. A Microsoft Windows Phone, circa 2006, sits next to the original mouse, circa 1968, on Douglas Engelbart's coffee table.

What they didn't count on was that Steve Jobs would return to Apple and with the help of Microsoft, who poured capital into the failing Apple of the late 1990s, brought Apple back, first by rejuvenating the Macintosh line to keep its faithful happy, then with the introduction of the iPod. Now, the iPod didn't seem to be a device that would help Apple compete with the Blackberries, Treos, and Nokias, but it helped Jobs build teams that could build small, hand-held devices and figure out how to market them. That effort crushed other portable audio players and did so in such a way to give Jobs the confidence, and cash, to invest in other devices like phones.

A few of the engineers who built the iPod were asked by Jobs to come up with ideas for a new device that would merge what they learned with the iPod and add in phone capabilities. The early prototypes looked much more like an iPod than the product we all know today.

That team all carried Treos and studied the other devices, Andy Grignon told us. He was one of the dozen who worked on the first prototypes. They saw that while early devices were useful because they could be carried around, they were hard to use for most things other than making phone calls. Many didn't have keyboards that were easy to type on, for instance, and even the ones that did have keyboards, like the RIM devices, were hard to use to surf the web or do things like edit photos on.

He told us that Jobs forbade him from hiring anyone who had worked on one of these competitive products, or even from hiring anyone who had worked in the telecom industry. Jobs wanted new thinking.

On January 9, 2007, Steve Jobs introduced the iPhone. That day, we were at the big Consumer Electronics Show getting reactions from Blackberry and Nokia execs. They demonstrated the hubris that often comes from being on top: "Cupertino doesn't know how to build phones," one told us. They totally missed that there was an unserved market—one that not only wanted to use devices while walking around, but also wanted to do far more than just make a call or take a photo once in a while. Their devices were too hard to use for other tasks, and their arrogance kept them from coming up with a device that made it easy.

Around that time, the web had become something that everyone was using for all sorts of things that Tim Berners-Lee, the inventor of the web, could never imagine. With iPhones, and later, Android phones, we could easily use the full web on our mobile devices while walking around, all by using our fingers to zoom into articles on the New York Times, just like Steve Jobs had demoed months earlier from a stage in San Francisco.

It was this combination of an easy-to-use device, along with sensors, that could start adding location-based context to apps that formed the basis of many new companies, from Uber to Instagram, that were born within years of the iPhone launch, which showed something significant had happened to the world of technology and that set up the conditions for the next battle over where the tech industry will go next: Spatial Computing.

Paradigm Four – Spatial Computing

You might notice a theme here. Each paradigm builds upon the paradigm that came before, bringing real breakthroughs in user experience. With our mobile phones, tablets, and computers, there's still one glaring problem—they don't work like humans do. Paradigm Four is bringing the perfect storm of all usability breakthroughs.

Even a young child knows how to pick up a cup and put it in the dishwasher or fill it with milk. But this same child is forced to use computing that doesn't work like that. Instead of grabbing with her hand, she has to touch a screen, or use a mouse, to manipulate objects on a flat screen.

In Spatial Computing, she will just grab a virtual cup like she would a real one in the real world. This will enable many new people to get into computing and will make all of our tasks easier, and introduce new ways of living.

This move to a 3D world isn't just happening in computing, either. We experienced an off-Broadway play, "Sleep No More," which was a remake of Shakespeare's Macbeth, where you walk through sets, with action happening all around. Even New York plays are starting to move from something confined to a rectangular stage to one that surrounds us in 360-degrees. It's a powerful move—one that totally changes entertainment and the audience's expectations of it.

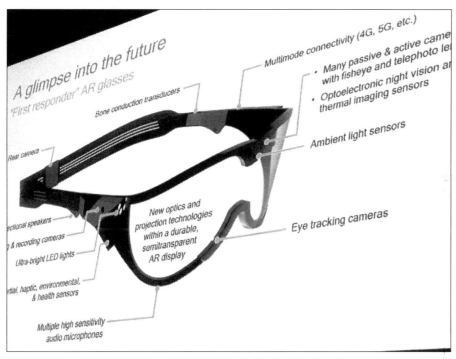

Photo credit: Robert Scoble. Qualcomm shows off Spatial Computing/AR Glasses of the future at an event in 2017.

If Spatial Computing only introduced new 3D thinking, that would be absolutely huge. But it's joined by new kinds of voice interfaces. Those of us who have an Amazon Echo or a Google Home device already know that you can talk to computers now and ask them to do things. Within a year or two, you will be having entire conversations with computers. Also coming at the same time are powerful new AIs that can "see" things in your environment. Computer Vision will make getting information about things, plants, and people much easier.

A perfect storm is arriving—one that will make computing more personal, easier to use, and more powerful. This new form of computing will disrupt seven industries, at a minimum, which we will go into deeply in the rest of this book. In the next section, we'll look at how this storm of change is to impact technology itself.

Six Technologies

The storm will bring major advances in six new technologies: Optics and Displays, Wireless and Communications, Control Mechanisms (Voice and Hands), Sensors and Mapping, Compute Architectures (new kinds of Cloud Computing, for instance), and Artificial Intelligence (Decision Systems). For the rest of this chapter, we'll explore the implications of the fourth computing paradigm for each of these technologies.

Optics and Displays

The purest forms of Spatial Computing will be experienced while wearing a head-mounted display personified in the form of glasses. In these glasses, you will experience either Augmented Reality (where you see some of the real world, along with some virtual items either placed on top, or replacing real-world items) or Virtual Reality (where you experience only a virtual world).

Paul Milgram, an industrial engineering professor who specializes in human factors, went further into depth than just dividing the world into these two poles. He said that these two were part of a reality-virtuality continuum, which included mixed reality (where both the real and virtual are mixed). People will continue to mix up all the terms, and we expect that whatever Apple calls them when it introduces its brand of Spatial Computing devices are what may stick, just like it calls high-resolution screens "Retina Displays."

Photo credit: Robert Scoble. DigiLens prototypes, as displayed at SPIE Photonics West 2019, a conference focusing on optics. As of early 2020, glasses like these still haven't gotten good enough, or small enough, but a raft of new technologies in R&D labs promises to change all that by 2025.

Other terms used to describe various experiences on the spectrum between Augmented and Virtual Reality? Computer-mediated reality, extended reality, simulated reality, and transreality gaming. Now, you probably get why we prefer to just lump all of these under one term: Spatial Computing.

There are already a range of Spatial Computing products on the market, from Google Glass on one side, with its tiny screen, to Microsoft HoloLens on another, with an approach that puts virtual images on top of the real world in a very compelling way. Yet none of these approaches have succeeded with consumers, due to deep flaws such as having a heavy weight, low battery life, blurry and dim screens, not to mention that since they haven't sold many units, developers haven't supported them with millions of apps like the ones that are available on mobile phones.

In talking with Qualcomm, which makes the chipsets in most of these products, we learned that there are two approaches that will soon dominate the market: one where you see through the virtual layer to the real world, and one that passes the real world to your eyes through cameras and screens.

Both fit into the Spatial Computing family, since they present computing you can move around in, but they have completely different use cases.

Examples of see-through devices are Magic Leap's ML1 or Microsoft's HoloLens, which let you see the real world through the lenses a wearer sees through, but that uses a Wave Guide to display virtual items on top of the real world.

In November 2019, it was leaked that Apple will bring HMDs that bring something else: a completely opaque display that, when worn, presents the real world "passed through" cameras to its tiny little high-resolution screens. This passthrough approach, first introduced in spring of 2019 in the Varjo VR-1, brings you a superwide field of view (FOV), something that the Magic Leap and HoloLens can't yet match, along with extremely high resolution and better color than Magic Leap and HoloLens can bring you. The same leak, reported in *The Information*, said that Apple is also planning a see-through pair of lighter glasses that will come in 2023. That matches plans at other companies, like Facebook, which has a four-year strategy for building its own pair of Augmented Reality glasses.

The passthrough designs, though, have some significant limitations—other people can't see your eyes, so they are not great to use in situations where you need to talk with other people in the real world, and, because you are seeing a virtual representation of the real world, they won't be good for military or police, who need to see the real world in order to shoot guns. The latency and imperfections in bringing the real world to your eyes in such an approach might prove troublesome in applications that require immediacy. Similarly, we wouldn't trust them in everyday situations where you could be in danger if your awareness is compromised, like if you are a worker using a bandsaw, or someone driving a car, or even if you are trying to walk around a shopping mall.

That said, a passthrough device would be amazing for replacing monitors. Another way to look at it is that passthrough will be biased toward Virtual Reality, where you see mostly virtual worlds or items and very little, if any, of the real world. See-through displays, on the other hand, will be biased toward Augmented Reality, where you are mostly seeing the real world with virtual characters or items, or virtual screens overlaid or replacing parts of the real world. Each is a member of the Spatial Computing family, and has different use cases and benefits.

We are hearing that, by 2022, these passthrough devices will present you with a virtual monitor that both will be bigger and have a higher resolution than most of our friends have in their homes in 2019, and we know many people who have 4K projection screens in their entertainment rooms.

We don't know which approach will win with consumers, but we have come up with some theories by trying out the different approaches for ourselves.

Enterprise workers who need to walk around machines, or police/military users, will tend to go with something like the HoloLens.

These devices, at least as of early 2020, use optics systems that guide light to your eye through glass with tiny structures, or mirrors, that bounce light projected from tiny projectors or lasers into your eyes, giving you an image. Why do we say workers or the military will go with these? Because they let you see through the glass to the real world. The analog world is hard to properly represent virtually with low latency, and these optics don't even try.

The devices that require lots of cameras, sensors, and powerful GPUs to properly align virtual images into the analog world will remain fairly big and heavy. The HoloLens weighs more than a pound and it doesn't even include a 5G radio, or batteries that can keep the thing powered for long enough for it to be used for more than a few hours.

We can't imagine running, or skiing, with such a big contraption on our heads, not to mention they make a wearer look antisocial if worn out in public, which explains why there are small, if not underpowered, devices like the Focals by North and Google Glass. We find these smaller devices lacking in the ability to present text in a satisfying way, and have many limitations from a very small field of view to not enough power to do Augmented Reality, which is where we believe the real power of on-face wearable devices lies. These are great for wearing while doing, say, inventory at a warehouse, or seeing notifications like a smart watch might display, but they can't display huge virtual monitors and can't even attempt to do virtual or true Augmented Reality-style entertainment apps.

Bigger devices with optics from companies like Kopin or Lumus, which makes the display in Lenovo's glasses, and DigiLens, which got an investment from Niantic, the company behind Pokémon Go, are pushing the bleeding edge, with many others coming soon.

You should be aware of these different approaches, though, and the pros and cons of each. For instance, people who mostly work at desks, whether sitting at a Starbucks, or a corporate office, won't often need to see the real world, so they may prefer the wider field of view, the better color, and higher resolution of passthrough devices like the Varjo, and what we expect Apple to be working on, among others.

Why do we see passthrough as the ones that may win with consumers by 2022? New micro LED displays are coming on the market from companies like Sony and Mojo Vision, which have super high-resolution displays that are smaller than your fingernails.

These displays offer better power utilization and some can do things like completely turn the sky you are looking at dark, or replace it with virtual images. That lets wearers experience both VR and AR, often one after another, in all sorts of lighting conditions with potentially wrap around screens at a lower cost than the techniques used in HoloLens.

We can see a world where we'll own two or maybe even three pairs of glasses for different things. Additionally, we might use a very different headset, like the Varjo, when we go to a shopping mall to play high-end VR in Location-based Entertainment retail settings like you see from The Void, Spaces, Sandbox VR, Hologate, or Dreamscape Immersive. These are places you pay $20-$30 or more to have much more immersive experiences than you can at home, but for the purposes of this book, we'll focus on enterprise and consumer uses of Spatial Computing and not these high-end uses—although you should try them out since our families and team members love them as well.

One thing we want you to realize is that much better devices will soon arrive— some may have even been announced in-between us finishing writing this book and the time you read it. Expect this section of our book to be out of date quickly after printing as technologies come out of the lab.

As we've been talking with people about these different approaches, many people believe that small GPUs will not be able to power such high-resolution displays. That might be true if displays behaved like the ones on your desktop, which have the same resolution all the way across the display.

VR pioneer Tom Furness told us that won't be true soon, thanks to a new technique called "foveated rendering." What he, and his researchers realized, is that the human eye can only perceive color and high resolution in the middle of the eye, the fovea. Since Spatial Computing devices will be worn and some include eye sensors, they can play visual tricks with our eyes, he says, by only putting high resolutions, or tons of polygons, right in the center where our eyes are looking. The outside screens could be lower resolutions, or, at a minimum, display fewer polygons, thus "fooling" your eyes that the entire display is, say, an 8K one, while it really is only the center of the display that is that high a resolution. Already, this technique is being used in some VR headsets, like the Varjo, and products that use this technique can double apparent resolution without putting extra strain on the GPU or computers driving them.

Other problems also need to be solved. With the HoloLens, you can't bring virtual items close to your face. Why is that? Because of two terms: accommodation, which is how the muscles in your eyes react to closer-focus items, and vergence, which is how your eyes move toward each other when focusing on something close. Those two actions are hard for current optics and microscreens to support.

The holy grail of displays was actually invented about 20 years ago by Furness. It uses a low-power laser to scan a single pixel across the back of your retina. No one has been able to manufacture such a monitor in scale yet, but Furness said prototypes in his lab actually helped a few people to add sight into their blind eyes, since the laser penetrates scar tissue that some people built up due to birth defects or injuries to the back of their eye. We hope to see a working version of such a monitor, which, if a company can build it, promises to use very little power and give amazing images due to being painted right onto our retinas. That said, display technology we will have on our eyes within a year of the publishing of this book will be very impressive indeed.

Now that we've discussed the future of Optics and Displays, let's look at the other pieces of the Spatial Computing puzzle that are also rapidly evolving.

Wireless and Communications

The screens mentioned in the previous section are going to be data-hungry. If our sources are correct, the wearable screens on our faces will need 8K and probably much higher resolution videos to give you a sharp view of the world around you. We are hearing of companies testing glasses with 32K videos that wrap around you in 360 degrees.

For such a viewing experience to be true, you'll need a huge amount of data—all while the glasses are also uploading data streaming from cameras and sensors up front.

Plus, engineers in labs are telling us that they are trying to remove as much computing from the glasses as possible and put that computation up on new kinds of cloud servers. For such a scheme to work, we'll need not only much more bandwidth than we have today, but we'll need very low latency.

Enter 5G. 5G brings us three benefits. First, very high bandwidth. Users are getting about 10 times more bandwidth than they used to get with LTE on mobile phones. Second, low latency. 5G has a latency of about two milliseconds to a cell tower. The current latency is about 10x slower. That matters if you are trying to play a video game with someone else. Imagine everything lags or is slow. The third benefit comes to bear if you visit sporting/concert arenas with thousands of other people. 5G promises many times more devices can connect per antenna. We remember the day we went to the World Series at AT&T Park in San Francisco and couldn't send a text message or make a phone call on our iPhones, despite AT&T putting the best radios it had into the park.

As of 2020, we don't expect many of you to have 5G, but it is already being put into sports arenas, and cities with high population densities. 5G also has some significant problems. The highest frequencies can't go through walls easily and you need to be much closer to antennas than with LTE. Telecom experts tell us that rollouts will be slow to most neighborhoods and you will probably need to upgrade your Wi-Fi in order to distribute such fast bandwidth inside office buildings and homes.

When will you get 5G in your home? If you live in a high-density city, probably by 2022. If you live in a rural area, though, you might not see it for most of the 2020s due to it being necessary for true 5G to be very close to a 5G tower. That said, in 2019, we got an AT&T fiber line and Wi-Fi 6 in our homes, which already gives us most of the benefits of 5G without waiting. WiFi6 is the newest version of the Wi-Fi standard and shipped on iPhones for the first time in late 2019. Unfortunately, very few people have access to a gigabit fiber line, our Wifi6 router cost about $400, and we bought another $500 worth of extenders. Very few people will want to put more than $1,000 into new Wifi6 equipment just so they can have the fastest speeds in the neighborhood!

Another place where 5G will be rolled out more quickly? Inside factories. Here, 5G pays real dividends because virtualized factory floors can make things much more efficient, and many factories have thousands of sensors and thousands of robots that can overwhelm older communications infrastructure.

It is the new software architectures that 5G enables, however, that will be most exciting. Google Stadia gives you a little taste. Instead of loading games on your phone or your glasses that can be many gigabytes in size, you just livestream them. This kind of scheme will enable much more complex processing to be done on huge server farms, serving just streams of pixels down to the optics on your eyes. We can imagine a day, soon, if it hasn't happened already by the time this book is published, where you say something like "Hey Siri, play Minecraft Earth" and the game just starts playing without loading anything.

The thing with all this bandwidth is that it's very hard to use on older equipment. Even with tons of 4K video streaming, we can't slow down our gigabit internet line. It's Spatial Computing that will use all that bandwidth that 5G, or a WiFi6/Gigabit internet line, will bring and to control that we'll need a much more efficient way to control the multiple video screens and the Augmented Reality that will surround us as we wear new Spatial Computing glasses. This is why Qualcomm is already building wearable devices that have seven cameras, most of which will be used for new kinds of controls for this new highly interactive world.

Control Mechanisms (Voice, Eyes, and Hands)

When we put a HoloLens on someone for the first time, what do they try to do? Grab for one of the holograms they see with their hands. Obviously, this is something that we would never attempt to do with a 2D interface such as a computer screen or a smartphone screen.

This human need to try to touch, grab, and manipulate is so powerful that it's easy to see that controlling computing inside an AR or VR headset won't be anything like it is on a traditional laptop or desktop machine with its mouse and keyboard. There are so many business and consumer uses in Spatial Computing for this direct kind of manipulation, that is, using your hands.

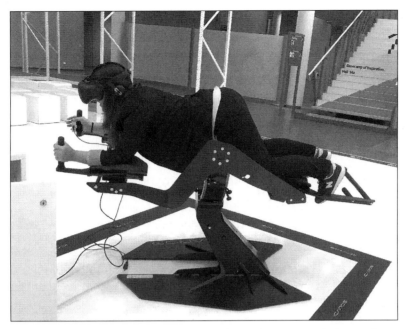

Photo credit: Robert Scoble. A woman uses the Icaros VR fitness device at a tradeshow in Germany in 2018. This shows that Spatial Computing controls will include not just hand controls, but sensors on the face, and other places that can enable new kinds of fun experiences.

At the same time, new voice-first technologies are coming fast and furious. At Apple's WWDC last year, Apple showed off new voice commands that could run the entire operating system of a Macintosh simply by talking. Many of us are already used to using voice for some things, either with Siri on iPhones, or Alexa on Amazon Echo devices, or with Google's Assistant on its Android phones, apps, or Google Home devices. Others, like Samsung's Bixby, are also coming along, and specialized voice apps and services, like Otter, are further encouraging us to talk to our devices to perform tasks, take notes, or do other work.

While most people will judge devices by how well they handle hand gestures, we see that it's the combination of input methods, whether it's using your voice, your hands, your eyes, or even typing or moving a phone, that makes Spatial Computing so powerful.

It's the first time we can really experience hands-free computing. Surgeons, for instance, are starting to use Spatial Computing because they can control the cameras and other devices by talking to their devices.

Haptic controls are also evolving quickly, which add realism to many use cases. The standard controllers that come with, say, an Oculus Quest or HTC Vive, do some, like shaking when you shoot a gun, but there's an entire industry springing up as Spatial Computing glasses and VR headsets become more popular, from companies that make gloves that let you touch and feel things, to suits that let you capture your entire body motion and, even, in the case of the $15,000 Tesla suit, let a wearer experience feeling hot or cold, along with other sensations passed to your skin through dozens of transducers.

That said, the standard sensors in headsets alone bring major new capabilities, even if you don't add on some of these other accessories.

What really is going on is that we're seeing a convergence of technologies that's making all of this possible. Sensors are getting cheap enough to be included in consumer-grade devices. AI is getting good enough that we are close to having full conversations with our computers, as Google demonstrated in 2018 with its Duplex demo. There, an AI called a local business and talked with the human answering the phone and the human was none the wiser.

Computer Vision and Machine Learning makes using hand gestures much more accurate. Andy Wilson showed us how gestures worked at Microsoft Research way back in 2005 (he directs the perception and interaction research group there: https://www.microsoft.com/en-us/research/people/awilson/). He wrote algorithms that could "see" his fingers with a camera. Another algorithm was taught how to tell if he touched his finger and thumb together. Then, he zoomed in a map just by using his hands in mid-air. Today, we see that same technique used in Microsoft's HoloLens, even though it has become much more advanced than the simple touch-your-fingers-together algorithm.

Back then, though, gestures only did one or two things and weren't accurate if the sensor couldn't clearly see your thumb touching your finger. Today, AIs pick up small patterns on the back of your hand from your muscles contracting so that many more gestures work, and the ones you try might not even be fully visible to the sensors on the front of your Spatial Computing glasses.

These capabilities make Spatial Computing devices awesome for remote assistance, hands-free work, and all sorts of new interactions with computing or robots. Snap your fingers and you can be shooting at monsters crawling toward you in a video game.

The thing businesses need to know here is that users will come at this world from where they are at, and you will need to do a lot more testing with people to make sure they can use your services well. Accessibility is a huge opportunity. Apple demonstrated this when a guy who had no use of his hands, working in a wheelchair, could still send messages, manipulate photos, and perform other tasks, all with his voice.

It is hard to imagine just how deeply user interfaces will soon change. Eye sensors will facilitate some major leaps in the way we interact with our technology. We can see a day when we are in the shopping mall and ask our glasses "Hey, Siri, what's the price of that?," totally expecting an answer about the shirt we are actually looking at. Indeed, all the major companies have purchased eye sensor-producing companies. In part, this is because eye sensors can be used to further develop high-resolution monitors that pack tons of polygons into the spot where you actually are looking using the foveated rendering technique, but we bet they see the business opportunities of making user interfaces understand us much better by knowing what we are looking at, along with the biometric security that will come, too.

Another need for eye sensors is biometric-multifactor identity. Turns out our eyes are like our fingerprints: uniquely ours. So, if our glasses are put on by someone else, they won't be able to access our private information until they hand them back and give them to us. Add that to identity systems that use voice, heart rate, and the blood vessels in skin that your cameras can see, where your human eye can't, along with patterns like gait and hand movements, and computing soon will be able to know it's you at a very high degree of accuracy, increasing the security of everything you do and finally getting rid of passwords everywhere.

Eye sensors will also be loved by marketers, since it's possible they will know if you actually looked at an ad or got excited by a new product display at a store. These new capabilities will lead to many new privacy and control concerns.

We've seen companies like Umoove, which lets us control phone screens using only our eyes, but that seemed clunky and not well integrated and, truth be told, not all that accurate. That won't be the case as more eye sensors get included into Spatial Computing glasses.

Speaking of Siri, as of 2019, she isn't all that good, but Apple is working on improving her to the place where you can do everything, from finding a restaurant to editing a video, just by talking to her. Ask her something like "how many people are checked in on Foursquare at the Half Moon Bay Ritz?" You will quickly learn her limitations. She understands us just fine (although if you don't speak English well or have a weird accent or other non-standard speech patterns, she fails there too).

Foursquare actually has an answer to that question, along with an API so other programmers could get to it. Siri, though, was hard coded and Apple's programmers haven't yet gotten around to such an obscure feature, so it fails by bringing in an answer from Bing that makes no sense.

Where is this all going? Well, Magic Leap had already started demonstrating a virtual being that it calls "Mica." Mica will stand or sit with you, and interact with you with full conversations, and she can even play games with virtual game pieces with you. Those capabilities were shown at the Game Developer's Conference in early 2019.

The thing about Mica is that it years away from being able to properly fool us in all situations that Mica is as good a conversationalist as a human, but that's not the point. Amazon Echo/Alexa and Google Assistant/Home demonstrate something is going on here: we are increasingly using our voice to control our computing, and much better AI is coming between now and 2025 that will adapt to even difficult-to-understand voices, as well as much more complex queries that go far beyond the Foursquare example.

As systems get more data about where we are, what we are doing, what we are looking at, what or who we are interacting with, and what our preferences are, these virtual beings and assistants will become much better. Businesses will increasingly run on them, and your customers will choose businesses that better support our assistants. A "Hey Siri, can you get me some Chinese food for lunch?" type of query might soon decide that your Chinese restaurant is the one it'll bring thousands of customers to. Why you, rather than a competitor? Maybe you put your menu online, maybe you are better at social media, maybe you got better Yelp ratings, or maybe your staff is wearing Apple glasses and can answer queries for Apple customers faster so Siri starts to prefer your business.

Put all of these together and you'll see a computing system that works the way you do with other people; by gesturing and touching, talking, and using your eyes to focus attention on things.

That said, a major way we'll navigate around is, well, by moving around, and there's some major new technology that's been developed for sensing where we are, and what surrounds us. You'll see versions of this technology used in robots, autonomous cars, and in Augmented Reality glasses.

Sensors and Mapping

We humans take for granted moving around the real world. It seems easy to us, something we've done ever since we were born after our parents bundled us up and brought us home.

Computers, though, couldn't understand this real world until recently. They didn't have "eyes" in which to see it and didn't have even a basic understanding of being able to move around, that is, until the mobile phone came along and we started teaching it by building digital maps.

At first, those digital maps were mere lines where streets are, with a few dots of data along the street. Today, however, our glasses, our cars, and robots in the street are mapping that street out with billions of points of data, and now this same process is happening inside our factories, hospitals, shopping malls, and homes.

Photo credit: Luminar Technologies. Here, a street is mapped out in 3D by Luminar Technologies' solid state LIDAR.

Mapbox, which is the map provider that hundreds of thousands of apps use, showed us the future of maps that was only possible once mobile phones became ubiquitous enough to get huge amounts of data on every street. It showed us how they could build an entire map of a freeway, including lanes, via huge numbers of mobile check-ins. Every time you open Yelp or Foursquare, or use Snapchat, among other apps, it gets another little point of location data, and if you get enough of these points, which they call "pings," a new kind of map is possible due to mega-huge databases of all that data, combined with Machine Learning to make sense of all that data streaming into its servers.

Then, there is data collected by cameras or new kinds of 3D sensors, like time-of-flight lasers, which measure the world out very accurately by figuring out how long a beam of light takes to reflect off of a surface and get back to it. Your 3D sensor in a modern iPhone works like that. Today, Apple mostly uses that sensor for Augmented Reality avatars or face detection to unlock your phone, but in the future, those sensors will do a lot more.

A Tesla car, driving down the same street, images the street as a point-cloud of 3D data, and there are many streets where a Tesla drives down the street every few seconds, gathering even more data.

Soon every stop sign, tree, pole, lane marker, restaurant sign, and far more insignificant details, will be mapped by many companies. Apple alone drove four million miles with 360-degree cameras and 3D sensors, in an attempt to make its maps better. Other companies have driven even further.

These early efforts in mapping the world are great, but the datapoints that all these companies have collected is going up exponentially. The next frontier will be to map out everything.

Our friends who have worked at Uber tell us it is keeping track of the sensor data coming from the mobile phones of its drivers. It can tell if streets have a lot of potholes just because those driver's phones are shaking. The auto insurance company, Go, says it has maps of which streets have more accidents than others. It and other companies are laying on top of the digital map all sorts of things, from sensor readings coming off of machines, to other location data from various databases, similar to how Zillow shows you the quality of school districts on top of homes you might be considering buying.

Luminar Technologies's CEO, Austin Russell (he runs a company that builds LIDAR sensors for autonomous cars), told us how his sensors work—they map out the real world with solid-state sensors that can see up to 250 meters away. The high-resolution point cloud that is generated is processed by Artificial Intelligence that quickly identifies literally every feature on the street. Other companies take that data and are building high-resolution contextual maps that future cars then can use. Russell explained to us how these maps are nothing like maps humans have ever used before. These maps, he says, aren't a simple line like you would see on your mobile phone, but a complete 3D representation of the street, or surroundings of where you are.

The glasses of the future will do something very similar. Companies like recently acquired 6D.ai had been using the cameras on mobile phones to build a crude (as of 2019) 3D map of the world. 6D.ai had been calling it an AR Cloud, but what it really is is a sheet of polygons stretched on every surface that a particular camera sees. AR Cloud is a new term that incorporates a technology called SLAM, which stands for Simultaneous Location and Mapping. That's the technique developed by NASA to have the Mars Rover navigate around the surface of Mars without humans being involved. Basically, it is how a robot can see the real world and move around in it. AR Cloud takes that further by giving a framework for where virtual items can be placed.

This is how Augmented Reality works at a base level. In order to put a virtual item onto the real world, you need a "digital twin" of that world. We don't like that term, because in reality, we see some places having dozens of digital twins. Times Square in New York, for instance, will be scanned by Apple, Facebook, and Microsoft, along with dozens of car companies and transportation companies, and eventually robots from Amazon and other companies, which will be rolling through there delivering food and products. Each building a digital twin.

This digital twin need not look anything like the real world to humans. At Niantic, the folks who make Pokémon Go, Ross Finman's team, have such a digital twin with only data of where people play games built on top of its platform—parks, shopping malls, sports arenas, that kind of thing. The data in its platform doesn't look like the real world to a human. Their "map" of the real world then converts that data into contextual information about the real world. Is there water nearby? Is this a park where children play, or adults hike? That data lets them build better games, by putting specific Pokémon characters near water, and others, where there are, say, tons of forests, and their world wide database is doubling in size every few months.

The holy-grail, though, is to have a detailed map of every surface that surrounds a human. Already at factories like the ones Audi or Volkswagen run, they have done just that. They used cameras and 3D sensors to build a high-resolution virtual version of their factory floors using a system from a company called Visualix, which tracks everything in that factory down to a centimeter accuracy, its CTO Michael Bucko told us. Why? For two reasons: training and design.

It can use that virtual factory floor to train employees using VR headsets on new jobs before they even see the real factory. It can also use that same virtual factory floor to see how to redesign part of it to hold a new set of robots, for instance, too, and design workspaces for the humans that will need to interact with the robots. It won't stop there, either. Workers, who wear Augmented Reality headsets, will be able to be assisted during their work while on the real factory floor. Re'flekt already built such a system for Audi workers. They can even leave videos on the real factory floor for the next shift to explain how to use a new piece of equipment. This is especially useful if a worker is retiring and will be walking out the door with dozens of years of knowledge about how said equipment actually works. These videos can be left on that real equipment by attaching it to the "digital twin" that is actually in a database up in the cloud. To the human it looks real, but it is all virtual and all enabled by sensors and cameras that have mapped out the factory floor.

Bucko says its hundreds of customers are using Visualix' SLAM-mapping and positioning technology to build the foundation for Augmented Reality, as well as the digital twin that thousands of robots will use to navigate inside, say, a huge warehouse or retail store.

Your kitchen will soon be the same as that factory. The cameras on the front of your glasses will build a 3D map of your kitchen (Microsoft's HoloLens and even the $400 Oculus Quest have four cameras that are constantly mapping out the room you are in, at a high resolution). It won't take your privacy away—that's how it works, so that you can play Virtual Reality or use Augmented Reality. On the HoloLens, sometimes, you even catch a glimpse of the polygon sheet that it's producing on your walls, tables, and floor. It then uses that sheet of billions of little triangles to put virtual items on top.

Today, we don't have enough bandwidth or power in our devices to upload that sheet to the cloud, but we can see how, in the future, you will want every room in your home mapped out this way, along with every place you typically use these devices in: your car, your office, even stores. Today, these maps, or sheets of polygons, are stored locally, partly for privacy reasons, but also partly because, again, the small batteries and processors inside just can't handle a lot of uploading and downloading and comparing of these sheets yet. That will start to change dramatically this year, as this process of seeing the real world and uploading and downloading a digital twin of it gets more efficient.

Visual mapping with cameras, LIDARs, and 3D sensors isn't all that's going on here, either.

Once these sheets of polygons, or even the higher-resolution point clouds, hit a computer, you'll see systems that categorize this data. MobileEye, at CES 2019, showed what we mean. This autonomous car company, started in Israel and now owned by Intel, not only builds a digital twin of the real world, but as users drive by, say, a restaurant, it ingests that data into its AI systems and then categorizes that data into a useful database that sits on top of the map. Now, it knows where your favorite Chinese restaurant is. It also knows what is next to it. So, future drivers can now say "navigate me to my favorite Chinese restaurant" and it will take you right there.

The dream is to go further than any of this—to a memory aide. After all, if these imaging and categorization systems are already able to map out where your favorite restaurants are, they can also do things like remember where you left your phone or your keys, even warning you if you walk away from a table in said restaurant without picking up your phone. They could say to you, "Hey dummy, you left your phone on the table inside the restaurant."

Soon, these databases will remember everything in your world and will notice if you move things around, or where you left your keys. Why? The demand on these companies will be to build much more realistic Augmented and Virtual Reality experiences. Virtual beings will even sit on chairs with you in your kitchen and will have conversations with you. To do that properly, it will need to be fully situationally aware. Not just know there's a chair there, but the context of a chair. After all, don't you behave differently when sitting in a chair at church, or school, or one at a noisy bar? So, too, will the virtual beings in our future glasses.

That sensor and map data will lead into new computing architectures, too, particularly when paired with the high bandwidth of 5G and new Wi-Fi.

Computing Architectures

Computing Architectures have also gone through major paradigm shifts, and as we move into Spatial Computing, will see another major shift: to decentralized systems. Databases that once used to be stored on a single server, then multiple ones, moved to virtual Cloud servers. We saw that move first-hand working inside Microsoft and particularly Rackspace. When Rackspace started in the late 1990s, it installed servers in racks for customers. Today, those customers buy virtual servers that can be started up in far less than a second.

This move led to Amazon Web Services being the dominant way that start-ups build their infrastructure. Today, Amazon offers dozens of different kinds of virtualized servers, from databases to ones with beefy GPUs to do image processing on. It also started out as having one big data center, to having many around the world in regions.

The goal is to get computing as close to users as possible. Some of that is for redundancy, yes, so if a data center in one region fails, the others kick in and the service stays up. Today, though, as we move into Spatial Computing, there are another couple of reasons—to reduce latency—and reduce costs of building systems that will see very heavyweight workloads. See, we are still controlled by physics. A packet of data can't travel faster than the speed of light, and, actually, it is slowed down by each piece of equipment it travels through.

Plus, as we move our businesses from, say, things that work like e-commerce systems that serve web pages, to ones that look and work more like interactive video games, traditional infrastructure that's centralized will start to crack and break, not to mention becoming very expensive.

This is why most companies no longer use Oracle to house their databases, preferring instead to house their databases on hundreds of virtualized servers, or even using serverless architectures that let companies like Amazon or Microsoft handle all that infrastructure work.

Photo credit: Robert Scoble. A bunch of wires serving 5G radios in Las Vegas' T-Mobile Arena. Just a very small part of how Spatial Computing experiences will get to your glasses and mobile devices.

As we move to 5G, which gets that packet from a cell tower to your glasses or your phone with very little latency, the latency elsewhere in the system will become the bottleneck. Already, we are seeing new computing architectures that push the systems that draw polygons on your glasses' screen out to the edge of the network—in other words, on the glasses themselves or a box that's sitting in your home or office or somewhere else nearby.

But some data still needs to travel elsewhere. Think about if you are playing a virtual shooting game in VR. Now, if you are playing a neighbor who lives on your street or in your apartment building, you might see everything slow down due to latency. Why? Well, that packet might need to travel from your home in, say, Mumbai, all the way to one of the mega-huge data centers in Las Vegas and back, passing through dozens of switches and routers, not to mention fiber or, worse, copper cable, to make it back and forth. Just because you have two-millisecond latency times to your cell tower won't mean that you have a good experience shooting at your neighbor in a video game, or collaborating with a coworker on a new product design.

As a result, businesses will increasingly be forced to buy cloud computing resources closer to the people playing the game. The standard architecture used by businesses is to spread data over three to ten regions, or data centers. That won't be enough, though, in this new highly interactive 5G-enabled Spatial Computing world. Packets getting to major data centers will still introduce too much latency and cost, because if everything is centralized, you need massive server power to deal with the loads that will soon come due to new customer demands like interactive VR experiences.

A new architecture is evolving that some are calling "fog." A new three-tier approach "cloud" for massive data centers far away, "fog" is for servers closer to you and "edge" is for servers that are built into your devices or are very close to you in your homes or offices. Your main servers might be on Amazon or Microsoft Azure hundreds or thousands of miles away, which we still will call cloud, but a new set of smaller data centers will evolve that will serve parts of cities, or neighborhoods. This new layer, since it sits between the huge data centers that Amazon, Microsoft, IBM, and Google run for their cloud infrastructure and users, is called fog. It's sort of between a real-world cloud (the huge data center) and the ground (for example, your computer), just like real fog is. In this way, many packets won't travel far at all, especially if you are only trying to shoot your neighbor virtually. These new smaller servers, or, fog servers, don't need to be massive machines because they will support far fewer users. So, this three-tier approach will scale to many new application types.

Businesses that come into Spatial Computing will need to build using this new three-tier approach, pushing as much computing power out as close to users as possible. Older businesses will find that moving from a heavily centralized infrastructure where everything lives on huge data centers to one that's decentralized will be culturally and financially challenging, but it must be done to support not just these new use cases, but to support the many new users we expect (and the increasing demands on infrastructure we expect they will bring).

While that is all happening, we foresee a new set of infrastructures needed—content management systems. Designing standard business web pages that keep track of the images and text that need to be translated to local languages is fairly simple compared to having, say, different Pokémon characters for each city around the world. We visited EchoAR to get a look at one of these new Spatial Computing management systems. They showed us how users could even change their avatars and that the system would distribute those new avatars in real time to other gamers, or even corporate users around the world.

Add it all up and CIOs inside businesses will need to learn new systems and budget differently for the new workloads that are rapidly evolving.

Artificial Intelligence (Decision Systems)

AI has gone way beyond telling the difference between dogs and cats. Today's AI, in the form of Machine Learning and Deep Learning, and often with the aid of Computer Vision, is used for everything from building virtual cities, to driving autonomous vehicles and robots, to helping answer your emails.

All of these elements provide the situational "awareness" that is necessary for software running in a machine to present the appropriate images, and possibly accompanying sound to the person who is viewing Virtual Reality or Augmented Reality experiences, or riding in an autonomous vehicle.

Before we go deeper into how AI is generally used for Spatial Computing, let's define what AI, Machine Learning, Deep Learning, and Computer Vision are.

AI is the simulation of human intelligence using software and accompanying apps or machines. Machine Learning, which is sometimes not included as a branch of AI since it is seen as its least robust form, automates analytical model building by identifying patterns in data and making decisions based on those perceived patterns.

Deep Learning is a more robust Machine Learning technique that uses multi-layered hidden artificial neural networks in a "supervised" or "unsupervised" way, having as many as hundreds of network layers that either train on large amounts of data (supervised) or not (unsupervised) and then makes decisions. Multi-layered neural networks are actually a system of mathematical algorithms that work together to come to a decision on what a pattern in a particular dataset is.

If the Deep Learning is supervised, it uses labeled data as training inputs, that is, data that has been identified, collected together, and labeled according to particular attributes, such as visual data labeled as "car" or "traffic sign" or "store front." The output of "supervised" Deep Learning is the determination of whether or not the new data that is fed to it matches with the training data in terms of particular attributes.

If the Deep Learning is unsupervised, it means that there is no labeled training dataset and the outcomes are unknown. The system learns on its own using its mathematical algorithms to see patterns. It is the unsupervised version of Deep Learning that has caught everyone's imagination. Both supervised and unsupervised Deep Learning are used for autonomous vehicles, but it is unsupervised learning that enables the vehicle to make a decision as to whether it should change lanes or suddenly stop. There is also a reinforced version of learning that mixes both supervised and unsupervised methods, but it is still the unsupervised "leg" that produces the outcomes that most mimic human decision-making.

Computer Vision plays a very big part in both basic Machine Learning and Deep Learning. Corresponding to human vision, it serves as a mechanism by which both digital images and real life images are "sensed," with image attributes then sent to the learning mechanism, which in this case is Machine Learning and Deep Learning; in the case of digital images, the use of Computer Vision is often called image processing. For instance, in the case of digital images, those that are in color are reduced to grayscale by the more advanced image processing algorithms, because this reduces the amount of data that the system has to deal with for identification. If color intensity is one of the attributes that needs to be categorized, then it is done by way of a digital tag. For real-life images, Computer Vision actually uses cameras that feed the visual data through its Computer Vision algorithms, which identify the elements of the images, reducing everything to computer code that could then be fed through supervised Machine Learning and Deep Learning algorithms, first as training data if the data is more finely labeled by the Computer Vision algorithms, or, otherwise, fed through unsupervised Deep Learning algorithms.

In Spatial Computing, AI algorithms coupled with Computer Vision are used extensively. It is not hard to understand why this would be the case since Spatial Computing often deals with first identifying and then predicting the movement of three-dimensional objects, and it can even work to identify and predict what you, a robot, or an autonomous vehicle will do next, or where you or it will look, within a Spatial Computing environment. This can be achieved because the AI algorithms, coupled with Computer Vision, produce a high level of situational "awareness" within the software that could then be used to make predictions about three-dimensional qualities and movements. New virtual beings, like "Mica," which was demonstrated in 2019 by Magic Leap, can even walk around and interact with real and virtual items in your room, thanks to this technology.

Other examples of where digital situational "awareness" is necessary for Spatial Computing are when drones and autonomous vehicles are operated. For drones, the need for situational "awareness" goes beyond what is needed to have the drone move in space without colliding with other objects. Drones used for the delivery of packages, such as what Amazon is championing, as well as those used for warfare, have objectives that need to be fulfilled regarding the identification of objects and the predictions of correct trajectory that could be determined by AI algorithms and Computer Vision. Similar types of machines along these lines that benefit from using AI systems are food and parcel delivery robots that travel on city streets, as well as robots used in manufacturing and logistics that operate in irregular environments.

Another example of a machine that benefits from using AI systems is an autonomous vehicle. There are many similarities between the smaller delivery robot and an autonomous vehicle in terms of them having to seamlessly navigate city streets; however, the complexities associated with the rules of the road and the more sophisticated machinery and human payload warrant a much more robust Deep Learning system, one that incorporates Computer Vision that uses reinforced learning.

Outside of these physical manifestations using AI systems are those that integrate the virtual with the textual.

Machine Learning really started to hit its stride when it became the system of choice for the user interface operation of bots; those textually-based, mostly reactionary "assistants" that companies ranging from insurance to telecom, to retail to entertainment, and others are still using on their website direct messaging systems and for customer phone calls.

Virtual assistants, such as Siri, Amazon Alexa, and Google Assistant, are just vocalized bots that have been encapsulated within branded machinery, such as the iPhone, Amazon Echo, and Google Nest Hub. Where these become relevant to Spatial Computing is when these voice assistants are paired up with devices such as AR glasses (to a lesser degree, they are currently useful spatially when used in collaboration with a smartphone and a mobile AR app).

When Apple comes out with their AR glasses, we fully expect them to offer a version of Siri as the voice interface. In the future, the expectation is that voice navigation and command, paired with natural hand manipulation, will serve as computing's user interface.

Characters that embody a bot virtually are called synthetic or AI characters, though it will be a long while before these virtual characters truly have unsupervised Deep Learning capabilities. These synthetic characters can be made three-dimensional, and thus spatial, and can be used in VR, as well as AR apps and experiences. Uses of these go beyond entertainment, into sales and marketing, training, customer relations, and other business uses—basically, anywhere where an expert is needed to provide relevant information.

In the further future, AI using unsupervised algorithmic systems could potentially create a culture and government for its own embodied bots, such as robots, which would ideally be in the service of humanity. These beings would be the ultimate in what Spatial Computing could bring. We choose to be optimistic with regard to this potentiality.

Back to the present. Since many tasks in Spatial Computing cannot be accomplished without the use of AI algorithms often coupled with Computer Vision, AI's impact on the business landscape cannot be overemphasized.

Evolution

The seven industry verticals that we will be covering in this book—Transportation; Technology, Media, and Telecommunications (TMT); Manufacturing; Retail; Healthcare; Finance; and Education—are in the beginning stages of being transformed by AI-enhanced Spatial Computing. We will go into more detail on these transformations when we address each vertical in their individual chapters.

The evolution of personal computing, from text-based interface to a three-dimensional one with Spatial Computing, fulfills our need for directness and ease that is produced via innovation. Spatial Computing's 3D interface jumpstarts a new higher curve for productivity.

The current technologies that fuel Spatial Computing will inevitably be enhanced and deepened with new technologies, all of which will take computing to new places that we cannot even imagine at this time.

In our next Part, Part II, we provide you with a roadmap for the disruptions caused by Spatial Computing that will happen in seven industries, starting with the transportation industry.

Part II

The Seven Visions

A Road Map to Spatial Computing Disruption in Seven Industries

3

Vision One – Transportation Automates

Soon, we will summon vehicles that will arrive without humans in them. This will have deep implications for humans and the cities and infrastructure we use. They will also collect data that will let us both see ourselves differently and develop new services that may affect everything, from how we go out to eat to how we shop and find other services like nightclubs. Here, we'll dig into these deep changes and the technology that will bring them to us.

A Future Vision

It is the 2030s. You are in front of Chicago's Navy Pier. It is raining, so you need a ride back to your hotel. You look into your Apple glasses and say, "Hey Siri, get me a ride."

"Okay, Mr. Smith, would you like your usual luxury ride?"

"Yes."

"A Tesla Model X will arrive within 3 minutes. Sorry, we are experiencing much heavier vehicle traffic than usual."

Within a few seconds, your glasses show you where your ride is. A letter "A/ Luxury" for "autonomous" is pointing to where your ride is, which is coming closer to you. You can see a map of your area and spin it with your hands in mid-air, just in case you don't like the default view. You see a 3D model of your Tesla driving toward you on a 3D map.

The reason you were spinning the map? You wanted to see the city from the top down to see what the holdup is. With this view, you can see thousands of other data sources, all showing the city in some form of 3D. There are little robots delivering things on sidewalks, showing you their surroundings. There are people walking around giving random bursts of 3D data to the map. There are tons of autonomous cars, each with a variety of sensors spraying high resolution 3D data. Finally, you can see data from cameras and 3D sensors hidden in light posts and stop lights. The city is awash with 3D bubbles of live data, which shows that there's a big wreck on the freeway. You can even see that an "M" caused the wreck—"M" for manually driven. Those cars give you data too, but it isn't 3D, just location.

Your Spatial Computing glasses or contact lenses let you see all the data. As your car gets closer to you (this one is in the Tesla network), you can see it glowing so that you can make sure to get into the correct car and not into someone else's Tesla. This visualization isn't the only thing that will change about the transportation system of the future, either. Thanks to combining databases, you will get directed from car to public transport to private drone to shared rides and back. In the next decade, major parts of the transportation systems in many countries will be automated. So, on that ride through Chicago, you'll see trucks, trains, buses, delivery robots, and many cars roll by that have no humans driving them.

Because we have many vehicles on the road that are automated, we'll start seeing major changes to the infrastructure we drive on, too. Special lanes for automated vehicles are starting to show up. Why? Dozens of vehicles can be chained together in a convoy that will make those lanes more efficient and reduce traffic. Already, Elon Musk is promising that Teslas will start cataloging potholes, both to report them to other drivers, as well as to report them to crews that will fix them. His fleet, while we were writing this book, added automatic lane changes so that you could see a car ahead of you finding a new pothole, and then report it to a cloud-based system keeping track and telling all other cars, for example, to "avoid lane number one because there's a big pothole there." Even alert human drivers might catch on that all Teslas are changing lanes in an area and join them too.

Vehicles will also be controlled by the central city government in conjunction with several corporate systems that have implemented an "air traffic control system" for watching each car get on and off freeways. It even tells those cars where to go to pick up riders, to do work like deliver food or packages, or go for a charge or a carwash.

How do we know all this? Well, we've talked with quite a few people who are building this kind of system. But the truth is that, in 2019, the system was built and was being tested in a very small number of neighborhoods, in cities such as Pittsburgh, Phoenix, Mountain View, or San Francisco, where companies such as General Motors, Mercedes-Benz, Uber, Waymo, and Tesla were testing new autonomous systems.

Cars have come a long way from the slow, smelly, and loud vehicles of the early 1900s to being something that we all rely on.

Photo credit: Robert Scoble. Early image of a Google self-driving car (now branded as Waymo) on Freeway 280 near Palo Alto with an early-model Velodyne LIDAR system on top, spinning furiously away back in December of 2009.

But that reliance will soon be far deeper as transportation systems turn into utilities where vehicles are seen less as something you own, but as something you put to work.

The Paths to Autonomy

If you sit in a cafe in Mountain View, or a variety of other places near San Francisco, and watch the world go by, you'll see a variety of autonomous cars roll by your table from companies like Zoox, Waymo, Aurora, Cruise, and others—as well as Teslas, which are more popular here than most other car brands. On the freeways nearby, you're likely to see semi-trailer trucks loaded with futuristic sensors.

It's clear from just watching the contraptions being tested on these roads (along with a few other cities, like Phoenix, Arizona) that the future of transportation will be different than it is today, but most people are still grappling with just how different it will be. Lots of us have arguments about when autonomous vehicles will be far more ubiquitous than the Waymos that you see pass through here every few minutes.

Today, even Waymos are limited to certain neighborhoods, and there's a technical reason for that; they can only go down streets that have been imaged a few times with high-resolution cameras and lasers and have been tested several times.

Autonomous cars aren't really something new. Industrialist Norman Bel Geddes created the first self-driving car in 1939. Back then, it was an electric vehicle guided by radio-controlled electromagnetic fields, which were generated with magnetized metal spikes embedded in the roadway for a "Futurama" exhibit. By 1958, General Motors took it further with a car that had sensors that could follow a wire embedded in the road. That project was aborted after the government stopped funding, even though it was shown that it would reduce accidents by 40 percent, and would also increase road capacity by 50 percent.

The idea didn't really come back into public view until Google started driving cars on Silicon Valley freeways in late 2009. Co-author Robert Scoble had the first video of that car on YouTube in December 2009 when he noticed a Prius with a weird spinning LIDAR on top (LIDARs have dozens of lasers that spin at 30 times a second, making a 3D map of the road and everything around the car). He didn't realize it was a self-driving car, because there was a driver who immediately put on the brakes to get away from his camera. It took until October 2010, when the New York Times wrote about the project, that people realized what those weird cars were doing on the local freeways around Mountain View.

Google's efforts actually came out of Stanford and Carnegie Mellon, but mostly Stanford, who, under Sebastian Thrun's leadership, had won the Defense Advanced Research Projects Agency (DARPA) Grand Challenge in 2005. That challenge was a 150-mile road course. It was a race to see if anyone could develop a car that could navigate by itself. The first time the challenge was held, no one completed the course.

What DARPA was hoping for was a new type of vehicle capable of navigating roads without needing to be manned by soldiers. They were losing tons of vehicles to crude roadside bombs. We visited Nellis Airforce Base in Las Vegas to visit with soldiers who had to deal with this problem while deployed in Afghanistan, and they showed us blown-up Humvees and supply trucks, and talked about fellow veterans who had been maimed or had died in these blasts. The trucks and supplies could be replaced, but the human cost was adding up.

On our own roads, the carnage was high, too. In America alone, more than 30,000 lives are lost every year to car accidents. When he was 18, Sebastian Thrun's best friend had died in one of these accidents, and it drove Thrun to study how to use computers to increase safety on our nation's roads.

He told us that he didn't realize the problem would prove to be so daunting. When he started out as a Stanford student, he thought it would take a few years. Turns out it will probably take 20, and, even then, it probably won't work on every road or path in the world, nor in every condition. That could take another decade. But as we talked with him in October of 2019, Waymo was just starting its first tests on real roads with no driver inside, taking real passengers around.

Which gets us to another path to autonomy that also started around the same time: Uber. When Uber was started it was just a year or so after the iPhone shipped in June 2007. It was partly invented in a Paris, France snowstorm. As we (co-author Robert Scoble, along with a group of other speakers at the conference) were coming out of the LeWeb conference, Travis Kalanick and Garrett Camp were talking with others about their idea. We were all stuck without cars and transportation in Paris, which had ground to a near halt due to the unusual snowstorm. Camp and Kalanick wanted to have a way to see where cars would be on their new iPhones. Within a year, the two built a company to do exactly that and Uber was born. Today, Uber is valued more than most car companies, which shows that investors are behind the idea, and it has major competitors in Didi in China and Lyft in the US, both of which also are valued at tens of billions of US dollars.

One reason that so many billions of dollars are being invested in autonomous cars is that the economics will dramatically change Uber and Lyft, because as you remove humans from driving, you radically change the potential economics and you get a far more consistent user experience, which is key to building a great brand. Riccardo Giraldi, who runs user experience for Zoox (a company that is building its own taxi vehicle from scratch based around autonomous driving), asks us to think about Starbucks. Starbucks is a great brand, not because of its amazing coffee, but because it's extremely consistent, ubiquitous, affordable, and personalized. All of those qualities, Giraldi tells us, will be possible once autonomous cars are rolling in enough cities.

Since Waymo started in its first one or two cities in 2019, we expect that it will take just a few years for automatic cars to be operating in 20 cities, and in 100 cities by the end of the 2020s.

Photo credit: Robert Scoble. A self-driving car in Velodyne's parking lot in Morgan Hill, California. Velodyne makes the LIDARs [the spinning set of lasers and computers on top of the car] for many of the companies doing self-driving research.

This race has already created a new ecosystem of sensor development and of companies who make the Machine Learning system and test suites. One of the more interesting people to meet in this area is David Hall. His company, Velodyne, sold the best subwoofers to audio enthusiasts back in the 1980s. As he moved his production to China in the 1990s, he found he still had a group of smart electro-mechanical engineers and a huge warehouse in Morgan Hill, California, which is in the southern part of Silicon Valley. He heard about the DARPA challenges and tried putting together a car to compete in it, but he quickly learned that he would be outspent by universities like Stanford and Carnegie Mellon, he told us, and so his entrepreneurial skills went into action.

Instead of building his own car, he decided to build the sensors that the other teams would need. His Velodyne LIDAR was the spinning thing on top of that first Prius that Google was driving around Silicon Valley, and today, Velodyne is moving to new semiconductor LIDARs that no longer spin and can be hidden inside car bumpers.

Falling Car Transportation Costs

Transportation is about to get dramatically less expensive. Insiders from Sebastian Thrun, who ran the first Google autonomous vehicle team before he went on to run Udacity and a new electronic flying vehicle start-up called Kitty Hawk, to Elon Musk, CEO of Tesla, talk about reasons why transportation will get cheaper. Biggest among them is that cars will no longer sit in garages most of the day but will go out and "work" on your behalf. There are other economic advantages, too. The original Stanford team told us that autonomous vehicles could save pennies while they drive because they would be more efficient than human-driven ones, even going up and down hills more efficiently, or joining in caravans on freeways.

If you buy a car today, you will probably buy a car that costs thousands to tens of thousands of dollars. You'll also be paying to maintain it and to keep it insured. And with all that expense, you'll only use it an hour or two a day; the rest of the time, it will sit in your garage. That's hardly a great economic decision. Imagine spending capital on a factory and only running it a couple of hours a day. That doesn't make sense, right?

Car sharing networks like Uber and Lyft have shown that a car can be used much more frequently, which shares the cost among many riders, but there are much deeper cost advantages coming due to electrification and the development of autonomous vehicles.

If you take the cost of buying a $70,000 car, and all the other costs, like insurance, fuel, maintenance costs of tires, filter changes, windshield wipers, oil changes, brakes, and so on, it comes out to around $4,000 a month if you drive it around the clock. Cheaper if you buy a $35,000 Toyota.

Now, divide that by the 733 hours in a 31-day month. That comes out to a little less than $5.50 an hour. Add $15 minimum wage and your wholesale costs come to just a little over $20 an hour. Uber or Lyft turn that into $60 retail. (The standard is to always triple wholesale prices to arrive at retail. You could easily check this if you so desired: order an Uber and ask your driver to drive you around for an hour. The bill will be more than $60).

If you could rent the same car out without a driver, your costs would only be $5.50 an hour wholesale, or about $17 retail. $17 versus more than $60. That is the economic power of driverless cars. It explains why so many billions of dollars are being invested into companies like Cruise (General Motors), Waymo (Alphabet [Google]), Zoox, Aurora, Tesla, and Daimler (Mercedes-Benz), not to mention many others, including Lyft and Uber themselves.

So, when self-driving hits, really hits, the economics will totally change. This change will be as big of a deal as when Henry Ford turned on the first assembly line and made cars available to a much larger percentage of Americans due to dramatically lowering the costs of buying a car.

When the economics change, so does the utility. As transportation gets cheaper, we will use it for more. If we could sleep in our cars as they drive, we could live further from our jobs. Our cars could do work while we sleep, or work. "Hey Tesla, pick up my laundry," we might soon say.

What does this have to do with Spatial Computing? Everything. First, the technology underneath a self-driving vehicle is very similar to the technology that makes Augmented Reality glasses possible. Eight cameras, sensors for gravity and movement, and 3D sensors—all joined together where AI does the work. These glasses will also be used to both control transportation and to enjoy it more due to virtualized screens and 3D social networks, games, entertainment, and education, which we'll go into elsewhere in this book.

There are already companies doing that, like Holoride, which spun out of Audi. Holoride won best of the Consumer Electronics Show in Las Vegas in January 2019 and gives passengers a way to play VR. Already it has some big names onboard, like Ford and Universal Studios, who see a new market opening up. As cars convert into electric, more minutes will be spent charging, and many more families will take VR headsets on long drives to make those charging stops more fun. As companies like Apple and Facebook introduce AR glasses, there will be much more demand for the kinds of games that Holoride is planning.

The co founder of Holoride, Marcus Kuhne, told us they have lots of plans to expand as more Spatial Computing devices like Augmented Reality glasses get introduced and as cars start to become more automated. Already, if you have a Tesla, you don't have to pay much attention as your car drives on freeways. Soon, people who have these bleeding-edge cars will want to do a variety of things while on the freeway, like watching movies or TV, answering emails, looking at social media or news, or doing deeper work like catching up on a PowerPoint presentation or a spreadsheet before getting into work.

This demand goes way beyond games. We expect Spatial Computing glasses to bring all sorts of utility to driving, being a passenger, getting deliveries, and being a passenger in a self-driving vehicle. Not to mention that lots of insiders say that the technology that will run the Apple glasses is very similar to the technology that lets a computer system drive a car. In many ways, they will overlap in the next decade, one adding to the other.

These same glasses will be used to fill in gaps in autonomy, too. Sometimes, autonomous vehicles may get stuck and will have to be handed over to remote drivers. Those remote drivers will be wearing Spatial Computing glasses to see what the car is seeing.

Even if you "own" your own vehicle, which many will still need—for example, if you are a mechanic who needs your tools to always be in the back of your pickup truck—the costs will come way down and you'll pay a per-hour and per-mile fee that will be lower than what you are paying today. Why? Electric vehicles are cheaper. Autonomous vehicles are too, and you'll be able to do more as you use it, since you'll be able to use your Spatial Computing glasses to watch movies, play games with your friends, or simply catch up on some sleep while your truck drives you to your next job. All of this dramatically lowers both the real costs for using transportation and will bring deep changes to every part of life.

Autonomous Vehicle Round-up

Each autonomous vehicle (AV) has a slightly different configuration of equipment and systems needed to make things autonomous, so we will review some of the major setups to give you an understanding of the technology. Public information regarding setups is extremely variable due to competitive concerns.

In addition, we will touch upon autonomous trucks and autonomous "flying cars"— officially called autonomous eVTOLs, which stands for "electric vertical takeoff and landing" vehicles.

Before going into companies' autonomous configurations and other information, we'll pause to explain exactly what we mean by "autonomous." The Society of Automotive Engineers (SAE) International is a global association of more than 128,000 engineers and related technical experts in the aerospace, automotive, and commercial vehicle industries, and it sets the standards for the five distinct levels of autonomous technology in vehicles:

- **Level 5** is full driverless automation, where human control will never be required and, in fact, may be outlawed on public roads.
- **Level 4** allows for full automation in most situations, within a specific geographic area and during appropriate weather conditions—needing driver intervention infrequently.
- **Level 3** allows for full automation in certain situations, notably freeway driving, with driver intervention needed frequently.

- **Level 2** offers a combination of autonomous functions, such as basic lane-keeping autonomous steering, in combination with active cruise control; passengers actively driving is the norm.

- **Level 1** includes some very basic autonomous functionality, including Electronic Stability Control and Active Cruise Control technologies, with drivers expected to maintain complete control.

Most autonomous vehicle companies are currently operating on Level 4 autonomy, most notably on known scoped and mapped-out roads and testing tracks. Tesla is currently operating at Level 2. Level 4 and above is typically marked as autonomous.

Now that we've covered the generally accepted meaning of autonomous, let's discuss some of the companies who are working on these autonomous vehicles.

Zoox

The major reasons for the existence of autonomous vehicles include safety, mobility, and sustainability. Looking at the US-based infographic from Zoox on the next page, you can see that 94 percent of car crashes have been attributed to human error, many millions of adults have disabilities that preclude them from driving freely, and massive amounts of greenhouse gasses are emitted by passenger vehicles, with much of that occurring during traffic.

SAFETY	MOBILITY	SUSTAINABILITY
37,133	42	96%
lives lost in car crashes in 2017	hours lost per commuter in traffic per year	amount of time cars sit unused
94%	53	1,113
crashes attributed to human error	million adults with disabilities in 2015	million tons of greenhouse gasses emitted by passenger vehicles in 2016

Credit: Zoox. Statistics that can be related to non-autonomous passenger vehicles.

Zoox is one of the companies who is pioneering the autonomous car revolution. They are one of just a few that are actually building the car from the ground up, rather than taking an existing car model and adapting to an autonomous system. We talked to Mark Rosekind, Chief Safety Innovation Officer of Zoox, and he told us, as an example of improving safety, Zoox builds the back seats of their vehicles to have the same form features as the front seats, which are safer by design. Additionally, Zoox cars are not built with a steering wheel. Steering wheels cause many injuries during car accidents.

Since it was founded in 2014, Zoox has raised about $800 million in funding. In addition to building its own cars, Zoox is developing its own autonomous-driving software, electric vehicle program, and urban ride-hailing system. Zoox has been testing its cars and systems in San Francisco and announced that, in Fall 2019, it will launch a limited robo-taxi service in Las Vegas. Though, up until recently, Zoox's protocols indicated that at least two operators must be in the vehicle at the same time, the company announced that they will be ready to go driverless soon, though COVID-19 has put a temporary stop to their robo-taxi plans.

Credit: Zoox. An example of a Zoox autonomous car – this one is an early version with a steering wheel.

Zoox autonomous cars come equipped with multiple cameras, four LIDAR ("light detecting and ranging" remote sensing method) systems, radar ("radio detection and ranging") and proprietary sensors, along with GPS and proprietary mapping data systems. LIDAR uses light in the form of a pulsated laser to measure distances and is the most expensive sensor system of the sensors suite used, typically upward of 10 times more expensive than radar.

The LIDAR units can be seen around the top of the car, along with radar and proprietary sensors and cameras. Radar units can be found near the front and back bumpers.

For all current autonomous vehicle companies, the cameras and sensor suite work together with Computer Vision software using Machine Learning in order to perceive surroundings and environments and predict future actions of road objects, in order to plan the car's movement accordingly.

All current autonomous vehicle companies navigate roads by way of a combination of virtual computer simulation testing and modeling, which uses Machine Learning as well and prior meticulous mapping of particular roads to be traveled on. All autonomous vehicles currently use LIDAR. Tesla, whose cars are not yet autonomous, does not utilize LIDAR as a part of its navigation systems (more on this later).

Ford

Ford is currently using Fusion Hybrid sedans for their self-driving test vehicles that are on public roads in the cities of Miami, Pittsburgh, Dearborn, and Palo Alto. All test vehicles have a two-person safety operations team while operating in autonomous mode. The two-person driving team will continue to be used post COVID-19 restrictions in vehicles to map the cities it plans to launch in 2022 and collect data prior to being allowed to operate autonomously. The plan after that is to launch with all-new autonomous vehicles that do not include steering wheels or pedals for a human driver. These Ford autonomous vehicles will only be available for use in commercial fleets and will focus on transporting people and goods.

Credit: Ford. Austin was chosen as the third city, behind Miami and Washington, DC, where Ford announced they will launch autonomous vehicles by 2021.

Ford has partnered with Pittsburgh-based Argo AI, an Artificial Intelligence and robotics company, with a $1 billion investment to develop what Ford calls the "Virtual Driver System" for its self-driving vehicles.

Earlier in 2019, Ford announced that it is teaming up with Volkswagen to build a system for a Level 4 vehicle, with Volkswagen putting $2.6 billion of investment into Argo AI.

Ford's explicit sensor types include LIDAR, radar, an inertial measurement unit sensor, far-field cameras, and near-field cameras.

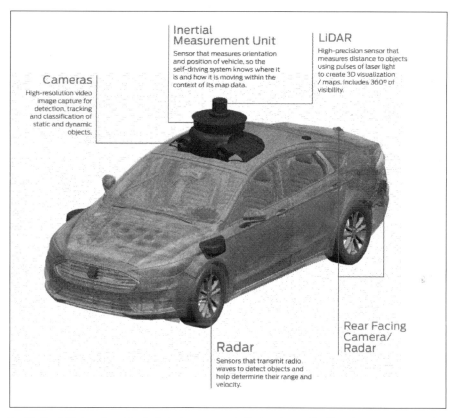

Credit: Ford. Pictured are the technical components that make up Ford's autonomous car system.

General Motors' Cruise

With regard to General Motors, their autonomous vehicle company is called Cruise. Each Cruise vehicle is equipped with five LIDAR units, 16 cameras, and 21 radar units and calculates its path on the road 10 times per second.

General Motors acquired Cruise in 2016 for reportedly over $500 million, and it has grown from around 40 employees to over 200 employees.

Photo credit: Cruise. A General Motors' Cruise self-driving car navigates the streets of San Francisco with a safety driver behind the wheel.

Cruise had originally planned to commercially deploy its autonomous vehicles by the end of 2019, but in July 2019, the company indicated that more testing than had been anticipated was needed and that they were working with Honda and General Motors to develop its autonomous vehicles. Cruise has raised more than $7 billion.

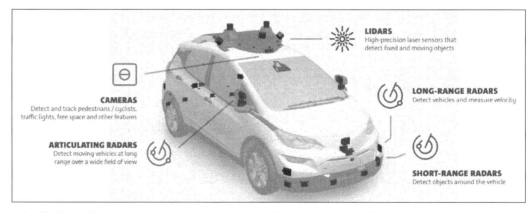

Credit: Cruise. Cruise's autonomous car system has relatively more radar units than other company systems.

Uber

All of Uber's current autonomous fleet are recent model-year Volvo XC90 sport-utility vehicles, upfitted with sensors and self-driving technology. The new version, which is its third-generation version, will be built to fit Uber's self-driving technology at the factory level. Uber will start testing this new car on public roads in 2020. It will still have a steering wheel and pedals; however, according to Uber, it has been designed to operate without a person behind the wheel.

In December 2018, Uber resumed limited self-driving car testing in Pittsburgh on public roads, following the death of a pedestrian in Arizona who was jaywalking in March 2018. The vehicle hit the pedestrian due to several reasons, though most notably due to the fact that Uber's software was not set up to recognize the possibility of jaywalking pedestrians. As a result, the pedestrian was classified as "other object," rather than a person.

Photo credit: Uber. An example of an Uber-branded autonomous car.

More redundancy with regard to the systems will be built into the new car version so that this, and other serious negative occurrences, can be avoided.

Credit: Uber. Some details on Uber's autonomous car system components.

Waymo

Waymo, the autonomous vehicle business under Alphabet (Google's parent company), has been saying for a while that its self-driving system is designed to operate without a human driver. In October 2019, Waymo sent an email to customers of its robo-taxi service in the Phoenix area that indicated, "Completely driverless Waymo cars are on the way."

Waymo's systems include three types of LIDAR that were developed in-house—a short-range LIDAR provides an uninterrupted view directly around it, a high-resolution mid-range LIDAR, and a powerful new generation long-range LIDAR. Other parts include a camera and Computer Vision system, radar, and self-driving software that incorporates Machine Learning trained on more than five million miles of on-road experience in six US states, and more than 25 cities and more than five billion miles of simulated driving. Waymo first began testing its technology in 2009 in and around its Mountain View headquarters.

Waymo has agreements to develop self-driving vehicles and services with Renault and its Japanese partner, Nissan Motor, and has deals to use minivans made by Fiat Chrysler Automobiles NV and Jaguar iPace sport-utility vehicles in its robo-taxi fleets.

Photo credit: Waymo. A portrait of a Waymo autonomous car.

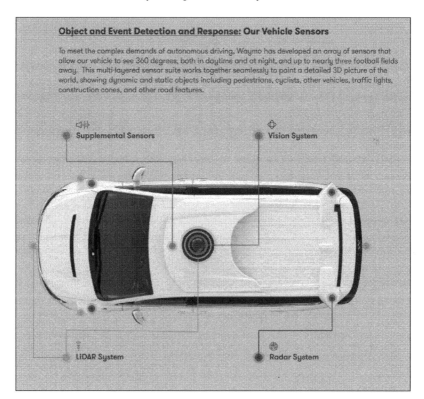

Credit: Waymo. Details of Waymo's vehicle sensors.

Tesla

We are including Tesla in this section, even though it is currently only at Level 2 autonomy. The reason we are doing so is to make it more clear what Tesla's current status is and what the possibilities are with regard to fully autonomous driving.

In comparison to others who use LIDAR systems, which can be 10 times more expensive than using radar, Tesla does not use LIDAR, but rather uses just radar, cameras, Machine Learning, ultrasonic sensors, and a custom computer system with a custom chip designed to enable full self-driving capabilities in the future. The next generation chip is said by Elon Musk to be three times better than the current chip and about two years away.

The current system has a forward-looking radar, eight cameras, 360-degree ultrasonic radar, and GPS.

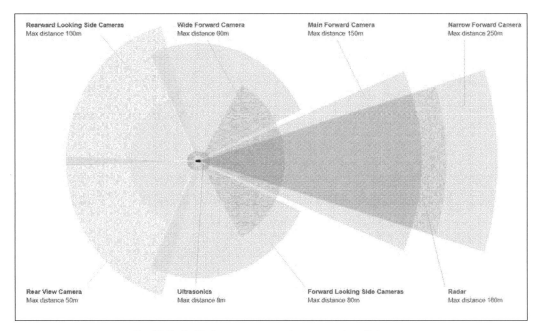

Credit: Tesla. Tesla car camera and sensor system distances.

Musk believes that it is possible for autonomous vehicles to rely solely on radar cameras, ultrasonic sensors, and GPS, rather than having to include LIDAR, which is expensive. And there are some key people that we have interviewed that also believe this to be the case, but they have asked us not to reference them or quote them.

Right now, there are only a few features that are part of Tesla's Level 2 automation: Navigation via Autopilot, Auto Lane Change, Autopark, Summon, Smart Summon, and coming later—system recognition and response to traffic lights and stop signs and automatic driving on city streets. Two terms, Summon and Smart Summon, need more explanation. With Summon, the car can move in and out of a tight space using the mobile app or key, and with Smart Summon, the car can navigate more complex environments and parking spaces—maneuvering around objects as necessary to come and find you in a parking lot.

Lyft, Magna, and Aptiv

With a $200 million investment from global supplier Magna, Lyft recently formed a partnership to co-develop fully autonomous vehicles. Lyft is developing the self-driving software system with a team of almost 300 engineers, while Magna is working to place those systems in the vehicles.

Photo credit: Lyft. A Lyft-branded autonomous car in action.

Lyft has finished a 10-week pilot testing period of their self-driving cars in Palo Alto with human safety drivers, utilizing technology from Blue Vision Labs, a London-based Augmented Reality company it has acquired. Blue Vision Labs' software uses cameras in smartphones to capture and perceive the environment, which could potentially lessen the requirement for more expensive sensors. Lyft also has a partnership with Aptiv, a company focused on mobile solutions. Together, up until COVID-19 restrictions, they were running an autonomous ridesharing pilot in Las Vegas, using BMW 540i cars. Aptiv has 75 of these cars deployed in Las Vegas, with 30 operating with Lyft since May 2018.

Aptiv's sensor suite is made up of nine LIDAR units (four short-range, five long-range), 10 radar units (six electronically scanning radars, four short-range radars), a trifocal camera, a camera specifically tasked with reading traffic lights, two GPS antennae, and two computers located in the car trunk.

Hyundai, Pony.ai, Aptiv, and Aurora

Hyundai has launched a pilot ridesharing service using prototype autonomous cars. A fleet of the autonomous Hyundai Kona Electric prototypes has started to provide free rides around Irvine, California.

Hyundai partnered up with Pony.ai, a Chinese start-up with Toyota ties, on the autonomous-driving system utilized in the rideshare cars. Pony.ai provided Hyundai with the sensors and proprietary software that enables cars to analyze data and make driving decisions. BotRide, the app that will be used to hail these cars, was co-developed with Via, a ridesharing company.

Photo Credit: Hyundai. Hyundai teams up with Pony.ai, Aptiv, and Aurora.

Hyundai also recently announced a $4 billion joint venture with Aptiv to develop Level 4 and Level 5 technology. Additionally, Hyundai has taken a minority stake (undisclosed amount) in the start-up Aurora.

Photo credit: Aurora. An autonomous car using Aurora's self-driving technology, with more than half a dozen visible LIDARs and sensors.

Aurora

Aurora has integrated its full self-driving technology into six vehicle platforms, including sedans, SUVs, minivans, a large commercial vehicle, and a Class 8 truck. Recently, it made a deal with Fiat Chrysler to develop self-driving commercial vehicles for its line of Ram Truck commercial vehicles, which is a portfolio that includes cargo vans and trucks. Aurora has not indicated any plans to ever launch a robo-taxi service.

Amazon participated in Aurora's $530 million Series B funding round, which was led by venture firm Sequoia Capital and was announced in February 2019. In September 2019, Volkswagen severed its partnership with Aurora, and recently stated that they are spinning out an internal start-up to bring robo-taxis and cargo vans to three continents by 2025.

Driven and Oxbotica

Driven, with its Ford Mondeos, is providing the first demonstration of an autonomous fleet driving in London. The UK tech firm Oxbotica is contributing its autonomous vehicle software system to the effort.

Oxbotica has a separate venture with the cab firm Addison Lee to produce an autonomous ride-sharing taxi service that is planned for June 2020.

In addition to Oxbotica, the Driven team is a combination of local authority planners, insurers, and cyber-security and data experts. They have been doing trials in Oxford and examining potential problems with hackers, communications technology, and the legal framework. The cars are currently operated with a safety driver in the front seat, ready to take control and intervene in difficult situations.

Photo credit: Driven. A Driven autonomous vehicle driving through Stratford, east London.

Autonomous Trucks

We've been told that **autonomous trucks (ATs)** could be 1.5 times more expensive than conventional trucks due to higher initial investment. And there has been a lot of talk about truckers losing their jobs due to ATs.

However, there is currently a massive driver shortage. As truckers retire, they are not being replaced. Younger generations are going for less-demanding careers in other industries.

Companies who operate ATs, and those who provide software for ATs, will be able to recoup the relatively higher initial investment needed to enter their markets in a number of ways. ATs are not subject to hours-of-service regulations, which limit the time a driver spends behind the wheel. With ATs, driving hours could be increased from 11 hours per day to 20. Trips will be faster due to more proficient driving due to optimized routing software and the elimination of the need for rest periods.

In terms of the kinds of change the trucking industry will undergo due to ATs, there will be a number of stages. The first two stages will feature "platooning," a technique used to wirelessly connect a convoy of trucks to a lead truck, which allows them to operate much closer together safely and increase fuel efficiencies. The first stage will be platooning with drivers at Level 3 autonomy. It will take three to five years to develop the networks of connected convoys.

Photo credit: Starsky Robotics. An example of a Starsky Robotics autonomous truck.

The second stage, coming in about in about five to seven years, will feature driverless platooning. While on an interstate, a driver will be in a lead truck and unmanned trucks will follow close behind. Drivers will take control of each vehicle once it leaves an interstate.

In about seven to ten years for the third stage, we predict that ATs will operate under Level 4 autonomy. Trucks will be unmanned on interstates and other "geofenced" areas without a platoon. Once off the interstate, drivers will take the ATs to their ultimate destination.

The first fully autonomous trucks, operating at Level 5, should appear in more than 10 years. This is the fourth stage, and over a long period of time, there will be a general move for a preference toward Level 5 ATs.

We are predicting the stages and timing for ATs, but not for AVs due to the complexities of city streets and political/legal concerns.

There are a number of companies who are working in the AT space, including Ike, Embark, TuSimple, Kodiak Robotics, and Waymo. Starsky Robotics shut down in March 2020 due to operational issues and a failure to get more investment.

Flying Cars (eVTOLs)

We recently talked with Sebastian Thrun, CEO of Kitty Hawk Corporation and chairman and co founder of Udacity, a for-profit online educational organization. Prior to this, at Google, Thrun founded Google X, home to projects like the Google self-driving car (now Waymo) and Google Glass, and at Stanford University, he was a research professor in the Computer Science department and director of the Stanford Artificial Intelligence Lab.

Photo credit: Kitty Hawk. One of Kitty Hawk's eVTOL vehicle types, Heaviside, navigating the skies.

Thrun is very passionate about eVTOLs and he believes that there is a great chance that operational autonomous eVTOLs will come before autonomous vehicles. The main reasons for this include the fact that airspace is much less cluttered than the roads on the ground, and that the technology for monitoring airspace has already been developed. Since eVTOLs travel in a straight line in the air versus having to follow non-direct and non-linear roads, they would be more energy efficient than AVs. Additionally, Thrun believes that it is possible that eVTOLs could navigate quite well without needing LIDAR, with a nod to the possibility of AVs not needing LIDAR due to the great strides the combination of Machine Learning, Computer Vision, and camera technologies have made.

Two of Kitty Hawk's eVTOL vehicle types, Heaviside and Cora, are being primed to become autonomous, with Boeing partnering up on Cora. A feature of Heaviside is technology that makes it roughly 100 times quieter than a regular helicopter. Being quiet is very important when it comes to taking off, navigating, and landing in urban areas, where vertical take-off and landing helipads, which are being called "Skyports," will be necessary. Both Heaviside and Cora are built to go no more than a little over 100 miles on a charge, with 70 miles being an average, and travel at 180 miles per hour, being about 10 times faster than travel on the ground by road. Charging is a breeze, taking no more than 15 minutes for a full charge, with the batteries being light and unremovable.

The US federal government, including NASA, FAA, and USDOT, all acknowledge that eVTOLs are coming. Los Angeles, Dallas, and Melbourne have signed on to launch eVTOLs by 2023.

Some other notable companies that are developing eVTOLs, and then autonomous eVTOLs, are Uber Air (which would enable four-person ridesharing flights in densely populated areas), Boeing's Aurora Flight Sciences (which Uber Air is partnering up with), and German start-up Volocopter GmbH, backed by Daimler AG and the Mercedes-Benz maker's biggest shareholder, the Zhejiang Geely Holding Group. Boeing CEO Dennis Muilenburg believes that commercial flying taxis could be a reality within the next five years.

Photo credit: Boeing. Boeing's first test of its Uber Air air taxi in January 2019.

Before any cultural or technological shift, particularly one as big as Spatial Computing looks to be, there's lots of arguing and resistance. Next, we will consider the extent of this "culture shock," what some of the arguments presented by skeptics might be, and how we foresee these arguments being overcome.

The Autonomous and Electric Culture Shock

When it comes to transportation's shifts, the arguments are varied and deep. Bring up electronic cars at literally any cocktail party and you'll hear a spectrum of reactions from "what a stupid idea—you have to charge for 40 minutes" to "people who stick with gas are destroying the earth."

Photo credit: Robert Scoble. New meets old: this book's co-author's family drove one of the first 10,000 Tesla Model 3s built to Detroit, where they visited Ford's first plant. Henry Ford, in this building, changed cars by building the first assembly line, which dramatically reduced the cost of buying one.

Add in talk about autonomous vehicles and you might experience an all-out brawl: "I love to drive."

The thing is, our culture is already changing due to early experiences, and while the resistance is deep, we look back to prior changes and every time there was a big shift, we heard the same kind of resistance. We look back at when the automobile first appeared in society and there were many who didn't like the contraptions, either. They scared the horses, for one. So much so that early owners had to have someone walk in front of the car to warn people one was about to come down the street.

How many people told us "I'll never carry a phone everywhere?" or "I'll never use social media"? As we wrote previous books about technology shifts and were among the first to try many a new technology, we can answer this for you: many.

That isn't to say that the resistance can be written off wholly. Not true—particularly when it comes to transportation. Their views, as expressed by especially conservative lawmakers, could bring a variety of legislative approaches. Already, we are seeing a vast difference in the technologies used on the streets. Some cities—London, for example—have blocked ride sharing, like Uber or Lyft, and still do. Others already have self-driving vehicles being tested out. In Phoenix, that brought tragedy, as an Uber car hit and killed a pedestrian in the early hours of one morning. Teslas have been blamed for a variety of deaths, including an Apple engineer who was tragically autopiloted into a barrier on a freeway offramp in Silicon Valley.

You might think that the federal government will decide, at least in the United States. That's not true, however, if you look at the vehicle code: each state decides on laws. This is the case even for interstate highways; states determine the laws upon any stretch of highway passing through said state. It's unclear how government administrations will work together to regulate autonomous vehicles, and there are many unanswered questions, from responsibility for deaths and wrecks, to whether or not you will be allowed to consume alcoholic drinks in an autonomous vehicle (today, that's not legal, at least in California, and if you are caught even in the back seat of a vehicle that's moving and you are intoxicated), you could be arrested for driving while intoxicated. Protestations of, "but hey, my Tesla is driving," have not yet been accepted by courts. We'll see many of these legal questions start to get settled in the 2020s.

You see this culture shift underway as people drive huge pickup trucks with horrible fuel mileage driving next to electronic cars from Nissan, Tesla, Chevy, and others, and you see the shifts on social media as people argue out which automaker produces the best product. While over the last few decades those arguments might have been between Chevy and Ford or American versus Japanese or versus European, the arguments in the 2020s will be about technology ecosystems, Spatial Computing apps, and who has the best AI and on which roads.

Already owners of Teslas have been captured on video sleeping on the freeways while their cars drive. The fact that these videos have gone viral and are discussed on TV news shows that a new usage pattern has started to arrive, and it's proving to be unnerving for many. There's a feeling that it's unsafe for everyone. Even owners of Teslas derided the first sleepers, but we posit that sight will be extremely common by the end of the 2020s, and it won't be done in just Teslas that only fairly well-off people can afford.

The next "weird" thing to get used to will be cars driving around without any humans in them at all. Tesla turned on the ability for cars to move around shopping mall parking lots this way, which generated another round of video derision. However, in 2019, an owner was always nearby, just in case something went wrong. Sometime soon, the owner will no longer be there, and our culture will continue to shift.

For businesspeople, these shifts bring new fears. Soft drinks and snacks are often consumed after a quick visit to a gas station, particularly on long trips. Consumer goods companies are already planning to see sales radically change as those distribution channels disappear and new ones appear. On our trip around the United States, we found that many Tesla supercharging stations were near restaurants, or sometimes even inside existing gas stations, so new patterns of traffic are springing up. When freeways were first brought through communities, similar changes also appeared. If there was an off-ramp, real estate values frequently went up and businesses appeared. The new off-ramp might include many charging stations or services for drivers on longer trips. Tesla already has huge stations with coffee, restrooms, and other services available in-between cities like San Francisco and Los Angeles, which didn't exist before people started using its electric cars to travel those multi-hundred-mile distances.

Electric vehicles also have an affordance for use as micro-offices, or even temporary homes. Lots of owners talk about using their Teslas as camping vehicles, asking how to keep the AC system running properly all night long, which is something that would seem dangerous in a gas-powered vehicle, or at least destructive to engines and environment. Now that electric vehicles run more like office buildings, you can keep them temperature-controlled and can work in a hot or cold parking lot while waiting. The silence from electric engines lets you do a variety of things, from videoconferencing to playing games on your phone or laptop. Already, a sizeable industry has sprung up with accessories for that kind of usage, and we know several businesses who have waiting lists for upgrades to cars such as tinting windows, which makes it nicer to use as a portable office.

Quite a few automakers, including new ones like Zoox, are seeing that trend and are even building new vehicles that will not have a steering wheel, but rather chairs and tables for having a business meeting or maybe a family meal inside as you are being driven around.

Only a few, like Brad Templeton—who was an engineer on Google's early autonomous efforts, and today teaches executives about technology shifts that are coming at Singularity University—has an idea of just how deeply American culture and the landscape itself will change due to the three forces of autonomous vehicles, electrification, and Spatial Computing glasses and devices. Since you will be able to sleep in these cars by the end of the 2020s, you'll drive overnight.

Imagine leaving San Francisco at 9 p.m., sleeping in your car, and arriving in the morning in Las Vegas or at midday in Salt Lake City. Those trips are uncomfortable to do by yourself, and quite dangerous due to the real possibility you'll fall asleep while on the boring straight highways that can numb even the most active of brains.

Trucks will also go through this transition starting in the 2020s. Yeah, it might take another decade after that to see autonomy hit literally every vehicle, but we can already predict the decimation of many a roadside diner or hotel focused on the more than a million truckers who drive in the United States.

On the other hand, those diners and hotels will see a steady stream post COVID-19 restrictions of new tourists who now see drives through United States as a sort of amusement park (the same for Europe, and many other places where the drives are long and there's lots of things to see along the way).

As these drivers approach cities, they will probably need to use a service to request permission to come into the city. Brad Templeton says that more and more roads will be metered. Why? Because as we automate transportation, more cars will be on the roads, particularly near city centers, because they will be asked to do more work than before, with people possibly asking things like, "Hey Siri, can you have my car pick up my laundry?"

That means more traffic and cities will have an impulse to both regulate that traffic and attempt to profit from it. A huge experiment in such a thing is underway in New York City. A 2021 plan will employ a cordon pricing system to charge drivers to access Manhattan south of 60th street. We predict that soon, cities will force drivers to get apps on their phones that will give them a pass to get on freeways into cities. Such a thing wasn't possible until literally every driver got a mobile phone, which brought us not only Uber, but new mapping services like Waze. Uber already works sort of like that, by the way. It tells its drivers where to go, all with a centralized "air traffic control system." That system knows where every driver and passenger is, and charges accordingly. We won't be shocked to hear that Uber is called upon to help build such a system for cities. Your glasses by 2030 might have you waiting outside of a city for a "slot" for you to drive in, just like airplanes are often held on the ground if there's a problem at a distant airport. This is yet another reason to have charging and other services available in stations near freeways.

This is why lots of new companies are springing up, too, to get around traffic. From Elon Musk's Boring Company, which is planning on drilling lots of tunnels underneath congested cities to open up new ways to move people around, to Hyperloops, which will offer high-speed transportation between cities, to companies like Sebastian Thrun's Kitty Hawk, which is developing new electronic flying machines that are much cheaper to operate per mile than planes or helicopters, and quieter, too.

Plus, you'll see more acceptance of ride sharing, particularly between cities. In 2018, we hitched a ride between Munich and Freiberg, Germany, in the back of an Audi thanks to BlaBlaCar, a service that sells seats in everyday people's cars as they commute between cities. Such a thing was impossible to implement before ubiquitous mobile phones arrived, and as Spatial Computing glasses gain acceptance in the 2020s, these kinds of things will become much easier to use.

We envision walking down a street and seeing tons of transportation options, when you want them, all displayed by your glasses—from scooters to flying vehicles, all overlaid in 3D around you so you can see what your options are. In many ways, this represents the purification of the vision that Garrett Camp and Travis Kalanick told us as they were thinking about creating Uber in a Paris snowstorm. We were stuck due to that snowstorm and no cars were coming to pick us up because traffic was at a standstill. Camp asked us, "Why can't we just see where the cars are?"

In the future, you might use your Augmented Reality glasses while sitting in traffic to get out of the cold and have a place for you to do a video call, which of course will be radically different in the future due to Spatial Computing. No longer will we be stuck to 2D screens. Your business meeting could have virtual whiteboards, desks with virtual items on them, plus lots of 3D designs. Think about being an architect—you'll be able to work on your building design while sitting in a car that's driving you across Paris. Even if you are stuck in traffic, you won't care nearly as much as you do today because the vehicle you are in will be much more comfortable and quieter, and you'll have hyper-fast bandwidth available to your AR glasses.

Photo credit: Robert Scoble. Google Maps now shows you an "augmented map" that better helps you navigate cities. This image was made in late 2019 in Rome, Italy. In the future, this augmentation, which uses Spatial Computing technology, will be expanded to be far more helpful and detailed.

Some other things that will shift about our culture starting in the 2020s? Where you buy your car, if you buy one at all. Let's say you need a new pickup truck for your plumbing business. Today, you need to go into a Ford dealership to get your car. Well, what if your truck can drive to you? Doesn't that get rid of the need for dealing with car salespeople? Yes. If we owned car dealerships, we would spend the next decade planning for this new way of buying a car or truck to hit our business hard. But it won't happen in one day—it'll be something you'll see coming for years. Just remember, these technologies are exponential. If you wait too long to get a different business model, it will be a lot tougher, particularly if you are the last one to make the move. The deeper issue for car salespeople will be the psychological move from needing to own a car or truck at all. A system like Uber (or Tesla's planned RoboTaxi network) could dramatically change vehicle buying patterns and, in fact, due to the huge gap in economics, we foresee a huge problem coming for car dealerships and salespeople by the end of the 2020s.

It is not only car dealerships that will be undergoing change, but also major parts of the cityscape.

The Future City

To get an idea of how deeply cities can change in a decade, we walked around old Barcelona, Spain in November 2019. Every store accepted Apple Pay. Taxis worked like Uber. We were guided by Augmented Reality on Google Maps down streets that were hundreds of years old. Apple has a store here. Every restaurant had tons of reviews and you could get reservations at many online. None of that existed in 2010.

Some cities like Rome or Milan will be harder to automate because of their lack of painted lines on streets, their much more chaotic pedestrian traffic, and unusual parking and traffic arrangements. Expect even these cities to see big improvements due to Augmented Reality glasses and the data collection from those and autonomous vehicles, however.

We asked many people who are building these technologies how cities would change in the future due to Spatial Computing technologies like robots, autonomous vehicles, and Augmented Reality glasses.

For one, as vehicles start to automate, the need for them to park and sit around unused for hours will go away. Templeton noted that about 20 percent of real estate in cities is for parking. We can see a world in, say, 40 years, where all that parking has been turned into either parks or housing to make living in cities more affordable.

The biggest change coming will be the 3D-ization of cities. Similar to what is being done inside factories, cities soon will have a "digital twin" or a digital copy. These digital twins will provide the virtual infrastructure for a whole range of new utilities and services that will be exposed in Spatial Computing/Augmented Reality glasses.

We are already seeing early evidence of this as Google Maps is adding Augmented Reality navigation and street signs onto city streets in many cities around the world (we tried it in Barcelona and Rome, for instance, and it worked well).

Today, maps still remain fairly static, though, and don't represent crowds or changing street conditions well. If a construction crew blocks off a street, people at home have no idea until they try to go down that street and find it blocked off. Soon, maps will turn "real-time" and show things like that in far greater detail and with far less "latency" or delay. These maps will be greatly helped by self-driving vehicles, which continuously map out streets in 3D as they drive down or, at a minimum, notice differences between a pre-scanned map and what actually is on the street.

The people building self-driving cars even could imagine that as cars drive down a street, they would refresh their data to include parking spaces available, what potholes are forming, construction underway, details on accidents or crowds, among other things that would be pushed immediately to maps. Not to mention the various agencies that could keep track of how to make roads better for citizens or, even, take note of new graffiti appearing or cars being left in one spot too long.

Particularly as 5G arrives in cities, both autonomous vehicles and this kind of "live mapping" will be seen as much more commonplace. Marketers might even develop a new kind of SEO. This extra data will also be used by both public authorities and transportation services like Uber, Didi, or Lyft, to move resources to places where there will be more demand. For instance, a nightclub with a line outside at 10 p.m. will probably need more vehicles nearby at 2 a.m. to give people rides home.

This new digital twin will be joined by other deep changes to cities brought by the combination of Spatial Computing glasses that users talk to, use their eyes or hands to control, and that present new visual information about the city around them.

Let's pop around the city to see some of the places where we predict we'll see the biggest changes.

The Changing City

For the remainder of this chapter, we will list some of the major changes that we foresee occurring within and around our cities over the next decade.

Auto Dealers

Let's start on Auto Dealer Row. You know, the place you go to buy cars. By 2030, we expect dealerships to start to shrink as more and more new cars come online that can be bought either by phone or by Spatial Computing glasses. Why will this happen? Cars by 2030 will be able to deliver themselves directly to users. Keep in mind that not all car sales will go away. Families who have car seats will want a "long-term car" for what the car services are calling them—the same for mechanics or plumbers who want to keep their tools in the back of a pickup truck and paint logos onto them. Either way, though, the car salesperson sure will look to have their jobs threatened.

Smart Roads

That new car will communicate a lot more with cloud servers, too, and infrastructure left around the city. In China, they are already building smart roads to get ready. Sensors along the side of the road watch for accidents or other problems and report to everyone what's going on. Speed limits can be changed, lanes opened or closed, and traffic light behavior changed by these smart roads, which will communicate with cars via 5G so cars can get real-time data about potholes, objects on the road, and changing traffic conditions ahead. Tesla is already starting to work like that, even without the smart road, by the way, because Tesla is making its own maps and updating those maps from its hundreds of thousands of cars. Many of these new "smart roads" will also have lots of cameras, for security, as well as to add new services. Your glasses and self-driving car might know exactly how many spaces are open on any given street before navigating you there, or where some of those electric scooters are so you will be able to continue your journey to your meetings for the day.

Interstates

As you drive along, you might notice that interstates in-between major cities are starting to look different. Hotels you might have seen in decades past are closing down, restaurants too, and they are moving to be near supercharging stations, which have changed traffic patterns through states like Kansas and Nevada. No longer do truckers need to stop to rest, so they've been flying by the hotels they used to stop at. They do need to charge their trucks and vehicles, though, so are stopping for 30 minutes at new charging stations, sometimes opting in for a meal nearby, or some shopping for the kids. At least that will happen until the transportation industry totally automates and gets rid of all the humans using all those services today. That might start happening in the late 2020s, but regulators and policy makers might hold humans into vehicles, mostly as a jobs act, until well into the 2030s.

Either way, we see countries like the United States getting a dramatic demographic shift over the next two to three decades due to all those interstate truckers being replaced by autonomous trucks and other changes, thanks to new "closer to home" warehouse farms and 3D printing plants, so lots of things may not need to be shipped such long distances in the future. 3D printing and Spatial Computing glasses fit together like peanut butter and jelly, too, since wearers can make and order 3D printed objects.

Factories

Other, more traditional factories, like the Louisville Slugger bat factory in Louisville, probably won't move from its historic location, but may see shipping costs dramatically reduce, and the time taken to get a product around the country might change due to autonomous vehicles so that they can open up new markets. The same will happen with a range of factories around America. Some companies, particularly drink or alcohol distributors, might be able to reduce the number of factories even further, and that could have an impact on communities.

Real Estate

You'll also see real estate developments further from city centers. Stockton, for instance, is about 100 miles from San Francisco. Now, residents there can take an electronic flying vehicle that looks like a drone (eVTOL, described earlier) for an affordable price directly into downtown San Francisco. The service can drop you off on top of one of a few buildings, and then you can take an Uber, Lyft, or maybe one of those new Zoox or Tesla robo-taxis to your final destination. Because this trip is less than 45 minutes, many people can see themselves commuting from Stockton to San Francisco, where before flying drones this would just be unfeasible. Basically, these are those big drones that can take off from small spaces, like a helicopter, albeit cheaper, quieter, and lighter, and will fly without a pilot. We interviewed Sebastian Thrun, who, besides running the first Stanford autonomous vehicle team that then got purchased by Google, now runs Kitty Hawk, a company that makes these lightweight flying machines. He says they will dramatically change the economics of moving people to cities that are around 100 miles away from city centers. Flying from Stockton to San Francisco, he told us, will take less than half an hour. In 2019, that trip can take two to four hours in a car, depending on if you are stuck in traffic or not.

Remote Working

One thing we expect to see radical changes to is how often workers will be expected to "come to headquarters" to work. Today, a worker at, say, VMware in Palo Alto, which is right near Tesla and many other employers who do the same, might skip many commutes altogether, due to new Spatial Computing glasses that will let that employee collaborate with other workers almost as effectively as if those workers were in a conference room together. This will be one of the ways that employers can do something real about housing prices, as well as making real inroads to climate change-mandated carbon reductions.

Travel Times and Ranges

Other changes are predicted to occur where people stop along interstates. In a gas-powered manually driven car, humans can only drive about four hours before they start getting dangerously tired. Today, a trip from San Francisco to Reno is pretty safe for a single driver to do in one shot. As autonomous vehicles get better, though, particularly at interstate driving, you will be able to go far further as a single driver will not worry about falling asleep on a boring straight road. So, you'll see many people travel from San Francisco to, say, Wyoming, which takes about 20 hours of travel time. Or, Salt Lake City in 13 hours. Even including bathroom breaks and charging stops, you'll see America (and many places, like Canada and Europe, which have an electric charging infrastructure and mostly straight, well-painted roads) turn into a new kind of amusement park. "Hey honey, why don't we go skiing tomorrow in Salt Lake City?," could mean hopping into an autonomous vehicle at 6 p.m. for a 9 a.m. arrival at the lifts.

Navigation

Back to cities, though. Street cleaning and other infrastructure will use 3D maps of everything to navigate and also figure out objects, cars, and pedestrians to be avoided. Museums and other popular tourist destinations will have intricate Augmented Reality audio tours. Already, Rome has audio tours from Rick Steves that you can listen to on your AirPods, and we used one tour in Yellowstone that automatically played as we drove around that National Park. It was magic and that was audio-only in 2018. Everything you look at will have an Augmented Reality nameplate with details such as, "Here is the Grand Prismatic Spring—as you look around, we'll show you the names of the mountains surrounding it and all the smaller geysers around too."

Green Thinking

Much more cities will electrify in the 2020s, too, due to climate change concerns. In China, they currently own about 90 percent of the electric trains and buses in the world. We expect that mix to change as other countries start investing in electronic alternatives in their mass transit plans.

This climate change awareness will be the excuse many cities will use to electrify and automate all sorts of services, from mail to garbage pickup. After all, turning those things from diesel trucks with humans that aren't as efficient to electric vehicles that are more efficiently operated by computers (and more safely, since they never will show up to work stoned or drunk) will be attractive to many cities as they struggle to meet carbon reduction goals and add new services for citizens wearing Spatial Computing glasses.

AI Assistants

Even as people use cars, they will use these glasses to join meetings, take classes, watch videos, play games, and get information on the world flowing by as their cars or drones take them places. Speaking of which, you will talk more and more to many computers almost at the same time. Where today you might say "Hey Siri" or "Hey Alexa," sometime in the 2020s, you might start talking to just one of them, or a generic "Hey 'cloud'" to command all services to figure out how to serve your query. Either way, by the end of the 2030s, we'll be very used to speaking with computers, if we even think of them in that way anymore. Why do we say that? By 2030, AI systems will be producing many things for us, including music, food, and running our transportation system, and they also will be presented to us visually as new virtual, or "synthetic," beings. Magic Leap first showed us its virtual being in 2019 at the **Games Developer Conference** (**GDC**) in San Francisco. Of course, that was heavily demoware, and couldn't talk with users, or do all that much except play a simple game on a simple table. We are sure that, by 2030, these virtual beings will actually sit in your car with you and will entertain you and assist you on your journey.

Entertainment

Speaking of entertainment, other changes in cities will be not just how cool they look. In late 2019, China had hundreds of drones flying over Guangzhou building a spectacular light show over its skyscrapers. That will seem quaint by 2030 as drones and Augmented Reality are mixed into nightly entertainment on top of cities.

Raves, virtual wars, and more will play out every evening in city centers this way, while participants play new kinds of virtual games, which will make the 2020 version of Pokémon Go or Minecraft Earth seem pretty simple, indeed. How? This will be aided by all the data that companies are grabbing off of cars, cities themselves, and those Augmented Reality glasses.

Fewer Cars

Finally, if you are walking around a modern city, you might notice two things: no more parking spots and no more cars in a city center, with a preference for bikes, electric scooters, or other public transportation, maybe including robo-taxis. Why? Europe is showing the way—as you get rid of cars, you make cities much more livable and attractive, not to mention safer. The city of the future will help you live better and will be designed by data that proves it so.

"Data Bubbles" Will Abound

Put it all together and we see the cities of the future with millions of newly-equipped autonomous vehicles on the road within a few years. In the San Francisco Bay Area, it already is very common to have two or three Teslas around you, with a Cruise from General Motors or a Waymo driving nearby, too. These all are like little "data bubbles." Each can see a couple of hundred meters around the car, building a 3D model and their AIs converting all that into component parts, like lane markings, stop signs, other cars, and pedestrians. These data bubbles soon will enable very detailed new maps, and bring radical changes to our cities as parking spaces get converted into drop-off zones, among other changes. Not to mention that we'll be wearing Spatial Computing glasses to summon new services from rides to food delivery because of the autonomous vehicles on the road.

This will bring deep shifts in our culture. Back in the 1960s, we sang "we drove our Chevy to the levy and the levy was dry." By 2030, we'll need a whole new set of lyrics. What a time to be alive!

In our next chapter, we'll attack the Technology, Media, and Telecommunications (TMT) vertical—one that goes to the heart of the Spatial Computing industry.

4

Vision Two – Virtual Worlds Appear

As we did in previous chapters in Part II, we will be looking at an industry vertical in this chapter. This chapter's vertical is Technology, Media, and Telecommunications (TMT). Since this vertical goes to the core of what Spatial Computing is very much about, it will necessarily be longer than the other chapters that focus on industry verticals.

New realities are appearing thanks to Virtual Reality and Augmented Reality. In a few years, though, the capabilities of VR and AR will change and morph into more sophisticated Spatial Computing glasses, which will arrive with massive increases in bandwidth thanks to 5G and new AI capabilities, which are due in part to the R&D being done on autonomous vehicles. Here we dive into some of the fundamentals of the TMT vertical, as well as the profound changes we expect.

From 2D to 3D

As we look back at the technology industry, especially when it comes to personal computers and mobile phones, which customarily present two-dimensional images on a flat screen, you can see that there's an underlying set of goals—beliefs, even. These include things such as connecting everyone together, giving you "superpowers" to analyze business data with spreadsheets, and the ability to communicate better with photos and videos. Previous generations were just about giving us better tools than the mechanical ones that existed before, whether the printing press or the old rotary phones that so many of us now-old people had in their homes.

Increasing the Bandwidth

Elon Musk puts it best: the goal is to increase the bandwidth to and from each human. Now he's investing in a new kind of computing with his company Neuralink that includes "jacking in" and hooking a computer directly up to your brain. That will take a lot longer to show up for most people than Spatial Computing, simply because of the cost of opening up a human skull and having a robot surgically implant tiny wires directly in a brain.

One way to look at it is via our current computing interfaces. If you have a thought that you want to communicate with other people, you probably use a mouse or a finger on a screen to open an application or a window, and you use a keyboard to type a message. That's pretty much the same whether you want to communicate in a Microsoft Word document, an SMS text message, an email, or a Tweet on Twitter. On the other side, your reader sees what you wrote on a screen and that person's eyes and visual perception system translates that into something their brain can understand, process, store, integrate, and then maybe reply to.

That process of reading is pretty fast in comparison to the process of writing. There's friction in communication. We're feeling it right now as we type these words into Microsoft Word and are trying to imagine you reading this book.

The process isn't a whole lot faster even if we use video. After all, you can even have someone, or, better yet, an AI, read this text to you while you walk down the street. That would be hard to do if we made a video. (Note: We previously discussed the relevance of AI, including Machine Learning, Deep Learning, and Computer Vision in *Chapter 2, Four Paradigms and Six Technologies*, so we won't replicate that information here.)

Plus, you can skim and do other things with text that video makes very hard. Your mind, on the other hand, would far rather watch a movie than read a movie script, or watch a football game on TV than read a report about it later.

Where we are going with this is that the tech industry is spending billions of dollars in an attempt to make it easier to communicate and work with each other, or even to better enjoy the natural world. We see the ultimate effect of this in the "jacking-in" fantasy that Elon Musk and others are trying to make a reality. Some take a more negative view, like John von Neumann and his term "the singularity," which was later popularized by Vernor Vinge in his 1993 essay in which he wrote that it would signal the end of the human era. Scary stuff, but the need to communicate our thoughts with not just other people, but machines, like we are doing now with Siri, Alexa, Google Assistant, and Facebook's Portal, are opening up new ways of communicating with machines. Elon Musk's Neuralink, which uses a robot to hook up tiny wires directly to a human brain, is the most forward approach we've seen actually being put to use. That said, we don't think we'll sign up for that in the early exploratory years of the company!

In its current form, such technology brings with it deep side effects and, as of today, costs hundreds of thousands of dollars due to the necessity of a surgical procedure to install something like Neuralink. If you have, for example, Parkinson's, you may get such a technology implanted by the end of the 2020s, but the rest of us will be stuck wearing some form of on-the-face computing, whether eyeglasses or contact lenses, for the foreseeable future.

Change is Coming

Spatial Computing is evolving quickly, with several different device types (which we'll go into more depth about in a bit), but they all require putting screens on your face. We dream of a lightweight pair of glasses that will bring the whole spectrum of Spatial Computing experiences that cover the reality-virtuality continuum introduced by researcher Paul Milgram, when he said that soon humans would be able to experience extended reality, or XR, along a spectrum from "completely real" on one side to "completely virtual" on the other.

Today we have devices like Microsoft's HoloLens 2 that give us tastes of VR, but they aren't really great devices for experiencing the "completely virtual" side of the spectrum, opting to let the user see the real world instead of presenting big, glorious high-resolution virtual screens.

Within the next three years, or certainly by 2025, we'll see devices that let you switch between real and virtual so quickly and seamlessly that some might start to lose track of the reality of what they are experiencing. We'll cover the pros and cons of that in the later chapters here but it's also good for us to slow down and revisit the technology that's here today so that we can have a decent conversation about where things have been and where they might be going.

We argue that it's easier for you to understand what, for example, a Macintosh could do if you knew what previous computers could do and the design constraints that were placed on earlier devices and ecosystems. Our kids forget why the Dodge tool in Adobe Photoshop looks like a lollipop, but those of us who used to work in darkrooms with chemicals and enlargers remember using a tool like that to make parts of photos lighter. The same will happen here.

First, we constantly get pushback every time we explain that you will soon be forced to wear something on your face to fully appreciate the higher communication speed that Spatial Computing brings to your brain.

Yes, why glasses? Why can't we get to this "high bandwidth to and from the brain" world with standard monitors?

Thomas Furness, the American inventor and VR pioneer, asked himself just that question back in the 1960s when he was designing cockpits for pilots in the military. He, and many others, have tried over the years to come up with better monitors. The US government funded HDTV research for just that reason. The answer comes in how we evolved over millions of years. Evolution, or some might say God, gave us two eyes that perceive the analog world in three dimensions and a large part of our brains are dedicated to processing the information our eyes take in.

If we want to take in more and get the bandwidth to our brains higher, we need to move our monitors onto our eyes. If we want to improve the outbound bandwidth from our brains to the computing world, we need to use voice, hands, eyes, and movement and add more sensors to let us communicate with computers with just our thoughts. All of this requires wearing sensors or microphones either on our faces or heads. There is no way around this except in special situations. Andy Wilson, one of Microsoft's top human/machine researchers up in Redmond, Washington, has a lab with dozens of projectors and computers where he can do a lot of this kind of stuff in one room—sort of like the Holodeck in Star Trek. But even if his room is successful, most of us don't want to compute only while sitting in a singular place, and most humans simply don't have the space in their homes and offices for such a contraption anyway.

We see this in high-end uses already. The pilots who fly the F-35 fighter jets tell us they are forced to wear an AR helmet simply to fly the plane. "I'll never lose to an F-16" one pilot at Nellis Airforce Base told us.

"Why not?" we asked.

"Because I can see you, thanks to my radar systems and the fact that your plane isn't stealthy, but you can't see me. Oh, and I can stop and you can't."

Soon many of us will be forced to follow the F-35 pilot in order to maximize our experiences in life. Those of us who already wear corrective lenses, which are about 60 percent of us, will have an easier time, since we already are forced to wear glasses simply to see. We see a world coming, though, where Spatial Computing devices bring so much utility that everyone will wear them, at least occasionally.

This will bring profound changes to humanity. We are already seeing that in VR. Users of VR are already experiencing a new form of entertainment and media; one that promises to be a bigger wave than, say, the invention of cinema, TV, or radio were in previous generations. This new wave builds on the shoulders of those previous innovations and even subsumes them all: wearing the glasses of 2025, you will still be able to read a magazine, watch a TV show, or listen to your favorite radio station (or the podcasts that replace them). As all of these improve, we are seeing new kinds of experiences, new kinds of services, and even a new culture evolving.

To those whom we have told this story, much of this seems improbable, weird, dystopian, and scary. We have heard that with each of the previous paradigm shifts too, but because this puts computing on your face, the resistance is a bit more emotional. We see a world coming over the next few years where we mostly will get over it.

Emergence as a Human Hook

So why do you need to put on a headset? Well, when you're inside the headset, you'll be able to experience things you've never been able to experience on a computer monitor before. But what's the purpose?

The Brain and VR

Why do human beings like playing in VR? Emergence is one reason, and we'll cover a couple of others in a bit. What is emergence? When applied to video games, emergence is the feeling you get from playing complex situations, and unexpected interactions show up from relatively simple game dynamics. The same feelings are why we go to movies. It's why we like taking regular drives on a curvy road. It's why we like holding a baby for the first time. That's why we like falling in love. All of these create positive chemical reactions in our brains that are similar to the emergence that happens in video games. VR enables this more frequently. Since the 1970s and 1980s, board games and table-top role-playing games such as Cosmic Encounter or Dungeons and Dragons have featured intentional emergence as a primary game function by supplying players with relatively simple rules or frameworks for play that intentionally encouraged them to explore creative strategies or interactions and exploit them toward the achievement of victory or a given goal. VR makes all that much more powerful.

If we have sharper and more capable screens we can experience things that make our brains happier, or, if you will, a flow state, which is the euphoria that both workers and surfers report as they do something that brings high amounts of emergence.

The Right Tool for the Job

The thing is, we're going to need different kinds of headsets for different things. VR headsets separate us from others. They aren't appropriate to wear in a shopping mall, on a date night, or in a business meeting. But, in each of these situations, we still want digital displays to make our lives better and to give us that feeling of emergence.

It's the same reason we would rather watch a football game on a high-resolution HDTV, instead of the low-resolution visuals of our grandparents' TVs. It's why we tend to upgrade our phones every few years to get better screens and faster processors. When we watch sports or movies on higher-resolution screens or bigger screens, or both, we can experience emergence at a higher rate.

Emergence is also why notifications on our phones are so darn addictive. Every time a new notification arrives, a new hit of dopamine arrives with it. Marketers and social networks have used these game dynamics to get us addicted and build massive businesses by keeping us staring at our feeds of new items. VR promises to take our dopamine levels from these mechanisms to new levels. In later chapters, we'll cover some of the potential downsides of doing that, but here we'll discover why Spatial Computing devices are seen as a more powerful way to cause these dopamine hits, and thus, a promise to build massive businesses.

These dopamine hits, along with powerful new ways to be productive, are coming from a range of new devices—everything from tiny little screens that bring new forms of your phone's notification streams, to devices that so completely fool your brain that they are being used to train airplane pilots, police, and retail workers.

The "Glassholes" Show the Way

It started with a jump out of a dirigible at a Google programming conference back in May 2014. The jumpers were wearing a new kind of computer: one that put a little screen and a camera right near their right eye. They broadcast a video feed from them to everyone. People jumped up to be the first to order one (we were amongst the first in line) the demo was so compelling.

Defeated Expectations

That said, the demo oversold what would actually materialize. Before we got ours, we thought it would be an experience so futuristic that we had to put down $1,500 to be the first to experience it. Now, don't get us wrong, the first year of wearing Google Glass was pretty fun, mostly. People were highly interested in seeing it. At the NextWeb conference, attendees stood in line for an hour to try ours out. Most people walked away thinking they had seen the future, even though all they saw was a tiny screen that barely worked when we talked to it with "Hey, Google" commands.

Photo credit: Maryam Scoble. This photo of coauthor Robert Scoble wearing Google Glass in the shower went viral and has been on BBC TV many times, along with many other media outlets.

As we got to wear ours, it became clear that Google Glass wasn't that futuristic and certainly didn't meet expectations. Robert Scoble's wife, Maryam, upon seeing it for the first time, asked, "will it show me anything about my friends?" Truth is: no, it didn't, but that was an expectation. There were other expectations too, set up by that first demo. The camera wasn't that good. Certainly, it wasn't as good as everyone thought it was, which later became a problem since people thought it was constantly recording and uploading, or, worse, doing facial recognition on everyone.

The expectations were, though, that it was a magical device that you could look at anything with and learn more about that person or thing. Those expectations were never really corrected by either Google or the people who owned them, who soon gained a derisive name: "Glassholes." This derisive tone came about after a journalist named Sarah Slocum wore a pair into a bar and was, in her words, accosted due to wearing them. After that, we saw more businesses putting up signs forbidding users from wearing them, and Google soon gave up trying to sell them to consumers.

Where Did Things Go Wrong?

We are frequently asked, how did Google Glass go so wrong? And what does it mean for the next wave of products about to arrive?

Photo credit: Google. Here is a closer look at the original Google Glass, which had a small transparent screen, along with a camera, microphone, speaker, and a battery.

We think it mostly came down to that dramatic launch and the expectations it caused, but there was a basket of new problems that humans had never considered until Google forced this into public view. Doing such a spectacular launch with people jumping out of dirigibles over a San Francisco convention center with thousands of people in the audience, all watching on huge screens, with millions of other viewers around the world, just set a bunch of expectations that it couldn't meet.

We list the main complaints many had here:

- The screen was too small.

- The three-dimensional sensors weren't yet ready.

- The Graphics Processing Units (GPUs) were very underpowered so the graphics that it could show were very rudimentary.

- The battery life wasn't great.

- It didn't have screens or cameras for both eyes, so it wasn't appropriate for doing more serious AR like what Microsoft's HoloLens 2 does today.

- The cameras weren't as good as in your standard GoPro.
- The screens were of far lower resolution and size than even your cheapest phone at the time (and compared to today's devices, are like a postage stamp compared to a letter-sized piece of paper).

Worse yet, Google didn't expect the social contract problems that showed up months after they shipped. Humans had evolved to look into each other's eyes to verify and communicate trust, and here was a new device messing with that. Many people focused negative attention on the camera. This touched on privacy expectations that hadn't been explored by previous technologies, and the lack of utility or affordability just added into a perfect storm of negative PR that it couldn't escape from.

That said, Google Glass was, and is, an important product that set the table for a whole range of new products. It was the first computer that you wore on your face that most people heard about, at a minimum, and got a whole industry thinking about putting computers on people's faces. But, this is a hard space to get right. Why? Because it's so damn personal. The computer is on your face in front of your eyes, or as we learned earlier this year from a new start-up, Mojo Vision, actually on your eyes in the form of a contact lens. This isn't like a desktop computer that you can hide in an office and only use when you aren't trying to be social. When fully expressed, these new computing forms change what it means to compute and what it means to be human.

What It Means to Be Human

Whoa. Change what it means to be human? Yes. Soon you'll be able to do things with these glasses that futurists have been predicting for decades. Everything from ubiquitous computing to next-generation AR that changes how we perceive the real world in deep ways. Qualcomm's new prototypes have seven cameras on a device about the size or smaller than Google Glass, which only had one camera. One of these cameras watches your mouth with Artificial Intelligence that was barely being conceived when Google Glass was announced. The others watch your eyes and the real world in high detail that bears little resemblance to what Glass' low-resolution camera was able to do.

It's important for us to pause a moment and take a birds-eye view of the Spatial Computing landscape though, and get a good look at all the devices and where they came from. Spatial Computing is a big tent that includes products that are small and lightweight, like the Google Glass, all the way to devices like the Varjo, which as of 2020, opened with an initial cost of $10,000 and needed to be tethered to a $3,000 PC. The Varjo is big and heavy, but the experience of wearing one is totally futuristic compared to the early Google Glass prototypes.

No longer are we stuck with a tiny postage stamp of a screen. Inside the Varjo, you have huge high-resolution screens. Where Google Glass is like a mobile TV on a kitchen counter, Varjo's device is like being in an IMAX theater. With it, you can simulate flying in an Airbus Jet's cockpit. Where the Google Glass could barely show a few words of text, the Varjo lets you feel like you are in the cockpit as a pilot, with tons of displays blinking away and everything so photorealistic that you feel like you are looking at hundreds of real knobs and levers in a real plane. Out the window, while wearing the Varjo, you can see cities and landscapes emerge, along with runways from a distant airport you were supposed to land at. All simulated, yes, but your brain sees so much resolution it thinks it is real.

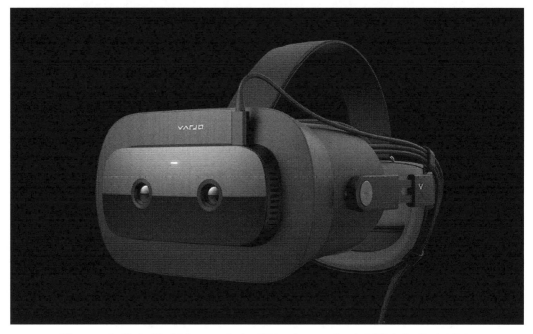

Photo credit: Varjo. The highest-resolution VR headset, as of early 2020, is the Varjo XR-1. This $10,000 device is used by Volvo to design and test future car designs.

As 2020 evolves, you'll see a spectrum of devices with far more features and capabilities soon escape from R&D labs—including a small pair of glasses. Focals by North is a good example, and one that's similar to what Google Glass tried to do. On the other side of the spectrum are VR headsets from Valve, Varjo, Oculus, and others. We'll detail them here to give you context on the market and the kinds of devices that fit under the Spatial Computing tent.

When we say these will change what it means to be human, we mean that soon, the way that you experience the real world will be completely changed by AR. Already Snapchat is changing faces, floors, and buildings with a simplified version of AR. Soon every part of your human experience will be augmented as new Spatial Computing glasses, headsets, and other devices appear. The Varjo is giving us an early taste of just how complete these changes could be—inside the headset, you experience a virtual world in such detail that you no longer want to turn it off. It is being used to train pilots, and when we got a demo, the virtual cockpit that was presented was so sharp and colorful that we imagine that someday we'll just experience the whole world that way. These changes will deeply change human life. We predict that the changes will be deeper than those brought to us by the automobile or telephone.

Embodiment, Immersion, Presence, Empathy, and Emergence

In February 2014, Mark Zuckerberg visited Stanford's Virtual Human Interaction Lab. Prof. Jeremy Bailenson and his students walked Facebook's founder and CEO through a variety of demos of how VR could change people's experiences. He walked across a plank that made you feel fear of falling off. He experienced how VR could help with a variety of brain ailments and played a few games. Bailenson ran us through the same demos years later and said we had the same experiences including being freaked out by finding ourselves standing on a narrow piece of wood after the floor virtually dropped away to reveal a deep gap. Bailenson adeptly demonstrates how VR enables powerful emergence, along with a few new ways to cause our brains to be entertained: embodiment and immersion, not to mention a few other emotions, like the vertigo felt on that wooden plank.

Embodiment and Immersion

Embodiment means you can take the form of either another person or an animal. Bailenson showed us how embodiment could give us empathy for others. In one demonstration we experienced life as a black child. In another demo, we had the experience of being a homeless man who was harassed on a bus. Chris Milk, a VR developer, turned us into a variety of forms in his experience "Life of Us" that he premiered at the Sundance Film Festival in 2017. We watched as people instantly flew as they discovered that they had wings, among other forms, from being a tadpole to a stock trader running down Wall Street.

Immersion is the feeling that you are experiencing something real, but in a totally virtual world, in other words, being present in that world. The perception is created by surrounding the user of the VR system with images, sound, and other stimuli that provide an engrossing total environment.

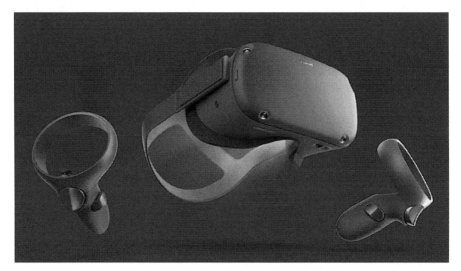

Photo credit: Facebook. The $400 Oculus Quest changed the market by making VR far easier thanks to having no cords and no need for a powerful PC to play high-end VR games and other experiences.

Within a few months of getting the demos from Bailenson and his team, Zuckerberg would acquire Oculus for $2 billion. Oculus was started a couple of years prior in Irvine, California, by Palmer Luckey, Brendan Iribe, Michael Antonov, and Nate Mitchell. The early VR device was a headset that had specialized displays, positional audio, and an infrared tracking system. Sold on Kickstarter, Oculus raised $2.4 million, which was 10 times what was expected.

Evolution

Since 2012, Oculus has evolved. The headset was paired with controllers that let a user touch, grab, poke, move, shoot, slap, and do a few other things inside virtual worlds. A new term, 6DOF, got popular around the same time. That stands for Six Degrees of Freedom and meant that the headset and controllers could completely move inside a virtual world. Previous headsets, including the current Oculus Go, were 3DOF, which meant that while you could turn your head you couldn't physically move left, right, forward, or backward. To experience the full range of things in VR, you'll want a true 6DOF headset and controllers.

Systems that aren't 6DOF won't deliver the full benefits of immersion, presence, embodiment, emergence, or the empathy that they can bring. That said, there are quite a few cheaper headsets on the market and they are plenty capable of a range of tasks. 3DOF headsets are great for viewing 360-degree videos, or lightweight VR for educational uses that don't require navigating around a virtual world, or the other benefits that 6DOF brings. It is this addition of 6DOF to both the controllers and the headset that really set the stage for the paradigm shift that Spatial Computing will deliver.

Photo credit: Robert Scoble. Facebook had huge signs when Oculus Quest first showed up, showing the market advantages Facebook has in getting its products featured.

As we open the 2020s, the product that got the most accolades last year was the $400 Oculus Quest from Facebook. This opened up VR to lots of new audiences. Before it came out most of the other VR headsets, and certainly the 6DOF ones, were "tethered" to a powerful PC. Our first VR system was an HTC Vive connected to a PC with an Nvidia GPU and cost more than $2,500. Today, for most uses, a $400 Quest is just as good, and for the few more serious video games or design apps that need more graphic power, you can still tether to a more powerful PC with an optical cable that costs about $80.

Facebook has the Edge

Facebook has other unnatural advantages, namely its two billion users, along with the social graph they bring (Facebook has a contact list of all of those users and their friends). That gives Facebook market power to subsidize VR devices for years and keep their prices down. The closest market competitor, Sony's PlayStation VR, is a more expensive proposition and requires a tether to the console.

The Quest comes with a different business model, though, that some find concerning: advertising. In late 2019, Facebook announced it would use data collected on its VR headsets to improve advertising that its various services show its users.

Photo credit: Robert Scoble. Here Scoble's son, Ryan, plays on Oculus Quest while his dad charges his Tesla at a supercharger.

This gives Facebook a near monopoly in sub-$500 devices that bring full-blown VR and it is the only one that brings this in a non-tethered way.

Yes, Sony's PlayStation VR has sold more units at five million sold, which seems impressive until you remember that device has been on the market since 2016, and the experience of using a PlayStation is far inferior to using the Quest with its better controllers, a better selection of things to do, and the integration into Facebook's social graph, which enables new kinds of social VR that others will find difficult to match. The Quest sold about half a million units between when it launched in May 2019 and January 2020. The Quest was one of the hottest products during Christmas 2019 and was sold out for months. Even well into April 2020, the Quest remained sold out and could be found on eBay for a hefty premium over its $400 retail price.

What is notable is the shifting of price points. When PlayStation VR first came on the market it was a lot cheaper for a kid to get when compared to buying a $2,000 gaming PC and a $900 headset, like the HTC Vive. The Quest obliterated that price advantage, and it's the business subsidy that Facebook is giving to its Oculus division that's turning the industry on its head. Anyone who wants to go mainstream has to figure out how to deal with that price differential due to the advertising-subsidized pricing that Facebook has. Google could also do the same, but its forays into Spatial Computing, including Glass and the Gear VR headset systems that used mobile phones, have fallen flat with consumers because they didn't provide the full VR magic of embodiment, immersion, presence, and so on.

Market Evolution

Our prediction is that Facebook will consolidate much of the VR market due to its pricing, social element, and the advantages that come with having a war chest of billions of dollars to put into content. Its purchase of Beat Saber's owner, Beat Games, in late 2019 showed that it was willing to buy companies that make the most popular games on its platform, at least in part to keep those games off of other platforms that will soon show up. Beat Saber was the top-selling game in 2019, one where you slice cubes flying at you with light sabers. This consolidation won't hit all pieces of the market, though. Some will resist getting into Facebook's world due to its continued need for your data to be able to target ads to you. Others, including enterprise companies, will want to stay away from advertising-supported platforms. For that, we visited VMware's Spatial Computing lab in its headquarters in Palo Alto.

Photo credit: Robert Scoble. A wide range of headsets hang on the wall inside VMware's Spatial Computing lab in its Palo Alto headquarters.

At VMware, they buy and test all the headsets, so they can see all the different approaches various VR and AR headset manufacturers are taking. VMware's main business is selling virtual machines to run the world's internet infrastructure inside data centers and manage all the personal computers that connect to it.

Why is it investing in Spatial Computing? Because it is building an array of management infrastructure for enterprises to use, and sees a rapidly growing demand for Spatial Computing. Walmart, for instance, bought more than 10,000 VR headsets for its training initiatives. Simply loading an OS on that many headsets is a daunting challenge—even more so if corporate IT managers want to keep them up to date, keep them focused on one experience, and make sure that they haven't been hacked and have access to appropriate things on corporate networks and other workers.

Inside VMware Labs, Matt Coppinger, director, and Alan Renouf, senior product line manager, walked us through the headsets and the work that they are doing with both VR and AR. They told us about enterprises who decided against going with Facebook's solution because Facebook wanted to control the software loaded on the headset too tightly. Lots of enterprises want to control everything for a variety of reasons, from the ease of use that comes from getting rid of everything but one app that's already running when you put on the headset, to being able to control which corporations the collected personal data is shared with.

They both split up the market into different use cases:

- **6DOF tethered/high end**: This means Varjo, with its ultra-high-resolution and low-latency reign, which is why Volvo uses it for car design. The headsets at the high end have sharper screens and a wider field of view, which makes them the best choice for architecture, design, and use cases where you have highly detailed and complex things to work on, like an Airbus cockpit simulation for teaching pilots to fly.

- **6DOF tethered/mid-market and lower market**: Valve Index, HTC Vive, HTC Cosmo, and Oculus Rift headset products fit here. These tethered headsets allow the use of Nvidia's latest GPUs, so are great for working on three-dimensional design, architecture, and factory work but are much more affordable than the $10,000 Varjo. Most of these will run $1,500 to $3,000 for a decent PC and about $1,000 for the headset systems.

- **6DOF self-contained**: The Oculus Quest. This is the most exciting part of the VR market, they say, because it brings true VR at an affordable price with the least amount of hassle due to no cord and no external PC being required.

- **3DOF self-contained**: The Oculus Go, which is a headset that only does three degrees of freedom, has lots of corporate lovers for low-end, 360-degree media viewing and training with a minimal amount of interactivity or navigation. This is the headset that Walmart did all its training on, although it's now switching to the Quest to get more interactive-style training and simulations.

Keep in mind we have been through many waves of VR devices. VR has existed in the military since the mid-1960s. In the 1990s, people had VR working on Silicon Graphics machines (if you know what those are, that dates you to at least 40 years old or so). We flew plane simulators on such systems. But the VR form factor back then was huge and a Silicon Graphics machine cost more than $100,000.

We tend to think of that phase as an R&D phase, where the only uses possible were either military or experiences that cost a lot of money per minute. One of our friends had opened a retail shop where you could pay $50 for a few minutes inside one to simulate flying a fighter jet. Since most of us couldn't afford the fuel for a real jet, this was as close as we were going to get and it was pretty fun. Today's version of the same is an LBE (Location-based Entertainment) experience, where you can pay $20 to $50 for an average of 15 minutes per person to be "inside a movie" at Sandbox VR, The Void, Dreamscape Immersive, and others.

2014's New Wave

Instead of looking so far back, though, we see the new wave of Spatial Computing really started in 2014 when Facebook bought Oculus. That purchase by Mark Zuckerberg really started up a whole set of new projects and caused the world to pay attention to VR with fresh eyes.

We still remember getting a "Crescent Bay" demo, one of the first demos available on the Oculus Rift headset, in the back room at the Web Summit Conference in Ireland in 2016. That headset was tethered to a PC. Two little sensors were on a table in front of us. Once we were in the headset, they handed us controllers. It started out in darkness. When the demo started, we found ourselves on the top of a skyscraper.

It was the first time we had felt vertigo; our brains freaked out because it was so real-feeling due to the immersive power of VR that we thought we might fall to our deaths.

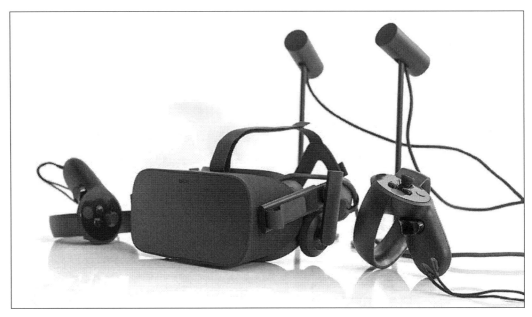

Photo credit: Facebook. The original Oculus Rift VR system, with its two sensors and controllers. Not seen here is the PC with a big GPU inside, usually made by Nvidia, that it's tethered to.

Now how did a computer make us scared of falling to our death? Well, the headset, as it was moved around, showed a 360-degree world. We felt like we were really on top of a skyscraper and could fall over the edge. This was far different than any computer or medium we had ever seen or experienced before. The power of putting highly tracked screens on our face that could reveal a virtual world was like magic. We barely noticed the cord that was hanging from a device over our head leading to a PC on the side of our play area.

Later, after we bought our own, we would get the limitations of the sensor system. It built a virtual room that we couldn't really move out of. In our case, in our homes, it was a virtual box that was a few feet wide by a few feet long. The cord and the sensors kept us from leaving that box and those limitations started to chafe. We couldn't play VR while on the road traveling. We couldn't take it to shopping malls. Trying to show people VR in their backyards proved very difficult. Getting even two of the systems to work meant getting black curtains to separate the two systems, since the sensors didn't like being next to another set that was trying to operate.

Photo credit: HTC. The HTC Vive was popular because of its superior tracking system. These black boxes, called "Lighthouses," were aimed at a VR player and sprayed a pattern of invisible light that let the system track the headset and controllers accurately. This type of tracking system is still used in many high-end headsets.

Let's talk about those sensors because how tracking is done is a key differentiator between headsets. HTC Vive is still a favorite amongst heavy users of VR, in part, because its tracking system is so good. It consists of two black boxes (you could use more, if needed, in, say, a large space) that spray invisible light on a VR user walking around. This invisible light is used to track headsets, controllers, and newer trackers that users could put on objects, their feet, and other things. These black boxes, called "Lighthouses," are better at tracking than the ones Facebook sold with its Oculus Rift system. The original Oculus ones were simpler cameras that weren't quite as exact and couldn't track as many things as the HTC system did.

Photo credit: Robert Scoble. A girl plays with an HTC Vive. Here you see the tether to a gaming PC.

A lot of these advantages, though, have been whittled away at by the Oculus team, who shipped quite a few updates to make its system work better and, finally with the Oculus Quest, this older "outside-in" tracking system was replaced by a series of four cameras on the front that implemented the newer tracking system that didn't require putting boxes or cameras around a VR user.

Inside-out

We believe this newer system, which industry people call "inside-out" tracking because the sensors are looking from the headset "out" into the real world, is better for Spatial Computing because it frees users from having to calibrate sensors and place boxes or cameras around, and it also means you have the freedom to walk around much bigger spaces, leading to wearing glasses in a few years where you can play virtually anywhere without worrying about the tracking.

The Oculus "inside-out" tracking also shows up in its Rift S model, which replaces the earlier Rift, with its two external trackers. Why does Facebook have three models – the Go, the Quest, and the Rift S? The Quest is optimized for low-cost 6DOF. The Rift S has the best performance. Compared to the Quest, graphics inside look sharper and nicer and the field of view is a little larger. The Go is a low-cost media viewer and we don't even like including it in a discussion about VR's capabilities because it is only 3DOF and can't let you do interactive games or experiences the way the Quest or the Rift S can.

Competing with the Rift S is the Valve Index, which got many gamers to salivate with its higher specs, including a sharp set of 2880x1600 monitors with a 130-degree field of view. The Oculus Quest, for comparison, only has 1440x1200 pixels per eye and a slower 72 Hz refresh rate and a smaller field of view at around 100 degrees. The negative for all that performance is that the Valve requires a user to be tethered to an expensive gaming PC.

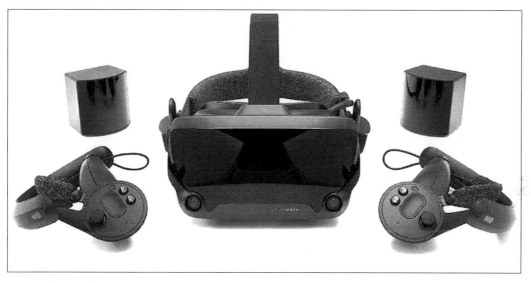

Photo credit: Valve. The Valve Index got a lot of great reviews from gamers, who valued its high-resolution screens with a wide field of view.

Finally, the road to bringing us this magic has been quite rocky. Even the best headsets haven't sold more than a few million units; the Quest struggled to get to half a million by the end of 2019, and many attempts at bringing the masses into VR have failed. Two notable failures are Google Daydream and Microsoft's Mixed Reality licensed headsets.

Why did these do so poorly in the market? Well, for different reasons.

Mistakes Were Made

The Google Daydream headset, and a similar idea from Samsung, let users plop their phones into a headset. This idea promised low-cost VR, but it didn't deliver very well. First of all, the mobile phones that were on the market three years ago didn't have hugely powerful GPUs, so the graphic capabilities were muted. Worse, mobile phones often got too hot because of this underpowered nature, and VR pushed the phone's capabilities harder than anything else could, draining the batteries quickly on devices people needed for a lot more than just playing in VR.

Ours crashed a lot, too, due to the processing demands that heated everything up. The weight of the phone, too, meant that these headsets weren't very comfortable, with a lot of weight out in front of your nose.

What really killed them, though, was that they were only 3DOF, and there just wasn't enough content to view and the people who might have hyped them up had just gotten their full 6DOF systems from HTC or Facebook and weren't likely to spend hours playing underpowered mobile-based headsets.

Photo credit: Google. One of the attempts that didn't go well with consumers was the Google Daydream headset that let you drop your mobile phone into this device to do VR. But it wasn't very full-featured; it couldn't do 6DOF, for instance, and only ever had very limited content developed for it.

The Microsoft Mixed Reality headsets tried to fix many of these problems but also failed due to a lack of customers, mostly because the people who really cared about VR saw these attempts as underpowered, with poor sensors, and not having much marketing behind them. Translation: the cool games and experiences were showing up on the HTC Vive or Oculus Rifts. Things like Job Simulator, which every child under the age of 13 knew about due to the brilliant influencer marketing of its owner, Owlchemy Labs, which now is owned by Google, were selling like hotcakes, and games like that needed the more powerful headsets.

We tend to think it was a mistake, too, for Microsoft to call these VR headsets "mixed reality." That confused the market since they came after Microsoft had released the critically acclaimed HoloLens, which we'll talk about a lot more in a bit, which was a true mixed reality experience where monsters could come out of your actual walls. These VR devices weren't that and confused the market and made the market wonder why they weren't just saying these are VR headsets. Either way, these are gone now except for the Samsung HMD Odyssey, and the Oculus Quest has set the scene for the next wave of Spatial Computing products.

We are seeing products in R&D that bear very little resemblance to the big, black headsets that are on the market as the 2020s open up. In fact, at CES, Panasonic showed off a new VR prototype that looked like a steampunk pair of lenses and was much smaller than the Oculus Rift. Oculus co-founder Palmer Luckey made some Twitter excitement when he posted a photo and praise of the Panasonic (which we doubt will do well in the market due to its poor viewing angle, lack of content, and lack of 6DOF).

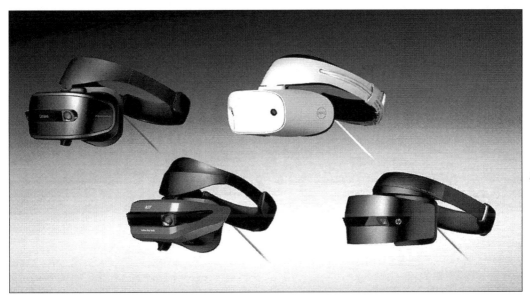

Photo credit: Microsoft. The original Microsoft-licensed VR headsets from Lenovo, Dell, Acer, and HP [from left to right and top to bottom]. The Samsung HMD Odyssey is missing from the photo, as it came out many months later than these, was relatively more expensive, and had the reputation of being the best quality of the bunch. Only the Odyssey is still available for direct purchase at a $499 retail price.

Either way, VR is here now, and the magic it brings of immersion, embodiment, and presence sets the stage for a whole range of new capabilities that will show up over the next few years.

The Spectrum – Augmented Reality from Mobile to Mixed Reality

The popularity of Amazon's Alexa and its competitors show us that humans are hungry for a new kind of computing. This form of computing lets us see new layers of information on top of the existing world. It is computing that surrounds us, walks with us through shopping malls and assists us while working out. This kind of computing could potentially even save our lives as it collects our visual, biometric and textual data.

Closer Computers

To make it possible to get this level of human-machine interface, we will need to get computers closer to our brains and certainly our eyes.

We can do some of this kind of computing by holding a phone in our hands, which is already used for AR by kids playing Minecraft Earth or Pokémon Go. Holding a mobile phone, though, won't get us to the promised land of true Spatial Computing. It must be said, however, that developers are using mobile to build a variety of things that are important to pay attention to.

As the 2020s open, we are seeing some of these wearables evolving in the marketplace with a spectrum of devices.

On one side, we have very lightweight devices that look similar to the Google Glass device. A good example of these lightweight devices is Focals by North, which got some hype at the Consumer Electronics Show (CES) 2020, but there are a number of them from Vuzix, Epson, Nreal, and others. These have screens that show you a variety of information overlaid on top of the real world and do it with a form factor that looks like a pair of sunglasses.

At the other end of the spectrum are devices that completely change our visual experience as we move around in the real world. These devices which include Microsoft's HoloLens 2 could be seen as a new kind of "mixed-reality" device that brings advanced graphical features and a ton of sensors along with a new form and Artificial Intelligence to see, process, and display all sorts of new experiences, both visual and auditory, that profoundly changes how we interact with the real world.

It is these higher-end devices that have us dreaming of a radically new way of computing, which is what we are covering in this book: Spatial Computing. With these devices, you're wearing seven cameras along with a bunch of other sensors and because of the amount of processing that needs to be done and the kinds of visual displays that need to be included, these devices tend to be both heavier and more expensive than devices, for instance, like Focals by North.

It is the near future, though, that has us most excited. Qualcomm announced a new XR2 chipset and reference design that will make powerful AR devices possible that will make the HoloLens 2 device soon seem underpowered, heavy, and overpriced. We're expecting a wave of new devices to be shipped in 2021 based on the XR2 with new optics that will be far better than anything we've seen to date.

Let's go back, though, to where AR came from.

The Origins and Limitations of Augmented Reality

For us, the potential for AR came up in 2011 as Peter Meier, then CTO of a small AR company in Munich, Germany, took us into the snow outside of its offices and showed us dragons on the building across the street. These virtual dragons were amazing, but the demo was done with a webcam on a laptop. Hardly easy to do for consumers. Earlier attempts, like Layar, which was an AR platform for mobile phones, didn't hit with consumers because the mobile phones of the day were underpowered, and most didn't appreciate AR on small screens. These early efforts, though, did wake up a lot of people, including us, to the possibilities of AR. It also woke Apple up, which started working earnestly on Spatial Computing.

Within a few years Apple had purchased that company, Metaio, and Peter today works there. Since then Apple has purchased dozens of companies that do various pieces of Spatial Computing, and that acquisition trend continues into 2020. While we were typing this Apple bought another company that does AI that will prove important to the future we describe here. Metaio's work was the foundation of a new set of capabilities built into iPhones. Developers know this AR framework as "ARKit." Google has a competitive framework for Android users called "ARCore."

There are now thousands of applications that use ARKit, ranging from apps to let you measure things to apps that radically change the real world in terms of everything from shopping to new forms of video games. If you visit Apple's store at its new headquarters in Cupertino you will be handed an iPad where you can see an augmented display of the building across the street from the store.

Touch the screen and the roof pops off so you can see what it's like inside. Touch it again and you'll learn about the solar panels that provide clean energy to the building. Touch it again and you can see a wind analysis layer of the building.

Photo credit: IKEA. IKEA Place lets you move furniture around in your house and try it out to see if it fits your lifestyle before you buy it and unpack it, only to discover it doesn't work.

It is apps like these that show the power of AR, but they also show you the limitations, of which there are many. Let's dig into a few of the limitations of mobile AR:

- **You have to hold the phone**: This keeps you from being able to use more capable controllers, or even your hands, to touch, manipulate, or shoot virtual items.

- **Tracking often doesn't work well**: This is especially the case in dark rooms or places that don't have a lot of detail or in moving vehicles like planes or buses, and tracking is almost impossible to get. Apple, even in its headquarters, put a grid pattern on top of the building model so that the camera on the iPad would be able to figure out where it was and align virtual items accurately and quickly.

- **Occlusion doesn't always work**: Occlusion means that virtual items properly cover up things behind them. Or, if a human or, say, a cat walks in front of the virtual item, the virtual item disappears behind that moving human or animal properly.

- **Virtual items don't look natural for a variety of other reasons**: It's hard for your iPhone to be able to properly place shadows under virtual items that match real-world lighting conditions. It's also hard to make virtual items detailed enough to seem natural. For things like virtual cartoons, that might not be a big deal, but if you want to "fool" your user into thinking a virtual item is part of the real world it's hard to do that because of the technical limitations inherent in today's phones and the software that puts these virtual items on top of the real world.

Photo credit: Niantic. Pokémon Go lets you capture characters on top of the real world in its popular mobile game, which generated about a billion dollars in revenue in 2019.

The other problem that most people don't think about when they are holding their mobile phone is that their screen is actually fairly small. Even the biggest iPhones or Samsung devices are only a few inches across. That hardly is enough to give your brain anything close to the immersion, embodiment, and other advantages of VR. The problem of having to hold the phone or tablet is the most daunting, actually, particularly for workers. Imagine working on a factory line where you need both of your hands to insert a part into a product. Now, imagine having to put down that part to hold up a phone to augment your work and see details on what you need to do next to properly hook that part up.

Or, if you are playing video games, imagine trying to play paintball, or go bowling with your friends. The act of holding a phone, especially with a tiny screen, limits your ability to recreate the real-world version of those games.

This is why companies like Apple, Qualcomm, Magic Leap, Facebook, Google, and others have already spent billions of dollars to develop some form of wearable AR glasses, blades, or head-mounted displays, if you wish to call them that.

Wearable AR

The industry has been attempting to have a go at this for quite some time and already there have been some notable failures.

ODG, Meta, DAQRI, Intel Vaunt, and others populate the AR "burial zone" and insiders expect more to come. This is really a risky game for big companies. Why?

Well, to really take on the mass market, a company will need the following:

- **Distribution, stores**: The ability to get people to try on these devices.

- **A brand**: Because these computers will be worn on your face, consumers will be far more picky about brands. Brands that are perceived as nerdy will face headwinds. Already, Facebook announced it is working with Luxottica, which owns brands like Ray-Ban, Oakley, and many others.

- **A supply chain**: If their product does prove successful, tens of millions will buy it. There are only a few companies that can make those quantities of products and use the latest miniaturization techniques, along with the latest materials science, to make devices lightweight, strong, and flexible to absorb the blows that will come with regular use.

- **Marketing**: People don't yet know why they need head-mounted displays, so they will need to be shown the advantages. This will take many ads and other techniques to get consumers to understand why these are better than a smartphone alone.

- **Content**: If you get a pair of $2,000 glasses home and you can't watch TV or Netflix, or play a lot of different games, or use them at work with a variety of different systems, you will think you got ripped off. Only a few companies can get developers to build these, along with making the content deals happen.

- **Design and customer experience**: Consumers have, so far, rejected all the attempts that have come before. Why? Because the glasses that are on the market as of early 2020 generally have a ton of design and user experience problems, from being too heavy to not having sharp enough visuals, to looking like an alien force made them. Only a few companies have the ability to get where consumers want them to be. One company we have heard about has built thousands of different versions of its glasses and it hasn't even shipped yet. The cost of doing that kind of design work runs into hundreds of millions of dollars.

- **Ecosystem**: When we got the new Apple Watch and the new Apple AirPods Pros in late 2019, we noted that turning the knob on the Watch (Apple calls it the Digital Crown) causes the audio on the headphones to be adjusted. This kind of ecosystem integration will prove very difficult for companies that don't have phones, watches, headphones, computers, and TV devices on the market already.

- **Data privacy**: These devices will have access to more data about you than your smartphones do. Way more. We believe consumers are getting astute about the collection of this kind of data, which may include analysis of your face, your vascular system (blood vessels), your eyes and what you are looking at, your voice, your gait and movement, and more. Only a few companies can deal satisfactorily with regulators concerning this data and can afford the security systems to protect this data from getting into the wrong hands.

This is why when Meron Gribetz, the founder of Meta, told us that he thought he had a chance to be disruptive to personal computers, we argued with him. He thought the $200 million or so that had been invested in his firm would be enough. We saw that a competitive firm, Magic Leap, had already raised more than a billion dollars and thought that meant doom for his firm. We feel Magic Leap, even with its current war chest of $2.7 billion dollars, doesn't have enough capital to build all eight of these required aspects from the preceding list. In fact, there have been news reports that indicate that Magic Leap is currently for sale. In April 2020, Magic Leap announced massive layoffs of about 50 percent of its workforce, or more than 1,000 people, and refocused away from attempting to sell to consumers.

We turned out to be right about Meta, for his firm was later decimated and sold for parts. Others, too, had the same dream of coming out of the woodwork and leaving a stamp on the world. ODG's founder Ralph Osterhout had quite a bit of early success in the field. He invented night-vision scope devices for the military and that got him the ability to have a production line and team in downtown San Francisco to come up with new things.

He sold some of his original patents to Microsoft where they were used on the HoloLens product. But, like Meron's company, his firm couldn't stay in the market.

Photo credit: Robert Scoble. Meron Gribetz, founder of Meta, shows off how his headset could augment the world and let you use your hands to work.

These early attempts, though, were important. They woke developers up to the opportunities that are here if all the pieces can be put together and they saw the power of a new way of working, and a new way of living, thanks to AR.

Photo credit: Intel. Intel Vaunt promised great-looking smart glasses with innovative digital displays, but didn't provide the features that potential customers would expect.

They weren't alone in their dream of changing computing for all humans, either. Some other notable failures tell us a bit about where we are going in the future. Intel's Vaunt aimed at fixing a ton of problems with the other early attempts. It had no camera due to the PR problems that Google Glass got into and the last version could only show two-dimensional overlay visuals in black and white. It also had no speaker or microphone. It looked like an everyday pair of glasses.

Too Much and Too Little

It was Intel's fear of the social problems of smart devices on your face, though, that doomed it. In April 2018, it announced it was canceling the Vaunt project. To do AR and the virtualized screens that would give these devices real utility beyond just being a bigger display on your face, the device needs to know where it is in the real world.

Not including cameras meant no AR. No microphones meant you couldn't use your voice to control the devices. No speakers meant you still needed to add on a pair of headphones, which increased complexity, and consumers just decided to stay away. Not to mention Intel didn't own a brand anyone wants on their face and didn't have the marketing muscle or the stores to get people to try them on and get the proper fit and prescription lenses.

DAQRI, on the other hand, went to the other side of the spectrum. They included pretty great AR and had a camera and much better displays. Workers wearing them could use them for hours to, say, inspect oil refinery pipes and equipment.

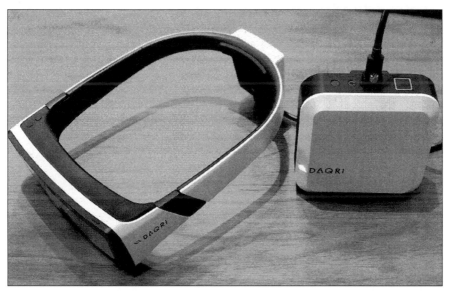

Photo credit: Robert Scoble. DAQRI's headset gathered hundreds of millions in investment and showed promise for enterprise workers, but never took off because of its tether and expensive costs.

Where Intel threw out any features that made the glasses seem weird or antisocial, DAQRI kept them in. It was big, bulky, and had a tether to a processing pack you would keep on your belt or in a backpack. This appeared very capable, and because they were aimed at enterprise users who didn't need to worry about looking cool or having a luxury brand associated with the product, it seemed like it would see more success. And for a while it did, except for one thing: the price tag.

Many corporate employees heard about this system, gave DAQRI a call, then found out the costs involved, which could run into hundreds of thousands of dollars, maybe even millions, and that killed many projects. In September 2019, it joined the failure pile and shut down most operations.

Getting Past the Setbacks

Now, if we thought the failures would rule the day, we wouldn't have written this book. Here, perspective rules. There were lots of personal computing companies that went out of business before Apple figured out the path to profitability (Apple itself almost went bankrupt after it announced the Macintosh). Luckily, the opportunity for improving how we all compute is still keeping many innovators energized. For instance, at CES 2020, Panasonic grabbed attention with a new pair of glasses. Inside were lenses from Kopin, started by John Fam.

Photo credit: Robert Scoble. John Fam of Kopin shows off how his lenses work in a demo. His lenses and displays are now in Panasonic's latest head-mounted displays and soon, he promises, others.

One thing that's held back the industry has been the quality of lenses and displays, and Fam is one of the pioneers trying to fix the problems. What problems? Well, if you wear a Magic Leap or a HoloLens, you'll see virtual images that are pretty dark, don't have good contrast, are fairly blurry, and are fairly thick. They also have disadvantages including a small viewing area, usually around 50 degrees, when compared to the 100 degrees on offer in most VR headsets. Because these new displays and lenses need to display virtual images while letting a user see through to the real world, they also are very difficult to manufacture, which is why a Magic Leap is priced at $2,500 and a HoloLens is $3,500 (as of January 2020, but we expect these prices to come down pretty rapidly over the next few years).

Today, there are only a few approaches to getting virtual images into your eyes. One approach is waveguides. Here, tiny little structures in something that looks like glass bounce light dozens of times from projectors until the right pixel gets to the right place and are reflected into your eyes. You can't really see these extremely small structures with the naked eye, but this process makes for a flat optic that can be fitted into a head-mounted display. It has lots of disadvantages, the most significant of which is that waveguides are typically not very efficient.

The ones in the first HoloLens presented virtual images that could barely be seen outdoors, for instance. They also present eye-strain problems because it is hard to make these kinds of optics present images at various focal depths. Getting virtual images close to your eyes? Forget it, but even ones that are a few feet away don't usually work at various depths as well as taking into account things in the real world, which puts strain on your eyes. Two terms optics experts talk a lot about are vergence and accommodation.

Vergence and Accommodation

Vergence is how your eyes move inward as you try to focus on things that are closer and closer to you. Cross-eyed? That's vergence and if your glasses don't align images well as they get closer, they can cause your eyes to get much more tired than when they have to focus on real-world items for a long time.

Accommodation refers to how your eye changes shape—and how the lenses in your eyes move to focus on things close up. The eye often uses cues from the real world to figure out how to do that and in smart glasses, these cues aren't available because everything is presented on a single focal plane. Eye strain appears again as an issue.

Microsoft with HoloLens 2, its latest AR device, went in a different direction— it is using a series of lasers, pointed into tiny mirrors that reflect that light into the back of your eye, which allows you to see virtual images. So far, this approach brings other problems. Some users say they see a flicker, while others say that colors don't look correct.

Either way, we haven't seen one monitor/lens system yet that fixes all these problems. The closest we've seen is one from Lumus, but because it stayed with waveguides, it needed huge projectors pushing light into the optics. This might be good for something as big as a HoloLens (which weighs about a pound) but the industry knows it needs to ship products that are closer to what Intel's Vaunt was trying to do if it wants to be popular with users.

We hear new optics approaches are coming within the next few years, which is what will drive a new wave of devices, but even those spending billions are no longer hyping things up. Both Facebook's founder Mark Zuckerberg and Magic Leap's founder Rony Abovitz have been much more muted when discussing the future with the press lately. Zuckerberg now says he believes we will get glasses that replace mobile phones sometime in the next decade.

Fast, Cheap, or Good

The saying goes that when designing a product, you can have it cheap, fast, or good, except you can only have two of the three. By "good," we mean well designed and appealing for the user: a good and intuitive user interface, appealing aesthetics, and so on. If you've got a "good," fast product, it's not going to be cheap. If it's both fast and cheap, it's unlikely that it's had so much time and expertise put into the design process to bring you a "good" user experience. Spatial Computing product designers will have to make other choices on top of this canonical choice as well. Lightweight or the best optics? A cheap price tag or the best performance? Private or advertising-supported? Split the devices up into their component parts and you see the trade-offs that will have to be made to go after various customer contexts. Aiming a product at someone riding a mountain bike will lead to different trade-offs from aiming one at a construction worker inspecting pipes, for instance.

Since we assume you, our reader, will be putting Spatial Computing to work in your business, we recognize you will need to evaluate the different approaches and products that come to market. These are the things you will need to evaluate for your projects. For instance, having the best visuals might be most important to you, and you are willing to go with a bigger, and heavier, device to get them.

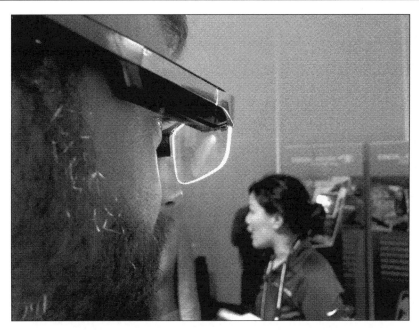

Photo credit: Robert Scoble. DigiLens Display at Photonics West in 2019. Photonics West is where the industry's optics experts go to show off their latest work and here a potential customer tries on DigiLens' latest offering.

Here are the 10 technology areas where devices will compete:

- **The monitors and optics**: These control what you see. The ones that present more data in a bigger field of view with more pixels, or higher resolution, are usually in the bigger and more expensive devices than the ones on the lightweight side of the scale.

- **The GPU**: GPU speed means how many polygons per second can be processed. The more powerful the GPU in your device, the more detailed the virtual items presented can be. Again, the more powerful ones will be in devices that can supply the battery power these will need and the heat handling that comes along with more powerful chips.

- **Battery**: If you want to use your devices for more hours without needing to charge, you'll need a bigger and heavier one. There will, too, be various approaches to charging said batteries that you will need to consider.

- **Wireless capabilities**: Will it have a 5G chip so it can be used on the new high-speed wireless networks? Or will it only have Wi-Fi capabilities, like current Microsoft HoloLens devices? That's great if you'll only use it at home or work, where Wi-Fi abounds, but makes it harder to use elsewhere.

- **The sensors**: Newer and bigger devices will have several cameras and a variety of other sensors—one to look at your mouth for data to build avatars and study your sentiment, one for your eyes, another to gather light data, so it can adjust the monitor to be brighter or darker depending on conditions, and four for the world, two of which will be black and white for tracking and two will be color for photography and scanning items. In addition, there's usually an Inertial Measurement Unit (IMU), which watches how the unit moves. An IMU actually has a group of sensors—an accelerometer, a gyroscope, a compass, and a magnetometer. These give the system quite a bit of data about how the headset is moving. The top-of-the-line units also have some three-dimensional sensors. All these sensors add many new capabilities, including the ability to have virtualized monitors that stick to surfaces such as real-world tables, or AR characters, masks, items, and such.

- **AI chip**: Newer devices will add on chips to decipher what the unit is seeing and to start predicting the next moves of both the user and others in their field of view.

- **Corrective lenses**: Many users will need custom lenses inserted, or systems that can change the prescription of the system. Apple and others have patented various methods to bend lenses to supply different corrective prescriptions.

- **Audio**: On some systems, we are seeing array microphones in some high-end units (an array has a number of microphones that can be joined together in software to make it so that they work in higher noise situations, such as a factory floor). Also, a variety of speakers are available, with more on the way. Some even vibrate the bones in your face, which passes audio waves to your inner ear.

- **Processing**: Some systems are all self-contained, like the Microsoft HoloLens, where everything is in the unit on your head. Others, like Nreal and Magic Leap, need to be tethered to processor packs you wear, or to your phone.

- **The frame and case**: Some design their products to be resistant to a large amount of abuse, others design them to be hyper-light and beautiful. There will be a variety of different approaches to water resistance and shock resistance, and trade-offs between expensive new materials that can provide flexibility and reduce device weight while looking amazing, versus cheaper materials that might be easier to replace if broken.

Each product that we'll see on the market will have various capabilities in each of these areas and trade-offs to be made.

Differences To Be Aware Of

We won't go into depth on each, since we're not writing this book to help the product designers who work inside Apple, Facebook, or others, but want to point out some differences that business strategists, planners, and product managers will need to be aware of.

For instance, let's look at the lenses. Generally, you'll have to know where you will attempt to use these devices. Will they be outside in bright sunlight? That's tough for most of the current products to do, so might limit your choices. Lumus, an optics company from Israel, showed us some of its lenses that would work outdoors. They said they are capable of about 10,000 nits (a unit of measure for how bright a monitor is), versus the 300 to 500 nits in many current AR headsets which only work in fairly low light.

The problem is that Lumus' solution, at least as it was presented to us in 2018, was expensive and fairly big. This is appropriate for a device the size of a HoloLens, but you won't see those in glasses anytime soon. The Lumus lenses were a lot sharper than others we had experienced before and since, and had a bigger field of view, but product designers haven't yet included those in products, in part because of their big size and higher cost.

At the other end of the scale were lenses from Kopin and DigiLens. DigiLens showed us glasses in early 2019 that were very affordable (devices would be about $500 retail) but had a tiny field of view—about 15 degrees instead of the 50 that Lumus showed us, which is about what the HoloLens 2 has, and not as much resolution either. So, reading a newspaper or doing advanced AR won't happen with the DigiLens products, at least with what we've seen up to early 2020.

So, let's talk about how these products get made. When we toured Microsoft Research back in 2004, we met Gary Starkweather. He was the inventor of the laser printer. That interview is still up on Microsoft's Channel 9 site at `https://channel9.msdn.com/Blogs/TheChannel9Team/Kevin-Schofield-Tour-of-Microsoft-Research-Social-Software-Hardware`.

In the preceding video, Starkweather talks about his research into the future of computing. Starkweather was looking for ways to build new kinds of monitors that would give us ubiquitous computing. In hindsight, this was the beginning of where the HoloLens came from. In a separate lab at Microsoft Research nearby, Andy Wilson was working on software to "see" hands and gestures we could make to show the computer what to do, among other research he and his team was doing.

He still is working on advancing the state-of-the-art human-machine interfaces at Microsoft Research today. Starkweather, on the other hand, died while we were writing this book, but his work was so important to the field that we wanted to recognize it here.

From Kinect to the HoloLens

This early research from the mid-2000s soon became useful as three-dimensional sensors started coming on the scene. In 2010, Microsoft announced the Kinect for Xbox 360. This was a three-dimensional sensor that attempted to bring new capabilities to its video game system. The system could now "see" users standing in front of it. Microsoft had licensed that technology from a small, then unknown Israeli start-up, PrimeSense.

Why was Kinect important? It soon became clear that Kinect wouldn't be a success in the video game world, but Microsoft's researchers saw another way to use that three-dimensional sensor technology. Shrink it down, put it on your face and aim it at the room, instead of players. That would let a wearable computer map the room out, adding new computing capabilities to the room itself.

That's exactly what Alex Kipman and his team did on the first HoloLens. That device had four cameras and one of those three-dimensional depth sensors that mapped out the room, then converted that map into a sheet of polygons (little triangles). You can still see that sheet of triangles once in a while when using the HoloLens and needing to do calibration.

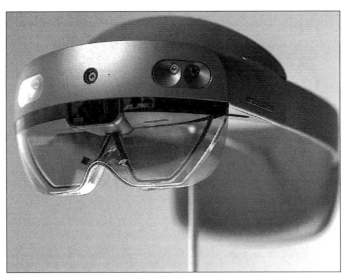

Photo credit: Microsoft. HoloLens 2 brings a much more comfortable headset with way better gesture recognition, along with a flip-up screen so workers don't need to remove it as often.

The sensors on the front of a Spatial Computing device, like a Microsoft HoloLens, build a virtual layer on top of the real world where virtual items can be placed. Software developers soon become adept at manipulating this virtual layer that many call the "AR Cloud." This database of trillions of virtual triangles laid on top of the real world provides the foundation for everything to come from simple text to fully augmented or virtual characters running around.

When the HoloLens was introduced, it brought a new computing paradigm. It's useful to look at just some of the new things it did that weren't possible before:

- **Screens can now be virtualized**: Before HoloLens, if you wanted a new computer screen you had to buy one from a retailer and hook it up. They are big, awkward, heavy, and expensive. With HoloLens you just gestured with your hands or told the system to give you a new screen. Then you could grab that virtual screen and place it anywhere in the room around you. There aren't any limits on how many screens you could get, either.

- **Surfaces can be changed**: When using RoboRaid, one of the games we bought for our HoloLens, aliens could blow holes in our real walls and then crawl through them to attack. The effect was quite stunning and showed developers that you could "mix" reality in a whole new way, keeping the real world but replacing parts of it with virtual pieces.

- **Everything is three-dimensional (and not like those glasses at the movies)**: The first thing you figure out when you get a HoloLens is that you can drop holograms, which are three-dimensional items that move, nearly everywhere. We have a clown riding a bicycle around our feet as we write this paragraph, for instance. Now that might not sound that interesting, but you can view your business data in three dimensions too. Over at BadVR, a start-up in Santa Monica, California, Suzie Borders, the founder, showed us quite a few things, from shopping malls where you could see traffic data on the actual floor to factories where you could see data streaming from every machine. This new way of visualizing the world maps to the human brain and how it sees the real world, so it has deep implications for people who do complex jobs, such as surgeons, for instance.

- **Everything is remembered**: Our little bicycle-riding hologram will still be here even a year later, still riding in the same spot; the monitors we placed around our office stick in the same place. Data we leave around stays where we left it. Microsoft calls these "Azure Spatial Anchors" and has given developers new capabilities regarding this new idea.

- **Voice first**: The HoloLens has four microphones, arranged in a way to make it easy for it to hear your commands. You can talk to the HoloLens and ask it to do a variety of things and it'll do them and talk back. While you can do the same with Siri on an iPhone, this was built into the system at a deep level and feels more natural because it's on your head and always there.

- **Gesture- and hand-based systems**: Ever wanted to punch your computer? Well, HoloLens almost understands that. Instead, you open your hand and a variety of new capabilities pop up out of thin air. You can also grab things with your hands, and poke at them now too, all thanks to the sensors on the front of the device that are watching your hands, and the AI chip that makes sense of it all.

Given this combination of technologies and capabilities, which are superior to those that the Magic Leap or any other current AR headset has, we believe that the HoloLens historically will be viewed as a hugely important product that showed the world Spatial Computing at a depth we hadn't seen before.

Technology Takes a Leap

All others would use the HoloLens as a measuring stick, which brings us to Magic Leap. Magic Leap gathered investors with a promise that it would make a big magic leap into this new kind of computing. In hindsight we don't think the investors knew how advanced Microsoft's efforts were. Its first round of $540 million came back in 2014, two years before HoloLens hit the market.

Photo credit: Magic Leap. The Magic Leap One is an attractive consumer-targeted product that has more graphical capabilities than HoloLens, but requires a tether to a processor pack, which HoloLens doesn't need.

The hype before Magic Leap shipped its first product, the ML1, was that it constituted a real graphics breakthrough, with optics that were way ahead of others in the market. That didn't come true, at least not in its first product, and as mentioned, Magic Leap's future as a continuing company as this book goes to press is an unknown.

As 2020 opens up, HoloLens is hitting some production problems of its own. It can't make enough devices to supply all the demand and some customers are reporting problems with the images seen in its devices, which has led to speculation that it is having a tough time manufacturing the laser/micro-mirror system that it uses to get light into your eyes. Microsoft now claims that those problems are behind it, but the delays show how difficult getting these products to market is.

Photo credit: Nreal. Nreal won praise at CES 2020, with some press stating that it was the best product there. This headset is expected to be released this year for $499.

Both the HoloLens 2 and Magic Leap ML1 feel like big elephants or whales, since having a whale jumping out of a gymnasium floor was how Magic Leap became known in a demo video that oversold its graphical capabilities.

This brings us to Nreal, and a lawsuit that Magic Leap filed against that company.

Patents and Problems

Nreal started when Chi Xu left Magic Leap in 2016, disappointed with the speed that the well-funded company was moving at He, along with Bing Xiao, co-founder and chief optical engineer, and Chi Xu, the founder, joined forces in China. The subtext is that China has long been seen as a place that plays loose and fast with intellectual property designed in the United States. Magic Leap promptly sued Nreal and accused Chi Xu of stealing AR secrets from his former employer. It was alleged that Magic Leap were using patents it acquired from Meta in its complaint against Nreal, and Rony Abovitz tells us that intellectual property rights are important to Magic Leap, which has invested billions in its product development. This case will play itself out, but for now, Nreal is getting products on the market that are fairly capable and a lot lower cost than Magic Leap—it was selling a $499 model like hotcakes at CES 2020. Having the Chinese supply chain at their back door will prove to be a big competitive advantage for Nreal, we think, and make it a company to watch.

This leads us to the elephant in the room: Apple. Apple has all the ingredients to make the meal already, from distribution to the brand to the supply chain. While there are a ton of rumors out there, it's good to note that no one really knows what will ship until Tim Cook calls the press in to see the new product. So far that hasn't happened, and even planned products can get delayed or radically changed. It's worth noting that the iPod, from conception to being on the shelf, took less than a year, which shows just how fast companies can move to make new products if motivated.

That said, Apple let details leak from an internal meeting where it detailed two new products. The first is a headset that would do both VR and AR and that will arrive in 2022. The second is a pair of lighter AR glasses, which will come in 2023. We expect when Apple does come to the market it will be with products that focus on what Apple does best: ecosystem integration and user experience.

We see that Apple plays a huge role in the industry and we believe that consumer adoption won't happen until they get into the market.

Compare Apple with Nreal and others, and you see the problem. While glasses from Nreal have pretty good optics with bright images and wide field of view, the company doesn't yet do very much that will get consumers excited, and it isn't clear how it will excite developers enough until it sells millions of units. In Silicon Valley, this is seen as a "chicken and egg" problem—how will it sell enough without apps, and how will it get apps without selling enough?

Can any company make the consumer market happen in a huge way without Apple? It's hard to see how, but after Apple arrives, the market will be open to alternative approaches, the same way that after the iPhone grabbed the market's attention, Google was then able to grab most of the market share with its Android OS and phones that ran it.

That all said, we have seen inside R&D labs and know that there are many products under development and that by 2025 we should see massive numbers of people wearing Spatial Computing devices. That will open up many new business opportunities and that's got us excited. For instance, there will be a hunger for new kinds of content, so we'll see new kinds of cameras and other technologies to help satiate that hunger.

Volumetric and Light Field: Capturing Our World in a New Way

DARPA had a challenge: can you take a photo through a bush?

That led to Computer Vision breakthroughs at Stanford University and other places that are still changing how we look at capturing images today. That challenge, back in 2007, caused Stanford University researcher Marc Levoy to move away from using a single lens to take a photo and, instead, build a grid of cameras, all connected to a computer where software would gather rays of light coming through a bush and collect them piece by piece from all the different cameras, creating a light field. Then, a computer would re-assemble those pieces, sort of like putting together a puzzle.

Shrinking Concepts, Expanding Horizons

Today, the light field concept has shrunk from using individual cameras arranged on a set of shelves to using pieces of image sensors, sometimes even putting microscopic lenses on top, and the field of Computer Vision has greatly expanded. Computer Vision is used in a variety of products, from a June Oven, which can tell whether you have put a piece of toast or a steak into your oven, to autonomous cars, where Computer Vision is used to do a variety of tasks.

The technique gathers data from a variety of sensors and fuses that into a "frame," which in Artificial Intelligence lingo is all the data from one specific point in time. A Tesla's frame, for instance, includes the data from its seven cameras, its half-dozen ultrasonic sensors, its radar sensor, and a variety of other IMUs that have motion, compass, and other data. Once a frame has been captured, then a variety of Computer Vision techniques, which are a subset of Artificial Intelligence, can be performed on that frame.

These new techniques have deep implications for entertainment, and, well, pretty much everything—since we'll soon see camera arrays in tons of products.

Photo credit: Robert Scoble. Part of Marc Levoy's photographic research lab at Stanford University in 2007. This research led to the development of new kinds of cameras that are still being improved today.

Already camera arrays are being used to capture dancers on "So You Think You Can Dance" and many other things, particularly important in Spatial Computing's VR and AR. When Buzz Aldrin talks to you in a VR headset, he was captured on a camera array with a new technique called "volumetric" video, which means you can walk around Buzz's virtual image as he talks to you.

Shooting Some Volumetric

Before we go on, we should define some terms. Volumetric video does what it sounds like: it measures volumes. When creative people say, "I'm shooting some volumetric," that means they are capturing video inside a special studio that has one of these arrays of cameras. We visited one multimillion-dollar studio, owned by Intel, near Hollywood to get a look at how it's done. There, a sizable room has a dome surrounding a space that can fit half a basketball court. In the dome, as we looked up, we could see more than 100 cameras.

The walls of the dome were green so that computers could get rid of the dome and easily insert virtual imagery later in editing. Under the dome, Intel had more than 100 cameras connected to a data center where the videos from each camera were stitched together to make something that editors could use and then distribute to people who would see that scene in a VR headset. This three-dimensional dataset is actually pretty useful for regular movies and TV shows, too, because there are infinite camera positions surrounding the action. So, a director could choose a different camera angle to include in the movie she is directing. If that one doesn't work, she could choose another of the same scene. There's a whole industry of volumetric studios, including Metastage, which was backed by Microsoft and utilizes Microsoft technology for Volumetric Capture for VR and AR experiences.

Photo credit: Intel Studios. This Volumetric Capture dome has 100 4K cameras around the dome, all pointed inside. When joined together the cameras make a three-dimensional image set that you can walk around, or through.

This is different from 360-degree video. Where volumetric studios include hundreds of cameras aimed inward, toward a single point, 360-degree cameras start at a single point and aim outward. This is a useful technique to capture, say, video of yourself skiing down a hill, since when you get home you want to be able to see the mountain in all directions, including your family members skiing in front of and behind you as you glide down the mountain.

This brings us to light fields. Strict volumetric cameras don't capture the data about all the photons of light streaming off of the subjects that are being captured. Light fields go further, to actually record the angles that light is reflecting off of subjects and entering a camera array.

This, in theory, will let you capture scenes in a much more natural way, which looks amazing to your eye if you view it in a Spatial Computing device on your face (light field lenses are just starting to be shown on visors, too—CREAL got critical acclaim at CES 2020 for its device that shows light field data).

The real magic of light fields, though, will be that they will enable far more interactive scenes and much greater editing control over objects and scenes. Today, a 360-degree video, and even most volumetric data, is not interactive at all. You sit there and you watch, or with volumetric video, you walk around while watching. But soon, in scenes with light field capture and lenses, you might be able to walk around things and even touch them and pick them up (given enough programming to enable that). Light fields are the holy grail of capturing light, as they do so in such a detailed way that you can do a ton more with that data later.

Google's The Relightables system already uses some of these techniques to let content developers edit three-dimensional images after shooting. That system uses 331 custom color LED lights, along with an array of high-resolution cameras, and a set of custom depth sensors to create volumetric datasets with a taste of light field-style features. Thanks to capturing light in a unique way the computer can separate out the color and luminosity data from the physical form of the subject being videoed. That way a producer could mess with how an object looks later on a computer screen.

Photo credit: Google. Google's The Relightables system uses 331 custom color LED lights, an array of high-resolution cameras, and a set of custom depth sensors to create volumetric datasets where the lighting can be changed later.

Video professionals are pushing even further into this field of using arrays of cameras to do new things. Michael Mansouri, founder of Radiant Images, a firm that used to rent cameras to movie studios and now does R&D on cameras for those studios, showed us his latest camera arrays that are doing things Ansel Adams never dreamed of doing with a camera.

Camera Magic

Mansouri's cameras can capture thousands of frames per second, for instance, and are synced with extremely fast strobe lights—this super-fast capture lets him build massive datasets that contain all the data to build light fields or volumetric constructions. He arranges about 100 of these cameras around an actor to capture him or her in ways that just weren't possible a few years ago. His cameras capture every ray of light and the angle at which it entered the camera array, so computers later can "remix" the data.

He said that he is doing tons of tricks to capture more data than the human eye can see, too.

For instance, TV images run at 30 frames per second. He can push his cameras to capture many more frames than is needed to satisfy the human eye and he oversamples those frames—the cameras he is using in one of his arrays can capture thousands of frames per second, which makes for great slow-motion captures, but he is using fast-frame captures to do new things and capture new data that helps Artificial Intelligence do new things with video. One frame might be overexposed, another underexposed. One might be black and white, another with color saturation pushed high. Then, the Computer Vision systems that he and others are building can find new detail in the data to make images not only sharper and clearer but also add capabilities that are hard to explain in a book.

The effect of all this light field work will be video that you could walk around in a very natural way. Imagine walking through a meadow in Yosemite at sunset. It won't be like a stage, where the facade is exposed as soon as you walk behind something and see that it's just a board painted to look nice from the front; here, you can walk around every plant and tree, and the deer 20 feet away looks real. You'll never find yourself "backstage."

Photo credit: Radiant Images. Radiant Images' Nebula Light Field and Volumetric system has dozens of high-frame-rate video cameras that it uses to both capture volumetric and light field data.

That kind of experience will arrive soon to our headsets. Michael says, "why stop there?" He sees a world where you will walk onto a virtual football field and watch the Superbowl from a new vantage point: that of the quarterback actually playing the game. His team actually shot a commercial for Oakley that gave a taste of how that would feel.

What comes after that might blow even him away: new datasets from the real world might let you walk off of that virtual football field and back into your seat, or even to places outside of the stadium, with lots of virtual holograms along the way. A decade from now, Hollywood could use these new datasets to bring us an entirely new form of entertainment. One that isn't delivered on film anymore, but, rather, a dataset we call an AR Cloud that streams to your headset as you walk around.

AR Clouds (3D Mapping) and Internet Infrastructure Including 5G

As we move into a world of glasses, we will want to move away from a world that requires so many apps. After all, do you want to load an app just to see where a product is when you get to a shopping mall? Or do you want to load another if you get to a ski resort just to see which runs are open? Or yet another to see the menu at a restaurant? No.

What strategists are planning is a new contextual system that brings you functionality where and when you need it, and that stretches onto the field of entertainment as we just discussed.

A New Kind of Map

When you walk into a shopping mall, you'll see all sorts of virtual helpers. When you go skiing, you'll see the names of the trails as you ski past. When you go to a grocery store, assistants will pop up, showing you more details on top of products, along with navigation to the products that are on your shopping list. When you drive, you'll see other things, like maps and controls for your car. When you exercise, you'll see your health apps contextually pop up. This contextual system will also let you experience new forms of entertainment from football to movies where you can follow an actor into, say, a burning building.

Now some of this can happen with simple location data, but in a true Spatial Computing world there will be virtual beings moving around, helping you out, plus you will want to play new kinds of games against other people, along with tons of augmented, or automated, things that either add data onto the world or keep track of the world to add new utility.

To get to this deeper augmentation, literally every centimeter in the world will need to be mapped in a new three-dimensional dataset that most people haven't yet considered. These maps barely exist today, mostly being built for autonomous vehicles or robots to use to navigate around streets. The Mapbox CEO, Eric Gundersen, laid out how this will all work. His firm already provides maps to millions of developers and if you use apps like Yelp, Snapchat, or Foursquare, you are already seeing maps provided by his firm.

He and others see a need for a new kind of map: one that doesn't just have a single line for a street, but that looks like the real world.

Mapping cars are building the skeleton for this new kind of map, which some of the industry has started calling an "AR Cloud." As vehicles roll by on the street, they are making high-resolution maps and ingesting, via AI, every sign and lots of other features. If you see Apple or Google's latest maps, you'll notice they are getting more three-dimensional features every day, and, in the case of Google, are able to use AR and Computer Vision to sense where you are, thanks to you turning on your camera, and show you navigation aids. This is using an early form of this kind of AR Cloud and gives us a taste of the world that will rapidly evolve over the next decade.

Some places, though, will need to be mapped out in a lot more detail. For instance, if you want to play games where monsters jump around your home, like you can with a HoloLens or Magic Leap, then those systems will need to build a three-dimensional map of your walls, ceiling, floor, and any objects in your home.

Building a Map

When recently acquired 6D.ai used the term AR Cloud (it was the firm that popularized the term), that's what they meant. That firm had up until recently shipped a Software Developer's Kit (SDK) that had let developers build AR Cloud capabilities into their apps.

What did 6D.ai's code do? It asked users to turn on their camera and then, as users moved their phone around where they were, it instantly built a three-dimensional structure of what it saw. Moving around enough, it soon captured a digital twin of your living room, it that's where it was being used. We've used this software in parks, stores, our yards, and at shopping malls. In each space, it built a new three-dimensional map.

Now this map, which usually is kept hidden from users, is quite special. It is actually a sheet of polygons, those little triangles that are built by computers to simplify a three-dimensional world to a dataset that a small computer can keep track of.

As Matt Miesnieks, co-founder and CEO of 6D.ai, showed us the app we noticed that it was building a virtual copy of the real world—all made from those polygons—and then all sorts of things could be done with that virtual copy. He showed us virtual things moving around that virtual room and new kinds of games where balls bounce off of these virtual walls. Keep in mind, this "copy" of the real world is laid on top of the real world, so the user thinks the balls are bouncing off of their real walls. They aren't; the code for the game is built to work with the AR Cloud, or digital copy, of the house that was just scanned.

Soon technology like that built by 6D.ai will map out almost everything as we walk around, or, at least, use maps that either a mapping car or someone previously walking around built for us. Often these new three-dimensional infrastructures won't be seen by users. After all, that's the case already. Do you really know how Google Maps works under the little blue dot that shows your phone on a street? Very few do.

We will share a bit about how Spatial Computing will work (autonomous cars, robots, and virtual beings will all need these new maps) because there aren't any standards today. Mapbox's data doesn't interoperate with the maps that Apple or Google are building, and we can list dozens of companies that are building three-dimensional maps for various reasons, from Tesla to Amazon, along with a raft of others that aren't well known by consumers, like Here Technologies or OpenStreetMap.

If you think about having a world where hundreds of millions, or even billions, of people are walking around with glasses and other devices that are using these maps, you start to realize something else: current LTE wireless technology, which delivers two to ten Mbps of bandwidth, just won't be able to keep up with the data demands of having to download and upload trillions of these polygons every time someone is moving around the world, not to mention all the other data that users will embed into this AR Cloud.

Ready for 5G

Now you understand why so many of us, like telecom analyst Anshel Sag, are excited by 5G. He explains that 5G is a spectrum of new wireless technologies that, at the low end, will increase our bandwidth more than three times and at the high end, provided by millimeter-wave radio, will give us hundreds of times, maybe even thousands of times, more bandwidth.

Today's 4K videos don't need that kind of bandwidth, but when you have a team of people playing a new kind of virtual football on a field made up of high-resolution AR Cloud data, you can see where 5G will be needed.

5G promises not just a lot more bandwidth, which can support these new use cases, but much lower latency too: it should take around two milliseconds to get a packet from your device to a nearby cell tower. That's way less than current technology. That means your virtual football will be much more in "real time" and the ball won't hang in the air while it is waiting for a computer somewhere else to render it on the way into your hands from your friend, who might be playing from a few miles away, or even somewhere else in the world, thousands of miles away.

There's a third benefit to 5G, too, where many times more devices can use a single cell tower. When we go to baseball games with 40,000 other people, it's typical that we can't even make a call because the wireless systems used just weren't designed for thousands of devices to be used at the same time on one cell tower. 5G fixes that problem, and also means that cities and factory owners, not to mention companies like Fitbit or Tesla, with their millions of users and products in the real world, can have millions of sensors, all communicating with new clouds.

The problem is that there are some downsides to 5G. To get the highest speeds (some journalists are showing that they can get around two gigabits per second, which is faster than a fiber line to your home) you need to be fairly close to a cell tower that has the newer millimeter-wave antennas on it (very few have these radios right now) and this new high-spectrum radio wave doesn't go through walls or other obstacles very well, so even if you live or work near one of these new towers, you will probably need to buy a repeater or mesh network for your home or business to bring that bandwidth indoors. At CES 2020, several manufacturers were showing off mesh networks that supported both 5G as well as the new Wi-Fi 6 standard, which brings a sizeable boost to Wi-Fi networks that get the new gear.

These downsides only apply to the high end of 5G, though. Most smartphone users won't be able to tell the difference anyway. Already on mobile phones, you can stream video just fine with only LTE, and any form of 5G will be just fine on a smartphone. It is when we move to new Spatial Computing glasses that you might notice the difference when you are connected to one of the high-end 5G networks, which provides more than a gigabit in bandwidth. Now, when you see the new iPhone, you'll know that it is really laying the groundwork for true Spatial Computing that will provide us with capabilities that are inaccessible on our mobile phones, such as interactive virtual football.

New Audio Capabilities Arrive

We are seeing an audio revolution unfold on two fronts: new "voice-first" technology that powers systems such as Siri or Amazon's Alexa, and new spatial audio capabilities with greatly improved microphones, processing, speakers, and the integration of these things into contextual systems. We are getting tastes of this revolution in Apple's very popular AirPods Pros, or Bose's new Frames, which have tiny speakers on the frame of eyeglasses that let you listen to new directional audio while also hearing the real world because they aren't headphones, like AirPods, that cover your ear drums.

Audio Augmentation

Apple uses the processing capabilities in AirPods (there's more compute power inside these little $250 devices than was shipped on the iPhone 4) to do a new audio trick: pass through real-world sound in a "transparent" mode. That gives you a hint at the potential augmentation that could be done with new audio devices. Apple and others have patents that go further, using bone transmission from devices touching your face, they promise private communication that only a wearer can hear, along with even better audio quality.

Photo credit: Apple. Apple AirPods Pro earbuds not only do noise canceling but can mix audio from the real world and from digital sources together.

These revolutions in voice and audio are hitting at almost the same time and once we get them built into our Spatial Computing glasses, we'll see a new set of capabilities that business people will want to exploit.

These new capabilities have been brewing for some time—it's just now that computing has shrunk and microphones have gotten inexpensive, thanks to the smartphone and its billions in sales, that we are seeing these new capabilities coming to consumers.

It was back in 2005 that we first saw array microphones on desks inside Microsoft. Back then, putting four high-quality microphones, and the computer to join those together to do new kinds of sensing, into a box cost about $10,000. Today a $150 pair of Pioneer Rayz headphones have six microphones embedded into their earbuds and along the cord that drapes around your neck. Why use these array microphones? The Pioneers have the best noise cancelling we have seen, that's why, and having better, low-noise microphone arrays helps the computer audio response systems that are evolving, like Apple's Siri, work a lot better. After all, if Siri can't hear you, it can't answer you.

Spatial Audio

The processing included inside the headphones can do much more, though. Early headphones had no idea where users were looking. Are they walking north, west, east, or south? The headphones had no idea. With Bose's new Frames, however, that no longer is true. Inside are sensors that tell the system which way the user is walking and the speaker system is designed to present audio from different places. So, if it wants you to go to the pizza place across the street it sounds like the voice is actually coming from that pizza place, which helps you get your bearings and makes new kinds of experiences, like virtual tour guides, possible.

Photo credit: Bose. Bose Frames present spatial audio. These can put audio on specific things in the real world. Imagine walking by a building and it is talking to you.

Think about if a system needed to get your attention—hearing "free coffee over here" means a lot more if that sound comes from your left or right, no?

This leads us to predicting a new audio-based operating system. You might have different audio assistants located in different places around you. Your email assistant's voice might come from two o'clock. Your social network one? Ten o'clock.

These new audio capabilities are also arriving as new Artificial Intelligence and much smarter voice assistants are coming. Apple is rebuilding Siri from scratch, we hear. It isn't alone. Amazon has 10,000 people working on Alexa, trying to make it better than similar systems from Google, Facebook, Samsung, and Apple.

In just a few years, it seems like everything has got Amazon Alexa built in. There are microwave ovens, locks, lights, phones, and much more that now have microphones and can do stuff when you say, "Hey, Alexa."

To those who have experienced Alexa in their homes, this is probably the first taste of ubiquitous computing—computing that's always on, and always waiting for commands. How did this happen?

We see that these "voice-first" capabilities align deeply with Spatial Computing. Already our Tesla car is getting voice upgrades that let us ask it to take us places. Soon consumers will expect the same from all of our computing experiences.

One reason we are excited about Spatial Computing is that it will provide a visual layer to these voice-first systems. A major problem with, say, Amazon Alexa, is that you aren't sure what it actually can do. For instance, did you know that the Internet Archive has the entire Grateful Dead recorded history for you to listen to just by talking to Alexa or its competitor, Google Assistant? It's there, the Internet Archive even wrote an Alexa Skill for it, but figuring that out is nearly impossible unless you already know it's there.

Add in a visual component, though, and voice systems get a lot more powerful. Yes, you could look down at your phone for that visual component, but what if you are skiing and want to talk to Siri? "Hey Siri, what run should I take to get to the lodge?" isn't nearly as nice as if Siri could actually show you which way to turn on your glasses' screen, and asking it "Hey Siri, what can you do with Foursquare?" would lead to a much more satisfying experience if you had some visual displays to see instead of trying to listen to all the commands it could respond to.

Put these all together and soon we'll get a quite different consumer: one that can find out anything nearly instantly just by asking for help and one that will be fed information via their ears in ways that seem impossible today. Where does that matter? Well, gaming is already using spatial audio in VR to make new experiences possible.

Gaming and Social VR Experiences

Ryan Scoble has a girlfriend he has met in VR. They play in Rec Room, the "virtual social club," every afternoon. Bowling, Paintball, and a ton of custom games. He has never met her, and doesn't know where she really lives. He doesn't know her real name (her screen name is LOLBIT) but they play together as if she were a 10-year-old living next door.

He isn't alone in this.

A World Without Rules

VR has brought its magic to gaming and even if you aren't a gamer, it's useful to try a variety of games in VR because of what they can teach you about where the user experience is going. These games are increasingly social and collaborative because VR lets you feel the presence of another person, the same way you would if that person was in front of you in real life.

Photo credit: Robert Scoble. Mark Zuckerberg, Facebook founder and CEO, talks about video game success stories at the Oculus F8 Connect conference in 2019. Here he highlighted the success of games like Beat Saber and then announced a new social gaming platform, Horizon.

This is the lesson that Lucas Rizzotto learned. He's a game developer and has developed several VR experiences including the popular "Where Thoughts Go," which lets you explore a virtual world populated by other people's thoughts. He says there's a generational shift underway between people who play VR games and those who don't. "Kids will talk with their parents," he says, pointing out that lots of weird conversations are soon going to happen due to this shift. "You won't understand, but I was an eggplant," he says a kid might try soon explaining to a real-world family member.

One of the magic things about VR is that you can be embodied in other forms, either animal, human, or vegetable. Anyone who is playing with Snapchat's AR face features, called filters, knows this, but in VR it goes to the next level. Chris Milk, founder of Within, a company that makes augmented and VR experiences and games, showed us how he could make people into a variety of things: birds, apes, or even fish. We watched him demonstrate this in his VR experience, "Life of Us," at Sundance in 2017 where people started flying within half a second of realizing they had wings instead of arms.

The next generation, he says, will grow up in a world where there are no rules. At least not physical ones. Want to jump off that building in VR? Go ahead, there aren't physical consequences like in the real world. Or, if you want to be an eggplant, you can be that too.

The Ripples of the VR Phenomenon

Some other shifts are underway, at least the major part because of gaming on VR:

- **Players expect more than just entertainment**: They want to pay for something they play through and where they come out with new insights about themselves.

- **Content creation will go mainstream**: Digital skills of the future will be artisanal skills. Already we are seeing a raft of new tools develop, everything from Tilt Brush, which lets people draw whatever they want in three-dimensional space, to modeling tools.

- **People will build their own realities and experiences**: We are seeing this trend well underway in Minecraft and other games.

- **Crafting will be done with digital materials that don't necessarily exist in the real world**: The new tools are letting people create anything their minds can come up with, everything from complex art, to entirely new cities. Already Rec Room has more than a million virtual places to play in, most created by the users themselves.

- **Gaming is now 360 degrees and much more interactive**: This is much closer to experiential theater, like the influential "Sleep No More," an off-Broadway play in New York where audience members walk around a huge warehouse and actors are all around, performing their lines. While enjoying the play you can take in the complex theatre set, even picking some things up and discovering what they do more.

- **We will be introduced to new, synthetic characters that are far more lifelike than before**: Magic Leap has already shown a virtual being, Mica. Mica looks like a human, and she plays games with you, among other things, yet she's completely synthetic. Rizzotto says he's already seeing people making digital pets in VR.

- **Collaboration is much better and deeper in VR**: You can already play basketball, paintball, and do a variety of other things together in VR, with more on the way, thanks to Facebook's announcement of "Horizons," a new social VR experience.

It is the collaboration part that's most interesting, though, and has certainly caught Mark Zuckerberg's attention. Rec Room has attracted an audience, and Zuckerberg knows that. Horizon seemed squarely aimed at Rec Room, with very similar kinds of games and social experiences, albeit with a promise of better integration into your existing friend pool.

This leads us to a key point: social software is only really fun if you know the people you are playing with. If you are like Ryan Scoble, you can invest the time in a game and make some friends there, but most of us just want to get in and do something fun quickly. Up until now, there just weren't enough other people on VR to ensure that you had someone else to play with, and almost certainly none of them would be your real-life friend. That's starting to change now as more people get VR.

Building a VR Community

It has been tough-going building a social experience for VR, though. Many studio heads expected VR to sell a lot better than it did. It turns out that this is another chicken-and-egg waiting game: the social aspect really works best if your friends can play with you, but most of your friends don't yet have VR. Lots of early social VR systems either sold for very little money, like AltspaceVR, which had announced it was going out of business and then was purchased by Microsoft at what were rumored to be fire-sale prices. Others have recently struggled to keep their doors open, but have had to shut down or sell off, like Sansar which comes from the company Linden Lab, developers of Second Life. Philip Rosedale was the founder of Linden Lab before leaving that company to start the VR-based company High Fidelity. Rosedale told us it is hard to get the critical mass to make social experiences work if only a few million headsets have sold.

Even Rec Room acknowledged that the lack of VR users is a problem and it now has apps on iOS and Android so that mobile players can join some of the fun. This is a smart strategy because this helps mobile users realize they are second-class citizens and aren't playing in an immersive, hands-on-the-ball kind of way. This brings us to a major benefit of playing in VR—you are forced to move around, which leads to greater fitness. In some games, like The Climb, you have to move your hands like you are climbing in the real world. We've found ourselves sweating after a few rounds in games like that, and in Rec Room, with its basketball, paintball, bowling, and other movement-activating games, you see this too. As we went to press, Chris Milk's company, Within, released "Supernatural" which is an exercise app, complete with volumetricly-captured coaches and a subscription plan that works like a gym.

Fitness uses of VR have even spread to gyms. A Boise, Idaho-based start-up, Black Box VR, has brought a new kind of weight training machine to its gyms. Founder Ryan DeLuca showed us how it works: you put on a VR headset and grab two handles at the ends of cables coming out of the machine. Then you select which exercise you want, and it walks you through that inside the headset. At the start of each round of exercises, it starts up a game. Keep up your exercise and the game gets more fun and intense, and you gather more points. It was so fun that afterward, we realized we were sore, but at the time we didn't feel like we were working out on the machine. It has since opened in other locations, including one in San Francisco.

Denny Unger, CEO and creative director of Cloudhead Games, whose VR game The Gallery won game of the year at VR Awards 2018, says this fitness effect surprised even him. Its latest game, Pistol Whip, has been used by people to get into shape and lose weight, and when Unger and his team started designing it they never thought it would lead to better health as a benefit, he told us. Pistol Whip is a rhythm game, which means you shoot and interact with things to the rhythm of music. This form has proven very popular with VR gamers. Unger even admits to being influenced here by Beat Saber, along with a few other games that you play to music. In Beat Saber, little boxes, and other things like bombs, fly at you to the beat of various music tracks that you choose and you have to slice them with a light saber to keep the game going and the music pumping. Both games are lots of fun and get you a good cardio workout as you get to higher and higher levels.

Great Expectations

Unger says even better games are in the offing. He is very excited by Valve's Half Life: Alyx which came out in March 2020. He says this game is a signal that the top game studios are finally building amazing experiences solely for VR. While the announcement of Half Life: Alyx caused a big controversy amongst gamers, many of whom didn't like being forced to buy a VR headset to enjoy this game, Unger sees that this is a forcing function that will bring many other people into the VR world, which will benefit all the studios.

Unger has a dream, however, of a decade from now, where you are walking around with glasses that do both VR and AR, or a newer form of both mixed together. His dream is that he wants what he calls "replacive environments."

What he means is that in the future you'll be walking around the streets and some bars will be decked out with virtual worlds that replace every surface. "It would be like walking into a bar that is set up like a medieval pub," he said. In such a world he sees a lot of controversy, maybe even regulation, because it would, he says, "radically change the economy of our planet." What he means is that in such a world everything will be virtual, creating less of a need for physical things to make the places we go to more interesting and more of a need for virtual worlds, which will drag with them all sorts of new transaction types. Even ordering a beer in one of these places will be quite different. Your server might be a synthetic being that comes over to take your order and a robot delivery system will bring you your beer. Virtual beings, like the one Magic Leap showed off at the Game Developer's Conference in 2019, named "Mica," have him thinking of new interaction types. "Get down to the primal instinctual experience," he says, while explaining that what he wants to build next is a VR game that feels like you are inside a movie.

The thing is, to get the full experience of what he's thinking about, you might need to head to your local shopping mall where entrepreneurs are opening new LBE experience centers, called LBEs. Here you get access to the best headsets, along with haptic guns that shake your hands when you shoot them, and other devices to bring your VR experience to a whole new level.

Location-based VR

There are places in shopping malls and other big venue areas that let you experience virtual experiences that are impossible to have at home. The idea of LBE VR experiences is not new—there were several exploratory versions created in the 1990s, but they were not successful due to the limitations of the technology available at that time. The latest iteration of LBEs started as the brainchild of Ken Bretschneider, one of the original co-founders of a company called The Void, which was started in 2014.

The Void

Ken's idea behind The Void was to enable several people, initially up to six, to be able to play and be immersed in a VR experience together. The technology needed to be able to do this was formidable and in many cases, proprietary technology needed to be developed, which included creating new batteries for the computers that people would wear as backpacks and were connected to the VR headsets and novel wireless system, among other items.

We have talked with Ken several times over the years since 2017, and he was one of the first people in the Spatial Computing industry to talk about using AI characters in VR LBE experiences, something that is currently still in the formative stages.

Photo credit: The Void. Players getting suited up to play the Star Wars: Secrets of the Empire experience.

The first public experience that was marketed at The Void was a *Ghostbusters*-themed VR experience called *Ghostbusters: Dimension*, which opened at Madame Tussauds in Times Square in New York City in 2016. The VR experience was created as a tie-in to the new *Ghostbusters* film. The cost for the experience was $55 a person. The Void eventually went on to be more controlled by Disney, who had been investing in the company, and several other VR experiences have been developed using Disney IP. There are currently 17 The Void locations in the world, with pricing for experiences ranging from $34.95 to $39.95 per person.

A total of six experiences are playing in different locations. Ken moved on to focus on building his immersive park, Evermore, as well as The Grid, an entertainment destination that includes proprietary VR technology, an immersive indoor karting race track and dining hall. The Grid's first location is in Pleasant Grove, Utah, very close to the location of Evermore, with further locations planned in 2020.

Dreamscape Immersive

Another LBE company featuring VR experiences is Dreamscape Immersive, which was started in 2016 by Kevin Wall, an Emmy-award-winning producer; Walter Parkes, who helped create DreamWorks; and Bruce Vaughn, who was Chief Creative Executive at Walt Disney Imagineering.

Their first location is located at the Westfield Century Mall in Los Angeles, along with another location in Dallas, with new locations opening soon in Dubai and Ohio. Their business model differs from The Void in that they are actively seeking franchise opportunities. The cost for their experiences is $20 per person and they currently offer four different experiences, one of which uses intellectual property from DreamWorks.

Photo credit: Dreamscape Immersive. Dreamscape's Westfield Century City mall location in Los Angeles.

One Dreamscape Immersive experience that we were particularly impressed with was *Curse of the Lost Pearl: A Magic Projector Adventure* due to its high-quality visuals and smart use of interactivity. For example, we were actively pulling a lever and reaching out to hold a "torch" all while in our VR headsets.

We talked with Bruce Vaughn, the CEO of Dreamscape Immersive, recently. He told us that the vision for Dreamscape is for it to produce originals that would spawn their own valuable IP. In his eyes, Dreamscape is an opportunity to build the next kind of entertainment studio—one that produces interactive experiences that most notably celebrate narrative storytelling.

Sandbox VR

Sandbox VR is another LBE company that shows promise. Sandbox raised $68 million in their Series A funding round led by Andreessen Horowitz, including an additional amount in 2019, bringing their reported total to $83 million for that year. The cost per experience per person ranges from $35 to $40. A differentiation point from other LBEs is that there is more interactivity that can be experienced due to motion-capture technology being worn by players.

Photo credit: SandBox VR

Sandbox currently has five experiences playing in two locations, Los Angeles and Cerritos, California. A total of 16 locations is planned by the end of 2020, in new cities including New York, Austin, San Diego, and Chicago.

There are several other smaller LBE companies all over the world, mainly catering to the countries and regions where they are located. A major difficulty of the LBE business model includes the high cost associated with creating a VR experience, which can range from $10 million to highs in the region of $500 million, based on the sophistication of the level of interactivity built into the experience. Another major hurdle is that revenues are very much tied to the throughput of people who purchase the experiences—that is, the shorter the experiences could be, the more people could potentially move through the experiences. Due to this, LBE VR experiences are generally short in nature, ranging from 10 to 15 minutes in length when longer experiences would be better at attracting people. However, longer experiences would have to be priced quite exorbitantly in order for businesses to recoup their costs.

Similar business issues befall the cinematic and interactive VR ecosystem, along with other issues, including opportunities to view and general distribution.

Cinematic and Interactive Experiences

Outside of gaming, social VR, and VR LBEs, there are Spatial Computing experiences currently made mostly for the festival circuit.

Festivals That Include VR

The reason why these experiences are shown this way is that the present state of digital distribution of Spatial Computing entertainment experiences is at a very initial unsophisticated state. We won't be focusing on distribution issues here, as it would take us further away from what the focus of this section is.

Cinematic VR experiences are those that are actually 360-degree experiences—that is, they are not actually VR. However, on the festival circuit, the term Cinematic VR has taken off, so we will briefly address it, as well as addressing those non-gaming experiences that are interactive, hence *are* VR. Additionally, there has recently been a very small and slowly growing body of AR experiences that are narrative in nature, shown at festivals.

Photo credit: SXSW. People at SXSW 2019 enjoying Cinematic VR in Positron Voyager chairs.

Major festivals where Cinematic VR, Interactive VR, and AR experiences are shown include the Sundance Film Festival in Park City, Utah; SXSW in Austin, Texas; the Tribeca Film Festival in New York City; the Cannes Film Festival; the Venice Film Festival; and the Vancouver International Film Festival. The Toronto International Film Festival did show Cinematic VR for a few years but discontinued it after having a change in leadership.

There has been much talk about how Spatial Computing festival experiences have been overly experimental and avant-garde and not made with the public in mind. We tend to agree with this characterization of the state of affairs. One of the major issues that impacts what kind of content gets made is how much money is made available to produce it. From 2015 until 2017, many VR headset companies, including Facebook, Samsung, and HTC, provided content funds to jump-start the industry. However, ever since 2018, much of this money has dried up.

Outside of self-financing narrative content for Spatial Computing environments (VCs and other kinds of investors do not generally have content funds), it is very difficult to have the resources necessary to make these kinds of experiences. As a result, only those that are extremely driven and also have access to funds are able to create them. The kinds of narratives that get developed, as a result, are not necessarily those that could actually be marketed for revenue. This brings us back to the original problem: that there is no real place to market Spatial Computing narrative experiences for profit.

Marketing the Unmarketable

In 2018, Eliza McNitt and her team received about $1.5 million for *Spheres*, a three-part episodic Interactive VR production that won the Grand Prix award in the Venice Film Festival VR section. The deal was struck at the 2018 Sundance Film Festival with a company called CityLights buying it.

Photo credit: Cannes Film Festival. Marketing for Cannes XR 2019. Cinematic VR experiences, over Interactive VR and AR, get the lion's share (over 90 percent) of the spots for showing at Cannes XR, even though the photo shows a person in a VR headset using controllers to interact in an experience.

This is one of very few deals that have happened so far for Spatial Computing narrative experiences. However, even after this, the company that bought *Spheres* did not know how to distribute it, effectively burying it.

Photo credit: Tribeca Film Festival. Marketing for the 2019 Tribeca Virtual Arcade.

Even when it comes to showing Spatial Computing narrative experiences at festivals, there is very little guarantee that ticket-buyers will have the opportunity to actually experience them. Although there were several Interactive VR experiences featured at the 2019 Tribeca Film Festival Virtual Arcade, most people who bought tickets were not able to view them due to the paucity of available viewing slots. This is actually the norm in general versus a special case when it comes to how festivals are featuring Cinematic VR, Interactive VR, and AR narrative experiences.

Every year, there are a few standout experiences. Two experiences that were featured on the 2019 festival circuit include *Gloomy Eyes*, an animated VR experience created by Jorge Tereso and Fernando Maldonado, and *Everest – The VR Film Experience*, a 360-degree documentary directed by Jonathan Griffith. Both of these were featured on the 2019 Vancouver International Film Festival's VIFF Immersed program (*Gloomy Eyes* also being shown at Sundance) and both won an award at VIFF in their respective areas.

Photo credit: Sundance Film Festival. *Gloomy Eyes* was one of the Cinematic VR experiences shown at Sundance 2019 and won an award at VIFF Immersed 2019.

We had the opportunity of interviewing Brian Seth Hurst of StoryTech Immersive and the organizer of VIFF Immersed for the years 2017-2019. The major takeaway from that interview was that most Cinematic VR, Interactive VR, and AR narrative experiences are made with the expectation that only a handful of people will ever get to view them, making the idea of broad appeal a very alien expectation.

Photo credit: Vancouver International Film Festival (VIFF). At VIFF Immersed 2019, the Cinematic VR experience *Everest - The VR Film Experience* won "Best in Documentary."

One Cinematic VR experience that actually approaches broad appeal is Seth Hurst's 2017 piece, *My Brother's Keeper*, which tells the story of two brothers fighting on opposite sides of the American Civil War and was backed by PBS. But, there have been very few in this category as of yet.

Photo credit: PBS. 2017's *My Brother's Keeper* incorporated several novel camera techniques using 360-degree cameras. The directors and directors of photography were Alex Meader and Connor Hair, with Brian Seth Hurst producing.

We have been impressed in general by what the immersive artist and producer Chris Milk, of the company Within, has created for festivals; as of late, his focus has moved from Interactive VR to AR narrative experiences, with one of them being *Wonderscope*, an AR iOS app for kids.

Engineering Experiences

Three studios that have produced some really good Interactive VR experiences are Fable Studio, Baobab Studios, and Penrose Studios. Former Oculus Story Studios people, including Edward Saatchi, founded Fable Studio in 2018. Fable went on to create *Wolves in the Walls*, a three-episode Interactive VR adaptation of the Neil Gaiman and Dave McKean story. In 2019, it was awarded with a Primetime Emmy for outstanding innovation in interactive media. It is one of a number of relatively few VR narrative experiences available for download online from the Oculus store. And it is free, which is the status of almost all the VR narrative experiences available online.

Photo credit: Fable Studio

In 2019, Fable announced that its focus will be on virtual beings using natural language processing and other AI technology. *Whispers in the Night*, which debuted at 2019's Sundance Film Festival, featured Lucy, the same character as in *Wolves in the Walls*. The experience was an Interactive VR animated experience where people who were in the experience could talk directly with Lucy, and together with her, we discover what's truly hiding inside the walls of her house.

Another studio that is pushing boundaries is Baobab Studios, founded in 2015 by Eric Darnell, an acclaimed former DreamWorks director and writer, and Maureen Fan, a former VP of games at Zynga. In 2019, Baobab won two Daytime Emmy awards for its latest Interactive VR animated experience, *Crow: The Legend*. It is also available on the Oculus store, along with an earlier VR animated experience, INVASION!; both are free.

In *Crow: The Legend*, which is based on a Native American folk tale, characters who are animals are made human-like—they can talk to each other and have human emotions. The interaction that the person has who is experiencing *Crow* is limited, but very well done. Using VR controllers, snow can be "sprinkled" into a scene turning it into a winter environment. Flowers, similarly, can be placed, creating a spring scene. As we travel through the virtual space, we can "conduct" a symphony while gliding through an asteroid shower, using VR controllers to elicit different musical sounds and tempos.

We talked with Jonathan Flesher when he was still Baobab's Head of Business Development and Partnerships in 2017. The company stance at that time on the level of interactivity a VR animated experience should have was one based on conservatism. The idea was to pepper the experience with choice possibilities for interaction, but leave most of it as non-interactive. Reasons for this include the high expense of instilling interactivity in an experience, along with the notion that interactivity is very potent. *Crow: The Legend* embodies this stance in a very high-quality way.

Photo credit: Baobab Studios

Another studio that is conservative in its approach to quality with regard to interactivity is Penrose Studios. Penrose was started in 2015 by Eugene Chung, former Head of Film and Media at Facebook. Chung and his team are highly experimental, and have made several VR animated experiences that did not go further than being tests. Penrose's latest VR animated experience, *Arden's Wake: Tide's Fall*, released in 2018, is a continuation of *Arden's Wake*, which won the first Lion for Best VR awarded at the 2017 Venice Film Festival. *Arden's Wake* and *Arden's Wake: Tide's Fall* are not available to download online, but two earlier VR animated experiences both from 2016, *Allumette* and *The Rose and I*, are available on the Oculus store for free.

Photo credit: Penrose Studios

Arden's Wake: Tide's Fall continues the story of Meena, a young woman who lives in a lighthouse in a post-apocalyptic world. Much of what used to be above ground is now underwater. Meena tries to unsuccessfully save her father after he falls into the water.

Even though *Arden's Wake: Tide's Fall* is not interactive, its visuals are stunning. Penrose is currently working on some experimental VR experiences that are interactive in unexpected ways.

The future for both VR and AR narrative experiences is one where more interactivity is used in a much more natural way, with more effects, such as haptics and smell being used artfully. Haptics is any form of communication involving touch, and it is the most difficult of the relevant Spatial Computing technologies to incorporate.

Photo credit: Venice Film Festival. An interactive VR experience that featured smell effects showcased at Venice in 2019.

The current use of smell is minuscule and when it is used, it tends to come off as gimmicky. Another entertainment form where haptics and smell would be useful is with VR LBEs, which makes sense since they would add more realism.

Content Production and Previsualization

Over a decade ago, while working on *Avatar*, the filmmaker James Cameron created a technique where actors wear motion-capture suits while being filmed inside digital backgrounds in real time. Even more recently, in films such as *Ready Player One* and *Solo: A Star Wars Story*, among others, filmmakers have started using VR assets and headsets to plan shots using a virtual world set. Cameron is also using VR for the previsualization of his *Avatar* sequels.

Another filmmaker, Jon Favreau, has been especially enthusiastic about the use of VR for content production and the previsualization of scenes. His most recent film where he utilized VR in this way is 2019's *The Lion King*, and he is actively using his technique, called "V-cam," for episodes of *The Mandalorian*, a Star Wars series for the Disney+ streaming service.

Favreau also used a more nascent version of his technique on 2016's *The Jungle Book*. Additionally, he partnered up with start-up Wevr to make *Gnomes and Goblins*, an interactive VR fantasy world.

The V-cam technology helps with fast turnarounds on schedule and on budget, allowing VFX supervisors to create the look of scenes in real time and providing major benefits to the actors and the crew, effectively, according to Favreau, turning the film's production process into a "multiplayer filmmaking game."

Except for a single photographed shot, *The Lion King* was filmed entirely in VR. In order to work out scenes, Favreau and others would put on their VR headsets to plan exactly where their cameras and lights should go, using handheld controllers to move the virtual equipment to create the scenes using the decided-upon calibrations.

Regarding the use of VR for previsualization, Favreau has also said, "We'll probably have to come up with some sort of new language... It's nice to be able to turn to these new technologies that could otherwise be a threat and use them to reinvent and innovate."

The future of the creation of movies and episodes points to actors in VR headsets doing their scenes inside a virtual setting, captured by virtual cameras controlled by a VR headset-wearing crew.

The Merging of the Virtual and the Real

What we've been showing you is how a new metaverse will appear. An entire set of virtual worlds, or layers, that you can experience with Spatial Computing glasses will soon be here. As you look around with these Spatial Computing glasses, you will see the real world and these virtual layers "mixed" with each other in very imaginative ways, and we just presented the pieces that are currently under development that will make this happen. Often the changes will be small, maybe a virtual sign on top of food, but other times they might be huge, like presenting a complete virtual world you can move around in and interact with. Over the next few years, we'll see an acceleration toward these new virtualized worlds as the devices that we wear get far more capable and lighter and new experiences are created for them.

For our next chapter, we will delve into the benefits that Spatial Computing brings to manufacturing. The use cases there have a much more practical nature than what we discussed in this chapter, though Spatial Computing's abilities will similarly change how we work.

5

Vision Three – Augmented Manufacturing

We have had the privilege of visiting Tesla's factory a couple of times. Over the space of just one year, we have observed some radical changes. There are more robots, sensors, and screens, as well as closer working spaces with hundreds, if not thousands, of workers siting around the factory looking at computers running things.

If you are paying attention online, you will see the hype about the changes: "Industrial Revolution 4.0" the headlines scream. The last two decades have seen much digitizing on the factory floor. That change isn't done yet; we still see lots of non-digital processes in many factories that have yet to change from paper and pen to computers.

That said, some major new trends have shown up and we haven't yet seen a world where a lot of workers are wearing Augmented or Virtual Reality devices on their faces. Those will come over the next few years, and we talked with manufacturing innovators about where things are going and what changes they are planning on.

The changes coming are extreme. A new kind of manufacturing is coming: one where humans are still involved, with new virtual interfaces to machines and new AI assisting in the work.

Robots and Other Augmentation

The factory at Tesla, for instance, already has 1,200 robots, and that's up from last year. And we can surmise that by the time you are reading this book, they may have hit 2,000 robots. Tesla isn't alone. Many companies are seeing more robots in their manufacturing lines.

The kinds of robots are changing too. It used to be that robots were things kept in cages. These robots were too dangerous for humans to get close to. They moved very heavy parts quickly. When we visited Ford's Rouge Factory, which builds a new F-150 truck every minute, we saw such a robot installing windshields into new trucks.

While many robots continue to work away from humans, a new kind of robot is showing up—"cobots." These new robots work right next to humans, and even with humans aiding them in tasks. Controlling these new cobots is difficult, though. After all, it's easy to tell another human "hey, can you help me hold this plate while I screw it down," but it's pretty hard to do that with a robot, especially if you have to touch a tablet or a mouse hooked up to a PC sitting on the workstation you are at. Soon, those who work in factories tell us, you'll be using Augmented Reality glasses with microphones and 3D sensors and software that can see what you are working on, who with, where your hands are, and where your eyes are looking, and then the "cobot" revolution will emerge in a big way on factory floors.

Photo credit: Steve Jurvetson. Tesla factory filled with robots building the Model 3.

As we talked with factory workers across different factories, we heard of a clash between using old and new technologies and systems. We define "old" as not using cameras or 3D image sensors to watch you work, worrying about the impact of privacy on workers, and not wearing Augmented Reality headsets or glasses to assist you in working. Also, "old" is not having robots integrated into your manufacturing lines working with humans, not using additive manufacturing, or 3D printing, to make parts, and not being able to radically change a factory floor within days (Tesla set up an entire line in a tent, for instance, within a few weeks to make a version of its Model 3 car).

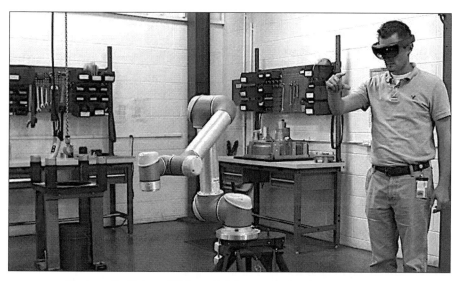

Photo credit: Universal Robots. HoloLens and cobot interaction testing.

Obviously, talking about the status quo in such a way opens a very controversial set of subjects: from the protection of jobs to privacy at work. Different companies and different cultures will come at these things with different sets of constraints. We have already found differences in how factory workers look at cameras on factory floors, for instance. Those in Germany are far more conservative than those in China. The same goes for workstations or glasses that "watch" worker performance. At Jabil in Silicon Valley, a company that makes many of the manufacturing workstations around the world, we saw Augmented Reality workstations that told people how to build items but that also watch and grade the worker at the same time.

Dennis Morrow, UX Design Manager at Radius Innovation, a subsidiary of Jabil, told us they are moving those augmented displays into headsets so that the worker is augmented all the time, not just while sitting at a workstation. Such a set of displays on a worker's face could even direct them to the shortest line in the cafeteria. When we visited factories in China, which often have tens of thousands—if not hundreds of thousands—of workers, simply moving people around more efficiently can create sizeable productivity gains.

When talking to innovators in factories around the world we keep hearing about "Industrial Revolution 4.0." When the World Economic Forum laid out the definition, it said "[the Fourth Industrial Revolution] is characterized by a fusion of technologies that is blurring the lines between the physical, digital, and biological spheres" and "the speed of current breakthroughs has no historical precedent."

Artificial Intelligence (AI), Robotics, the Internet of Things (IoT), Autonomous Vehicles, 3D Printing, Nanotechnology, Biotechnology, Materials Science, Energy Storage, Quantum Computing, and Augmented and Virtual Reality are all exponentially evolving and are bringing the perfect storm of changes to literally every part of human life. But how we design and make things may see the biggest changes, and, certainly, have deep implications for employment and what jobs look like.

A future car company might ship a potential customer a pair of Augmented Reality glasses before the car is even introduced. Those glasses may let you see the experience of owning one, let you order one, and let you watch it being built in real time. Think that's impossible? Well, we are seeing a world by 2030 where Augmented Reality glasses will be fairly low cost, subsidized by advertising. We are reminded that Tesla doesn't spend much on advertising and we talked with hundreds of people standing in line overnight to buy a Model 3 without having seen the car yet.

Tesla, in a way, provides great insight into how quickly work is changing. We visited its factory in Fremont, California, several times between 2018 and 2020, and each time we visited we noticed more robots, more sensors, more computers, and a higher density of workers working with robots.

Photo credit: BMW. Using a HoloLens to put together a BMW car engine.

In talking to innovators who are designing new factories like the ones Tesla runs, we found that they are planning to introduce new technologies at a rapid rate.

Volkswagen, for instance, has a complete virtual copy of its factory floor. It isn't alone; we heard this from many manufacturers we interviewed, from Coca Cola to Audi. This "digital twin" lets workers redesign factory workstations, get trained on new jobs, and soon even control machines and processes on the factory floor from anywhere—not to mention get remote assistance from vendors and other employees. The digital twin can be walked around using Virtual or Augmented Reality headsets and is being made smarter every day.

We heard of many who are letting workers make digital documents, videos, audio recordings, and 3D objects accessible via their digital twins so that future workers would get the benefit of past learning. At many factories, managers are worried about a new "silver tsunami." That is, older workers who are retiring in droves, leaving the factory floor with dozens of years of knowledge about how things are run. New workers are currently learning from those workers digitally while navigating to their workstation. The digital twin can be overlaid on top of the real factory floor and can be used as the basis for adding all sorts of new capabilities both to factories and to workers wearing new Spatial Computing devices.

Photo credit: Volkswagen. Digital twinning – Florian Uhde (left) and Christopher Krey (right) from the Virtual Engineering Lab of Volkswagen Group IT look at the chassis construction of the current Golf using HoloLens headsets.

Just one of these new capabilities, remote assistance, doesn't sound that significant, but when you consider Boeing's factory in Everett, Washington, where they build 747, 777, and 787 airplanes, it takes nearly 30 minutes to walk from one end of the factory to the other. The building is so large it has its own weather pattern inside. If technology can save a worker a trip, you're saving the company money and making the worker happier.

That same factory has workers wearing devices that "augment" their work, showing them where one of the thousands of wires in an average airplane should be plugged into thanks to a camera on the front of the device that sees a barcode on each wire and on each piece of equipment that needs that wire to be connected to. Think through the trends hitting consumer expectations. Things will be done with higher quality, fewer materials, lower cost, and more choices—all faster.

All of those expectations are forcing factory owners to constantly add new technologies to make things cheaper, better, faster, and with more transparency. Political concerns and human rights are driving many of these. Want to make sure children aren't making your shoes? We can see future shoes coming with a video of every step of their manufacture to prove that. Why will that be possible, if not probable, in the 2020s? When we toured Tesla's factory, we met some LG employees who make cameras, and they said that cameras are getting cheaper and with a higher resolution because of the billions of dollars being spent in R&D by the smartphone industry. We are seeing this dramatic decrease in the price of technology hitting nearly every product, from June Ovens that have cameras inside, to Monopoly board games that now have voice commands thanks to a little computer that ships with its latest game.

Photo Credit: Boeing. Using HoloLens to view a wiring application displaying digital engineering drawings inside a Boeing airplane.

Where robots inside factories used to be big, expensive machines that were kept separate from humans in cages, robots now are integrated across the factory floor and are delivering parts to workstations in such a way that they navigate around humans walking the corridors. Spatial Computing technologies are making those robots "see" and are giving them much better navigation skills, just like the same technologies being used in autonomous vehicles on the road.

To ensure really deep integration between human workers and robots, though, requires new Augmented Reality glasses that haven't shipped yet. These glasses will allow a worker to, say, install an air conditioning pump in a new car while talking to and controlling a robot that's holding that pump. Today's computers that need to be touched, or wheeled over to, just aren't up to the job.

The iPhone coming later this year has a sensor that can "see" 300,000 points of data. That gives us a hint as to what's coming to the manufacturing floor. Those sensors won't be limited to just iPhones. Microsoft, with its Azure Kinect sensor/camera, can already be used to do new things on factory floors, from watching product quality to building new systems for robots to do new work. We are told by many innovators that Computer Vision will be used across the factory floor and will provide data to know where everyone and every part is in real time.

Already these techniques are being used while building planes at Boeing, but the cost of the systems means, as of 2019, they are only used in very complex situations. We expect that as costs come down, thanks in great part to including them in mobile phones, we'll see them used in much more routine work where the return on investment isn't nearly as high as figuring out which of the 20,000 wires needs to be plugged into a certain outlet inside a Boeing plane.

We've laid out the context somewhat. Manufacturing is becoming more hypervigilant. Hypervigilance means that fewer mistakes will be made and work will become more efficient because the technologies used are more detail-oriented, digital, and data-based. Jabil's Dennis Morrow told us of a new kind of screwdriver that is used to put in screws so small that the worker (and the robots who will also use it) needs to work under a microscope. We visited a watch factory in Switzerland where $100,000 watches are hand-built using similarly small screwdrivers and devices that magnify the work. "Today a user has to look on a 2D screen to see that screw," he says, while pointing out that they are building an Augmented Reality system that lets users zoom in without looking away from the work. It goes further than just magnification, though. It shows the right process, which screws to put in and in which order, then checks the work while it's being done, warning you if the work is being done wrong. "How can we empower them to have these kinds of superpowers at their fingertips?"

This new system, driven by data and AI, with visuals in Augmented Reality devices on workers' faces means a huge improvement in quality, Morrow says. It also means that QA people down the line have fewer things to reject and fix.

Yes, there will be job shifts, many factory managers told us, but they see a new opportunity for workers to be rapidly trained for newer, more interesting, jobs due to this hypervigilant manufacturing capability. Some of the major new Spatial Computing tools that will enable workers and factories to become more productive and efficient will now be discussed further.

Augmented Reality Visions and Informed Robots

Within a decade, working in a factory will probably be very different than it is today. Many, if not most, workers will probably be wearing Augmented Reality glasses. They will be working with a lot more robots and will be guided by a connected system that will track everything, including machines, humans, robots, and parts flowing into the factory. Additionally, production itself might be quite different thanks to additive manufacturing (3D printing).

Let's go back to the new devices being worn on the face by many workers. We call them Spatial Computing visors, but others call them Augmented Reality or Mixed Reality glasses or visors or HMDs (Head Mounted Displays). These new displays let you see computing in 3D and all around you. They also include microphones, 3D sensors for your hands, for your eyes, and for the world around the worker, along with sensors inside the devices that track up and down, left and right movement and other things, from a potential heartbeat to the brightness of the room.

On little displays, workers see 3D and 2D images overlaid on top of the real world, or, as optics get better, replacing pieces of the real world. Bruce Dickenson, Vice President and General Manager of Boeing's 767/747 program, commented about Boeing's use of Augmented Reality in their factories: "The cross-functional team working on this technology has made a step-change breakthrough in our quality and productivity by following their passion to pursue a great idea. We don't often see 40 percent improvements in productivity, and I'm convinced that it was a culture of innovation and leaders who are willing to say 'yes' that enabled this idea to come to life."

While today's Spatial Computing devices are big and have low-resolution monitors (which is why you don't see many workers using them for coding or writing reports, for instance), in a decade they will be small and have a much larger field of view, with sensors that will see 100x more points of data than they do today, and with GPUs that are much more powerful.

They will also be connected with wireless systems that'll be 10x or more faster than what we can get today. These glasses will also have eye sensors, which haven't really shipped in devices as of 2019, and will have voice recognition systems that make the Siris and Alexas of 2019 seem pretty stupid indeed, along with hyper-sharp optics that will replace all sorts of physical screens.

"Applying Computer Vision and Augmented Reality tools to the manufacturing process can significantly increase the speed and efficiency related to manufacturing and in particular to the manufacturing of automobile parts and vehicles," Tesla's application for a patent for a future Augmented Reality device reads.

Elon Musk, Tesla's CEO, noted in an interview with Marques Brownlee, technology journalist/YouTube star, that many jobs are still not appropriate for robots because they are too complex or still have too much variability. He pointed to a harness of wires being strung along the roof and sides of the car. "If a robot faults out you have to have a 24/7 technician," he said, while pointing out that such a robot failure had him woken up at 2 a.m.

However, much work is being done by robots, but they need to be programmed and dealt with as a machine, and not in a very human way. In a decade, robots will be responsive, much more like a human, thanks to much better voice commands, but the worker will be able to interact with the machines around them in a much better way because the glasses that worker is wearing will let the worker point, grab, and control the robot virtually and probably even remotely.

Giovanni Caturano, CEO of SpinVector, spins it around (he builds AR and VR software for factories). He thinks the robots will train us humans on what they need through these glasses. He sees that AI can learn new things faster than we can, which is why AIs are beating us at Go and other games, but lack lots of other skills, or are unable to physically reach and grab something. So, the AI needs to ask us for help, he says, and that's the kind of system he's already working on.

Think about moving a heavy box with a friend. There's a lot of visual information you both are sharing. Is one side of the box going lower? Is your friend's face straining? Don't you watch for gestures? Listen to voice commands? Yes. Today's factory robots have the beginnings of such human interaction styles, but they will pale in reaction to tomorrow's robots and factory automation types. Caturano explained that robots can watch humans far better than humans can watch robots. Additionally, they won't get distracted, they won't get scared and drop an expensive part, they can see in all directions, and they are better at seeing very small changes in temperature, angles, distances, or pressure than humans are.

To really understand the changes, we talked with Rebecca Johnson and Bettina Maisch of Siemens. Johnson is head of the research group and builds UX prototypes and platforms there and is the CT senior key expert for ambient intelligence.

Maisch was, until very recently, the Portfolio Project Manager for Industrial Design Thinking. Together they paint a wild picture of factories of the future.

Maisch notes that such tools will become "exponential learners" in that they will be hooked up to a cloud system that will watch everything about their use, and any learning will be pushed back out to not only the humans but to the networked robots "learning" while using those tools. The whole factory system will become more reliant on data and AI systems that will make that data useful.

Siemens' Maisch and Johnson surmised that some jobs of the future, both for AIs as well as humans, will be dealing with what goes wrong. Humans are pretty good about keeping things moving, even when all else goes wrong. One worker who left Tesla wrote about duct taping a part together to keep the line running. Not exactly good for quality scores, for sure, but if your line is building a new $60,000 car every 60 seconds would you stop the line for a part that could be fixed later? Maisch says one of the attributes humans have is working around rules and figuring out how to keep things moving, where robots might just get stuck.

Some of the factory thinkers we talked to even expect that many factory workers will be able to work, at least some of the time, from home, controlling robots from their living rooms—maybe on call just to fix those weird problems that crop up in factories from time to time; whether it's a belt on a machine breaking, or some traffic accident holding up deliveries of parts on the freeways outside of the factory. But that's a bit too sci-fi even for us. We just see that factory floors are about to radically change thanks to a raft of new technologies, and that these technologies will make it a lot easier to retrain robots to do new things and make it a lot easier to work next to, and with, robots.

One problem with trying to predict exactly what will happen in factories as more robots and Spatial Computing technology shows up is that not every factory will get them at the same rate. We learned that in several interviews. Some factories will cling to the old ways of doing things for years, while some, particularly in, say, the automotive industry, will advance much more quickly. Audi, for instance, already uses Augmented Reality devices on its factory floors to assist workers with a variety of things. Ashim Guha, Vice President of Consulting and Enterprise Solutions at Tech Mahindra, told us that Augmented Reality is already being used quite a bit in Germany and China on such lines, while admitting that other factories he visits are using the same techniques they've used for decades.

On the other side of the spectrum of factories are ones that will be completely automated with no humans in them. Already, there are "lights out" factories, particularly in warehousing and picking. "Lights out" means there is no need to keep the lights on for human beings.

Fuji Automatic Numerical Control (FANUC), one of the largest makers of industrial robots in the world, has been operating a "lights-out" factory since 2001, where robots build other robots completely unsupervised for nearly a month at a time.

The focus of this section is in the middle of the spectrum: where humans will need to continue to work alongside robots, but where there is enough force to get workers to wear Augmented Reality devices. Already that's happening at Audi, Boeing, and other factories—usually where there is a complex enough job, like keeping track of tens of thousands of wires inside a plane and where they need to go or be plugged in. A human can do that job better than a robot, at least so far, but the human wears a device like Google Glass that shows a barcode on each wire and displays where that wire needs to go.

In the past few years, though, a new kind of work has arrived thanks to the cobots that we already discussed. These cobots, we'll see, will get more intimate with humans as we get better spatial tools on our eyes to be able to communicate with them, and program them.

It's hard to understand how deeply this new worker will be "augmented," because, well, when we visited factories in 2018 and 2019, whether Boeing, Ford, Tesla, or even Louisville Slugger, we saw very few workers wearing computers on their faces and most robots were still things kept in cages because they were too dangerous for humans to be next to. One set of memorable robots at Tesla, that lives in such a cage, lifts an entire Model 3 in the air, spins it around, and places it on a new track. This is something that, if a human were in the way, would be quite dangerous indeed.

This new way of 3D working goes beyond design and to the work itself. At Siemens, Maisch told us her team built an app that lets a worker wearing a Microsoft HoloLens work underneath a train engine and it warns that worker if they try to plug something into the wrong socket. Even before that, Augmented Reality is changing how things are done. If you buy tools for the factory floor, or robots, you now can pick them out of a virtual catalog and see how they would work alongside the other robots or tools you have already purchased for your manufacturing line.

The complexity of thousands of robots and humans working together in a modern factory is something that will need new user interfaces and new approaches too. BadVR's founder, Suzanne Borders, showed us a virtual factory floor where you could watch it run from anywhere in the world and see all sorts of data streaming off of the machines.

In the old days, a part might travel around a floor with a simple paper trail kept on a board. Modern factories are moving toward a computing system, one might say an "air traffic control" system, keeping track of literally everything on the floor, and even keeping track of those things outside of the factory, such as incoming component shipments.

Maisch and Johnson say having new kinds of wearable devices will help workers not just see where the load of parts they need to build something are, but could also build a new kind of interface with the robots and the factory floor.

Several factory workers we talked with say that the need to bring new tools, particularly Augmented Reality devices, is coming from two trends: first, younger workers are staying away from factories that don't use them. Second, older workers are retiring and leaving factories with decades of knowledge about how they work. So, many factories are bringing this technology onto the shop floor to record older workers, getting them to leave their knowledge directly on the shop floor through videos, drawings, and 3D captures of what they actually do. Then the factory managers appeal to younger workers by showing them how useful the new tools are and how exciting working in such a "smart" factory is.

Photo credit: Microsoft. ZF Group, a German car-parts manufacturer, is using Microsoft Layout (https://aka.ms/Esw053) to help them lay out equipment on its factory floor.

As a part of a "smart" factory, wearables could bring some great benefits. By putting sensors, computers, and displays on workers (or similar tech into robots), and by giving them hands-free interaction, in terms of its benefits "it's very convincing," according to Caturano. The bigger payoff, though, he says, is the lack of disruption and the ability to do quicker upgrades: "The client (a big soft drink company) liked this approach because they didn't need to shut down the factory for days to wire up lots of sensors." Also, workers can charge up batteries every night, while if sensors were built onto factory floors, new electrical wiring might need to be run, or those sensors would need to run for a year without having batteries changed, he says.

Sensors are upgrading at a very fast rate, too; the 2019 iPhones only had sensors that could "see" 30,000 points of data, while the ones that are being announced in 2020 will be able to see 10x more, or 300,000 points.

Morrow says that the real advantage to all of this, though, is that factories will get rid of 2D screens, and move to a system that makes both a human and robot smarter at the same time.

What really makes a robot "smart" is the combination of Computer Vision and AI in the form of Machine Learning software. Computer Vision has to do with systems that enable a computer to "understand" digital images, videos, and live-streaming visuals. Part of that understanding has to do with matching and recognizing shapes, colors, and textures. Machine Learning software enables Computer Vision systems to do that. Before a system can do recognition matching, it has to be trained on many thousands of image datasets. Supervised, unsupervised, and reinforcement Machine Learning, as described earlier in this book, as well as other forms of learning, could all play a part in making a robot "smart." The predominant kinds of features/areas surmised through Machine Learning include object classification, object identification, object verification, object detection, object landmark detection, object segmentation, and object recognition. Frank Loydl, CIO at Audi AG, emphasized: "Artificial Intelligence and Machine Learning are key technologies for the future at Audi. With their help, we will continue to sustainably drive the digital transformation of the company."

As expertly explained by Everette Phillips, Director, North America, of Lyric Robot, one of the major issues, though, when it comes to creating a "smart" robot is that the software that includes both the regular instructional and Machine Learning parts almost always has to be tailor-made, specifically taking into account the robot and the situational environment the robot is in. Some robots come with ready-made software, but then have to be majorly modified, while others do not. In both of these cases, in-house engineers and/or outside consultants have to be utilized to modify and extend existing software or completely build custom versions. An improvement from the past that could be helpful in dealing with this issue is that general manufacturing processes overall have become more flexible so that a robot system might also be partially accommodated by a change in process and even a change in factory floor layout. Beforehand, both the change in process and factory floor layout could be virtually tested by using Augmented Reality software. The case for the use of Spatial Computing in manufacturing has never been clearer.

According to Deloitte, by 2028, as many as 2.4 million manufacturing jobs may go unfilled, causing $454 billion in production to be at risk. The main reasons for this are potential workers lacking in relevant skills and the retirement of current workers. Spatial Computing could be used to re-skill current workers and then place them in jobs where they work alongside robots.

Arnold Kravitz, Chief Technology Officer at Advanced Robotics for Manufacturing (ARM), told us that there are novel tests that are being developed for the joint use of cobots and workers using Augmented Reality glasses that measure and determine how the two could most efficiently "learn" from each other and, once those configurations are discovered, processes could then be updated to take these into account. Similarly, the concept of a virtual digital twin, mentioned previously in this chapter, could be instituted to figure out the best product and manufacturing design and also to find out what the culprits are when a process or system fails.

The Mirror World Comes to Factory Floors

What really is going on is that there's a new boss of the factory. It used to be that there might be someone like Henry Ford walking around, watching everyone working, prodding and pushing the workforce, keeping track of parts that hadn't shown up yet, and so on, but those days are long gone.

The boss of the factory is being replaced by data and AI, along with Augmented Reality glasses or visors. These cloud computing systems keep track of every little thing in their surroundings. This will likely include even facial recognition to ensure that only the correct workers get access to the factory floor, and the position of the wearable device, down to fractions of a millimeter, along with everything that said wearable device's 3D sensor is shining on.

This new boss is displayed in these Spatial Computing devices as a "digital twin." On one level, the digital twin is just a virtual copy of the factory floor. Every display, lever, switch, motor, and part is there. This makes it really easy to train new workers. You just take them into the digital twin, and they learn how to do their jobs on the virtual copy of the factory floor.

Photo credit: General Electric. General Electric is developing digital twins of major portions of its factories and products built to actively aid in machine planning, implementation, and error recognition.

If that's how you look at a digital twin, you'll miss something deeper that's going on: these virtual copies of factories are actually new kinds of databases and virtual interfaces, where both physical IoT devices can be hooked into, but also other data can be laid onto the virtual floor.

This virtual floor, or rather, digital twin, can then be laid on top of the real factory floor. This new "Mirror World" brings radically new capabilities that simply can't be replicated using older techniques.

For instance, Nucleus VR founder Alexander Bolton showed us how workers can leave training materials, and even instruction manuals and videos, for workers right on top of the real factory machinery. New workers coming into work wearing a Microsoft HoloLens, or another similar device, could "see" the digital instruction manual that got an update since the last shift. They could also see and watch a video left there by the crew that just left, explaining a problem they had with the machinery and how they fixed it.

Also, on top of the digital twin, they could see all sorts of information about the machinery itself. How hot are its engines? How many products a minute are being built? Which machines are running low on supplies? Which ones will need to be taken offline in the next few hours for some maintenance?

Remote workers are even seen moving around the digital twin, and others can be called in with just a command (think about "Hey Siri" or "OK Google" and how that impels a system that is listening for those commands to listen for other commands).

This new digital twin doesn't just affect the operation of the floor, though. It can save millions of dollars when designing the factory floor. Giovanni Caturano, of SpinVector, told us that they now start building the digital twin first. In fact, the digital twin can be designed through AI in a process called "generative design." Autodesk walked us through this and so did Siemens. A computer will give hundreds, or even thousands, of possible configurations and a human will pick the best one, or refactor and try again. This "generative design" process is already being used by architects. This process would be best done in Augmented Reality glasses where a factory designer could walk through a virtual factory and see iteration after iteration of factory designs and pick the best ideas that AI comes up with. One example of how this can impact a company is discussed below.

Caturano explained how one problem came up in a factory before they got these new 3D tools to design the factory floor. He told us they thought they had designed it all well, but there was a pesky post in the middle of one factory. Yes, the product and the carriages they were being moved around in (think of robot trolleys that can move around, say, soft drinks in pallets) could technically fit, which is why the design got through approvals. But, every once in a while, one of these carriages, when turning, would hit the post, damaging thousands of dollars of product and making a mess. It turned out that moving that post would cost a lot of money. This problem, Caturano says, won't happen again now that they are designing factory floors on a Microsoft HoloLens where they have a 3D "digital twin" to test everything on before they build the factory floor.

Siemens' Maisch, mentioned earlier, told us that her team designed an app for a mining operation. It turned out that workers usually took one path through the mine, but once in a while molten steel would flow over the path.

Sensors in the machinery would pick up that the path would be unsafe to navigate, and worker's headsets and mobile apps would navigate around the danger.

This "Mirror World," has many new superpowers. For instance, on a real factory line, you might need to build 100,000 parts before you'll see your first defect. Caturano says that on a digital twin you can force virtual defects down the line, which can be used to train all the AIs to look for these defects and become far better at spotting them than any human could, even with years of experience. The AI could have dealt with hundreds of forced, simulated defects, while even the most experienced of workers may have only encountered a handful of such problems. The digital twin will soon have extraordinary smarts hooked into each polygon of data that's overlaid on top of the real factory floor.

Everette Phillips, Director, North America, Lyric Robot, says: "What you are seeing is an evolution of a change in approach where AI is leaking into industrial systems." He says: "What has been improving is the cost of computational power. That allows more sophisticated code to be run without bringing in more sophisticated programmers."

Photo credit: Robert Scoble. Apple's new headquarters Augmented Reality app shows a "digital twin" on top of a real physical model.

To get a taste of what a digital twin can do, you should visit Apple's new headquarters in Cupertino. There, it has built an Augmented Reality application, that includes a digital twin. On top of a physical model, this digital twin shows you how the headquarters works and looks. You can touch the digital twin to get it to show you various new virtual views.

As you walk around the model with an iPad, you can see how the solar system works, and you can remove the roof and walk around the interior of the building. You can even see a simulation of how wind flows over the building.

This is all while dozens of other people walk around you with their own view of the same thing.

It shows the magic that can come from placing a virtual layer on top of a real-life plant. You can see data flows of humans and equipment in new ways. You could simulate what the plant would look like with a new lighting system installed. You could simulate the impacts on getting workers from parking lots if you built a new shuttle system. That and much more, and, of course, if you have this kind of work done, you automatically get much better training systems and are way ahead in terms of enabling new ways of working.

As factories are increasingly virtualized, they could fundamentally change a lot about what we think of as "work." Imagine having your morning coffee and signing into your factory floor and watching your robots in your area doing their work. Imagine saying "Hi," virtually, to your coworker Joe. Then checking up on all your inventories and data streaming from the machines working…even making an adjustment or two to speed or temperature, or checking in a new protocol for one of your robots.

As you walk around the virtual factory floor, you will see updated information, and even a new menu for the cafeteria—all virtually. And you can help Joe virtually figure out a problem he's having with one of his robots—all while having morning coffee.

The digital twin will enable all this, plus new virtual interfaces for machines (and other humans) that are pretty hard to comprehend today, but Apple's Augmented Reality demo at its headquarters gives us a little taste of just how much will change in the next decade thanks to digital twins.

The Human Robot

Imagine being able to safely work alongside robots on the factory floor and being able to communicate with them on a human level. Eventually (maybe sooner rather than later), we have been told, robots on the manufacturing floor and elsewhere will be able to display human characteristics. Siemens' Maisch and Johnson talked very eloquently about how robots could be visibly humanized for the benefit of humans and how Siemens is running tests along the following lines.

Robots will be able to use "facial" expressions that show whether or not what they are doing is going well or if there is a problem, as well as using language that is colloquial. An answer to the question of whether or not everything is going well could be: "Not really…" They could also answer in a depressed tone if there is a problem. This would greatly help in assessing if there is an issue more directly than checking robot diagnostics.

Another kind of humanness that could be integrated into robot systems is the ability to create products that very closely mimic human randomness. Currently, it is very easy to tell the difference between a piece of clothing that has been knit by human hands and one that has been made by factory automation. It is also very easy to tell the difference between a piece of furniture that has been fashioned by a master woodworker and one that has been crafted by a factory. In the future, by using AI algorithms, robots will be able to very successfully mimic human randomness in the making of products, making them appear to have been made by human hands.

This is just the start of making a robot display human-like external and internal characteristics. The question of how far this could go is not the focus of this book, but the forward motion in this direction shows the promise of how far the elements of Spatial Computing could be taken for the benefit of humans.

The arc of where manufacturing is going is clear. Where robots could clearly do a better job than human beings, they will replace them. Where productivity is higher when robots and human beings cooperate together, they will be kept as a unit. Computer Vision and AI will continue to be used by both humans and robots in greater frequency and for wider uses. Augmented Reality could be used as the bridge between the human and the robot; however, we do see a day when the robot will be much more human and vice versa.

This chapter has dealt with how manufacturing is in the process of using augmentation in the form of robots, Augmented Reality, and AI to improve productivity and efficiency. Our next chapter tackles how the retail industry does the same with regard to logistics and presentation to consumers.

6

Vision Four – Robot Consumers

Retail still defines the face of America and indeed the whole world, and you can still see this yourself if you visit small towns or big city malls, whether in Chicago or Dubai. Soon, though, that face will radically change as tons of new technology is brought to all parts of the retail world, from robots to Spatial Computing glasses that consumers will use to shop in new ways. Here, we look at both the past and future for lessons about how deeply our culture and businesses are about to change due to Spatial Computing.

What Drives Consumers?

People buy emotionally, not rationally. That is what we learned while working at consumer electronics stores in the 1980s. What do we mean by that? Let's say you are a grandfather who is tasked to buy some headphones for his granddaughter for, say, a Christmas gift. He goes into a store, say, a Best Buy, and is overwhelmed with choices. He can't hear well, so he can't tell the difference between, for example, a Sennheiser or a Sony. The salesperson isn't much better at figuring out what will put a smile on the granddaughter's face when she opens her gift, either.

He remembers that he saw Beats on American Idol and that Apple had bought them, so he walks out of the store with one of those. Why? Because he knows that on Christmas morning that if she doesn't like the Beats, he can defend the purchase by saying, "Hey, if they are good enough for American Idol, they are good enough for me" and that, as Apple's premier brand, he feels good about that, too.

Now, those of you who understand headphones will know that Beats are hardly the best-sounding headphones out there. A rational person would do research on audio profiles and buy coldly based on which headphones sounded best for a particular budget, but that's not how most of us buy, which explains why Beats continues to outsell other brands.

As we talk to retailers, we see that they understand this, and are looking to more deeply figure out how to engage your emotions when you shop, which explains a whole raft of changes underway in retail thanks to Spatial Computing technologies. How do they change retail?

Getting Emotional

Well, these technologies are changing the consumer electronics that people want, which you can see by visiting the Consumer Electronics Show (CES) in January in Las Vegas, with its huge booths for devices that use Spatial Computing—from Virtual Reality to drones to autonomous cars to devices in your home that track you and products. These technologies are changing everything about the retail supply chain, store, and e-commerce experiences themselves. For the grandfather, though, buying a set of headphones will mean that not only will the headphones be different (already, Bose has augmented headphones that use new Spatial Computing sensors inside that know which way a wearer's head is aimed), but the way he buys them will be, and how they get made and delivered to him will be, too.

Augmented Reality is changing the media he sees. Soon, he will be able to watch American Idol on Spatial Computing glasses and walk around the singers and coaches. Even on current TV shows, we are seeing Spatial Computing technology used in shows such as "So You Think You Can Dance." Now, a few dozen cameras surround dancers so that producers can spin the view all the way around the dancers. Soon, that effect will seem as quaint as black-and-white TV. He'll be able to touch products he sees, and ask questions like, "Who made these?" or "Alexa, can you put these on my shopping list?" or "Alexa, what's the price on these?" or "Alexa, can you deliver these to my car?"

Speaking of cars, someday in the next decade, he might even ask his car to go pick them up, all thanks to Spatial Computing technologies. That is a bit further out, though, from getting the glasses, which will arrive by the mid-2020s. We cover more of those scenarios in *Chapter 3, Vision One – Transportation Automates*, our chapter on the transportation industry vertical.

Now in 3D

Already you can get tastes of how the buying experience is changing by using AR apps on your mobile phone. Before the late 2010s, you would have to go to a store to see how, say, a new couch would fit into your home. Now, you pull up an app and you can see a three-dimensional version right on top of your real home and see how it fits. You can even now use many apps to measure your room accurately to see whether that new couch would fit. Lots of apps from stores such as IKEA or Amazon already have these features as we write this book, with many more on the way.

We see a deeper meaning to three-dimensional visualization in retail, though: the act of looking at three-dimensional versions of products and experiences at home hits your emotional triggers far better than looking at grids of two-dimensional products. Amazon and other stores have seen increases in sales by converting their products to three-dimensional visualizations, and newer stores, such as Obsess (https://obsessar.com/), take it a lot further. With Obsess, you see sets of new products in a three-dimensional representation of a real home or office. No more grids of product results.

The result sells way better, particularly groupings of products like, say, art that goes with pillows that goes with a vase on a coffee table. You can instantly change how a room looks just by clicking a button and then you can see all the products that go together in that look. This dramatically increases engagement, fun, and the ability to sell groupings of products. There's a reason why so many companies are hungry for consumers getting Spatial Computing glasses, and this new kind of "virtual showroom" is a major part of it.

There are many other apps that let you visualize in some form of 3D before you buy, including Argos, VADO's Viv, to car companies such as Audi.

Photo credit: Audi. Audi has deployed over 1,000 VR showrooms in dealerships worldwide.

This virtual showroom also decreases product returns due to products not fitting right or not matching what the customer saw online. With AR, for instance, you can try shoes out on your own feet and see how they look. That's quite different, both emotionally and in reality, from trying to imagine a two-dimensional shoe and how it might look on your feet.

At Sephora, they are going further. Its Virtual Artist product came out of its R&D labs in San Francisco. It lets you try virtual makeup on your own face with your mobile phone. If you like what you see, you can purchase the real thing, and they were careful to make sure the colors match. This lets you play around with (and emotionally bond to, retailers hope) different looks and makeup styles without worrying what others are thinking about you before you buy.

Photo credit: Sephora. Illustration of "Sephora Virtual Artist" AR app.

"Since 2010, Sephora has built our mobile experiences with the store shopper in mind," Bridget Dolan, Senior Vice President, Omni Experience and Innovation, has commented. "Our customers are very digitally savvy, and constantly have their phones in hand when shopping in the store."

Finally, three-dimensional product visualizations will bring with it a new kind of virtual shopping, one that you can walk through just like you walk through a real-life mall, like the ones in Dubai and Minneapolis we visited to prepare for this book. One thing, though, is that when Spatial Computing devices arrive, you'll be able to "call up" your friend and walk through the virtual mall with them. Retail is about to see some deep changes due to digital twin technology that we talk about elsewhere in this book, and when we talk to people inside consumer goods companies, such as Red Bull, they are salivating to do new kinds of three-dimensional shopping experiences because they know that these will cause much deeper brand engagement and emotional attachment to brands, if done right.

The visual and emotional side of shopping is just the tip of the iceberg of change that's coming to retailers in the next decade. Let's dig into some of the other changes that are already underway with regard to Spatial Computing.

Retail Destruction? No, But Radical Change Underway

During the Fall of 2019, one of the biggest Fry's Electronics locations in Silicon Valley announced it would close. This retail store used to have dozens of checkout lanes and it often had long lines during its heyday in the 1980s. John Fry gave us a tour on opening day of its Sunnyvale store when it did its first million dollars of revenue in one day. Those days are long gone now.

Photo credit: Google Maps. The Palo Alto location of Fry's Electronics that will have closed as of January 2020.

We all know the reason why it closed: Amazon crushed it. The truth is that Fry's didn't change, but the competition did. It was disrupted, as we say in Silicon Valley.

Trying to Keep Up

Amazon and other online retailers, like B&H Photo, took away Fry's unique position of having everything from soldering irons to computer processors. Back then, it was "the place" to buy the stuff you needed to build the products that made Silicon Valley famous in the 1980s as a place to start a technology company. Now, you can get all those online and have them delivered to you, often within an hour or two and for a cheaper price.

Online is not only cheaper, it's better organized, and comes with reviews to help you choose between dozens of products and is better at reminding you of associated things you might also need. One of the last times we visited Fry's in Palo Alto, there was a huge set of shelves with dozens of drones. There was no help to choose. No salespeople nearby. If you did pull one of the drones off of the shelf, you might not realize what batteries you need to buy, or cases that will work, or even what other devices you would need to go with it. Amazon is different—it shows you all of these things when you buy a drone or, really, any product. The experience of shopping at Fry's is poorer in real life than it is online and online is getting better at an ever-increasing pace thanks to the move to three-dimensional product visualization.

Worse, Fry's didn't have two things that are keeping some brick-and-mortar retailers thriving, like Bass Pro Shops, which sells a variety of outdoor goods from boats to tents to fishing rods and guns: things you want to try physically before buying, and a showroom attitude that teaches you about the products you are buying. We predict that retailers such as Bass Pro Shops won't disappear in the next decade, but can imagine dozens of ways they will be changed as customers adopt more Spatial Computing. We can imagine a virtual stream where you can try out fishing rods and lures and see how they feel, and work, in the stream you are planning on soon fishing.

This goes way beyond the emotional triggers of changing how we can demo things, now that applications of three-dimensional visualization are becoming more interesting.

We can already see the early signs as we visit stores such as Amazon Go, which have no checkout counters. Or in Las Vegas hotels, where small robots deliver things to rooms. Or in warehouses that retailers own, like Kroger, that have hundreds of thousands of robots scurrying around, moving products on their way to both storage shelves and delivery vehicles. Or in the Amazon app, which has a feature where you can get more details by using your camera. Aim your phone at a product and it tells you more. Soon, Computer Vision features like this will bring new capabilities into your lives.

These changes will really be felt in retail stores as consumers move computing from two-dimensional screens to three-dimensional glasses or visors that bring virtualized stores into living rooms and offices, and even if that doesn't happen, three-dimensional product visualization is already changing how people can try on products, or see how they fit into their rooms in real life. All of a sudden, you won't need to walk into a store to see displays like you would see in today's shopping malls or grocery stores. These will show up virtually literally anywhere and be much more customizable and personalized.

Looking Ahead

We dream of a world where everyone is wearing Spatial Computing devices on their faces and where Spatial Computing technology also drives around robots, virtual beings, and autonomous vehicles, including drones.

These on-face devices will bring massively new visual experiences into people's homes, and the same devices, when worn by retail workers, can enable new kinds of service, new, more efficient warehouses, and new delivery systems that will get products to you via robots, drones, or autonomous vehicles.

If you have worked in previous versions of retail stores, like we did back in the 1980s while running consumer electronics stores in Silicon Valley, you can see the shifts. Back then, we didn't take inventory on computers. We didn't have cash registers that allowed people to pay via their mobile phones (heck, our customers didn't have computers or phones for the most part, either, apart from the rich executives or real estate agents).

Already, Walmart is training its employees with VR, a trend we expect to greatly accelerate over the next few years because the early examples are proving not just to be profitable, but lifesaving (the company claimed that the VR training saved lives during a shooting in one of its stores, which you can read more about at https://fortune.com/2019/08/20/walmart-ceo-vr-training-helped-save-lives-in-el-paso-shooting/).

In quite a few warehouses, we are seeing Spatial Computing devices and systems being used to make them more efficient. AR glasses can show you exactly where a product is in a huge warehouse, saving seconds on every trip. Things like dwell time, touching, and transaction data all help manufacturers build products that better serve consumers, and even design packaging that gets their attention on busy store shelves. Soon that will be augmented or, in fact, already is. Walk into a Lego store and you can see three-dimensional models of what is inside each box thanks to an AR system originally built by Metaio, which was later bought by Apple to form the basis of its ARKit platform.

Photo credit: Nathaniël de Jong. Nathaniël plays Bait! on Oculus Quest on his popular YouTube channel. This game lets you "shop" in two virtual stores, and then head out to a virtual lake and go fishing with your virtual gear. Soon, this kind of experience will be just a preview of the real gear you'll use on real trips.

As of 2019, if you want to buy something like a fishing rod from the huge retailer Bass Pro Shops, your experience at home is limited to searching on Google and poking around mostly two-dimensional images of rods and text reviews.

If you have an Oculus Quest, though, you might have played one of the new fishing games like "Bait!," which gives you a pretty good preview of what it's like to fish in real life. We imagine that soon, fishing rod manufacturers will give you virtual looks at their rods, just like the ones in Bait! Already the game has two stores, showing that the designers of this game already are preparing to disrupt Bass Pro Shops. After all, who wants to drive a distance to one of these stores, then wait 20 minutes for help, as we did when we visited? Not to mention the fact that we didn't get a good introduction into how to actually use the fishing equipment at the store, something that will be part of the experience when shopping in VR or AR.

Aspects of retail are changing their roles in several ways due to Spatial Computing. The store itself is morphing into something that serves you in new ways, while augmented stores will let you experience shopping in the comfort of your home in a way that will look and feel pretty close to real stores, and then the retailer can serve you via rolling robots or autonomous vehicles. Let's dig into how the stores themselves are changing due to these new technologies.

Variations on a Retail Theme

The camera functionality in Amazon's app is worthy of checking out and gives a good taste of where things can go in the future. What's funny is that when we ask people if they have tried it, even techie people, very few have. Yet it's been in the app for a couple of years, at least. What does it do? It lets you visually search. Google and others have competitor products, but because it's from Amazon, which has the most highly-developed retail store, it works better with the products there.

Aim it at a logo, say the Starbucks logo on your coffee cup, and Amazon will bring up all sorts of merchandise with the same logo on it. Aim it at a friend, wearing, say, a black turtleneck shirt, and it will find you similar shirts to buy. Aim it at a product, or, particularly, a box, like that of a coffee maker, and you will find lots of coffee makers to buy.

When still at Amazon, Chris Hargarten, who ran the largest team of people categorizing all sorts of things, told us they tried to use techniques like these to make the shopping experience even better and faster. "We want users to go directly into the product page they want," he explained to us. That takes some work, given the millions of products and pages, and the visual search feature inside the Amazon app gives us all another vector to do that.

It isn't perfect, though. With clothes, it does usually get the style right, but rarely gets the brand right. We hear that over in China, the competitor for Amazon there has a similar feature that's much more accurate. We notice that in China, people use cameras far more frequently than in other countries. This leads us to a new point: if you have more users and even more aggressive users of your technology, you will have more data, and more data leads to more accuracy when you try to do things like figure out the brand of the suit someone is wearing that you like and want to buy for yourself.

The camera, too, could enable a new kind of "showrooming." This is what they call when people go into a local retail store, only to go online to buy the product they are checking out for, presumably, a cheaper price. Retailers hate showrooming, and with good reason; Fry's has been decimated by the practice, and so have lots of other retailers.

But do retailers fight back with technology of their own to help customers build highly customized shopping experiences that lead back to their stores? Very few have the capabilities to hire the software teams that Amazon has. We learned that about 10,000 people are working on the training of Amazon's Echo line of products alone. What kind of retailer can deal with that kind of technology investment?

Not to mention that Amazon is putting that kind of investment into the entire supply chain. Visit its warehouses and you will find hundreds of thousands of robots scurrying about, moving products from truck to truck for delivery to customers.

Amazon, Hargarten explained, is aiming at making every part of buying and receiving a product more efficient. To see how, let's walk back into B&H Photo in New York City.

When you walk in there, you have a few choices. Do you just wander around going aisle by aisle, looking to see what is there? Sometimes. We did just that because we enjoy consumer electronics so much, and it reminds us of stores we shopped at, or ran, in the 1980s.

Or, do you know exactly what you want and want to go straight to that section, like we did the time we needed to get another set of Rode Wireless Go microphones? Yeah, there's even a greeter/security guard at the front door who can direct you right to where you want to go.

The same applies online. Amazon tries to make it very easy for you to go directly to a specific product, and if you don't know exactly what you want yet, it also makes it easy to shop by category, like microphones in the B&H Photo store.

There are points of friction, though. One is that product visualizations are being converted to 3D, but they are stuck on small glass screens where you can't get a satisfying look. Ever try to see how a refrigerator would look in your kitchen by looking at a three-dimensional version on a mobile phone? We have, and the experience isn't satisfying at all.

The problem is that while retailers would *love* for us all to have Spatial Computing visors on our faces, we don't, and even the ones that are out there, like Magic Leap or Microsoft's HoloLens, are simply too cumbersome and don't have the software anyway to browse a three-dimensional store. Those days will have to wait for lighter, smaller, cheaper, and more capable devices. We predict that much of that will happen by 2023 or 2024, but even if it takes 5 years longer than that, we are already seeing a huge revolution in retailing thanks to sensors on mobile phones, three-dimensional imagery on mobile, and new kinds of stores that use sensors, whether from Amazon or Standard Cognition, which promise to get rid of slow, cumbersome checkout lines, making shopping a seamless, magical experience with much more human-computer interaction.

We think the changes are deeper than just trying to bring back brick-and-mortar stores. Everything about retail is changing, from how inventory is ordered to advertising, warehousing, delivery, in-store services, and customer expectations. All of this is being driven by the technologies that drive AR, autonomous cars, or robots. Cameras, Computer Vision, AI/Machine Learning, three-dimensional sensors, and more are changing literally every piece of the retail puzzle. A glimpse of this future can be had if you check out an Amazon Go store.

Amazon Go is Watching You

Going into an Amazon Go store, you feel something is different even before you enter it. First of all, you probably are there to check out the future of retailing, either because you heard about it from a friend or from media reports. Second, you have to load up an app just to get into the store. Third, as you enter the store you might notice hundreds of computers and sensors over your head.

Photo credit: Robert Scoble. An Amazon Go store in Seattle – a 1,800-square foot convenience store with no checkout lines. You just take a product off the shelf and leave and it automatically charges you. Note all the cameras and sensors in the ceiling, under shelves, and behind the walls.

Every part of the store uses Spatial Computing technologies to track everything you step in front of, look at, touch, or take. As you walk out of the store with items or even consume them in the store, you will be charged, and new AI is being trained for new product lines all the time.

If you look closely, there are sensors behind the walls and even scales under shelves, so this store is very hard to fool. It knows if you take a product off the shelf and leave it on another one somewhere else.

It is tracking every move you make through your mobile phone and the cloud computing it is connected to. No facial recognition is necessary. Of course, we won't be shocked if facial recognition is added in the future, so you won't even need to carry your phone anymore into these stores. Already in China, facial recognition is being used to let customers buy drinks from vending machines.

As you walk out, your mobile phone has a receipt of all the purchases you made and even how many minutes you spent in the store.

A competitor, Standard Cognition, makes claims that Amazon's stores are over-engineered, claiming it allows retailers to turn on the same kind of stores that Amazon does by using just standard video cameras. Dozens of them aimed at customers in its retail store concepts do pretty much the same thing Amazon does with tons of extra sensors.

Why are Amazon and Standard Cognition operating these kinds of stores? Well, for one, to cut down on shrinkage loss. Employees every year steal millions of dollars' worth of goods from store shelves and warehouses and shoplifting continues to produce huge losses in retail, despite putting tags on many products and sensors at doors. These kinds of stores will see far fewer shrinkage losses for sure.

A bigger reason is that these stores don't require checkout lanes, which means smaller stores can display more products and customers will be happier because they won't need to wait to buy, say, a banana and coffee for breakfast simply to check out. Yes, eventually, stores will see additional savings due to having fewer employees in the store, but so far it isn't clear how many employees can really be eliminated. Most 7-Eleven stores have only one employee at most times to cover the register anyway and these new stores still need employees to make sure the stores remain clean and stock is carefully placed on shelves.

The biggest reason, though, could be the AI training and visualizations that can be made by operating a physical store, not to mention that there are lots of places, like airports, that would benefit from the instant satisfaction of such a store, and one run by fewer people is very attractive to investors. At Facebook Oculus Connect 6 in 2019, executives walked through a volumetric scan of a real store and that gave us a glimpse of how we will shop in the future. We can pull up a virtual representation of a real store while we sit, well, anywhere, and start looking around. Obsess is already giving us a taste of that on mobile phones, but Facebook demonstrated that it will be far more real when we get VR or AR headsets in the future.

Amazon is using the data it is recording by watching real customers come into a real store to better know how to lay out virtual stores in the future and what affects buying behavior. So, it will have much better virtualized stores (and physical ones) in the future.

Standard Cognition founder, Jordan Fisher, explains that they are even using this data to train the computer to know if you are eating food at, say, a salad bar or a display of, say, berries. Be honest, you do try some once in a while, right? Well, now it can charge you as you try them. No more getting away with sneaking a berry or two as a "free sample."

A similar revolution has been happening for retail logistics with regard to Spatial Computing, albeit in a less public way. Let's take a look at what's going on behind the scenes that will, in the coming years, revolutionize the way you receive your goods.

Spatial Computing for Logistics

Logistics is undergoing its own emerging mini-revolution when it comes to utilizing Spatial Computing. Companies like Seegrid, who make **Vision-guided Vehicles (VGVs)**, help in reducing the high accident rates associated with human-manned forklifts. These VGVs use Computer Vision and sensing technology to know where to go on the floor and to be able to avoid obstacles in their way. Companies such as BMW, Jaguar, and Whirlpool, among many others, use Seegrid's VGVs on their warehouse floors.

Photo credit: Seegrid. Examples of Seegrid's VGVs that replace human-manned forklifts.

Another Spatial Computing warehouse helper is the GreyOrange Butler robot, which GreyOrange calls a "Decision Science-Driven Robotic Goods-to-Person System" for "automated put-away, inventory storage, replenishment, and order picking in fulfillment and distribution centers." GreyOrange Butler customers are mostly retailers with physical and/or online stores, in addition to apparel makers, third-party logistics providers, and consumer electronics companies. Potential competition for both Seegrid and GreyOrange logistics products comes from start-ups like Fetch Robotics and 6 River Systems, as well as larger established players such as Swisslog.

Photo credit: GreyOrange. GreyOrange Butler robots working inside a warehouse.

In terms of logistics' use of AR headsets, there has been some version of AR used in warehouses since at least 2008, though the overlay visuals used were in 2D versus 3D up until the last few years. Companies such as RealWear and Microsoft, with the HoloLens 2 headset, along with the now-defunct companies ODG and DAQRI, have catered to this market that we predict will have exponential growth within the next 5 years due to a fast-growing need for logistical warehousing systems.

Photo credit: ARM23. Example of an AR program for logistics using a Microsoft HoloLens headset.

Underlying this demand is an ever-increasing growth in online sales for a wide diversity of products.

Spatial Computing Delivery Methods – Robots, Drones, Future

Starship Technologies is a venture that was started in 2014 by Skype co-founders, Janus Friis and Ahti Heinla, to address the "last mile" of delivering goods such as groceries, restaurant take-out, and packages. Their product is an autonomous electric robot that navigates city streets and paths using six wheels, Computer Vision, and a sensor suite that includes cameras, GPS, and an inertial measurement unit. It does not use LIDAR in a bid to cut down on costs to the customer.

We talked with Sean Eckard, Senior Manager of Business Development of Starship Technologies. He says it is "supreme in every way" to deliver things with a 50-lb electric robot instead of delivering things with a 2,000-lb car.

Funny enough, it isn't the technology we mostly talked about while we were with him. Rather, it is the regulatory approach that he's seeing from different cities. Some cities meet his company with open arms, recognizing the benefits that delivery robots will bring to their citizens: lower costs and more consistent delivery times, along with new jobs that come from companies like Starship. Others, however, refuse to consider letting Starship's robots roll down its streets, seeing them as too dystopian, or a threat to existing jobs, or a potential safety hazard.

Eckard says the job is harder for some of Starship's competitors since they made their robots bigger and uglier. Starship has overcome some of these objections, Eckard says, because of its fun low profile and attention to detail when it comes to pedestrian safety, which is mostly due to a ton of AI training on what to do around, say, kids or dogs. He says that is why they started on college campuses before going to entire cities. They wanted to have the ability to watch and train the robots in a constrained space, which also gains the trust of people using them.

Photo credit: Starship Technologies

Oh, and by going to college campuses, they assumed they would have a lot more trouble with thefts and abuse, which turned out not to be true. In fact, they are having trouble getting anyone at all to rip them off (and were actually hoping for more so that they could train the robots on what to do if someone carted one off in, say, a pickup truck). It turns out that even most criminals are smart enough to know that the cameras onboard are recording them, just the same as a new Tesla records someone breaking a window or doing other damage to the car.

Enough cities have signed up, though, as of 2019, to note that delivery robots are a trend and give us some insight into how retail will change due to them, along with the other "last mile" delivery technologies that are coming, such as drones.

It was Eckard's opening argument, though, that's going to be most interesting to watch: why are we driving cars around to go pick things up, or deliver them, when a 55-lb robot can do it just as well? One, presumably, that will take a lot less energy to move around, which means less carbon put in the air for each package delivered?

Climate change is, as of 2019, heating up as an issue, as it were. Where in 2018, 16-year-old climate activist Greta Thunberg protested alone, by the end of 2019, she was joined by millions in protests around the world every Friday.

This increased pressure to do something about climate change will lead more companies to use these delivery robots, it seems to us, and make other changes as well to reduce the amount of carbon that they are putting in the air as they move products to people's homes.

Photo credit: Amazon. An Amazon Scout robot reported to have been built on the acquired IP of a company called Dispatch.

Amazon announced a very similar-looking autonomous robot (also called a self-driving delivery device, or just a robot) in January 2019, and is running small field tests with it on getting packages to customers in Snohomish County, Washington, and Irvine, California. It predominantly uses LIDAR as its remote sensing method, which Starship feels is overkill.

Some are definitely looking at the delivery robots as a way to completely rethink business.

Take, for example, pizza.

Alex and Julia Garden noticed that the average delivery took about 20 minutes; about the same length of time it takes to cook. In a bid to completely disrupt the pizza supply chain, they outfitted their Zume delivery vans with dozens of robot-controlled ovens. The pizza is cooking as it drives to your house. This reduces the capital, since they don't need an expensive kitchen and building to house it, and their pizzas arrive hotter than their competitors, literally coming out of the oven at your front door. Zume, alas, will no longer be doing these kinds of operations due to internal mismanagement.

We can imagine they won't be the last business to completely rethink retail, delivery, or both thanks to Spatial Computing.

Photo credit: FedEx. An example of a FedEx's last-mile delivery robot, Roxo, the SameDay Bot.

Roxo, FedEx's SameDay Bot, is its answer to the last mile delivery issue. In August 2019, it completed a two-week test in Memphis, Tennessee, following its initial test in Manchester, New Hampshire, earlier in August. FedEx has been working with AutoZone, Walgreens, Target, Pizza Hut, Lowe's, and Walmart to adapt automated delivery technology to customers' needs. What makes Roxo a little different than the other delivery robots is that it can travel upstairs to arrive directly in front of a person's door.

Amazon's vision of 30-minute or less package delivery is encapsulated in its design for its drones. Its drone operation is run by Amazon Prime Air, a subsidiary of Amazon, and it is currently still under development. In the Summer of 2019, Jeff Wilkie, Amazon's Worldwide Consumer CEO pledged that Prime Air drones would be delivering packages "in months." Time will tell if this indeed has transpired by the time this book is printed. Our friends who have gotten a look at the Spatial Computing technology inside say that what's really fantastic is the paper-thin radar sensor inside that maps out the world in 3D and can fly to your door the same way your AR glasses will soon bring all sorts of virtual fun to you: through new technologies such as "AR Cloud" and Simultaneous Location And Mapping (SLAM). Already, consumer drones are starting to use the same techniques to navigate through trees or around obstacles.

Photo credit: Amazon. An example from Amazon Prime Air: a future delivery system designed to get packages to customers in 30 minutes or less using unmanned aerial vehicles, also called drones.

In April 2019, Wing Aviation, the drone delivery arm of Google's parent company, Alphabet, became the first American company to be granted FAA approval for commercial delivery. In addition to Amazon, Uber and UPS have applied for air carrier certificates from the U.S. Federal Aviation Administration to launch commercial drone operations.

Prior to having deliveries of goods come to you, Spatial Computing experiences could be used to visualize what furniture and other goods would look like in your living room and anywhere else.

In Your Living Room and Elsewhere – Spatial Computing Marketing Experiences

We *wrote* this part of the chapter by talking into a microphone to produce text (elsewhere, we generally just used a keyboard). This is to get ready for the world that Amazon and others are bringing to us. Alexa listens to us and brings us whatever we want. "Hey Alexa, put a box of Cheerios on my shopping list." "Hey Alexa, can you deliver some Chinese food?" "Hey Alexa, can we watch Halt and Catch Fire?" "Hey Alexa, I want to buy some clothes."

Starting in the Living Room

Ubiquitous computing is already changing our living rooms. Robert Scoble says, about his living room: "I have a Google device listening to me. I have many Apple devices listening to me. I have a TV that listens to me. I have a Sonos soundbar and a Facebook Portal device that listens to me and, of course, we have Amazon boxes listening."

Soon, we will have three-dimensional sensors on our face and in our living rooms and new kinds of displays on our eyes, potentially replacing our television sets and computer displays. Hooray! There's a company called Looking Glass that has a flat display that gives you a three-dimensional look at a three-dimensional objects. And other devices or technologies have been shown to us that include three-dimensional contacts that don't need to be on your face. But it is the on-the-face wearable devices that are the most interesting. They also are the most controversial, because of the privacy implications of having a three-dimensional sensor that can literally see everything in your house. If you take it to the utmost, there are wearable devices that are going to remember where you left your keys. Or where you left your Pepsi, or how many bites of food you've taken in the last hour.

They also could know who has been in your house or how many times you've actually interacted with your children or your spouse. What music you listen to. What things you bought. What tasks you put on your task list. What things are on your calendar. What you're wearing on a daily basis. Or if you're wearing anything at all. They might catch wind of your emotion. Did you just yell at your children? Do you feel guilty about it? Did that cause you to buy some Ben & Jerry's ice cream? Soon Taylor Swift might start playing in your ears singing "You Need to Calm Down" and ice cream ads might pop up with messages "need a break?" because you are raising your voice.

By the end of 2020, we're going to be playing new kinds of board games. Already from companies like Tilt Five, there are AR glasses that let you play games with your family and friends gathered around a coffee table or a kitchen table. But we see the changes yet to come to the living room to be very profound thanks to these personalized viewing devices.

Already, we can use an Oculus Quest to watch movies on Netflix, or TV shows, music videos, or other kinds of content on our personal devices.

The children can watch SpongeBob while the adults watch something a little more racy. What does this mean for personal interaction? And what does it mean for retail?

A Personalized Experience

We are heading into a hyper-personalized world where Amazon, Google, Facebook, Apple, and others will know a ton about our lifestyles, our family structure, and our favorite media choices. Adding to that, Amazon already knows everything you've purchased from Amazon and now, its member brands, such as Whole Foods.

As Jeff Wilke, Amazon's CEO of Worldwide Consumer, says, "We're going to see AI and Machine Learning embedded in all kinds of different products, so it makes personalization better. We just launched an enhancement to the iOS app that lets you screenshot a fashion look that you're interested in and find something on Amazon that matches."

So, let's go back to the three-dimensional store that soon will be shown to us in our living room. It can predict what you're going to buy next with some level of confidence. Planning a trip to Rome? It will suggest new luggage. Running low on groceries? It might suggest you look around a new kind of Amazon store where you could put pick out strawberries and Cheerios and your favorite coffee.

All to be delivered in an hour or less by a robot.

Many people will find this very attractive because heading to the store often means being stuck in traffic in cities or stuck in lines at grocery stores and this opportunity cost of time ends up being quite a high cost indeed.

Of course, as you use more of these services, they learn more about not just your shopping behavior, but everyone's shopping behavior. This is already how Amazon works and why Amazon is already beating the experience of shopping at a real store like Fry's.

These new three-dimensional stores that are going to be in your living room are also going to mean that marketers are going to have to think differently. Soon, we will be able to have conversations with virtual beings: things that look like real human beings and can actually have a pretty good conversation with you because they know everything about what you're buying. Magic Leap, for instance, has already started showing off a virtual being called Mica. We can imagine a world where you are wearing a Spatial Computing device and have these entities show up in your home to discuss things with you and help you out.

"Hey Mica. Can you help me buy a new camera?"

"Sure!"

She could ask the same questions I asked thousands of people in a retail store in the 1980s. "Would you like a small pocket camera? Or a big DSLR?" "Would you like to see a Nikon or a Canon?" "Do you know the difference?"

Mica can warn you that some of your product choices are not in line with your new intentionality. You could tell Mica, "Hey, I want to lose 10 pounds within the next month," and Mica could tell you that it's not a good idea to buy that Ben & Jerry's ice cream that it "knows" you want to buy.

Facebook and other big companies are already planning for such a world years in advance. We've caught wind of design documents for this kind of future world. The designers inside these companies are already thinking about how your buying behavior will change thanks to these new technologies in your living room.

Steve Conine, co-chairman and co-founder of the online retailer Wayfair, says, "My belief is, at some point in the not-too-distant future, every home in America will have a three-dimensional model tied to it. If you give us access to it, we can use that to show you styles and designs in that space that look amazingly good."

That's for the near future and the farther-out future. Let's now go back to what is currently happening with regard to Spatial Computing. In this case, we will focus on how some major select furniture and accessories stores are using AR, and, in some cases, VR.

The VR World

In 2016, IKEA came out with its Virtual Reality Kitchen Experience, where potential customers could browse the IKEA catalog to place items around the virtual kitchen, open drawers and oven doors, fry and toss around meatballs, and make pancakes. The app was developed for the HTC Vive and released on Valve's Steam game platform. The experience was not widely known, however, as an article published in the Financial Times in April 2018 made it appear that this experience was a new one.

In December 2017, for the opening of its newest store near Dallas, IKEA partnered with media and technology agency Wavemaker to offer VR games and experiences to potential customers entering the store. Close to 300 people played a "pillow toss" game or hung out with a virtual panda. With this, IKEA was able to test what types of VR content would attract potential customers. This is part of a larger effort to test and learn what kinds of investments should be made with regard to IKEA's stores, logistics, digital capabilities, and services.

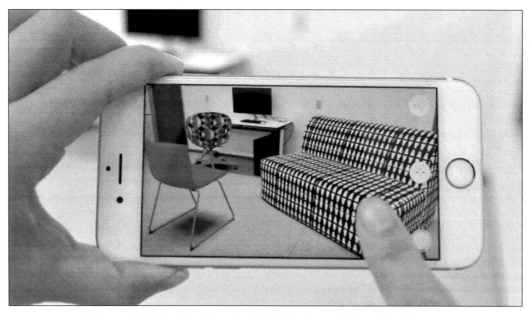

Photo credit: IKEA. Advertising for IKEA's "Place" app. IKEA updated their app in Fall 2019 to allow for placement of several digital furniture items in a room.

With regard to its mobile AR app, IKEA has collaborated with many partners, including ad agency 72andSunny, to help prospective customers better visualize IKEA furniture in their homes and to foster strong consumer loyalty.

In September 2017, IKEA launched its AR app, IKEA Place for Apple iOS devices. Over 2,000 products—nearly the company's full collection of sofas, armchairs, coffee tables, and storage units—were available to view and place. In contrast to the catalog AR app IKEA launched in 2013, the placements were more stable, staying put to the floor, and in their proper measured proportions. Also, in 2013, there were only about 100 products versus the more than 2,000 products currently available to view and place. Also, the products appear with about a 98-percent accuracy in scale and true-to-life representations of the texture, fabric, lighting, and shadow.

As of March 2018, the number of IKEA products in IKEA Place available to view grew to 3,200 with the AR app now available for Android mobile phones. Also available now for both the iOS and Android versions of the app is "Visual Search," which allows users to match photos of furniture they like to similar or identical IKEA products through the app. For the IKEA Place app, you need an iPhone 6S or above with iOS 11 or an Android phone with ARCore.

IKEA's VR strategy has not been as clear as its AR strategy. Wisconsin's first IKEA opened on May 16, 2018, in Oak Creek, Milwaukee. As part of the store's opening festivities, visitors to a pop-up event close by in McKinley Park could participate in a VR experience that displayed an IKEA showroom and designs, as well as some of its latest products.

As the world's largest retailer, Walmart is also a company competing on multiple fronts. Its culture is nearly the opposite of Amazon's, having begun in the U.S. South, and building significantly on a foundation of price-sensitive rural shoppers.

Photo credit: Walmart. Two screenshots from the original Spatialand (now spelled "Spatial&") app. With this app, consumers could try outdoor products in a Yosemite National Park VR experience.

Yet Walmart transitioned well into the online space, where its website is the third largest after Amazon and Apple, better than all of its traditional shoppers in terms of visitors and sales. Its e-commerce business, which accounts for 3.6 percent of its U.S. sales, has incurred much expense to grow. Its website has about 100 million unique monthly visitors, versus 180 million for Amazon.com. However, recent reports indicate that despite significant and continuous online growth, investors remain unsatisfied that it can stop Amazon's relentless rise.

Walmart keeps trying and expanding, showing it is unafraid to take risks with new technologies, particularly AR and VR. In 2017, it acquired Jet.com, an online shopping network often compared favorably with Amazon. Marc Lore built Jet.com and came on board as head of Walmart's U.S. e-commerce business in September 2017 following Jet.com's acquisition. In the third quarter of 2017, Walmart's U.S. e-commerce sales grew 50 percent year on year. However, for the fourth quarter of 2017, those sales were up only 23 percent year on year, which was a great cause of alarm for the company and the investment community as it showed weakness during the holiday season.

Making an Impact

To devise new technologies that have an impact on the way people shop and thus hopefully increase sales, Lore created an in-house start-up incubator called Store No. 8, named for the store that founder Sam Walton had once used for experimentation. The incubator currently holds at least four start-ups. The focus so far has been on VR solutions. Spatialand (now spelled "Spatial&"), the VR start-up that had been funded by Store No. 8, was fully acquired by Walmart with the founder, Kim Cooper, and about 10 employees joining Walmart. Other Store No. 8 start-ups include a personal shopping service run by Rent the Runway founder Jenny Fleiss; an initiative for a cashier less store like Amazon Go, run by Jet.com co-founder Mike Hanrahan; and Project Franklin (no other details provided), led by Bart Stein, the former CEO of Wim Yogurt.

According to Dave Mayer, president of shopper-focused design firm Chase Design, "there are two types of Walmart shopping trips: replenishment, in which a customer runs out of a given product and is likely to buy a familiar brand again; and discovery, in which consumers know they've run out of a given product but aren't loyal to a particular brand."

"When you compare digital to physical, physical is still predominant when it comes to discovery … no one has found a way to make discovery easy online," he said. "What's attractive about VR is its potential to create immersive experiences in the digital realm that will open up and enable browsing."

In other words, if you go shopping in VR, you won't just see a single product—perhaps you'll see a whole suite of brand names for that product, and you might discover something new.

We have heard that two California units will be working closely together on innovations to digitize Walmart product lines. In our brief research related to this project, we gained some sense of the strategic imperatives taking hold. We heard that the Labs' top priority in immersive technologies is to prioritize three-dimensional scanning for millions of SKU units and that centralizing operations for this to occur is paramount. However, we found out from multiple sources that ideas from Silicon Valley are being stalled by decision makers in Walmart headquarters in Bentonville, Arkansas. Yet, Walmart is still actively hiring for the immersive industry area, as evidenced by job postings for recruiters, projects managers, and engineers.

With regard to AR, it is not clear when Walmart will ramp up efforts there. There is a clear verbal mandate within the company to provide something meaningful in that area; however, as of today, there has not been much movement there. There has been a Super Hero AR app that was launched within the stores as part of an Angry Birds retail and gaming marketing integration, as well as *The Avengers* AR in-store experience.

According to Sarah Spencer, Walmart Director of National Media Relations, "Walmart is committed to creating engaging and fun experiences for their shoppers, across multiple channels of engagement...The Super Hero AR app is part of an ongoing "retailtainment" initiative for Walmart. In March 2016, we launched the Angry Birds retail and gaming integration, and now *The Avengers* AR in-store experience are examples of how Walmart is integrating technology and gaming directly into the retail shopping experience."

As the world's largest online retailer, Amazon's strategy and culture have always been to use technology to become more efficient and improve customer experiences. It has been lethal to competitors on virtually every consumer-facing front. As always, Amazon moves successfully in multiple directions: it has expanded successfully into B2B with AWS, a wholly owned web services subsidiary. It is building brick-and-mortar stores and has acquired Whole Foods, the supermarket chain: now it is buying large goods producers to lower grocery costs for consumers. On another front, according to job postings, Amazon is creating statistical three-dimensional models of human bodies, which it will then match to images and videos of people via Deep Learning algorithms and other tactics. That will have a "wide range of commercial applications" for Amazon customers, the company says in the job ad.

Among the company's many competitive assets is that it probably has more data on what people buy than any company on Earth, and with the addition of Amazon Echo, it now has a friendly device that people talk to—and in doing so, provide massive amounts of additional data on a growing number of the world's households.

Like all major IKEA competitors, Amazon has an AR application called "AR View" for both iOS and Android; we tried it for a few minutes on a Pixel phone and found it to be pretty similar to IKEA Place. Amazon's many thousands of items to view is welcoming. If the current app was the end-game for Amazon in AR and VR, IKEA could comfortably remain the leader of a small, but aggressive pack of competitors. But Amazon's historic long-view strategy would make that possibility unlikely. Where they are headed, we can only guess, but we speculate that a future iteration of AR View will include headset applications. Even more significant is that it will eventually link Echo to AR View. It does not appear that Amazon will be utilizing VR for retail purposes, with earlier indications pointing to its interest there solely for the entertainment industry.

In a few years, pattern recognition will be able to predict what consumers will need next, whether that is another quart of milk or a new couch. Alexa could actually suggest that it is time, and suggest they look at AR possibilities of an 84-inch couch that would fit properly in a certain space, then show colors that would match the curtains behind it. This could all happen before a family even considers shopping for the couch online or in a store. While competing with Amazon on this level, we also see an opportunity for partnering elsewhere via AWS, Amazon's B2B web services subsidiary.

Photo credit: Irena Cronin. A chair sold on Amazon being viewed through
the company's AR app, "AR View" (iOS version).

AWS' Amazon Sumerian is a non-technical platform for creating AR or VR applications without programming. Imagine that we have a room hosted by an AI-enriched host avatar. The rooms are easily filled with three-dimensional objects and, from what we can discern, the room can be as large or small as developers wish to make it. Perhaps this could be a furniture showroom. The host can be a sales representative who shows online shoppers selections from any chosen category. Sometime in the near future, haptic technologies could be added on, perhaps in the form of a glove. Then, shoppers could actually feel textures and surfaces.

A "No Install Needed" AR World

In late 2016, Amazon began planning for what AR and VR should look like for AWS customers, with a preview debuting at AWS re:Invent. They then bought Goo Technologies, a bankrupt Swedish company. Goo Create, its three-dimensional creation platform, became the foundation of Sumerian's Integrated Development Environment (IDE). One of the biggest benefits of a scalable cloud infrastructure is to be able to dramatically reduce latency, a feature that is very important for quality presentation and manipulation when using mobile AR apps. Another huge benefit is that you won't need to load up a new app just to, say, see some functionality in a shopping mall.

With regard to open standards, Sumerian supports several of them: WebGL, WebAR, WebVR, and the emerging WebXR framework that brings AR/VR apps universally to all devices and browsers across platforms.

Photo credit: Wayfair. Advertising for Wayfair's "View in Room 3D" app

In many ways, Wayfair Furniture is the cultural opposite of Walmart: It prides itself on having its engineering team at the core of its organization and credits engineers for "creating customer experiences that we would enjoy ourselves."

Founded in 2002, it fits the classic start-up model. Two high school pals go off to college together and fall in love with technology. They start on a shoestring with a single home furnishings boutique, then another, and another. They consolidate into a single online home-furnishings superstore, go public, and become one of the most successful retailers in modern history.

Today, they offer over 10 million products from over 10,000 suppliers and yet the two founders who continue to head the company see Wayfair as a tech company, rather than a home furnishing merchant.

They are sometimes credited with inventing the term "v-commerce" to replace the older "e-commerce" term because the concept of a virtual store for real shoppers is what they say they are all about. We point to this because we believe it gives insight into their corporate culture and priorities.

Accordingly, the company has been early to introduce AR over VR apps. Since 2018, Wayfair has partnered up with Magic Leap to test out new AR experiences for its customers. Wayfair Next, the company's lab, has been aggressive in working on evolving from two-dimensional to three-dimensional renderings in catalogs and online. It introduced an app with the ill-fated launch of Google Tango for the Lenovo Phab 2 phone in 2016 that allowed shoppers to see how a piece of furniture fitted and looked in their homes.

While that attempt was limited, it came back to be introduced as the "View in Room 3D" app that was launched with ARKit at the same time as the IKEA Place app. While it did not receive the coverage and favorable reviews that IKEA Place received, it was generally perceived as a quality offering with a broad selection of three-dimensional rendered items for sale. As with other competitors included in this report, Wayfair introduced an Android version of its AR app based on ARCore in early 2018, following its iOS ARKit version introduced in the fourth quarter of 2017.

Wayfair has also been quick and aggressive on all popular social media platforms, where 71 percent of all consumers say they are influenced on buying decisions. Understanding that visual product representations are extremely important to marketing and sales, it has made Instagram a top priority and achieved its greatest growth on any social platform there.

Photo credit: Houzz. Advertising for Houzz's "View in My Room 3D" app.

Founded in 2010, by a Silicon Valley couple who became frustrated with trying to find useful information online to help them with home renovation, Houzz is a community of home improvement people, architects, contractors, furniture, and home accessory providers.

It started on the iPad and did not get to Android until 2013. By then, the community had helped more than six million people. Houzz is focused on helping buyers and makes most of its money through commissions from selected vendors and from its online marketplace.

It began to go international in 2014. Today, it has localized versions for the UK, Australia, Germany, France, Russia, Japan, Italy, Spain, Sweden, Denmark, India, Ireland, and New Zealand.

Since its start, the online-only community platform has been prolific with innovative products, most of which are not currently on AR or VR, but have the potential to be used in that way moving forward.

These include:

- **Real Cost Finder**: An interactive tool that helps users plan home renovations and calculate total costs based on data collected from the Houzz community

- **Site Designer**: A free website-building and publishing tool for home professionals

- **Houzz TV**: This is essentially videos on room designs that we assume will be immersive in one form or another

- **Sketch**: A feature that lets users upload their own photos or choose any from the platform to add products from the Houzz Marketplace and see how they would work in rooms being redesigned

- **Visual Match**: A visual recognition tool that uses Deep Learning technology to analyze more than 11 million home photos on Houzz and drag and drop two-dimensional versions into the "View My Room 3D" app

Each of these items would clearly work better in AR than they do currently. Based on Houzz's embrace for emergent technologies, we assume that development work is already going to upgrade one or all of these.

As is the case with every company mentioned so far, the Houzz "View in My Room 3D" AR app for iOS and Android does essentially what IKEA Place does, and from our testing of it, it works quite well, offering over 500,000 images rendered in 3D. Houzz's focus is on AR, not VR, though an earlier version of "View in my Room 3D" was also available to be viewed in VR.

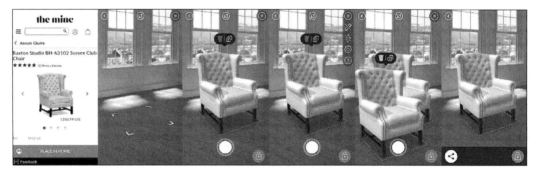

Photo credit: Lowe's app for The Mine. Lowe's high-end luxury furnishings operation.

In March 2018, *Fast Company* named Lowe's the most innovative company in AR, VR, and MR (followed by Houzz and Wayfair). They cited an ongoing campaign of using internally developed immersive technologies to make all aspects of home and office improvement easy and accessible. The publication specifically cited Lowe's Measured app for the iPhone, which essentially turns handheld devices into digital tape measures and lets users share a visual measurement of the height of a chandelier or the distance to the hot tub in the backyard with friends on social media. Almost simultaneously, The Mine, Lowe's high-end luxury furnishings operation, acquired and renamed in 2017, introduced Envisioned, a shopping app that lets anyone browse a catalog of furnishings and then digitally superimpose items in their own homes using AR. Unlike competing apps, iPhone users can view furniture objects in the spaces they will occupy at home from 360-degree perspectives.

The retail Spatial Computing experiences discussed here are helpful when trying to make a decision as to whether or not to buy something. They tie into our view that in the future, physical retail stores will eventually be non-existent, except for, perhaps, those that sell high-priced luxury and/or unusual items.

The Past and The Future

Much of the future of retail has its roots in what exists today. People will continue to have a need or desire to buy something, whether it be a pear, a pair of pants, or a sailboat. It also seems that the need and urge to buy things in stores traverses time. Going back a few thousand years, archeologists have found remnants of stores that were set up in Ancient Greece and Rome. Currently, we still have physical stores where people go to buy things. Going back to the early 1900s, there were some mail-order catalogs where you could order items. The Sears, Roebuck and Company catalog was a very prominent example. Sears, Roebuck and Company had actually started in 1892 as a completely mail-order company, with its physical retail stores only opening up starting in the 1920s.

The idea of ordering something without having to go to a store and having it delivered directly to you is certainly not a new one.

Photo credit: Sears, Roebuck and Company. Early 1900's Sears, Roebuck and Company Household Catalog.

The clothing company, J.Crew, from 1983 to 1989, existed only as a mail-order company. The modern incarnation of the mail-order company is one that places its full catalog online exclusively, such as Amazon. More commonly, hybrids exist where physical stores, physical catalogs, and internet sales all contribute to a company's revenues.

Commonly heard, though, are stories of companies who want to have a much more fully fledged and thriving digital presence above all, such as Nike and Walmart. This is just the start of the digital model fully eclipsing the physical model when it comes to retail operations.

Photo credit: Los Angeles Public Library. Pedestrians crowd the intersection of Seventh Street and Broadway, Downtown Los Angeles, circa 1937.

It used to be that the downtown areas of major cities were where people would congregate to go on regular buying sprees and have their fill of social interaction. Retail tasks would need to be planned for and lists were made so that nothing would be left out—each trip made was usually coordinated and well thought out.

The downtown areas of major cities thrived on this constant influx of retail buying power. Whole industries and businesses grew around it—movie theaters, restaurants, and circuses, to name a few.

Photo credit: Public domain. B. Altman and Company department store in New York City, circa 1948.

Department store buildings were made so large so that they could accommodate the vast variety of different objects for sale, as well as the large number of prospective incoming shoppers.

Most of these large behemoths have ceased to exist, though Macy's Herald Square in New York City is still standing since 1901 (albeit some of the original space has been leased out to other companies).

It appears that these days, the large spaces for retail are its logistics spaces—non-public warehouses that hold items in a very organized and project-oriented way. Spatial Computing appears to be getting a major toehold not only in warehouse and packaging logistics, but also along the full arc of retail fulfillment, which includes the sampling of goods via three-dimensional visuals followed by the ordering of them—all done digitally.

Photo credit: Amazon. An Amazon logistics center in Madrid.

The future of retail belongs to those companies that seamlessly and transparently offer Spatial Computing systems that allow for frictionless retail fulfillment. When goods are received faster, something resembling joy could ensue.

Photo credit: Apple. The glass window design of the Apple Park building that is prescient of the AR glasses Apple had leaked will come out in 2023.

One company that is due to capitalize on this is clearly Apple, with its devoted loyal customer base. When Apple's AR glasses come out, as it is rumored they will in 2023, an "army" of people using their Spatial Computing technology will be ready to purchase retail goods seamlessly, using eye-gaze selection and voice commands. The days of going to a physical store are truly numbered.

Will Anything Remain the Same?

As we look at all the changes coming to retail in general, we see that Spatial Computing will bring major changes to the supply chains that feed goods to stores, to the stores themselves, to the experience of using the stores, either in physical locations or at home, and to the distribution networks of trucks and robots that will bring goods to our homes and offices. There are lots of changes ahead—ones that are keeping many an executive up at night. These changes might seem fairly mundane compared to what's potentially coming to healthcare—all hitting in the 2020s. Will anything be the same again? "No" is our prediction, as you'll discover in the next chapter.

7
Vision Five – Virtual Healthcare

As we imagine a world where every doctor, nurse, administrator, and patient wears Spatial Computing glasses, we see five changes: the medical system becomes more efficient, existing patient care gets better, those who provide care are better trained, the patient experience improves, and healthcare becomes more predictive and personalized.

Spatial Computing will eventually redefine what we think of as healthcare and the medical system that delivers it. Every part of it will be touched, from the surgery rooms to the doctors who save your life. They already are starting to use devices like Microsoft HoloLens 2 to prepare for or perform surgeries.

Nurses will be assisted by robots bringing them drugs, needles, or other supplies without forcing them to walk down the hall to gather them. All of this directed by glasses flashing visuals about their job process and their patients into their eyes, and audio into their ears providing information and commands.

Patients will see their waiting room experience transformed thanks to VR, not to mention they might not need to wait at all, thanks to new kinds of telemedicine that they will be able to get from home or work. What we think of as healthcare might turn into a new kind of virtual coach, that is, a virtual being that helps you make better choices in life, for example, directing workouts so you meet your fitness and health goals.

Administrators will finally see efficiencies from the move to electronic health records, and will see nice returns on investment on systems to actually change patient behavior, getting them to exercise more and eat better, thanks to games on their glasses.

We will have a new understanding of healthcare, one that's more predictive and can anticipate your healthcare needs based upon your current lifestyle, all thanks to devices you wear, much like today's Fitbits and Apple Watches. This will bring us a world where healthcare is more readily available, much improved, and cheaper to afford. This will be a particularly radical change for the world's poor, in contrast to their current experience of healthcare.

Although this pipe dream is probably a decade away, our discussions with doctors, administrators, and others demonstrate that R&D is already well underway to bring about a new kind of healthcare, which will bring us new techniques that early studies show is even changing our ideas of how pain will be dealt with. Someday soon, instead of being prescribed opioids or other types of prescription drugs to tamp down your pain, researchers see a new kind of practitioner prescribing that you use VR instead. This may seem an odd way to relieve pain, but we'll describe how promising results are already being observed for pain relief in the *Brain Tricks/Virtual Medicine* section of this chapter.

Even better, we are about to head into a world where the healthcare system isn't reactive like it is today. Today, we mostly go to a doctor because we aren't feeling well, or to get annual checkups, which mostly include blood workups, weight and blood pressure checks, and some other simple procedures to look over your body. Worse, hospitals primarily deal with patients who are having heart attacks or other health failures. Many of the researchers we talked with see a new, predictive healthcare that will see problems in advance of a major issue, or even work to get you to live in a more healthy way, which would save many dollars and lead to better outcomes for everyone.

If your glasses say "hey, you need to get to a hospital now," that is a far better situation than having to be brought to a hospital by an ambulance later, which costs thousands of dollars and may already be too late. Even in a situation where you might need surgery, the doctors will have your heartbeat and other data from the past few weeks available, allowing them to see much more of your history than if they were to hook you up to monitoring equipment and have to guess what's been going on based on a far smaller amount of data.

With all of these highly significant applications for Spatial Computing in healthcare, we will now give you a sweeping overview of what changes we can expect to see in the coming years, based upon our research and discussions with medical professionals.

The Virtualist

Dr. Sherylle Calder in South Africa is, in our eyes, the prototype of a new kind of medical practitioner who works with Spatial Computing technologies to improve her patient's lives—one that Dr. Brennan Spiegel, director of health research at Cedars-Sinai, calls "the Virtualist." Spiegel cofounded a conference that deals with the changes coming to healthcare thanks to Spatial Computing and is writing a book of his own where he details this new kind of specialty.

Dr. Calder is an eye doctor who has found a new way to improve her patients' lives by manipulating their eyes—all with digital patterns on screens. She is the first sports scientist to be awarded a doctorate in visual motor performance and works with professional athletes, and now everyday people, thanks to the company she started: EyeGym.com. The aim of her product is to improve her patients' eyes and the part of the human brain that deals with visual input from them. She does her work with patients completely on digital screens and has had remarkable results. The owner of the South African cycling team told us that she took its worst rider, in terms of falls per race, and, after spending a few minutes a day with Calder's system, the rider went from the worst to best within a few months. Her digital system fixed a flaw in his brain that caused him to fall during races. While not purely "spatial," we believe her system demonstrates how computing can be used to heal the human brain and we will see applications like this greatly expanded as more people wear computing on their eyes.

She explained that more than 30 percent of our brains have to do with visual processing and that she found ways to identify flaws in that system and "exercise them" with patterns and colors on screens. She's the first doctor we saw using a completely digital approach to medicine, which is why we see her work as being groundbreaking. Working with the 2003 England Rugby World Cup team, her system brought huge changes. They ended up winning that year in the final against Australia. She also told us she worked with Ernie Els during a low period of his golf career, and her work helped him to win a major within six months.

Her story of finding ways to improve human brains with digital screens was verified in our discussions with many doctors who are doing the same to find ways to provide relief to those who suffer from depression, pain, autism, dementia, PTSD, and other maladies, and we see her and her work as a prototype of this new kind of specialist.

She won't be alone—several doctors and medical researchers have told us. If you walk through a modern hospital, you will see dozens of specialists, from radiologists to pediatric surgeons. Dr. Spiegel says that to understand this new field that is in its beginnings, we have to see the Spatial Computing R&D being done in surgery rooms, waiting rooms, burn recovery centers, mental health clinics, and other places in the healthcare system.

Photo credit: Robert Scoble. Dr. Sherylle Calder, left, in her South African office, explaining the work she does to improve professional athletes' perception systems.

For instance, UCSF Benioff Children's Hospital uses VR to do patient consulting with children who have brain tumors, which improves the patient's experience. That kind of usage gets patients to relax. There, Dr. Kurtis Auguste, chief of the department of surgery at UCSF Benioff Children's Hospital Oakland, gives children and their parents a fly-through of their brains. He can zoom in on their tumors and the nerves and blood vessels surrounding them and explains whatever procedure he will use on them. This gives the patent much more detail than can be provided by a standard MRI or CT scan.

"This technology is unlike any visual platform I've ever experienced—it is an actual immersive experience," Auguste reports on the UCSF website. "I can use this to plan a surgery and determine the best roadmap to a target in a way I never could before." The system he uses was created by Surgical Theater, Ohio.

It also helps him see things that he would have missed with earlier technology. It's a win-win all the way around and that visualization pre-surgery is bringing us this new kind of "Virtualist" specialist. We will see if the term sticks, but the healthcare practitioners we talked to agree with him that VR and AR are showing up in many places inside hospitals and they can see a role for doctors and nurses who work only with virtual tools.

These "Virtualists" are the ones setting up 3D sensors and putting HoloLens and other wearable technology into surgery rooms, and the ones who are using VR to relieve pain in burn clinics and using VR and AR to treat phobias, phantom limb pain, eating disorders, and other things. These include surgeons like Dr. Shafi Ahmed, who uses a variety of devices to teach surgery and enable new kinds of surgery to be done.

Dr. Ahmed, who the press has anointed "the world's most-watched surgeon" due to his broadcasting of surgeries on YouTube and other social media, told us about his work and the work of others who are leading the way to democratize surgery and healthcare by making better education available to surgeons. He wears devices like HoloLens during surgery, which lets him share that with others, but he says the changes coming are far deeper.

Other places "the Virtualist" will see jobs is in training and putting new brain research into use, and looking for ways to get efficiencies out of the healthcare system as more Spatial Computing glasses, along with AI running it all, and robots, are brought into hospitals and labs.

Technology coming from companies like MediView, Dr. Ahmed says, will let surgeons actually plan for and perform surgery in whole new ways.

Fixing Humans – Surgery Preparation and Surgery

The crown jewel of many hospitals is its trauma center. Here, patients arrive with various injuries or illnesses, and many are quickly operated on in high-tech surgery rooms. Dozens of machines, with teams of doctors who run around working on saving lives, which is very similar to what you see on various TV shows like *Chicago Med*.

What they don't show you on TV is the preparation time that surgeons go through to prepare for complex procedures. That used to be done by calling other surgeons who might have dealt with a similar condition. That led to incomplete learning, and no way to practice a procedure over and over until the surgeon gets it right.

Today, surgeons like Dr. Shafi Ahmed are using VR to view the data coming in from MRIs and other scanning systems, planning out their complex moves, and then practicing them on 3D printed "virtual" organs with either VR or AR glasses before they get into the surgery room. In this way, they can call in other surgeons and ask for help learning a complex move that they might never have done before and they can practice it over and over until they get it right.

Then, when they move into the surgery room, new systems are showing them the scanned data wrapped right onto, and in some cases into, the patient's body. One system from MediView in Boston even works like a guidance missile system. It tells the surgeon if they have their cutting tool on the right tumor and at the right depth with a series of video and audio prompts that are showing up the lenses of a Microsoft HoloLens.

A company in Ohio, Surgical Theater, too, gives surgeons a very detailed view of, say, a patient's brain, and the surgeon can plan out a path to a tumor, or a group of cells causing epileptic seizures, and then show the plan to the patient and their family.

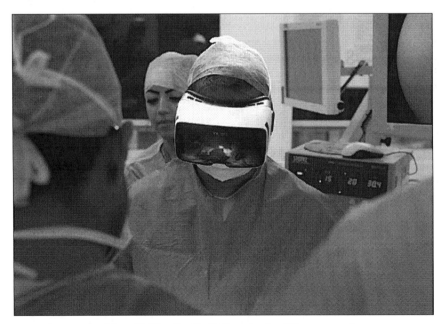

Photo credit: Edward Miller. Dr. Shafi Ahmed using VR to prepare for surgery.

In addition, using VR for surgery preparation and during the surgery itself, Dr. Ahmed has made a name for himself by using VR to train other surgeons. "When I train, what other surgeons need to know very quickly is depth perception," he says, while extolling its benefits for showing many other budding surgeons how to do a new procedure. Getting a cutting tool into the right place inside the human body often takes great skill and that learning used to be passed along surgeon to surgeon. "This takes years and years of experience. What Spatial Computing allows us to do is see the depth." This changes how the medical system can share techniques and the benefits go way beyond surgery. As this technology comes down in cost, you'll see Spatial Computing surgery spread throughout the hospital system. Why? Dr. Ahmed says that the secret sauce is that VR can improve retention of learning by 80 percent.

Dr. Daniel Kraft, who is the founder and chair of exponential medicine at Singularity University, tells of how he uses tools like OssoVR to train other doctors (he has a long list of accomplishments and was the first to implement a text-paging system at Stanford University's hospital). He uses it along with Precision OS, Surgical Theater, and FundamentalVR. Surgical Theater lets him plan surgeries. Precision OS and FundamentalVR let him practice it. Osso lets him teach it to others. Currently, a small but growing raft of companies, including Boston Scientific, EchoPixel, and Medivis, provide similar capabilities for the planning of different kinds of surgeries.

Further, there is at least one company that goes way beyond visualization, collaboration, or simulation—to actually helping the surgeon do the surgery itself: MediView.

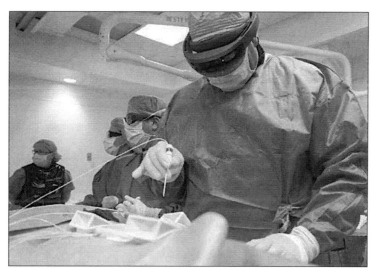

Photo credit: Cleveland Clinic. Dr. Charles Martin, III, Head of Interventional Oncology at Cleveland Clinic, uses a Microsoft HoloLens to overlay AR images on a patient during surgery.

MediView's technology is like a missile guidance system for surgeons. It joins data from MRIs and ultrasounds and overlays that in three dimensions on a patient's body to show where a cancer tumor is. Then it even guides the surgeon's cutting tools toward the tumor and tells them when they are in the right place to cut it out. This technology will even save the life of the surgeon. MediView's founder told us he lost a partner to cancer caused by ionizing radiation used to locate tumors with older technology and that he knows of lots of surgeons who have gotten cancer from the older techniques, which is what drove him to find a better way to figure out how to visualize tumors on the surgery table. MediView has already passed through one patient trial of five patients and is about to go through another one.

Additionally, MediView is focusing its AR surgery system for use on soft tissue surgery, which is a much harder thing to accomplish than, let's say, a surgery that focuses on the bone that tends to stay stable and stationary during a procedure. Another company, SentiAR, uses AR to overlay 3D images of a patient's actual anatomy during interventional procedures that deal with the treatment and analysis of cardiac arrhythmias, so it does deal with soft tissue procedures, but its system is currently utilized for this narrow use only.

Philips' Azurion Platform concept utilizing the HoloLens 2 was announced in February 2019; its focus is on using AR for image-guided minimally invasive therapies, rather than for major surgeries. MediView and SentiAR, as well as HoloSurgical, are developing their platforms for eventual FDA submission. Philips' Azurion Platform is still in the concept stage.

The first related system that was cleared by the FDA was the Novarad OpenSight Augmented Reality system in October 2018; however, the system is for pre-surgical planning use only.

Other companies besides HoloSurgical with its ARAI system, which have a Spatial Computing system that focuses on surgery on hard tissue such as bone, are Augmedix (xvision spine [SVS] system) and Scopis (Holographic Navigation Platform).

What is common among most of these company surgery systems is the use of the HoloLens AR headset. Most of these companies will have moved forward to use the new HoloLens 2 headset, announced in February 2019, by the time you read this book. The HoloLens 2 offers much better functionality in comparison to the first HoloLens, unlocking far more potential benefit for pre-surgery and in-surgery Spatial Computing systems.

The improved functionality has to do with an increased field of view, a more ergonomic and balanced design, direct and natural hand manipulation of 3D images, improved natural language speech processing, and direct access to the cloud and AI services from Microsoft.

The lesson here is that Spatial Computing is already radically changing surgery, and will soon do the same for the rest of the hospital—and eventually for the entire system. For both pre-surgery planning and in-surgery procedures, the aim of the use of Spatial Computing is to reduce operating time, cost, and complications caused by suboptimal surgical execution. Let's look at the use of Spatial Computing another way—how it actually works with patient's brains to open up new treatment methods.

Brain Tricks/Virtual Medicine

Pain management is one piece of the healthcare puzzle in which Spatial Computing, particularly VR, is showing its most promising results. At the University of Washington, researchers working with Tom Furness and burn victims found that playing in a virtual snowfield was better at managing pain than morphine. You can read their studies at: http://www.vrpain.com. This and other discoveries, which we call performing "brain tricks," have deep implications for healthcare and show us a path to a new kind of healthcare that many can experience outside of a hospital, saving time and stress for patients, saving money for the healthcare system, and solving problems better than the drugs of old.

These new anti-pain brain tricks work through multiple methods—the two most understood are distraction and getting the brain to shut down the nerves delivering pain signals to the brain. Putting light into your eyes is a powerful thing, it turns out. "It is a photonic trojan horse," Dr. Brennan Spiegel says. "If the brain is anxious or upset, it wants to keep track of pain. If the brain is calm and relaxed, it doesn't have time to feel pain."

Dr. Spiegel explained to us how it works. Pain, say, from your finger touching a hot stove, travels from nerves in your finger along nerve highways up your arm and into your brain, passing through several "gates" or "handoffs from nerve to nerve." When those signals arrive at the brain, he says, it is possible to either distract yourself from those signals, or you can go further and get your brain to actually close the gates between your finger and brain so pain signals never arrive at all. A snowfield app mostly works through distraction.

When you are having fun throwing snowballs your brain's attention centers are more focused on the fun than the pain, but Spiegel is seeing several other pain-blocking effects. He says VR actually effects how serotonin gets used by your brain and nervous system.

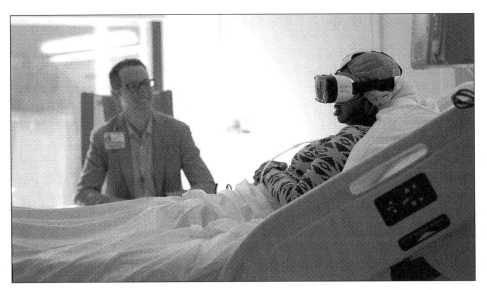

Photo credit: Cedars-Sinai. Dr. Brennan Spiegel attends to a patient using VR to diminish pain.

People who play Beat Saber, a VR game, note that they go into an enjoyable "flow state" after playing for a while. That effect people experience, Dr. Spiegel says, is deeper than just distraction, and that VR works just like opioids: they block those nerve handoffs.

"Many people are not in pain even after the headset gets removed," Dr. Spiegel says. "That suggests there are other mechanisms than mere distraction at work. Engaging people in a flow-engaging activity is the goal." So, don't be surprised if your doctor prescribes a VR headset soon and asks you to play some games similar to Beat Saber!

This set of discoveries has a deep impact on not just the opioid crisis hitting America, but it provides hope that a whole range of mental issues can be fixed simply by having patients put on a headset.

"We are all searching for safer analgesics," Dr. Spiegel says, explaining that in the United States there are lots of research dollars chasing new ways to deal with pain that don't require using opioids, which are killing close to 40,000 people per year in the United States alone. Some companies that have VR apps that address pain management include AppliedVR, Psious, and Firsthand Technology.

Dr. Spiegel and other researchers say that their understanding of these brain tricks are far enough along that they are starting to ask questions about how to use VR with more patients. How do we pay for it? How do you keep the equipment clean? How do we offer a VR consultation service? How often do you need to use VR to treat various conditions? Who owns the equipment and software to make it happen? The field of VR pain management is developing into a standalone discipline. "VR works. This tool cuts across all of healthcare."

An example of another area where VR is being used in healthcare is dementia. With dementia, the "tape recorder" of the mind has stopped working. Dr. Spiegel says "They have lost their sense of self. That is disorienting and depressing." Often, dementia patients develop severe depression. Here, a different brain trick is used called reminiscent therapy. He explained that often he deals with patients that are barely coherent and are extremely depressed by their fractured mind. Pulling out a photo of a childhood memory reminds them of something before their memories stopped working, which makes it far easier to work with the patient to get them to further fix their brains. He says this process works better in VR, because you can quickly immerse a patient in childhood memories.

Another area for VR's use in healthcare is schizophrenia. Schizophrenics are hearing voices in their head. Most of us hear voices, but we understand them to be ourselves. People with this condition hear other voices that have them living in their own form of VR, Dr. Spiegel explains. "[These voices] aren't real. Ironically it takes Virtual Reality to access their virtual reality." Researchers have found that using avatar therapy helps to climb into the mind of the schizophrenic. Patients are shown recreated faces and minds so they can see their demon—and maybe turn that voice into something that helps them out. Dr. Spiegel says that they are seeing statistically significant results that are much better than the drug therapies currently being used.

Another place where the relaxation technique works is during childbirth. Mothers who wear VR see not just a sizeable decrease in pain but perceive that time moves faster, similar to how a Beat Saber player sometimes loses track of time. Tripp VR, a meditation app, is another good example of using the brain to enhance cognitive flow.

Relaxation isn't the only brain trick that comes with VR, though. We are seeing other researchers unlocking brain tricks that come to play with stroke victims, PTSD sufferers, and eating disorders.

In a visit to Stanford University's Virtual Human Interaction Lab, we saw how researchers are using brain tricks to help stroke victims and other people who have lost control of one of their limbs. Jeremy Bailenson and others are doing a ton of research on other VR effects, from environmental education to studying whether it can be used to increase empathy for others.

Inspired by Bailenson, Dr. Sook-Lei Liew, who is director of the Neural Plasticity and Neurorehabilitation Laboratory, also uses avatars to help stroke victims. They have worked for years on a study where they give stroke survivors who can't, say, move a limb, a virtual avatar controlled via EEG, or electroencephalography signals gathered by sensors placed on a patient's skin. She's found that can help their brains and nervous system to rewire, which would eventually lead them to moving that limb again.

In addition, Bailenson told us about studies that use VR to "mirror" a healthy limb onto their other limb and, often, patients regain some movement and control of the limb that previously didn't move. VR actually can cause new brain pathways to be built, it appears to researchers. This research is exciting for all sorts of other conditions, like PTSD or autism.

"It's very easy to fool the brain," says Dr. Albert "Skip" Rizzo, while explaining his work into using VR exposure therapy to treat PTSD. Dr. Rizzo is the director of Medical Virtual Reality at the Institute for Creative Technologies (ICT) at the University of Southern California. He takes patients into a traumatic event, like a simulation of a battle for a veteran who is suffering. He and clinicians can use that visual to trigger them to talk about what happened, and then they can treat it. He reports that VR brings remarkable results.

Photo credit: University of Southern California Institute for Creative Technologies (ICT).
Dr. Skip Rizzo serves as the project leader for ICT's Bravemind project, which incorporates VR as a part of exposure therapy to provide relief for post-traumatic stress. A still from the VR experience is above.

Dr. Rizzo started the Medical Virtual Reality lab in 1995 after getting excited in the early 1990s about an experience that opened his eyes to the possibility of game-based rehabilitation. He found that a 22-year-old male who had injuries to his frontal lobe had improvements in cognition after playing video games.

VR could also help with autism. In autism, the cells that deal with the ability to correctly discern emotions, for instance, haven't formed properly. Spatial Computing can solve that problem with brute-force methods. Someone with autism might have glasses on in the future that simply say: "Your friend is sad." However, studies are underway to see if some of VR's brain tricks can be used to actually get patients to build new pathways to understand when their friend is sad even without being told via glasses. Dr. Rizzo is also working on reducing anxiety in people who have autism, with a combination of VR experiences and video. The primary scenario that is being used is that of a job interview, where patients can practice going through an interview over and over until they are confident and relaxed.

Another brain trick is feeding it some education or changing the perspective of a patient. This works particularly well on eating disorders. A little education in VR goes further than other approaches, several researchers told us. How can they get patients to eat less salt that would lower their blood pressure? It turns out that by showing patients how their body works in VR and what happens as salt begins to destroy their organs, it got a study group to eat less salt and saw an average seven-point drop in their blood pressure, Dr. Spiegel reported to us. Other studies are seeing an effect if food sizes are virtually made bigger or smaller. If your glasses make those Oreos look bigger, you will eat fewer of them.

Another method of dealing with eating disorders includes getting patients to see their bodies differently. Often when presented with someone who isn't eating enough, it is because the patient sees themselves as too fat, as what happens with someone who suffers from anorexia nervosa. Researchers are using one of the magic powers of VR: embodiment, which is where you can become something you aren't, either another person or, as Chris Milk, founder of Within, showed us, various animals. In the case of eating disorders, they take patients into the bodies of normal people so they can see that they are sensing their bodies improperly. This remaps their brains so that they no longer feel fat or skinny, and start eating better.

These brain tricks work with a whole range of conditions, Dr. Rizzo reports, from Parkinson's, where VR's brain-relaxing conditions help, to women trying to avoid birth pain. Dr. Melissa Wong, of Cedars-Sinai, uses them when performing difficult procedures on pregnant women. She showed attendees at the Virtual Medical conference how one procedure had women screaming in pain, but with VR on, the patient never winced and was more bothered by having the game she was playing being interrupted.

Additionally, researchers like Bailenson and doctors like Rizzo say they are seeing amazing results while the patient goes through rehabilitation too. VR gets these patients to not only move more, say stretching an arm that had been operated on, but do it more often. Many of these exercises are to be done at home and researchers say they are seeing better results because exercising in VR is more fun; something many VR users are discovering after they buy a VR headset and start playing games that require physical activity. Robert Long, a VR fan, reported on Reddit that he lost about 200 pounds mostly by playing Beat Saber.

Dr. Diane Gromala does chronic pain research at Simon Fraser University and found that adding in biofeedback loops improves the results even more. By changing the scene you are in, or the avatar you are interacting with in relation to, say, your heart rate, it lets you reduce pain levels to an even greater extent.

We tell you all these stories (which are only a small fraction of the good news being reported) to show that a new kind of healthcare is coming: one that uses Spatial Computing technology to solve a wide range of health issues. The techniques being discovered here could be delivered to patients as they sit at home, or even as they move around the world. How? We see a new kind of virtual coach that will help deliver this new "virtual" healthcare to you. Add that to the "Virtualist," who works inside the healthcare system, and you'll see healthcare administrators get excited as they see costs come down and fewer patients experiencing negative results due to addiction to opioids. This can only be a good thing.

We've seen how VR can be used to fix problems with the brain; now let's look at how it could be combined with other applications to give us a "check engine light" to further improve our health and healthcare.

Photo credit: Black Box VR. A new kind of gym you use while wearing a VR headset.

The Virtual Coach and the "Check Engine Light"

When Facebook founder and CEO Mark Zuckerberg goes running, he has a real coach. You see this coach running next to him in photos he uploads to Facebook. That coach pushes him and keeps him company on runs, and probably doubles as a security guard. Most of us can't afford such a coach, which is why so many of us join fitness classes at gyms. Now, however, a new virtual coach has emerged on our watches that cajoles us into doing more steps or performing mental health tasks like remembering to take a few deep breaths once in a while. You see that virtual coach in today's Apple Watch, for instance, as a circle of lines. It tells you that you haven't taken enough steps today, or it's time to take a break from sitting in front of a monitor.

When we've run with a real coach, that coach often rode a bike next to us, pushing us on runs, or getting us to do interval training up hills. A virtual coach could easily take over those roles and more.

This new virtual coach will appear in your Spatial Computing glasses. A virtual being, like Magic Leap's Mica, might run along with you, pushing you to keep ahead of last week's run pace. As of 2019, Mica only sits at a table and plays puzzle games with you—but you can expect virtual beings to do a lot more over the next decade. This coach will have access to all your data, or at least the data you want it to have access to. It will have access to your location, gait, and heart data at minimum, and will know whether it is pushing you hard enough to reach your fitness goals.

It will go a lot further, though, in motivating you to do better. On YouTube, you can see a video of 6,000 people running across Central Park in New York to catch a Pokémon. That wasn't a very compelling visual when users of Pokémon Go stared into their mobile phones, but it shows how computing visuals can be used to motivate people to exercise. With glasses that bring us AR, your healthcare provider will go a lot further we predict—helping you choose the right foods, smoke fewer cigarettes, exercise both body and mind, and more. This leads to lower healthcare costs, healthier lives, and more information for the coach itself to have a chat with your doctor about, if you allow such a thing (and you probably will, given the benefits). The games it will play will make that early Pokémon Go game seem quaint soon. Already we know of people who have lost many pounds playing Beat Saber in VR. Imagine games that can improve your eyes, like the one that Calder has built, or exercise your body, or get you to eat better. These are just a few examples of how healthcare is about to get more intimate, personalized, and in many ways "built in" to daily life.

Research already shows that if food portions are made bigger in either VR or AR, you will eat less of that item (the research study, funded by the University of Tokyo, used a variety of foods in its tests to show participants different serving sizes). Imagine a virtual coach who assisted you with your food goals this way with you all day long.

Dr. Ahmed explains that this kind of social reengineering is bound to happen and that patients will be persuaded to take the journey into a preventative world. "Your glasses will look at your food and the Augmented Reality will show you calories," he told us.

"Getting people to change is the Holy Grail," Dr. Spiegel says. "Human beings understand concepts better when presented with more direct evidence, such as that which is visual and made more accessible by being three-dimensional." Translation: a virtual coach could get you to learn and change faster, which will lead to massive changes ahead for everyone in the healthcare business, and more fun for patients as their virtual coaches entertain them while exercising or eating out.

These kinds of virtual coaches might not look like anything human, either. If you visit a new gym in San Francisco or Boise, Idaho, run by Black Box VR, they have weight-lifting machines that you use while you are participating in a VR experience. If you pull harder on the cable coming out of the machine, the visual in the headset plays a new kind of game with you. As you work out, the machine increases the resistance as you "level up." We tried it and it uses all the pain distraction techniques that the University of Washington used with burn victims. While exercising we didn't notice how hard we were working while playing a variety of games, for instance. Most of the games are things like punching out a monster. Once out, though, we were sore from the day's workout. On return visits, it remembers us and pushes us to go further in its game. They promise "every minute is optimized through Artificial Intelligence and adaptive workout prescription." They use visuals where your brain perceives an actual danger—virtually—and get you to work out harder to achieve your goals. The AI even watches your workout so it knows not to push you past injury levels.

The age of virtual coaching and preventative healthcare. To enable all this, we need a ton of data to drive the future of personalized, predictive healthcare.

Data, Data, Everywhere

In 2020, as we still write this book, there still are many hospitals around the world that haven't digitized their patients' health data yet, and even those that have are struggling to make these **EMR** (**Electronic Medical Records**) systems useful or the data in them clean and understandable.

Doctors aren't famous for using clear, consistent language, and they often use tons of shorthand and very specialized terms that can contain lots of typos upon entry. We heard tons of stories about problems when we attended Ray Wong's influential Healthcare Transformation Summit for CIOs of healthcare organizations about how medical systems are struggling to not just get the data in these systems into a useful form, but how to get doctors back to focusing on care rather than inputting a ton of data that doesn't lead to better healthcare for patients.

We see Spatial Computing glasses as a potential answer. It is in the supporting technologies, whether to listen to doctors' and nurses' intent and language, support new kinds of Computer Vision that can look at various things and come up with better data inputs, or connect all the systems in a hospital to talk to your health record. The pressure to improve the efficiency of the system so more people can afford good healthcare will push administrators to continue investing in new technologies like the ones we've laid out.

How many hospitals still have a ton of machines that don't talk to each other in a patient's care room? Most, if not all. All of these problems give skeptics the encouragement to say it's impossible to get to the world we are laying out, and other skeptics are worried the surveillance systems that are under development will lead to dystopian outcomes (your glasses could soon see that you eat too many donuts and could increase your insurance costs accordingly, they worry, and their fears get worse from there). We will take on these fears, and the balance between utility and dystopian control, elsewhere in the book.

Many parts of the healthcare system will be slow to upgrade, like changing a simple drug dispensing machine that might take years to transition to a new always-connected digital model. Connecting machines to a cloud is necessary for the complete overhaul of the medical system, but Douglas Purdy, who used to run Facebook's Platform, gave us another place to look at just how deeply data and Machine Learning could affect healthcare and all of our lives. He did this by showing us that data is already changing in how we can provide healthcare in ways that were hard to dream about only a few years ago.

Purdy built an AI that monitors heart rate variability (which is the signal in between the electrical pulses that pump your heart) and told us that, if you train a computer correctly, it can detect patterns in the information between your heartbeats that can tell whether or not you are getting enough sleep, or taking care of your mental health, among other things.

He explained that the heart doesn't actually pump all at once, which is why there's so much untapped data here. What actually happens is an electrical signal starts in one nerve pathway in your heart, causing the muscles to contract, and that signal passes literally cell by cell through your heart.

Humans simply can't watch this—the same way humans had a hard time telling whether a horse's feet totally left the ground until motion pictures came along. But now, our sensors are getting so good at recording the heart that new patterns are being found in between the heartbeats. AI can see those patterns where humans couldn't.

Purdy is using that AI inside an app called Zendō (`http://zendo.tools/`) to watch your health and tell you if you are meditating right, or enough, among other things that are on the way, including sleep, diet, and more. Dr. Spiegel and others validated that heart rate variability is something new, and an exciting place to use AI that has only recently became usable for consumers because of the widespread use of watches that have heart-beat sensors built into them, and said there's exciting new research that is underway now that we have powerful computing tools to analyze patient data like that in real time. Even Apple now has a "Research" app that you can download and use to add your own experience—data, essentially—to a variety of medical studies underway. This, along with other data, is doing something new, and could lead to the "check engine light" kind of functionality discussed earlier. Will it lead to your glasses telling you in advance that you will soon have a heart attack? That's a bit presumptuous for us to say today, but we can see how data will lead to that kind of system.

Dr. Brandon Birckhead put it clearest in our discussions: "A new era of precision VR therapy is here," he says. "We will be able to tailor things precisely down to the person."

That kind of hyper-personalized, intimate healthcare is possible thanks to wearable devices like Spatial Computing glasses along with watches and other devices, like a pacemaker that Boston Scientific developed that listens to your heart directly, leading to benefits. Said pacemaker can save your life if you aren't following doctor's orders to get enough exercise, or are eating unhealthily, for instance.

Dr. Rizzo told us he is seeing in his studies with PTSD sufferers that many actually share more when they think they are talking to a computer. "They self-disclose more information," he says. "Contrary to popular belief, people are less concerned about shame [when talking to a computer]," he told us. They worry less about consequences. Even spoken words contain data that can be quite revealing. At SRI International, researchers showed us an AI-driven system where you read a few hundred words from a card, and it identifies whether you are suicidal or not. Stress in your voice can't easily be detected by other people, but a computer can see patterns most will miss.

Dr. Daniel Kraft explained the role of data best, and it probably comes from his work in the military; he was a flight surgeon, but did a bunch of other work, including conducting research on aerospace medicine that was published by NASA. He says all this data will lead to a new kind of situational awareness machine that will watch all parts of the healthcare industry.

Today, he says, you are in the dark with a lot of healthcare. From staffing, to triage, to people pushing food trays around, inefficiencies abound within the hospital infrastructure. Worse, this could be compounded by poor communication, and in a critical environment such as healthcare, this can lead to tragic results in the worst-case scenario. He sees a lot of misaligned incentives, which lead to bad outcomes, but this "situational awareness machine" could exponentially learn as doctors, nurses, administrators, hospital staff, and patients themselves teach it new things and correct old, bad patterns of work.

Dr. Rizzo sees that all this will build a new virtual environment that will help us in every step of our healthcare journey. He says: "The future of this is a companion, buddy, or support agent. Medicine is always about dose/response, and if you can quantify those things better, without compromising patient privacy, we are going to find relationships, or causal things, that go beyond our brains' ability to read journal articles and learn with traditional techniques."

Precision and Personalization

Data collection will only increase as time goes on. Our modern-day society is obsessed with precision and personalization. All of this data collection combined with AI and Spatial Computing is bound to produce healthcare that saves many more lives than it does now.

Spatial Computing brings many changes to not just the healthcare system of labs and hospitals, but heralds a new move to very personalized medicine that can both help you avoid the healthcare system longer, but, once you are in it, can watch your care, and even deliver new care through AR or VR headsets that was impossible only a few years ago.

This brings us to the end of our journey through healthcare and the changes that are expected to come. In the next chapter, we'll take a look into a very different world—banking and trading—and how Spatial Computing is also making waves in this sector.

8
Vision Six – Virtual Trading and Banking

The future uses for Spatial Computing in the financial industry are vast. There is very little Spatial Computing currently being utilized in that field, however. The main reasons for this include the general conservatism of the industry and the number of regulations that would need to be addressed relating to customer interfaces and trading. We believe that the great benefits that Spatial Computing could bring to the financial industry will enable the hearty adoption of its technologies in the future.

Since almost all of the views for the use of Spatial Computing in the financial industry included here are forward-facing, this chapter will be much shorter than the other six chapters we have written that address industry verticals. The functional areas we touch upon here include 3D data visualization, virtual trading, ATM security and facial payment machines, and virtual branch functionality and customer services. Let's start off by discussing 3D data visualization.

3D Data Visualization

One area where a start has been made is in data visualization. A company that has focused on using Virtual Reality as a medium to visually present data is a start-up called Virtualitics, based in Pasadena, California. Over the last year or so, it has added a demo using Augmented Reality as well. Many of the management team and employees went to Caltech; their understanding of data science is extremely good.

A major focus for the company has been to cater to financial clients that need to have complex data represented in a more visual way in order to simplify finding the possible solutions they are looking for. However, the software that Virtualitics has built is not specially built to handle certain problems or industry verticals—it is very open-ended.

Another company that had a 3D data visualization product, albeit at a very early stage, was a company called Looker. In 2019, Google announced it was acquiring Looker for $2.6 billion.

There are skeptics we have spoken with who are very enamored with the uses of Spatial Computing, but they do not see the usefulness of an open-ended 3D data visualization product. Since there are no companies that specialize in 3D data visualization products just for the financial industry, a big opportunity exists in this area. Virtual trading, that is, trading that would happen with a person using a VR or AR headset, cannot happen without these kinds of specialized 3D data visualizations. Any company, whether it be a bank, a hedge fund, an over-the-counter options and futures trading house, or any other financially-oriented company that wishes to do virtual trading, would need to have programs that have 3D data visualization capabilities integrated into them.

Currently, many kinds of trading that are not automated are accomplished only after a trader has looked at several sources of information and come to a decision. Most of the time, these traders have to view all the different kinds of information across many screens as simultaneously as possible. Due to this complexity, the rate of human error can be quite high. With the right kinds of 3D data visualization software capability, the numerous screens could be reduced to just one 3D representation, which would enable a trader to make a faster, more informed decision about a particular trade.

Photo credit: Bloomberg. A typical hedge fund trader's desk.

At this time, traders tend to use 19-inch monitors, in multiples of 4, 8, or 12. What is interesting is that there are still innovations being developed for traditional computer monitors. During CES 2020, Dell came out with a new 43-inch monitor aimed at traders that need to track multiple tickers or charts simultaneously.

However, with 3D data visualization software, multiple charts (literally, an almost limitless number of charts) could be viewed and manipulated in both Virtual and Augmented Reality. These could be placed side by side, tiled from top to bottom, tiled backward and forward in space, and in combinations of these at different angles in space.

Photo credit: Dell. Dell's new 43-inch monitor geared toward traders.

In addition to virtual trading, 3D data visualizations would also be useful in portfolio management since the intersection of many different kinds of information is often needed to make a decision there as well. Since much of what could be applied to portfolio management could be used for virtual trading, with even more specialized visualization being used there, we will focus on virtual trading in our next section.

Virtual Trading

There has been much talk among tech and financial insiders about how Spatial Computing, especially Augmented Reality, could be applied to virtual trading, but very few tests so far have been done yet with actual traders. Both Bloomberg and Reuters experimented early on with initial mock-ups for trading desk software using Google Glass and then, more recently, using a HoloLens headset. We've heard that a mid-2018 test that Reuters ran using a HoloLens on 30 or so traders was not successful, because they found the headset to be too clumsy and not wearable enough.

The HoloLens 2 could very well start to solve this issue, as well as future iterations and other headsets—such as those that Apple has leaked—that will be coming out in 2022 and 2023.

In 2016, the consultancy 8ninths (now a part of the Valence Group) was engaged by Citibank to provide a proof-of-concept mock-up for a trader's workstation that utilizes AR and a HoloLens headset. This proof-of-concept became very popular, with many believing that an actual software app had been developed, but it had not been.

Visual aspects of 8ninths' proof-of-concept mock-up include 3D bubbles of individual trading vehicles (these could be stocks, options, and so on) of a given market. The idea is that when a trader clicks on a bubble, they will be able to access its up-to-date trading information. 3D tabs appear to be able to be tiled in space and could provide all kinds of other information, including news. There is also a space for 3D data visualizations.

What is not evident in the mock-up is how a trader would be able to execute a trade using AR software and an AR headset. It also appears to us that there could be consolidation among the kinds of information that an individual 3D object could offer. For example, clicking on a 3D bubble could present both trading information and access to news, as well as other relevant information, such as access to a list of a financial vehicle's competitors that could be clicked on from there.

What does work very nicely is the idea that the size of a 3D bubble, as well as the color of it, could indicate different discrete features, such as the relative market size and industry vertical, respectively. Other novel ways could be integrated into the user interface so that many other types of features could be easily visually evident.

Photo credit: 8ninths and the Valence Group. This is a proof-of-concept workstation mock-up of what a trader could potentially access using AR and a HoloLens headset; developed for Citibank.

Besides wearing an AR headset, another possibility (though a little further in the future, by three-to-four years) is wearing smart contact lenses made by Mojo Vision, called Mojo Lens. Mojo Vision, a Saratoga, California start-up with dozens of PhDs and engineers, came out of stealth mode in January 2020. Even though the Mojo Lens is initially being marketed for healthcare purposes, many other kinds of use cases are very evident. The company calls what you are able to do with their lenses "invisible computing." Mojo Lens would be able to make trading even more efficient—no need put on and take off or swivel up a headset, and eye-tracking and voice capabilities would make information gathering and trade fulfillment faster and more intuitive.

Using an AR headset or Mojo Lens and specialized software, all kinds of trading support could be accomplished, which includes equities, options, futures, REITs, commodities, and any other tradable financial instrument. Where the most benefit would be gotten, though, are those instruments that require the analysis of many different streams of information in a fast manner before making a decision to trade. These include options and futures, both at times when decisions have to be made as to whether or not to purchase the instrument and also as to whether or not to "roll forward," that is, to extend the expiration or maturity of an option or futures contract by closing the initial contract and opening a new longer-term contract for the same underlying asset at the then-current market price.

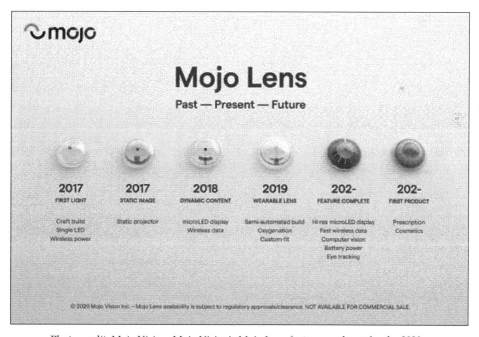

Photo credit: Mojo Vision. Mojo Vision's Mojo Lens feature roadmap for the 2020s.

The amount of information needed for these decisions would normally necessitate the use of many monitors. The stress of having to consult these monitors and then have to make very quick decisions as to what to do has worn down many traders. Before reaching trader burnout, traders can make very costly errors. Using an AR headset or Mojo Lens with software that supplies 3D data visualizations with plotted relevant points based on criteria input previously could cut down on burnout and errors. News and information could be pulled up alongside the 3D charts, with elements there added as criteria for the charts themselves. Actual trade order execution could also be achieved.

Some delay in using AR headsets and/or Mojo Lens and specialized software for information and decision-making, as well as trade execution, will come from financial regulatory authorities. Getting their "OK" will take time, because of the potential risks involved. If information from Reuters, Bloomberg, or any other company that provides financial quotes and news is not updated in exactly the same timely manner in the new software as it is in existing systems, then the new system will not be reliable. And if trade execution lags by even a millisecond compared to existing systems, there would be a major issue. The new software would have to match with existing systems when running tests; it would have to match at all times in every instance.

Having said this, there is no technical reason why systems using AR headsets and Mojo Lens would not be able to match existing systems' reliability. We believe that the future of trading is one that relies on Spatial Computing.

Management from the New York Stock Exchange, Nasdaq, and the hedge fund Bridgewater Associates expressed interest in our book but declined to comment. We know of at least one very large global financial services firm that has a great interest in Spatial Computing and has started developing technology for it, but we have been asked to keep it confidential.

Different aspects of Spatial Computing, including Computer Vision and associated AI, make the next section we are focusing on in this chapter possible.

ATM Security and Facial Payment Machines

It is now commonplace to unlock smartphones and computers using fingerprint and/or facial recognition. In some countries outside of the US, such as China and Spain, facial recognition has already been implemented for ATM security.

When we spoke with Brett King, the author and founder of the banking service company Moven, he became especially animated when talking to us about the developments happening in China. In China, facial recognition is even being used to pay for vending machine items. A TikTok video from August 2019 shows a woman doing just that. Chinese technology expert Matthew Brennan has reported that he found another TikTok video that shows that non-Chinese people are blocked from using that facial recognition payment system, presumably because they don't have IDs issued by mainland China.

Photo credit: TikTok. A still from a video uploaded to TikTok that shows a woman paying for a vending machine item using facial recognition.

In 2015, China Merchants Bank launched an ATM that uses facial recognition, eliminating the need for the use of cards. It was the first time that this had been made available for public use. The company claimed that the system would be able to distinguish between twins since several parts of a face were used to create the profile used for facial recognition comparison.

Wearing glasses or different makeup was tested and shown to not make a difference.

Photo credit: China Merchants Bank. An advertisement for the China Merchants Bank that tells users they can now use their face to withdraw money.

Several banks in mainland China now, including the Agricultural Bank of China, China Construction Bank, and China Merchants Bank, have ATMs that use facial recognition as part of their security process.

Taiwanese bank E.Sun partnered with NEC to provide ATMs that use facial recognition; the ATMs were made available to the public in February 2019. In order to set up facial recognition cash withdrawals, customers must first insert their cards and then have a photo of their face taken with a camera installed within the ATM. They are then sent a one-time password to their mobile phone, which must be entered into the ATM within a minute, thus registering their facial image.

In Spain, in February 2019, CaixaBank started offering ATMs that use facial recognition. Trials conducted among customers before indicated that 70 percent would use it as an alternative to entering their personal identification code on a keyboard. Registration for the facial recognition system is conducted in a bank branch and takes a few minutes using tablets.

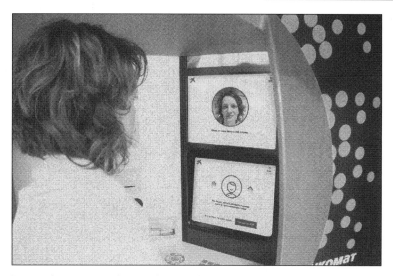

Photo credit: CaixaBank. A CaixaBank ATM that uses facial recognition instead of a card to access its system.

Outside of banking and ATMs, facial recognition could be used to pay for products. Again, in China, this has already been achieved with "facial payment machines."

Mobile payment in China is already the most advanced in the world, with customers making a purchase simply by posing in front of **point-of-sale** (**POS**) camera-equipped machines, after linking an image of their face to a digital payment system or bank account.

With devices in already over 300 cities, Alipay, the financial arm of e-commerce giant Alibaba, has been leading the facial payment machine business in China. Its facial recognition system comprises a screen that is as about as large as a mid-sized iPad, its AI software and Computer Vision components, and mobile payment software called Dragonfly. Alipay has earmarked $420 million over the next three years to roll out its technology.

Photo credit: Alipay. Pictured here are two Dragonfly facial recognition systems, which are currently actively used in China to make mobile payments.

Additionally, in August 2019, Tencent, which runs the WeChat app with 600 million users, announced its new facial payment system called WeChat Pay. Besides Alipay and Tencent, a growing number of start-ups in China are focusing on the facial payment machine business.

Facial recognition technologies can also be used to facilitate virtual banking, which is the topic of our next section.

Virtual Branch Functionality and Customer Service

Second Life, the virtual world, shut down all the virtual banks that had been built and operated there in 2008. Now, almost none of those banks were real financial institutions, but rather individuals who had deigned to create a bank out of thin air and put it in operation among the denizens who populated Second Life. However, Second Life virtual banks actually had deposits made with real money, and ultimately, they were shut down due to a lack of regulation.

Photo credit: Second Life. One of the virtual banks that operated in Second Life before they were all shut down.

Nowadays, talk of a virtual bank refers to a real financial institution that operates without any physical bank branches—basically, an all-digital bank. A good example of this is Simple, which calls itself a "neobank."

CaixaBank, in 2017, became the first bank in Spain to incorporate the iPhone X's Face ID technology so that customers could access their accounts solely using facial recognition on their mobile devices. Now several banks around the globe offer this capability.

With many of the major banks around the world closing down physical bank branches due to a lack of customer foot traffic, there has been some movement around the idea that all bank branch functions could be digitized, such as those associated with opening up a first bank account and mortgage paperwork.

Shaun Moore, cofounder and CEO of Trueface, a company working with top global banks on facial recognition uses, has commented that "We are seeing the financial services sector test face recognition as a part of multi-factor authentication for ATM withdrawals, mobile banking enrollment, and mobile account access and transactions. By implementing face recognition as the key step in multi-factor authentication, banks are able to mitigate their exposure to risk and fraud, saving themselves millions of dollars in the process."

Along with bank services being available post-facial recognition check are those available using voice technology, with USAA being the first to offer limited voice banking. Capital One offers banking by voice via Amazon's Alexa, on devices like the Amazon Echo and Amazon Dot. Capital One customers can check balances, review transactions, make payments, and more, using simple voice commands. Bank of America's "Erica" works similarly, but off of its own app, versus using Alexa-reliant apps.

What we envision is virtual banking that combines the use of facial recognition and voice commands and is accessed via an AR headset and also on Mojo Lens (though, features that would enable that to happen haven't been built yet, but are expected to be). This would also allow both virtual AI assistants and real bank customer service reps to be tapped by the customer on demand when needed.

Future Adoption

Even though the use of Spatial Computing technologies for virtual trading and banking is at such a nascent stage, we are confident that given the great benefits that Spatial Computing could bring, these technologies will be adopted on a large scale in the future.

Spatial computing has the potential to make trading and banking functions take less time and make more money—particular outcomes that are shared with other industry verticals, including manufacturing, retail, and healthcare.

In our next chapter, we turn to how Spatial Computing could be used for education and training across several industry verticals.

9
Vision Seven – Real-Time Learning

Bill Hill told us how he escaped poverty. He grew up in Scotland in dire circumstances and later went on to invent, at Microsoft, the font-smoothing technique that is used on all computers and phones today to make text easier to read. Back when he grew up, instead of playing on the streets like other kids, he went to the library. He told us that he read a new book every day and that helped him be "educated" about how the world works.

In the past few decades, the world has changed. Now, everyone has the world's libraries at their fingertips. You can talk to a Google Home device and ask it "what is the latest in breast cancer research?"

Google Home has an answer. Yet most people aren't "educated." The truth is our kids don't know how to be curious. Worse still, there are massive new distractions to absorb their attention. YouTube has more videos being uploaded every minute than most humans can watch in 100 years. Fortnight, Roblox, Minecraft, and many other games captivate children's imaginations far more easily than books can. This is hurting their ability to be curious while removing any chance of being bored, which is when creativity really comes out.

In this chapter, we'll talk about how Virtual and Augmented Reality is already being used in schools and corporate training. These technologies can provide the same kind of learning, or in fact better learning, many people tell us.

Experiential Digital Learning

Educators report to us that Spatial Computing technologies are already radically changing how our kids are learning and they see even more change coming. Virtual Reality can show kids things that only rich kids in the best schools could see before. When we've met educated people, part of what makes them educated is that they are well traveled, well cultured, and often know about diverse sets of music, theater, dance, along with a deeper specialization, whether retailing, farming, engineering, law, or medicine. Getting more kids to have the same opportunities is something that Virtual and Augmented Reality are showing is not only possible, but probable. In VR, you can remotely attend an amazing university class and "feel" like you are there. Already that's starting to happen in social software like AltspaceVR.

But remote learning is only a small piece of why education is about to radically change. Once learners have Spatial Computing devices on their faces, they will find that learning itself is radically different than what most of us experienced in classrooms. Experiential learning will not only reach kids who haven't had any boredom in their lives. To fill their free time, kids are now constantly on their iPads or iPhones, and many are spending hours a day in VR already.

Even if kids could find the books that would educate them, learning is slow, isn't personalized, and isn't often the best way to learn. Research done by James M. Clark and Allan Paivio shows that learning done in 3D in VR or AR is about twice as likely to be remembered as learning done using books or old-style videos.

Take a John Steinbeck novel, which talks about Monterey, California, that could be made much more "real" to today's kids by taking them there. The problem is that getting that kind of education is only open to the wealthiest. When we did a 9,000-mile-road trip in the summer of 2018 to take our kids to learn about America (and to do the same ourselves), that trip cost about $12,000 in hotels, electricity for our Tesla, and a month of our time. That simply is not an avenue open to most people.

But here comes Spatial Computing, with a new way to learn, which we call "experiential digital learning." Want to understand how something works? Or visit a historical site? You can do that in your new head-mounted displays, or even while looking at Augmented Reality on a mobile phone screen. Already we are seeing that kind of learning happening in classrooms around the world and, yet, a bigger shift is coming, one that will let many more kids excel and get the kind of education they will need to fix the huge problems that are appearing, such as climate change or social problems due to opioid addiction or terrorist attacks, not to mention new aspirational goals like doing more space exploration.

Photo credit: Robert Scoble. Third-grade students at Forest Hill Elementary School in Campbell, California use VR in their classroom. They were using Google's Tilt Brush inside Oculus Quest headsets to discover new ways to make art.

Jesse Schell, CEO of Schell Games and Principal Investigator of *HistoryMaker VR*, remarked in a statement: "The most recently published National Assessment of Educational Progress report (NAEP, 2014) cites only 18 percent and 23 percent of eighth-grade students performed at or above the proficient level in U.S. history and civics, respectively. What's more, students commonly report they find history to be boring and they lack motivation to understand or remember the content," Jesse went on. "The generous grant from the IES coupled with the talented *HistoryMaker VR* development team could play a significant role in helping those numbers climb in the near future by offering students an entertaining way to learn about the past."

Why is Virtual Reality so important to education? Well, for a few reasons. One, it lets you experience learning as if you have experienced something in the real world. Learning archeology? It's better to walk around Rome or Jerusalem with an archeologist. VR can do that. Learning chemistry? What if you could visit a virtual lab and experience chemical reactions firsthand? VR can do that. Learning physics? What if you could visit the particle accelerator at CERN and talk with one of the physicists there? VR can do that.

No Teachers, Books, or Movies? New Approaches in the Offing

It isn't just the classroom that's about to radically change, though; learning at work or even in your kitchen is about to change due to both Virtual Reality and Augmented Reality. The same set of questions apply. What if you could learn to do surgery without having a human patient? VR and AR can do that. What if you want to learn to fix a tractor? AR can do that and do it while you actually have your hands on the tractor. In fact, companies like Caterpillar are doing exactly that. What if you want to learn to cook a meal in your kitchen? AR can do that. What if you want to learn how to do a job on a factory line? Both AR and VR can do that.

A perfect storm is coming, not just because of VR, AR, and AI/Machine Learning, but some of that is due to new kinds of schools bringing new approaches, like 42 Silicon Valley, which teaches people to do new jobs. We predict that all four will collide in the 2020s to bring massive changes to education and corporate training and, we predict, will even offer an answer to the massive numbers of people who will need to be retrained to do new things as automation causes many jobs to go away. Truck driving, for instance, is America's number one job, with 1.3 million drivers. Many of those jobs, if not all, will go away in the next one-to-three decades. And that was before the job shifts that were completely unanticipated due to the COVID-19 pandemic. Huge unemployment currently exists and Spatial Computing, along with new educational approaches, offers an answer.

42 Silicon Valley, a peer-assisted and immersive school located in a big building near Tesla's main factory in Silicon Valley, is an example of a new educational approach. The school is unique in that it has no teachers and charges no fees. It reminds us of how Uber disrupted taxis while owning no cars or how Airbnb disrupted hotels while owning no properties. It was donated by a French billionaire and is packed with Macintoshes and tons of students, who agree to spend more than eight hours a day there.

Yet the school took a chef who had never coded, Danny Saetern, and got him to the level that he started a VR game studio and, today, he is working as a software engineer at Schlumberger. We visited that school and saw students grouped together, learning from a curriculum and on computers the school provided, but learning mostly from each other. Students, when they hit upon something they didn't understand, asked the other students for help figuring it out. By doing this and immersing themselves on-site for about 10 hours a day, the students learned very fast. Danny, the former chef, told us he learned to program in about a year.

Another example of shifts in the way schools operate can be found at Lambda School, which is a school teaching computer science. Here, the change is in how students pay. Since this school is more traditional, with a teacher walking students through their learning, they pay a portion of the wages that they get when they get a job.

Yet another shift is coming from the start-up sector with entrepreneurs like Nick Smoot in Idaho and investor/entrepreneur John Borthwick in New York who are building "Innovation Collectives," which have daily classes that teach students a variety of topics (often for free) to build stronger companies around the ecosystems they are working to prop up. At both, we saw classes teaching VR and AR, among many other topics.

At Salesforce, Phil Komarny, VP of Innovation, tells us he is seeing these educational shifts even inside traditional institutions like Harvard. He says that there will be new efforts to help upskill a disrupted workforce and is seeing lots of new technology to do it, from blockchain to track a student's progress, and sees great advancements in the ability to co-learn, like 42 Silicon Valley does, thanks to Augmented and Virtual Reality. Blockchain and new collaborative Augmented and Virtual Reality systems, he explains, will be used to build a new learner network that will bring many of the same advantages that, say, attending a school like Stanford or Carnegie Mellon does today. A huge part of the value of going to those schools is the network you build with other students, many of whom will go onto build important companies and technologies.

It is this combination of both technology and new approaches that have us most excited about the future of learning, training, and upskilling. Current workers, students, and future generations will need this because many jobs will be automated and because of major new challenges due to climate change and globalization.

Many of us learn best by doing, or, at least, visualizing what we are learning. How many of us, when reading a math equation, visualized inside our minds so that we could better understand what we were learning? Watch children learn math, for instance, and they will often count on their fingers. Why? Fingers are physical and can be tracked.

Brainier Learning

Spatial Computing is the most important learning technology humans have ever invented. Why? It goes back to how the human brain learns. We learn a lot faster when we are engaged and when we can visualize. Spatial Computing brings both of those ingredients in big doses. Today, learning something out of a book, say a chemistry equation, might take an hour.

Using Spatial Computing, it might take a minute to grasp the same knowledge—not to mention we will probably learn the concepts better. In VR, you can be embodied in someone or something else. You can experience life through the eyes of another, which, in studies done in Stanford and other schools, builds not only empathy for those others, but as deep a memory as if you experienced the learning in the real world. You can also slow down time and take a different view; walk around a chemical molecule, for instance, or look at the results of a math equation in a way that would be impossible with any other method.

That shift is also joined by another one: the learning can be delivered in real time on top of things we need to learn to manipulate. Let's say you need to learn how to take an oil pump out of a tractor. In the old world, you would have needed to either read an instruction manual and go step by step or sit in a classroom where you would have memorized the steps. With Augmented Reality, the steps can be shown to you right on top of the real tractor. In some instances, it can even watch you work and warn you that you are about to do something wrong. We've seen manufacturing workstations in place in China that do exactly that, but over the next decade that kind of learning will come to a consumer's face. Imagine an IKEA-bought piece of furniture that actually shows you how to assemble it, and watches you work to make sure you did it right.

Tractors aren't the only place we are seeing this new kind of learning. Students are using Augmented Reality to learn everything from how to do math equations, to chemistry, to biology on virtual cadavers, to learning to drive a forklift, and to how to play football better. Football? Yes, at Stanford University, Jeremy Bailenson's students (who included Derek Belch, today founder and CEO of STRIVR, a company that trains many people in both sports and corporate jobs) took a 360-degree camera onto the practice field and recorded a bunch of plays while the camera was next to the quarterback. The quarterback then watched those plays at night to prepare for the next day. They found his stats got better. So, they tried it on more than 700 other players and learned that people who initially trained in Virtual Reality versus using a 2D tablet had a 20 percent decrease in reaction time and were correct more often too.

Why does this work? STRIVR's Belch says that it's partly because it's the same view a player will have on the field, but also partly because when players are on the field their brains pay attention to things that will do them harm. When a 250-pound defender is running toward you, it's hard to pay attention to other patterns that are taking shape on the field. However, partly because you can play the 360-degree replay over and over, you can learn to see patterns taking shape and train your brain to see them. You actually learn better. Belch agrees and says: "The effect on your brain says this [technology] is legit. Having the headset on is more effective than 2D learning. This stuff works when people buy in and do it right. There is real research behind this."

The learning goes deeper, though, because the system and observers can see where a player, or, really any user is looking. That way, others who are watching along with the one wearing the headset can see that they are looking at the wrong thing or see why a mistake is being made and fix it right there. These effects simply aren't possible with 2D video.

What comes next with that data is a really interesting play. STRIVR is recording that data from the controllers that people being trained are holding, along with the sensors on the headsets that can show all sorts of things, potentially including heartbeats and where the user is looking. That data can be used to train new AI systems that can potentially let managers know who won't work out, or who is better suited to a warehouse job than one working with people. Already STRIVR has announced a system that will help decide whether an employee should be promoted, and we can see quite a few other HR tasks that could be done in the future, building on data that comes from tens of thousands of people running through its HR training. This technique has moved to other sports. The New York Mets are using it to prepare for tomorrow's games. If you search Google, you will find lots of examples from soccer to basketball.

Others we talked to agree that a new kind of learning has arrived and will radically change the learner's experience and even bring more people into lifelong learning and retraining that other methods simply can't dream of. Classrooms are already seeing teachers use Merge Labs' Cubes to teach everything from astronomy to frog dissection.

Why does it all work? The brain experiences presence. In other words, it treats VR as real as the real world, and that strengthens neural pathways. The same way you can remember, in detail, some events like a car crash or an earthquake, so too can you remember the training you received in VR, while studies show that the same training delivered in books, videos, or slide decks can't be remembered nearly as well.

This has huge implications for training and the simulations that come with training. So, why aren't we doing more of this? It mostly comes down to cost. Overall, VR hardware costs when HTC Vive or Oculus Rift first came on the market ran about $3,000 and needed a room where sensors could be permanently set up. In 2019, the cost came down to $400 with the Oculus Quest, and we saw a great increase in the numbers of companies that started using VR for enterprise uses. As costs continue to come down, and headsets get more capable, watch for exponential increases in the numbers of places we'll see both VR and AR used. The one room that might be more changed than any other by this technology is the classroom.

The Future of Education

How do you learn? Some can learn well from a book. The two coauthors find that they learn far better by actually seeing how something works, or, better yet, building it and teaching it to others. That is why we chose the line of work that we are pursuing, choosing to talk to people who are making the world work and seeing how they do it.

Virtual Reality and Augmented Reality bring us a very powerful new education technology that can do just that: give you the ability to see, build, and learn about something in a way that closely maps how we learn.

Even better, because it maps to what we already know about the real world, like how to grasp a cup, this learning will be open to far more people, even those who struggle to read. We observed just this as we watched a four-year-old girl use VR. She learned how to use the controllers, how to open an app, how to copy a file, all within a few seconds of putting on the headset for the first time. What did she see inside the headset that was nearly as big as she was? She could pick up a cup just like she could in the real world. She could navigate around from space to space very much like she does in the real world. And the visuals she was seeing were being perceived by her brain the same as she sees the real world; the whole process was intuitive.

Virtual Reality means all you see is this virtual world, but your brain perceives it as being just as real, or at least much more so than, say, a book or 2D video, as the real world. You can "immerse" yourself in what you are learning, for instance, by taking a virtual tour of archeology, or getting a tour of the solar system as if you were an astronaut on a spaceship flying past.

If you study how people learn like Lisa Petrides does, who is the founder and CEO of the Institute for the Study of Knowledge Management, ISKME, an education nonprofit, you are excited and scared by the changes coming due to AR and VR to not just the classroom, but for lifelong learning. Some of the change coming might mean virtual classrooms move from physical spaces to being wherever a student is, whether a living room or a coffee shop. Already, we have experienced new classrooms (both as a teacher and as a student) in virtual spaces like Nanome or AltspaceVR, now owned by Microsoft.

Lisa is scared because she sees yet another round of kids left behind on another round of technology due to cost and other factors. She told us of walking through a township in South Africa and seeing electronic smart boards rendered useless because in some neighborhoods power is up only a few hours a day.

Even in richer countries, she told us, lots of the educators who come to her yearly conference are seeing huge problems in student preparedness. Many students, she told me, are born into harsh circumstances and are coming to school unprepared to learn. Think about the student who is malnourished, or growing up in a homeless shelter, or has opiate-addicted parents, she said, listing some of the huge problems that her institute faces every day.

She sees that AR and VR, even while being huge accelerants in the speed of learning for many kids, could leave lots of kids behind and, worse, tear open new societal wounds that are already straining. Some kids, who now are in special needs programs, might be simultaneously helped and left out by such technologies as other kids race ahead with their learning due to new Spatial Computing devices on their faces or in the classroom.

Even where new technology could lead to some answers, her educators will be asked to figure out how to deal with new privacy fears as the new Oculus Quest has four cameras on the front of it, mostly to see the real world to do inside-out VR tracking, and so it can see where the controllers are in space and even more sensors and data privacy issues are to come.

While these are serious issues that we feel must be considered, we believe that the potential benefits of VR and AR will lift up many kids into being educated, who would have otherwise fallen through the cracks. Many more stories like Bill Hill's will be heard after this technology arrives in more classrooms.

Fears aside, she says, she is excited by the tons of great news and new approaches for educators thanks to these new technologies and she isn't alone. She sees that these technologies could bring major advances in how schools could bring new approaches to mental health, to teaching empathy for others, and how students could learn to collaborate better with others and learn new critical thinking skills, all of which, she says, society desperately needs more of. Most importantly, she says, the teaching of science in the classroom will see huge improvements due to VR and AR.

The Grabbable Classroom

A simple rubber cube already is demonstrating that. When Franklin Lyons and Andrew Trickett started Merge Labs, which makes that cube, they had no idea that a simple cube would turn out to be their biggest seller. For a time, even after they launched the product, it looked like it might not sell well enough to support the company. They told us that Walmart had an oversupply back in 2018 and discounted the Merge Cube. They wondered if their business was done.

Luckily, schoolteachers swooped in and bought dozens, clearing the shelves. Since then, they have gone on to have a bona fide hit with educators and, in 2019, passed a million cubes sold.

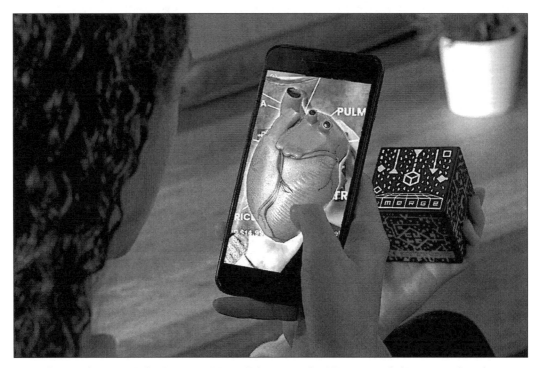

Photo credit: Merge Labs. By using a Merge Cube you can lay 3D scenes and objects on each surface and control them by turning the cube in front of a phone, camera, or Augmented Reality glasses.

The company launched in 2013 with a foam holder for mobile phones that turned them into VR headsets. Smart idea, because foam was very low cost and could take the beating that students could dish out. That led to asking the question: "What can we do with VR or AR?"

Merge came out with a handheld controller for that early headset, but it was too expensive and too hard to make work to garner a huge audience. Plus, Oculus and HTC came out with more capable products around the same time that took away any potential attention they could have gotten.

A better idea was about to come as they looked at the camera on the front of phones: to build a foam cube that had a unique pattern on each side of it as a sort of controllable marker system for AR. The camera sees that pattern on each face of the cube, and the phone would know which side it was looking at and how the cube was oriented in front of the phone. Then, the phone could replace the cube's faces with all sorts of fun AR visual imagery.

At first, when they released the cube at the 2017 Consumer Electronics Show, they thought it might find a market with parents who wanted new kinds of games or new kinds of stories for their kids.

Today, on the Merge Cube, you can dissect a frog or explore the universe. These new apps and new customer bases quickly went exponential and, as of 2019, they have sold more than a million cubes. Lyons and Trickett's Merge Cube product is an early sign that huge changes are coming regarding how we educate not just our kids, but ourselves.

This new education is coming, particularly in places where classroom training just didn't fit well before, if at all. For instance, police training is best done in VR, says Steve Grubbs, CEO of VictoryXR, an education platform: "All learning is immediately in front of us wherever we are. This radically changes learning. This changes the ballgame." This new kind of training is actually a simulation of the real world that police officers move through. This makes learning far more experiential and immersive, and the learning happens much faster and sticks much deeper. Grubbs tells us there's a huge difference between being taught something, like to check a potential suspect for a weapon before moving in, and experiencing the same thing in a Virtual Reality simulation.

It also is coming to homeschoolers.

Why are both cops and homeschoolers using this technology? This new kind of learning is much faster and lower cost than buying books, watching videos, or trying to videoconference into a classroom.

Homeschoolers fall into a few camps, Mark Andersen, co-founder and President of Lifeliqe, a 3D education company, tells us. One camp has one, or more, amazing children that need more education than regular schools, even private ones, can offer. Another camp wants strict religious schooling. Yet another camp doesn't fit into regular schooling. Maybe they are anti-vaxxers who don't want to comply with, say, California state laws. Maybe they had a troubled kid who was getting bullied at the regular school. Yet another camp, one that is growing, doesn't want their kids in a regular school due to the threat of gun violence. All of these camps have one thing in common, however: they are looking for better ways to educate their kids at home. And, in 2020, yet another camp appeared: millions of kids who all of a sudden were forced to stay home due to COVID-19. Increasingly, Augmented and Virtual Reality will provide some major solutions.

The homeschoolers, Andersen says, are flocking to new approaches to teach their kids faster. He surmises that this might force more traditional educators to change, since traditional parents will expect their kids to be taught using these techniques too.

As homeschoolers buy more recent curriculum tools, and are looking for more experiential learning to bring into their homes, they can experience the same learning other kids might be performing physically (say, frog dissections, but without the mess of the actual frog). This will provide the funding that companies like his need to turn more lessons into 3D sessions. There's a downside, though, Grubbs reports: the customer acquisition cost of homeschoolers is higher, because you have to convince them one at a time, in contrast to convincing a school administrator to, say, buy a bunch of Merge Cubes for the entire school in one purchase.

There are lots of examples of curriculums inspiring 3D learning environments for lessons, though. The University of Alberta is teaching cell biology via Virtual Reality that presents cells that students can walk through, watch, and interact with. Preston's College is using 360-degree videos to teach dance. Virtual Reality is helping children with autism learn in Bristol, UK, by dealing with their emotions and learning in a way that they take to very quickly. Mohawk College in Canada has built a $5 million interactive digital center featuring a curriculum from EON Reality. In New Zealand, they have built an AR app to bring graphic novels to life. At a start-up, Explore Interactive, affiliated with Purdue University, students are being taught science, technology, engineering, and mathematics using a series of animated virtual cards that dance on top of tables. "Collaborative Augmented Reality is one of the most innovative things happening in education," CEO Amanda Thompson said. "It allows teachers to challenge students to work together to troubleshoot and solve problems. The potential topics are limitless."

Explore Interactive got a $225,000 small business innovation research grant from the National Science Foundation, among other funding, and it, like other companies, is bringing students into this new way of learning. "Elementary school-age children can't work with a Bunsen burner, but with Augmented Reality they can turn on a Bunsen burner and boil water and see how water reacts and changes," Thompson said. "Future development will allow them to zoom in to the molecular level and see the atoms heating up and moving apart from each other."

AI is playing a major role in this new learning, too. At Rensselaer Polytechnic Institute, a university based in Troy, New York, they are teaching students Chinese with a variety of AI and VR apps in a special "immersive" classroom that was partially built to study these new interactive learning environments. Inside, students talk and interact with virtual images that are actually in front of cameras that are tracking their movements and gestures as they talk with virtual beings or agents. AI analyzes whether they said the right thing at the right time in the right way. An article in MIT's Technology Review reports that the team is still in the early stages of understanding how effective it is, but in a pilot, at the end of 2017, the researchers found that it qualitatively increased the student's engagement and enjoyment in language learning.

The American Museum of Natural History has an interactive multi-player Virtual Reality experience to learn more about dinosaurs. Music instruction goes virtual with the Jam Studio VR, which lets students play around with a variety of musical instruments. With DebuggAR, students in electrical engineering courses can build complete circuits and test them out, all without buying separate components and greatly reducing the time required for trying new things out.

"It's really [moving fast] and it's hard for teachers and librarians to wrap their mind around," Lifeliqe's CEO Andersen says. But to get to the place where every student is wearing Spatial Computing devices, he says that a ton of friction has to be removed from the process. The cost is too high. Lots of wireless infrastructures that many schools don't have need to be built. It's too hard for already overworked, and underpaid, teachers to figure out which apps and services could be used in their classrooms. Often, they are required to teach within the confines of tests and curriculums that aren't flexible enough to allow new approaches to be brought in. Equipment to do VR or AR, even if it's as simple as a tablet with a Merge Cube, needs to be maintained, updated, and dealt with, if broken. VR headsets often can be even more confusing than traditional learning methods and paper tests since a child who is having problems can't show others what trouble they are having inside a headset. Lots of friction that will make school system adoption slower than some parents might like, but we might see an effect like Apple caused with the iPhone: students might bring their own technology to school.

How? Well, consider the new Statue of Liberty Augmented Reality App that was released in 2019 to celebrate the opening of a new museum at the Statue. It is educational. Parents will be more than happy for their kids to use it to take an audio tour around the statue. You can put a virtual version of the statue in your living room and learn all about how it was built, who built it, and why. If you visit the actual statue it's even better, since the audio tour in it is the same one you can do when you get off the tour boat, except it sounds better and is easier to use than the one on the audio tour device that you get when you get off the boat.

This app is free, too, but unfortunately only available on iPhones. It was developed by Yap Studios in association with the Statue of Liberty-Ellis Island Foundation and took a year to scan the statue and gather all the media and photographs used to generate a highly detailed 3D model. We talked with one of the developers who worked on it, Ollie Wagner, and he used a variety of Apple technologies to build the app, including its ARKit foundation. That work will move easily into Apple's future Spatial Computing devices too, and then you'll be able to experience it in a much more immersive way. (Search for "Statue of Liberty AR" to find links to it in the online Apple Store.)

Renowned French engineer Alexandre-Gustav Eiffel (of Eiffel Tower fame) devised an ingenious new support system of an iron, skeletal structure, built around a central pylon for the Statue of Liberty's interior framework.

TAP TO DISMISS

Photo credit: Robert Scoble. Here, the Statue of Liberty Augmented Reality App, used on a visit to the real statue, which is in the background on the capture of our screen, shows how it was built internally and teaches you the history behind the statue. You can use the same iPhone app anywhere in the world.

The Statue of Liberty App shows that changes to education will come from unexpected places over the next decade, and both homeschoolers and curious parents looking for a way to connect to kids who are already heavily using computers, phones, or tablets, will get kids new kinds of rapid-learning technology at home. Like we saw when corporate users started bringing iPhones to work, even against the wishes of management, we predict changes will come to education whether the educational establishment wishes it or not. Parents, innovative teachers, and kids themselves will bring the best tools to school, or, if forced to, use them at home to advance their learning faster and in a more entertaining way.

Another challenge is coming for educators, though, and the needs will be bigger than they can satisfy. We all know that if trucks start fully autonomously driving that that technology will put 1.3 million drivers out of work in the United States alone. As we were writing this book, tens of millions of people lost their jobs due to the COVID-19 pandemic and many will need to be retrained for new jobs because their old jobs simply won't reappear. There aren't enough schools ready to retrain just that population. China is facing a similar problem: there simply aren't enough teachers to train the kids who are being born every year. As a result, China is building Virtual Reality classrooms with AI assistants by a company called NetDragon Websoft to fill this gap in available teachers and classrooms to hold them.

This may sound scary to many Western parents, but to a laid-off truck driver who needs to find a new skill to keep food on his or her family's table, this prospect will be a lot less intimidating. Go back to 42 Silicon Valley, the school that took a chef and helped him learn to be a programmer. Today, that school still needs an expensive building and rows of expensive computers to provide an environment for learning to take place. We predict that, by the end of the 2020s, schools like that will take their curriculum, and methodology, to the virtual, where students will meet in virtual classrooms and learn from each other—all without having to travel to a school. These new learning environments, whether in something like AltspaceVR or other virtual places that we haven't yet seen developed, will provide another nudge for the existing education system to change. Already those changes are showing up in the workplace with new kinds of training and simulation.

Workplace Training and Simulation

When you mix computing that you, a robot, or a virtual being can move through on top of a physical machine, you get a whole new level of ability to learn a new job quickly. Whether we call this Augmented Reality, Spatial Computing, Mixed Reality, or Virtual Reality doesn't matter too much. It's the fact that we can get visual simulations of, say, a factory floor, and we can learn a new job as if we were on the factory floor doing the actual job, or having someone standing beside us assisting us in learning that new job.

Workplace needs are going to increase, Accenture predicted in a report on Immersive Learning for the Future Workforce. It shared research from the World Economic Forum that estimates that, in 2020, nearly 35 percent of the top skills needed across all job families will change. The signals are strong that a lot of people will soon need to be retrained and Spatial Computing offers the answer.

The same report says that learning through experience, which is what Spatial Computing brings, increases learning quality and improves retention by up to 75 percent. That number comes from studies at Stanford University and Technical University Denmark. According to ABI Research, the same Accenture study reports that the enterprise VR training market will grow to $6.3 billion in 2022.

What else does virtual training bring? Well, much better analytics so that you can prove your workers were trained, for one. By 2025, our Spatial Computing devices will capture a ton of data from eye, motion, behavioral, and gesture sensors, and that will all be used to ensure that training is being understood and can even make sure that the job is performed properly on factory lines, in mines, and in many other jobs.

It also lets you learn without fear of the consequences of mistakes. At Boston Scientific, they showed how doctors can practice heart surgery over and over again without fear of messing up and costing a patient their lives. VR and AR provide real-time 3D views of human anatomy that can be significantly more effective than how we learn from diagrams or 2D training videos. Immersive learning experiences like this are also what today's tech-savvy generation of students expect from healthcare education. Other companies that are using Spatial Computing for healthcare, surgical learning, and simulation include Dr. Shafi Ahmed's company, Medical Realities, Medivis, and Osso VR.

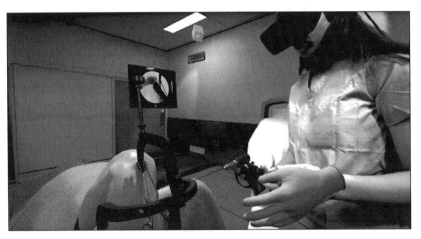

Photo credit: Osso VR. A surgeon practices, in VR, a new surgical technique using Osso VR's surgical preparation system.

What is wonderful is that the benefits of using Spatial Computing for learning are applicable for workers doing far more mundane jobs like putting an air conditioning unit into a car. Or a toilet in a bathroom. Why do we bring that up? Because Accenture reports that workers who had to learn to do that task completed it 12 percent more accurately and 17 percent faster after doing training in VR rather than watching similar training on a 2D video.

We have dozens of such stories of companies using VR to enhance training for these mundane tasks, but something deeper is underway. As we talked to people who are doing VR training, we kept hearing about training that was hard to do before VR came along.

If you visit Ford's plant in Detroit, like we did, where they build F-150s, you will see a new one is built every minute or two—24 hours a day. They rarely stop the line. After all, if you owned a system that spits out $40,000 every minute would you ever stop it? This shows why so many factories are already using VR to train their workers somewhere away from the factory to do difficult and often dangerous jobs. In VR, you can slow down the line virtually. If you make a mistake, there aren't consequences like there are on the real line.

You hear factory workers learning new terminology because of this shift. "Digital Twin" is one you frequently hear. This is a virtual version of the entire factory floor; one you can experience in either a VR or AR headset.

Training isn't the only thing that's changing on manufacturing lines, and we cover more of them in *Chapter 5, Vision Three – Augmented Manufacturing* about how manufacturing and warehouse work will radically change over the next decade, but it's worth digging into workplace training here. It's not the only change happening to how workers are learning new jobs either.

Another factor at play here is that older workers are retiring at a fast rate from many jobs, often leaving factories with decades of knowledge. Using Spatial Computing, they can leave lots of that learning on the factory floor by recording videos and leaving those videos on top of the digital twins that are now being built. That's helpful because, mixed with other types of training, you can find that wisdom more easily than using a search engine and it's on top of the machine you are being trained to run.

We see many workers wearing devices like RealWear's devices or Google Glass, which doesn't really present much of an augmented view of the world, rather these devices mostly augment work by presenting information on small displays, even video, and open up new kinds of remote training capabilities. These devices augment jobs in real time, helping workers do things around factories, oil refineries, and other enterprises, and they also let you learn remotely from experts elsewhere in the enterprise. Imagine you are installing air conditioning units on, say, that F-150 truck, and you hit an issue you never have seen before. Quick, you can't stop the line for long since every minute of stopped time costs your employer at least $40,000. Do you reach for a paper manual? Or, do you call your boss or another expert to ask for help? That's exactly what's happening now. Microphones on the RealWear device let you talk and a camera on the device lets the remote expert get a look at the problem via videoconference.

There's a screen on the device that lets you see any visual solution to the new problem, too. This is all in a head-worn device that lets you continue to work with both of your hands.

Workplaces are changing already because of Spatial Computing technologies. Today, we are designing things in 3D, like new kinds of architecture and new kinds of products, yet many of us are seeing those things on 2D screens, which really don't map to how our brains work very well and it's hard to visualize how those products will be used in real life. Architects took to VR very quickly. We were shown one home completely in VR and we could walk through it and even visit the pool outside and see how it would look in the real physical space where it is being built (the home is being built for Lynda Weinman and her husband. She started Lynda. com, which was one of a group of companies that radically changed learning thanks to the internet, and their new home should be completed in 2021).

Others are having to learn new kinds of jobs very quickly or deal with engineering changes to existing products or lines. Other kinds of jobs, like firefighting, criminal justice, or police work, are changing every day because of new science or new technology, and here, too, VR and AR are already seeing radical new uses. The New York City Police Department is using VR to train their police on how to act during high-stress events, such as terrorist, hostage, and mental health emergency situations.

That brings us to the role of simulation in workplace training. Some things happen so infrequently, are so dangerous to train for, or are so costly to recreate in real life, that real-life training is, for the most part, intractable. Learning to defuse a bomb, for instance, is a bit hard to do on a real bomb, yet we met people who had to learn how to do that when we visited Nellis Airforce Base in Nevada where we were taught to defuse such a bomb. We imagine that learning that skill in VR is a bit more comfortable than having to learn on a real device. Even if you say learning on a real device is better, it's hard to teach a large number of people quickly about a new kind of device. Virtual training can be passed to your entire workforce immediately, which can save lives and money, and ensures that everyone is on the same page.

These are similar changes to those that will roil the previously stable waters of classrooms over the next decade. These changes are already starting to happen, but will greatly increase as Spatial Computing devices get released by companies like Apple, Facebook, Microsoft and Sony, which consumers and workers can afford and that are light enough to wear for hours every day. Already our kids are spending hours every day inside our Oculus Quests, which costs $400, something that many workers can afford.

Photo credit: Robert Scoble. A defused bomb for training purposes at Nellis Air Force Base with an X-Ray of the scan. Now training like this can be transmitted to soldiers in the field via Spatial Computing systems, and when one base discovers a new kind of bomb, that training can be sent to teams all over the globe within minutes.

Why will this happen? As we already explained, humans tend to remember things better when they are experienced more directly, as they do when experiencing VR or AR. Because of this, less time is spent on learning and more can be spent on the job. STRIVR says that VR training improves employee confidence and has boosted test scores by 10 to 15 percent, even for trainees who simply watched others experience the training.

Additionally, we are seeing a move to more jobs being done remotely, even those who coordinate with people on factory floors. With the use of VR and AR, this will only increase. Younger workers are hoping to work this way, and if factories can keep some people working at other locations or working using VR and AR headsets at home, traffic and carbon footprint problems could be alleviated.

Another reason for the increasing adoption of VR and AR for workplace uses is that you can experience things from various points of view. For instance, you can become a woman experiencing sexual harassment, or the boss that is dishing it out. This increases empathy, which could be an HR training objective, and the same hardware could be used for factory training so you can walk around a machine and see how you would work on it from any angle.

Photo credit: BMW. A worker uses VR to both build and train on a new manufacturing line.

At BMW, workers use VR to practice their jobs before they get onto the factory floor. They can grab virtual parts, see how to install them, practice doing that with virtual tools, and after that is all done the system gives them a score on how well they did each task. BMW's Armin Hoffmann, project manager at BMW's group plant in Landeshut, says that this lets his teams learn how to build new cars, or get updated on new part designs, faster, which saves BMW money and reduces error rates on its factory floors.

Verizon uses VR to train employees on what to do during a robbery in its stores. The New York Mets use VR to practice hitting against tomorrow's pitchers in hotel rooms the night before games. Norway's World Cup soccer team used it to prepare against its opponents. In STRIVR, you can practice firing an employee. In Ireland, the military practices sweeping for mines in VR. In some medical centers, you can learn to deliver a baby. We have hundreds of examples of training and simulations already being used on many other jobs.

VR training isn't just replacing previous methods of training, although, in some cases it is, like with sexual harassment training, where VR can bring new approaches to getting into someone else's shoes so you can feel how your words and actions might hurt, but it is excelling in new, more dangerous, areas, where previously the best thing you could do was read a book about it.

Walmart, for instance, takes new hires onto the retail floor during Black Friday, which is its busiest day of the year. You can watch as much video as you want, or read entire books about what it's like to deal with customers who are fighting to get a deal on a TV, but VR can actually take you there and give you a much more real experience.

Lockheed Martin's Shelley Peterson, who is the emerging technologies lead there and principal investigator for Augmented Reality, reports that their efforts to get training out of the "rectangles" that represent paper or screens that most of us use are already paying off big time: "It has a significant impact. You can capture a concept much more thoroughly when it's not in that rectangle of data. It changes when you are picking up a new concept."

She explains that often when building spacecraft, workers have to crawl through tight, confined spaces, sometimes with potential hazards, and other workers have to work in clean rooms that take minutes to undergo sterilization procedures and suit up so as to meet requirements. Even then, workers going into such areas can introduce defects to the manufacturing process, and still other workers have to crawl up and down lots of ladders, and, if a class is following a worker to learn a new task, that alone can take minutes away from learning.

Augmented Reality makes learning much better because it shows the students all sorts of things that they need to be aware of, and now virtual interfaces actually make many physical tasks easier. Then, the Augmented Reality headsets, in Lockheed's case Microsoft HoloLens, actually show whether or not you did the job properly.

"Where it normally would take 8 hours (to comprehend), now it takes about 45 minutes," says Shelly. This saving of time is there even with seasoned technicians, she reports, while pointing out that Augmented Reality even saves time when building the instructions, and that they saw gains in cost, quality, and time to get the job done.

Lockheed isn't alone. Research by Capterra found that almost a third of small and midsize U.S. businesses were expecting to use Spatial Computing in employee training by 2021 and projected that it will get employees up to full productivity 50 percent faster than traditional instruction. By comparison, in early 2018, 32 percent of retail employees said they didn't receive any formal instruction, which shows there's a big potential market for Spatial Computing technology to be used here.

The PR consequences for not doing training are extreme now. Sephora closed all its doors for an hour to perform "inclusivity workshops" following accusations of racial profiling. Starbucks similarly captured headlines when it closed 8,000 stores for an afternoon of racial-sensitivity training after two African-American men were arrested at one of its stores while waiting for a friend, Forbes reported.

The list goes on and on. Lowe's is using it to help employees learn about how to better perform do-it-yourself projects. Chipotle is using VR to help with food safety. In VR, you can learn to drive a bus, be a railway engineer, get chemical industry training, and, at Airbus, they are using HoloLens headsets to virtually test their designs to see if they are ready for manufacture. It reports that using Spatial Computing speeds up the process substantially, decreasing the time spent in training by 80 percent.

We've seen this ourselves. In Bailenson's lab at Stanford University, his students wanted to teach people about climate change and have the facts "stick." We wore a VR headset and were taken underwater where we experienced first-hand the damage being done to the oceans. It showed us how carbon dioxide molecules, when absorbed into the sea, created acidic conditions and were killing the reefs. That memory sticks clearly in our minds even two years later.

Speaking of climate change, so much corporate training requires students to fly long distances to training rooms. Just flying a short distance from San Francisco to Los Angeles for a one-day training costs $300 for the flight, $250 for the hotel, and $75 for a meal. That's already more than a single Oculus Quest where you can experience the same training in VR and that's not counting the value of the worker's time spent traveling. If you have to fly your workers internationally, the cost savings become even more extreme. With VR, you can teach everyone remotely, at the same time.

We saw a class for real estate agents that was done completely in VR. No travel required. More pressure will be put on companies to do this kind of training due to the carbon costs of flying workers around the world as climate change becomes a much more serious issue for both customers and investors. As a benefit, your workers might get together in Rec Room and play some games too, which will increase the bonding your team has without the problems that come with tons of alcohol consumption in the hotel bar.

Other benefits? The "teacher" never has a bad day or forgets to communicate something important. It's there every time for every student and, due to the sensors that watch where a student is looking and virtual tests that can be done, you'll have proof that the job was understood, and remembered, at a far higher rate than if you don't have VR and/or AR training.

With trades such as healthcare, military, and police that could inherently provide safety risks, VR provides a safe training alternative. For example, the New York City Police Department is using such simulations to train for new kinds of terror attacks and this technology is rapidly developing, thanks to not just the better visualizations that are possible in Spatial Computing headsets, but the AI that can run all sorts of things. We learned about this by studying autonomous cars. Car companies like GM and VW are running billions of miles where a virtual car drives around virtual streets that are so realistic now that they even have virtual puddles due to recent rain. That same technology is currently being used in workplaces.

Commenting on VR workplace training that uses simulation, Andy Trainor, Senior Director of Walmart U.S. Academies, says the following: "We can create scenarios that may never happen (like severe weather training) or situations that happen all the time, but we don't want to disrupt our stores to give associates firsthand experience. VR lets them explore these sorts of scenarios in a firsthand way."

The workplace location where Spatial Computing could be used for simulation could be anywhere, including a factory, logistics facility, retail storefront, or even U.S. military and air force training facilities and battlefields. The Pentagon awarded a $479 million contract to Microsoft in November 2018 for HoloLens headsets, in order to have soldiers in training and on the battlefield interact in simulated battle scenarios. Login to the headset can be accomplished via iris recognition so that the simultaneous sharing of experiences and movement updating among multiple people is fast, easy, and secure.

HoloLens helps Airbus aircraft designers to virtually test their designs to see if they are ready for manufacture. Use of the HoloLens sped up the designing process prior to manufacture substantially, decreasing the time spent by 80 percent. In addition to this, Airbus has identified more than 300 use cases for Augmented Reality and they will be continuing to use the HoloLens 2 headset.

Given that there are close to 35,000 serious injuries involving forklift accidents each year in the United States alone, the Raymond Corporation, which is a leading manufacturer of forklift trucks and pallet jacks, created a VR simulation for forklift operator trainees. 3M, Caterpillar, and UPS are other companies using VR simulations to enable workers to know how to operate in situations that are potentially not safe.

Another example of Spatial Computing simulation being used in the workplace is at Paccar, the parent of Kenworth, which makes semi-trucks. Paccar ordered 50 Microsoft HoloLens 2 headsets, after the success of a Kenworth worker who understood how to do a new task while using the HoloLens in less than 20 minutes. The plan is to now train more than 2,000 workers on at least two dozen tasks at that particular plant.

This brings us to a new kind of training that was hard to do before: teaching humans to manage and behave better, both while working with other humans and while working with other machines. It turns out that early science shows that if you have an emotional connection to the robot working alongside you, you will perform better yourself.

Photo credit: Walmart. Here, a Virtual Reality image shows you what a user of Walmart's training app shows as they walk around a virtual store and are evaluated by their reactions to common tasks. The app, built by STRIVR, can even recommend which simulation users are ready for a promotion.

A Virtual Arm for Human Resources

As anyone who has worked in a corporate organization can tell you, one of the first stops when you get a new job is the company human resources department. There is a terrific amount of work that a human resources department does for a company, but it usually flies under the radar of most workers since its touchpoints are seemingly on the periphery of what is considered to be the main company business. However, if a company's human resources department is lax and careless, workers will inevitably suffer—from minor issues such as losing an accounting of a due vacation day or two, to losing large sums of money due to sloppy equity options paperwork.

A company's culture is usually governed through its human resources department. Empathy, diversity, and sexual harassment training comes under its purview. Official workplace safety is another area. If there are problems in these areas, upper management and human resources are the first entities to be blamed.

Additionally, a company's human resources department has a large part to play in developing and enforcing the rules and standards for pay grades, reviews, and promotions.

In all of these areas, Virtual Reality has already been implemented, sometimes as a complete replacement, and other times as an adjunct, for a company's human resources tasks. Examples of tasks covered by Virtual Reality include recruiting and onboarding, benefits training, empathy and diversity training, sexual harassment training, workplace safety, and guidance on reviews and recommendations for promotions.

Regarding workplace safety ran through the human resources and HR department, over 11,000 Intel employees and contractors are required to take an Electrical Recertification course every year—this course is now given in Virtual Reality.

A very interesting area that HR is using VR for is workplace empathy via a tool that VR offers natively, which is embodiment. A company called Somewhere Else Solutions allows a person in VR to swap bodies so that they could role-play as their manager and a manager could role-play as their employee. Additionally, people could swap genders for sexual harassment and unconscious bias training.

Talespin offers VR workplace simulations so that employees at all levels of a company hierarchy could practice and learn how to deal with others in workplace situations.

A company that has taken the VR role in HR further than most is Walmart, with its training vendor STRIVR. Walmart is using VR to determine their workers' skills and overall potential on the job using VR simulations. The data gathered during the simulations is then used as part of the decision-making process to determine who will get a promotion or a pay cut. Currently, data gathered is based on how workers answer questions put to them while in the VR simulation. However, plans have been made to gather workers' body movement and attention data while in VR, which early research has shown provides a relatively more accurate picture of future on-the-job performance.

This VR implementation at Walmart is in addition to the one that was instituted in 2018 where they added headsets to 4,600 U.S. stores to train over a million workers on how to stock shelves and use new online pickup machines. It is very clear that there is a place for the use of Spatial Computing for learning both in and outside the workplace.

Our Learning Futures

Thanks to Spatial Computing technologies, we'll see a deep change in how we educate both our kids and ourselves. Soon, we'll be learning on top of tasks or via simulations. Our learning will be far more immersive and interactive than anything we've experienced before, and we predict eventually far faster and at a lower cost too.

As we learn we can teach too. The AI systems that will study our every move can learn from us and even start predicting what we'll do next. That will further take our learning to a much more efficient place because soon we'll be learning while doing. Imagine a pair of glasses that notice you are about to touch a hot stove. "Hey, that's going to burn," our systems might say just before we put our hands on that hot surface. Think that's impossible? Not for computers that are starting to do a variety of things from driving cars to helping us shop with these predictive systems. Let's go into that next.

Part III

The Spatial Business

Productivity, Efficiency, and Making Profits Are About to Undergo Radical Changes

10

The Always Predicted World

Humans are predictable. If we go to church, we are there at the same time every weekend. We head to work at the same time. Kids have to be dropped off at the same time, to the same place. Even things that seem somewhat random, like going to grocery stores or for dinner at restaurants, have a pattern to them.

What is your next best action? Humans are pretty good at figuring that out, right? But computers can assist you even more by warning you of, say, an accident ahead on your route, or some other pattern you can't see ahead of time. "Ahead, there's a new pothole in the left lane."

Here, we'll explore the predictive capabilities that will come with Spatial Computing and how these technologies will change almost every part of our world, from transportation to education.

The Predictive Breakthrough

Predictability goes beyond knowing that if it's 8:45 a.m. on a Monday, you probably are headed to work. Vic Gundotra, who used to be an exec at Google, told us that Google realized that if you walked into a store, that act predicted you would end up buying something in that store. That might seem obvious, but it was a breakthrough in thinking through how to advertise to users. Kelley Blue Book, among others, used that learning to put car advertising in front of you once you walked onto a car lot, via your mobile phone's notifications or by sending you an email based on your previous login to Kelley Blue Book, sometimes even convincing you to leave that lot to get a better deal elsewhere.

If you are visiting a Volvo lot after doing a bunch of searches on Kelley Blue Book, another car company might even offer you $50 to come to their dealership and take a test drive in an attempt to get you to leave the Volvo lot without making a purchase.

Glasses That Understand You

Those early uses of contextual data and predictive systems will soon seem pretty simple when compared to what's coming next. That's a world where many users will wear Spatial Computing glasses, with tons of cameras and sensors to watch what the wearer is looking at, talking about, and interacting with. This world will arrive at about the same time as autonomous vehicles and delivery robots start showing up on our city streets. Each will have a ton of sensors as well, gathering data about the street and sharing it with a new type of cloud computing that can learn exponentially and deliver radical new services and even virtual assistants, all due to massive amounts of data being collected about the real world and everything and everybody interacting in it.

The software of Spatial Computing glasses will get a very good understanding of the context that a user is in. We call the engines that will watch all of this "exponential learning systems." After all, you will want to do different things on computers if you are shopping than if you are trying to work in an office, and those two things are quite different than if you are in a restaurant on a date night.

These glasses we soon will wear will have three new systems: data collection, contextual deciders, and exponential learning systems that are constantly using data and user context, along with other predictors, such as who you are with, with the aim of making your life better. These systems have been under design for at least 15 years, but are now getting much more complex due to new technology, particularly on autonomous vehicles, which have AI that does all sorts of things, including predicting whether a pedestrian at the intersection ahead will cross the road or not.

At Microsoft Research, back in 2005, researchers showed us how they built a system that could predict traffic patterns in Seattle 24 hours a day. It knew, for instance, that it was pretty likely that you would get stuck in traffic coming across the I-90 bridge during rush hour. This might seem pretty obvious to most humans, but it was an important breakthrough for computers to be able to predict traffic conditions before they happened. With Spatial Computing glasses, similar Artificial Intelligence-based systems might make thousands of similar predictions for their wearer. These predictions, and the assistance they will give, will change human life pretty significantly, and provide the ability to build new assistants that go even further than the human assistants that executives use today.

(Human) Assistance Not Required

To understand how these changes will occur, we talked with someone who is an experienced executive assistant. She doesn't want to be quoted or have her name used, but she was an executive assistant to Steve Jobs and still is an assistant to an executive at Facebook. Executive assistants do everything from getting other executives on the phone to doing complicated travel planning, to maybe something simple like ordering lunch for the team. She told us stories about getting the CEO of Sony on the phone and helping to fix problems for Steve Jobs. In other words, she cleaned up messes, since he was famous for getting angry when something didn't go right. She has a deep Rolodex of other executives' cell phones and their personal assistants' details that she could use to make such meetings and other things happen.

The thing is, her kind of job is quickly going away. The Wall Street Journal reported that more than 40 percent of executive assistant positions have disappeared since the year 2000. Why? Well, think about your own life. In the 1970s, travel, for instance, was so complex that you probably would have used a travel agent to do it. Today, mobile phones and services like Google Flights have made that job much more simple, so you can do travel planning yourself. Heck, you can even get a ride to the airport by simply using a mobile app and you know if that ride is on its way, which wasn't true back just a decade ago. The same is happening to all parts of the executive assistant's job; after all, now that you can say "Hey Siri, call Jane Smith," you probably don't need an assistant like our source to get someone on the phone.

Soon, virtual assistants in our glasses will have a lot more data to use to help us than just looking at the number of steps you are taking or your heartbeat. We've seen AI-based systems that know how many calories you are consuming, just by taking a few images of the food you are looking at, and Apple has patents for its future Spatial Computing glasses that watch a number of different health factors, including listening to your voice, heart rate, and other biometric data to predict how your workout is going. Apple has a set of patents for a bunch of sensing capabilities for looking into the human eye for a variety of ailments too.

These aren't alone—Robert Adams, the founder of Global e-dentity™, showed us how his patent that looks at your vascular and bone structure could be used for a number of things, from verifying your identity to assessing your health. Future glasses will have cameras aimed at different parts of your face for just these kinds of things. Our virtual assistants will have a number of helpful features made possible through Spatial Computing, which could allow them to see to most, if not all, of our assistance needs.

Pervasive

Now, imagine the other data that such a system would have if you are almost permanently wearing a camera on your face—developers could build systems to play games with you about your eating habits that would say to you, "Hey, don't eat that donut, but if you do, we will remove 400 points from your health score and that will require you to eat 10 salads and go on two extra walks this week."

Already we are seeing Computer Vision apps, like Chooch, that are starting to identify every object you aim the camera at. It's using the same kind of Computer Vision that a self-driving car uses to know it is seeing a stoplight or stop sign, or another object on the road (while writing this chapter, Robert's Tesla started recognizing garbage cans, of all things).

If you use Amazon's app on a mobile phones, there's a camera feature that does something similar. Aim the camera at a Starbucks cup and it will show you things you can buy from Starbucks. Aim it at someone's black-collared shirt and it will show you other collared shirts. In the Spatial Computing world, you will see these capabilities really come to bear in new kinds of shopping experiences that can take a single 3D object, like a scan of a coffee table, and show you lots of other things that will fit with that table.

What if, though, it knew you needed a shirt before you even started looking for one? How would that work? Well, if you put a new job interview on your calendar, a predictive system might surmise that you will need a new suit to look spiffy for that interview. Or, if you learn you are pregnant, such a system might know that you soon will need a new car, new insurance, and a new home. In fact, such predictive systems already are running all over the place and are the reasons why after a big life event, we get a ton of junk mail advertising just these kinds of things. The New York Times reported that a system at Target knew a woman was pregnant before she told her family because she started changing the products she was buying and a computer system recognized the change in her patterns.

We can see these systems at work in tons of other places, too, including inside email systems, like Gmail, that start answering our emails with us and giving us predetermined answers that often are pretty darn accurate.

The world we care about, though, isn't the one of email, it's the new computing world that's 3D and on our face. Here, predictive systems will be watching our eyes, our hands, our movements, and watching everything we touch and consume. Now, don't get all Black Mirror and dystopian on us.

Truth is, the early devices won't do that much due to the small batteries that will be in them and the sizeable privacy concerns, but over the next decade, these devices will do more and more and, when joined with devices in our homes, like Amazon Echo or Google Home, will start doing a sizeable number of new things, including changing the way we go to the store, using what we call "automatic shopping." Heck, we are pretty close to that already, and in our research, we visited Amazon and its Amazon Go store where you can buy things just by picking them up and walking out with them. There were hundreds of sensors watching every move in that real-world store. Soon we'll have versions of that store virtually in our living rooms.

Proactive

Going back to the human assistant, if you really had an assistant that knew you well, especially if you had one who lived with you, that assistant would know if you were running out of milk or cereal. Well, already, making a shopping list is easier than it used to be. In our homes, we just say "Alexa, add Cheerios to my shopping list" and it does. But within a few years, the glasses you are wearing will just make note that you have had your seventh bowl of Cheerios this month and that there are only two bowls left in the box in your kitchen, so it will just add another box to your shopping list. Yeah, you can take it off if it gets too aggressive, but we bet that most of the time it'll be pretty accurate. Added onto new delivery robots, you'll see almost a total change in how we stock our kitchens.

Already, when we were writing this book, our Tesla started doing something similarly automatic: "automatic navigation." Instead of having to put an address into the car's navigation system for, say, heading to a doctor's appointment, the car now looks at your Google Calendar and then automatically navigates to your next appointment when you simply get into the car. Hey, it's pretty accurate. After all, you did add that appointment to your calendar. Where it wasn't accurate or didn't have enough data to work, it trained us to make sure our calendars were accurately kept up to date with the street addresses of appointments.

This two-way feedback system proves very effective and its accuracy increases our trust in, and love of, our car. Other owners have reported the same. One thought it was the most amazing new feature because it saved her trying to find addresses while driving or touching the screen while her nails were drying on the way to work.

That's one level of prediction—a system that just does pretty simple stuff, but what will really change radically over the next decade is when you hook up the exponential learning systems of Artificial Intelligence and Computer Vision, along with millions of cameras and sensors moving around the real world.

Connected

What do we mean by "exponential learning system"? Well, one night when walking home from band practice, a fellow student back in 1982 was hit in front of the school and died. The next year, a stoplight was erected in front of Prospect High School in Saratoga that is still there 35 years later. That system was a linear-learning system. It improved that one intersection. If you lived in, say, France, though, it didn't improve your life at all.

Now, compare that to how a June Oven gets its information and makes appropriate changes. The June Oven has a camera inside and an Nvidia card that lets it do Machine Learning. Why do you want an oven like that? Well, if you put a piece of fish into the June Oven, it says "salmon" and correctly cooks it without you needing to look up the recipe. What if, though, you put something into the oven it can't recognize, such as Persian kabobs? Well, then you can set it manually, which teaches the oven about something new. The thing is, a photo of that kabob, along with the temperature and time settings, are sent up to June's servers, where programmers there can then add that to everyone's oven, which makes everyone's oven exponentially better.

It's the same for Tesla cars. When we slam on our brakes in our Tesla, it uploads the video from that part of our drive, along with all sensor readings. Programmers there can then work that into new Machine Learning training, improving the system for, say, understanding what a pedestrian looks like, and improving the system for the entire fleet on the next update. These new products that have neural networks inside learn exponentially and get dramatically better after you purchase them, and do it fleetwide. So, unlike the stoplight example, which only improved one intersection, next time something goes wrong, the programmers will fix the program for the entire fleet. It gets better exponentially and as more users get these products, the time to new features goes down exponentially as well. Within a decade, these exponential learning systems will dramatically change almost every part of our lives, particularly inside Spatial Computing glasses, which have an exponential learning system built in.

Back to Spatial Computing glasses, then. When you first get them, they might not recognize much in the world, but if millions of people have them and teach them one new thing a week, that means your glasses will recognize millions of things within a few weeks, exponentially learning and getting better with a rate that will speed up as more people get the glasses.

What this means is that we will soon have virtual assistants and coaches who get smarter and smarter every week. Our virtual running coach might start out only understanding simple runs, but within a few weeks might be taking us on back-country trails that are poorly marked.

Our virtual nutrition coaches might start out only understanding major brands but soon will recognize unusual candies from far off places. Our shopping services might start out not knowing our favorite brands, but within a few weeks, will learn exactly what brands and colors make you happiest.

Our Spatial Computing glasses will bring this kind of new utility, along with some that might even save your life and take the fall detection feature of the 2019 Apple Watch family way further. Let's dig into just how deeply human life will change because of this data collection, contextual decision-making, and processing, and the exponential learning systems that Spatial Computing will bring.

Data Dance With Seven Verticals

We'll present here some visions of how the intersection of data collection with Machine Learning and 3D visualization will benefit the seven verticals that we have been addressing in this book: Transportation; Technology, Media, and Telecommunications (TMT); Manufacturing; Retail; Healthcare; Finance; and Education. Let's begin by getting into how the world of transportation is set to change due to the influx of data, and our increasing capacity to utilize and learn from it.

Transportation

When you need transportation, you'll see that tons will have changed by 2030. Your Spatial Computing glasses will radically change the way you approach transport. These changes will be bigger than the ones that Uber, Lyft, and Didi brought as they enabled people to order a ride on their new mobile phones. Uber is worth looking back at, because we believe transportation, even the vehicle that sits on your own driveway, will act and work a lot more like Uber than like the Chevy that was memorialized in the 1971 anthem, "American Pie."

When Travis Kalanick was starting Uber, he told us that his goal was to have a single car near you. Not none, because that would mean waiting, which wouldn't be a good customer experience. Not more than one, because that would mean drivers were sitting around not getting paid and getting angry.

This is accomplished by data collection, smart data analysis, and proprietary algorithmic software. It knows, contextually, where rides are. In fact, drivers are urged to move around the city, and sometimes further, in anticipation of new demand. We watched its organization at the Coachella music festival, where they had drivers from across the Western United States—thousands of them—converged in Palm Springs by this system that controlled transportation.

The transportation system of 2030 will be different, though, because most of the pioneers we talked with expect autonomous systems to be well underway. In fact, as we open the 2020s, Waymo is just starting to drive people around in these, now named "robotaxis." At least it is in a few cities, like Phoenix, Arizona, and Mountain View, California. We cover these robotaxis in depth in the transportation chapter elsewhere in the book, but it's worth explaining how the data that these systems are slurping up everywhere will be used, processed, and displayed, all in an attempt to predict what the transportation needs are so that Kalanick's impulse of having a vehicle waiting nearby whenever you need it will become true, even without a driver involved.

Further, your glasses, and possibly Augmented Reality windshields, will see layers of other utilities, all built by the data being gathered. For instance, it's very possible that you will be able to see what the street looks like during the day from these glasses or windshields. The maps that are being built by autonomous cars are so detailed, and have so much data about what surrounds the car, that you might be presented with a "day mode" so that you can more easily see what surrounds the car.

The maps themselves, which the industry calls "HD maps," for "high definition," already go way beyond the maps most of us use in mobile apps, whether from Google or Apple. They include every stoplight, stop sign, tree surrounding the route, lane information, speed information, and much, much more.

The autonomous car system needs all that data to properly be able to navigate you from your home to, say, work—stopping correctly at intersections, accelerating to the right speed on freeways, and turning smoothly on mountain roads. All this is controlled by the HD maps underneath, usually invisible to the driver. Although, if you are in a recent Tesla model, you get a taste of these maps on the car's display, which, as we are writing, now shows stoplights and even things on the road like garbage cans. The data these maps are collecting, though—or rather, that the autonomous car groups, whether Cruise at General Motors, Waymo, or Tesla, are gathering—goes way beyond what you might think of as data for moving vehicles around.

Because they need to track literally everything on the road, their AI systems have been taught to recognize everything from a ball to a child riding a bike, and their systems predict the next likely action of each of these things. These systems have also learned how to recognize parking meters, parking spaces, curbs, poles, and other things that they might need to navigate into and out of.

Now, think about when Spatial Computing glasses and autonomous cars work together. The car system itself can watch how many people are waiting in line at, say, a nightclub. It can tell how busy a downtown district is, or whether a restaurant is either lighter or busier than usual.

At Microsoft, 15 years ago, they showed us how predictive systems could use huge amounts of data to predict just how busy a freeway would be at a certain time, long before you would leave on your journey. Today that kind of prediction seems pretty quaint as Spatial Computing glasses and autonomous vehicle systems are gathering 10,000 times or more data than was gathered by early AI-based systems, and the amount of data is increasing exponentially every year.

So, what is possible as these systems mature and as more and more data is gathered, either by fleets that grow from hundreds of thousands of AI-outfitted fleets to millions of cars, all assisted like an ant farm with millions of people gathering other data on their wearable computers that are also mapping the world out in 3D?

You'll be able to see literally everything about the street in real time. Is there a wreck ahead? You'll see it within seconds of it happening, and potentially even be able to watch it happen in 3D on your glasses. Lots of other news will also be displayed on maps in the future this way. Everything from bank robbers to fires. Already, lots of cars are able to display video captured from dashcams or the cameras included in, say, a Tesla, which has AI that senses that humans are moving around the car in a way that they shouldn't, so it starts playing loud music and records them in an attempt to get them to move away from the car.

Systems like Waze have long warned of things like potholes or objects on the road ahead, but in a world where cars have 5G radios and can transmit huge amounts of 3D data, by 2030 you will be able to see changing road conditions sent to you by cars imaging those conditions ahead. The thing is, most of us around that time won't care about road conditions at all, except maybe in some extreme weather situations where sensors stop working, or the road can't properly be sensed. Even then, the autonomous car network might "hand over" control of your vehicle to an employee wearing an expensive Virtual Reality headset and they would remote control your car without the passenger even knowing about it—all thanks to the data systems that are gathering, processing, and sharing a 3D view of both the real world and a digital twin, or copy, of the real world.

Speaking of that digital twin, with your Spatial Computing glasses, you will be able to see a whole raft of new kinds of games, along with new kinds of utilities. Pass by a historical marker? Well, grab a virtual version of that with your hand and pull it closer to you so you can read the sign, all while your car zooms past. Want a hamburger? Tell your glasses your needs and they will be satisfied but not just with a "McDonalds is 2.5 miles away" but with a full 3D menu of the food options so you can have your order waiting for you when your car navigates you there and you'll know exactly what to expect, whether it's a salad, a hamburger, or something more complex like a Vietnamese soup.

The kids, too, will have their own Spatial Computing glasses and will invite you to join in their game, where they are manipulating a metaverse, or virtual world, that you are driving through. Toyota, and others, have already demonstrated such Virtual and Augmented Reality games that are under development.

It is the predictions that are possible because of all the data being collected as you navigate, stop for food, go to church, head to work, that are really set to shake things up. Remember, a system that has hundreds of thousands of cars, each with eight cameras and a variety of other sensors, can "see" patterns humans just can't. The system can predict what's next, knowing that a baseball game is about to finish, for instance, and can reroute everyone within seconds. Humans just aren't that good at knowing things like that. These predictions, done on a mass scale, will save millions of people a few seconds a day, sometimes minutes. Add those all up and it's the same as saving a life's worth of time every day, and at a bigger scale will truly revolutionize transportation.

Already, Tesla is giving a taste of how magical predictive systems are. In late 2019, Tesla cars started automatically navigating you to your next appointment, thanks to hooking up to your work and personal calendars, whether on Google or Microsoft systems.

These predictive databases and the AIs that are working on your behalf will make the transportation system itself much more efficient, safer, and more affordable. For instance, if you were to take a car on a long trip, these systems would know that long before you left, probably because you put something about the trip on your calendar, or told social media friends "Hey, we are going to New Orleans next weekend. Anyone want to meet up?" Or, even without any signals, it would figure out that you were on a long-range trip as soon as you crossed a geofence 30 miles out of town. All the way, the master in the sky would be able to route you the fastest way and even hook you up in a convoy to save everyone some money on electricity for your vehicles.

Fleets like those owned by UPS are already starting to move toward being completely automated and electric. UPS, in January 2020, announced that it will buy 10,000 electric vans and install Waymo's autonomous driving package onto each (Waymo is the autonomous vehicle start-up spun out of Google's R&D labs, and was the first self-driving vehicle system we saw on Silicon Valley roads).

The predictive system taking care of you on trips, and preparing the car for you automatically, saves a few seconds of typing of an address into a phone-based map or clicking around on a screen to get it to navigate, an act that can be very dangerous if you attempt it while driving, which many people do. It seems like something minor, but over the next decade, our glasses and car screens will add dozens, if not hundreds, of little features like these to make our lives easier.

After all, we are creatures of habit. Sam Liang, who used to work on the Google Maps team, told us just that. He now runs an AI speech recognition engine. He recognized years ago that the context that humans were trying to do something in matters to make computing systems work better.

After all, if you are wearing your glasses while driving a car, you will expect a different set of functions to be available to you than, say, when you are attending church, and that will be different than if you are watching a movie.

The cloud computing infrastructure that is watching your glasses, and all the cars moving around you, is about to make life itself much different than it was a decade ago when Uber seemed like a big idea. Let's discover how it'll work, not just when you are ordering a car, but in the technology you utilize, the media you consume, and in the communications systems you use.

Technology, Media, and Telecommunications (TMT)

Where and what you pay attention to is already paid a lot of attention. Teams of engineers at Netflix, YouTube, Hulu, Spotify, Disney, and other media and entertainment services, have developed systems to pay attention to what media choices you make and where and what you watch, and they have already built extensive prediction systems. You can see these systems come to life when your kids use your accounts for the first time and all of a sudden you start seeing suggestions that you watch more SpongeBob.

In the Spatial Computing world, though, the data collected will go far beyond what movie, TV show, or website link you click on. There are seven cameras on the devices that Qualcomm's new XR2 chipset enables: four for looking at the world, one for watching your face for sentiment, and two for watching your eyes.

It is the ability to see user sentiment and watch where users are looking that will open up many new predictive capabilities that will change even the entertainment we see. Knowing you actually looked at a door in a game or interactive movie of the future, for instance, could put you down a different path than if you looked elsewhere. Thanks to the incredible download speeds that wireless will soon bring with 5G, the device you are wearing itself could load quite complex 3D models before you even open the door to look through.

Already, games like Minecraft Earth are loading assets based on where you are located, and if you walk down the street, it predicts you will continue walking down the street and loads characters and game pieces ahead of when you need to see them.

Microsoft's Flight Simulator has worked this way for more than a decade. As you fly your virtual plane, the system loads scenery and city details ahead of you so that everything is sharp and doesn't stutter when you fly over, say, New York. Entertainment makers are planning out new kinds of entertainment that let you choose a variety of paths through the entertainment. Netflix already has shown how this will work with its TV project "Black Mirror: Bandersnatch." There, you can make choices for the characters that shape the story as you go. In Spatial Computing glasses, touching things, looking at other things, and moving around your real-world living room might impel movies and games you are enjoying to show you different story paths.

Lots of pioneers in the industry refer to an off-Broadway New York play, "Sleep No More," which is a new version of Shakespeare's Macbeth, except it isn't performed on a stage. Audience members wander through a huge warehouse, with action happening all around as you walk through the set.

Innovators like Edward Saatchi, who is the cofounder and CEO of Fable Studio, see this as foundational to the future of entertainment. Soon, he says, audiences will be walking through virtual sets, similar to in "Sleep No More," and will be interacting with virtual beings that can talk with you, or even play games with you, amongst other interactions. Fable's "Wolves in the Walls" is an example of just this and introduces a virtual character, Lucy, that can do just this. This Emmy-winning project has Lucy talking with you, and interacting with you, and is the first example of a virtual being we've seen that makes you feel like you are inside a movie.

Others are coming, say investor John Borthwick, who has invested in a variety of synthetic music and virtual being technologies. He sees the development of these new beings as a new kind of human-machine interface that over the next decade will become very powerful, both in terms of bringing new kinds of assistants to us, like a Siri or Alexa that we can see and almost touch, to new kinds of musical and acting performers for entertainment purposes. We spent a day at his Betaworks Studio, where we saw early work on an AI-based musical performer. Everything she sang and performed was developed by AI running on a computer. It is still pretty rough, but on other projects, Borthwick showed us AI is good enough to automatically generate elevator "muzak." You know muzak as the crappy background music in elevators and other public spaces. If an AI can generate that, it'll decrease the cost that hotels and shopping malls have to pay for public versions of that music.

Virtual beings like Lil Miquela are entertaining millions of people, though that version of a virtual being is an impoverished one of what the future will bring. Soon, in glasses, we will see volumetrically-developed characters who entertain you.

It's hard to see how this will happen because Lil Miquela isn't very good, and isn't truly interactive, and isn't run by an AI-based system; rather, she's more like a puppet with humans pulling her strings. Still, she has caught the attention of marketers and others who use her (or it, since she exists only in virtual space) as an example of advantages to marketers and entertainment companies. She'll never get arrested, or die in an accident, and she won't complain about poor contracts or having to work around the clock. Plus, marketers can make sure she'll never damage their brands, or cause them to get woken up early on a Sunday morning because she said something disturbing on Twitter in a drunken rage.

These virtual beings will be programmed to interact with you, asking you questions, presenting you with choices, and constantly feeding an exponential learning machine running behind the scenes. "Would you like to listen to Taylor Swift or Elton John?" she might ask one day. The answers you give will change every interaction you have from then on, and you might not even know, or care, just how deeply your experience has been manipulated, or how much a company behind the scenes is learning about your preferences and passions.

Give an exponential learning machine enough of these interactions and it quite possibly could figure out that you are a conservative Republican, or that you will soon be a full-blown country music fan, or even that you are of a particular sexual orientation—even if you've not yet been entirely honest with yourself about it. Each can be used to both addict you to more things that interest you, but there's a dystopian fear that the system could, even by accident, divide you from other humans and radicalize you into having potentially negative beliefs. We'll discuss that more in *Chapter 12, How Human?*

For now, know that Spatial Computing glasses are arriving at the same time as extremely high-speed wireless networking and Artificial Intelligence that can drive cars and predict the future moves of hundreds of people, and animals, around you. Add this all together and you'll be experiencing new kinds of movies, new kinds of games, and will see the real world in quite different ways with many augmented layers that could show various things both above and below the street, including other people's information.

Don't believe us? Facebook has a strategy book that it built for the next five-to-ten years, where it details how people will use Spatial Computing and describes how you will know whether someone is a friend, or connected to a friend, on the street, and enable you to play new kinds of video games with them. Already, in Virtual Reality in Facebook's Oculus Quest product, you can play paintball and basketball, amongst dozens of other games, with friends and random people.

Next, let's think about how Spatial Computing and the data associated with it will impact the world of manufacturing.

Manufacturing

We predict that within the next five-to-seven years, Virtual Reality and Augmented Reality combined with Computer Vision and ML-massaged data will be used much more in manufacturing than they are currently. The drivers for making this happen have to do with efficiency, quality, and safety.

Efficiency, quality, and safety will all increase when more Spatial Computing systems are integrated into manufacturing processes because the humans working in manufacturing could then focus less on the repetitive aspects of their jobs that are currently taking up much of their time, to focus on other tasks where human decision-making processes could be used. The negative aspects of human rationale when encountering repetitive tasks could be avoided—those associated with a lack of focus and tiredness that lead to slower productivity, lower quality assurance, and injuries.

Additionally, these Spatial Computing systems, most notably those using Augmented Reality, will be fully integrated to work with robotics and other machinery so that currently existing setups could be improved upon. Besides being used for making products, both VR and AR will be used for training purposes, as well as for accessing machine breakdowns and recommending solutions.

Porsche Cars North America has rolled out an AR-based solution for service technicians at dealerships, for instance. Why? Porsche, and its vendor that built the system, Atheer, says that the system connects dealership technicians to remote experts via smartglasses for a live interaction that can shorten service resolution times by up to 40 percent.

In complex assembly, using Augmented Reality sees even bigger gains. As Boeing builds a 747-8 Freighter, its workers keep track of 130 miles worth of wiring with smart glasses and the Skylight platform from Upskill. The result? Boeing cut wiring production time by 25 percent and reduced error rates effectively to zero.

At BAE, they are using Microsoft HoloLens headsets to build the motors for their electric busses. The software system they used, Vuforia Studio from PTC, let them train new people from 30 percent to 40 percent more efficiently and build these motors much faster and with lower error rates.

Once a few more large corporations adopt Spatial Computing in their manufacturing operations, they will become even more operationally efficient, which will lower their operational costs and give them market advantages. This will cause other companies to adopt Spatial Computing technology for their manufacturing operations until it becomes a business standard.

Having covered manufacturing, let's now move on to think about the world of retail.

Retail

As you walk into Sephora's R&D lab in San Francisco, you see the depth to which they are thinking of using technology to improve the customer's experience there. They built an entire copy of the store so they can run tons of customers through the store and study every interaction. This shows up on perfume displays that have been digitized, so you can smell each product without spraying it on your skin, along with Augmented Reality-based signs, and even virtual makeup that you can try. All of these experiences are improved through the use of data on all sorts of things that happen in the store, from the dwell times that customers spend hanging out in front of displays to real-time sales that provide feedback loops, to promotions and store changes.

Another example of a retail store that integrates Spatial Computing is Amazon's Go store. The Go store has hundreds of sensors overhead, and in the store, there are sensors on the shelves and cameras above tracking everything. When a person grabs a product off the shelf, the store automatically charges them through the Go app. Gathering data on people's buying habits has never been easier.

Today's e-commerce stores have trouble vividly showing you how a product will actually look when you receive it. Spatial Computing glasses change all that deeply, by bringing you 3D visuals of products, and we predict 3D stores where you will be able to grab products off of virtual shelves, spin them around in your hands, and even try them out.

This will give retailers whole new sets of data to study and use to improve their presentations and the products themselves, but it is the predictive possibilities of these new displays that have the retail industry most excited says Raffaella Camera, Global Head of Innovation & Strategy, XR and Managing Director, Accenture Interactive.

What do we mean? Well, let's say you add a wedding or a baby shower to your calendar; these systems can bring new shopping experiences to life. Imagine a wedding registry, populated with 3D products that your friend has picked out, along with maybe 3D images of your friend explaining why they added that item. Touch an item or show some interest in it, and it can change the entire display. For instance, touch a china plate and it could instantly show you all sorts of other things that pair with it, from glassware to silverware that you might also purchase for your friend.

The industry is salivating at getting this new data, which includes where you look, what you touch, and what you buy.

"Give me eye-tracking data of you in the real world for a week, just going about your business," says Roope Rainisto, Chief Design Officer and cofounder at Varjo, which makes the high-end VR headset that Volvo is using to design new car interiors. "The value of that data for learning about your preferences is so immense—behaviors that are currently not visible to these online services."

What will that data be used for? Rainisto sees a new shopping assistant. "There is far too much information for one person to understand and to even keep track of. The personal assistant will swoop in, help us by telling us things we should know or would like to know, do menial tasks, like keeping track of the prices of particular goods, put items on a wish list for the future, etc.

"How does the assistant become good at its job?" he asks. "Through learning us. This learning is fundamentally the exact same learning as what is used in ad targeting. Once the assistant knows me, then it can properly help me. Before that, its services will 'feel like ads'—pushing stuff I do not find all that relevant or helpful."

Retail itself will be changed deeply by these predictive systems and by workers who use Spatial Computing devices. For instance, today if you buy something in, say, B&H Photo in New York, an order goes into a warehouse and a worker grabs the camera you want and puts it into a tray that goes on a conveyor belt to where you complete your purchase. If you are buying online, the same process happens, except your product goes to a separate packing warehouse. Soon these systems will be made more efficient thanks to workers who are directed what to do by wearable computers that can see the products via Computer Vision and show the worker all sorts of detail via Augmented Reality.

These warehouse workers using Spatial Computing devices and hooked into a system of retail helpers (both real humans and virtual assistants) will radically change retail.

Logistic robots are already doing this, but not as efficiently as a human because Computer Vision for a robot, along with Machine Learning, is not sophisticated enough to recognize novel objects and objects that are not uniform. There are researchers already working to make this possible, but it will take another five years.

When this happens, very few humans will be working in logistics. Even with today's limited technology, this process of automating everything is underway; we've met warehouse owners who tell us they turned on completely automated warehouses in 2019.

Like with transportation, retail too will have a cloud computing system watching literally everything. Soon, such a system might even save your life; let's talk healthcare.

Healthcare

The combination of data, ML, and 3D visualization will be a great boon to healthcare. The data and ML combination have been used by practitioners, as well as non-practitioners, as in the case of the Apple Watch, for a few years already. The inclusion of 3D visualization, paired with location and situational awareness, makes a big difference, even saving a few lives as the systems watching sensors can tell whether you have taken a terrible fall or are having a heart attack.

Healthcare practitioners will be able to view patients' current conditions, including 3D scans of their internal organs, as well as run simulations of conditions, to plan and predict how surgery and other kinds of interventional procedures should go for those patients. As we mentioned in our chapter on healthcare, a company called MediView is already using Augmented Reality actively during cancer ablation surgeries. In the future, decisions about whether or not to perform surgery could be made using Spatial Computing methods.

The big change that will enable this to happen is the massive digitization of patient data that is currently underway now by hospitals and other organizations. Issues regarding this are the different systems that are being used by the different organizations and how they might not be universally accessible, and privacy issues having to do with bulk data. Without data being generally accessible, applying ML will not provide trustable outcomes. We believe that eventually, perhaps by the mid-2030s, medical data sharing via patient opt-ins will become more ubiquitous due to the immense benefit to society that would occur as a result.

Moving on from healthcare, let's take a look at how change is coming to finance.

Finance

We envision a day when many types of financial analyses and trading will be accomplished using Spatial Computing glasses or even contact lenses, as in the case of the Mojo Lens, a prototype smart contact lens from a Saratoga, California-based start-up, Mojo Vision.

Much of this could be accomplished because of the massive amounts of raw data streams that will be made available to make decisions, as well as data that has been characterized by ML. All of this relevant data could be portrayed in 3D, so that decision-making could be made even faster.

Virtual assistants could also be used in combination with voice querying, as well as proactive and opted-in suggestions honed in by ML to aid in making decisions as to whether or not to participate in a trade.

In addition to financial analyses and trading, and 3D data representations, Spatial Computing can also be used for customer-financial service rep interfaces. The combination of the use of voice, data, ML, and 3D visuals could make figuring out thorny financial issues much easier and faster.

Add in cameras and Computer Vision, and now we have facial recognition technologies that use ML, as well as body gait analysis technologies. With these, security is greatly increased, and all kinds of financial transactions could be more efficiently accomplished.

Finance is truly one of those areas that will be completely disrupted by the use of Spatial Computing; as it is with something like this, it is difficult to completely foresee all the different kinds of new apps and technologies that will emerge as a result of Spatial Computing's disruptive force.

Education

Not only will there be millions of people that remain unemployed for a significant amount of time post COVID-19, the coming increased automation in manufacturing and cars will bring on even more upheaval in society. Truck drivers, for instance, will largely lose their jobs in the next few decades. To America alone, that means a pretty deep restructuring of the landscape because trucks will no longer need to stop at small towns along interstates, which allowed hotel keepers and cafe workers to be employed, alike. Millions of people will see their livelihoods threatened and will need retraining to remain relevant in the modern world.

Even if you aren't struggling to put food on the table, though, Spatial Computing will radically change what it means to "be educated." Everyday activities like travel, cooking, learning about the latest science, watching the news, and even participating in civic duties, will change deeply because of Spatial Computing. We can see education changing dramatically in our discussions with founders of companies who are already planning ahead with 3D lesson plans and are building exponential learning engines to teach us everything from how to save a life to how to cook a certain meal. Our June Oven already has a camera in it and an Nvidia card, running Artificial Intelligence so it can automatically detect the kind of food we place in it and properly set the cooking temperature and time. On its app, it is already exposing us to an exponential learning engine that gets better over time, showing us more and more recipes, and properly recognizing more and more food types, from different kinds of fish and meat to different kinds of bread.

In our chapter on education, we cover how extensively the field is being changed by Spatial Computing. Here, we explore some things that are coming due to always-connected data engines that we call "exponential learning engines," which will soon change every part of our world, including how we learn.

For instance, in China, students are being checked in via facial recognition. In other places in China, teachers are starting to be replaced by AI and Virtual Reality. Well, actually, not replaced, since there aren't enough teachers to keep up with demand. Soon, the same might happen here, and what we call exponential learning systems, which are a combination of data and applied Artificial Intelligence that constantly learns from an increasing collection of data, will take over the act of educating.

Even here in the United States, these exponential learning systems will take over the act of educating many people. Why? We won't have enough teachers to keep up with demand soon, either. Look at truck driving, which is the number one job in the United States with 1.3 million people driving today. What will happen over the next decade or two when their jobs go away? Who will teach them to do something else? Already, companies like Caterpillar are using Augmented Reality glasses to teach people how to fix tractors in real time through visual overlays on top of the tractor itself. Mercedes-Benz is using AR to teach first responders how to cut apart a car without touching an electric line or fuel line. This app, designed by Germany's Re'flekt AR development firm, works on a tablet today, and glasses tomorrow, and shows firefighters arriving on scene at a car wreck where it's safe to cut.

The use of AR alone will make education better but think about any task. Could it be made better by hooking it up to an exponential learning machine? Even the Mercedes app could be made better, by studying, say, how a firefighter in Japan uses it on a custom rebuilt car. That learning could be shared with the cloud computer in the sky and shared instantly with all the other firefighters in the world, making everyone's skills and knowledge better.

Can such a system learn via ML that humans aren't doing a task right and gently nudge them with visuals in their glasses that there is a better way to do something? Even something as difficult as, say, learning a language, how to play an instrument, or how to make a complicated meal, can be made better by joining an exponential learning engine with Spatial Computing glasses displaying Virtual Reality and Augmented Reality to its wearer, and mundane things, like cooking an egg, or replacing a tire, are made much simpler with Augmented Reality assistants. Yes, you can look those up on YouTube already, but if you were wearing Spatial Computing glasses, you would be able to see assistant images and directions right on top of what you are trying to learn, and the sensors on the glasses could watch to make sure you took the right steps too.

Classroom teachers are currently getting a taste with the Merge Cube, a low-cost plastic cube you hold in front of a camera on a phone or tablet that overlays AR images. But this is a very elementary example of what could be accomplished with Spatial Computing in the future. Keeping you immersed in the digital world makes learning better, and letting you use your hands on top of a real task will enable new education that is hard to imagine today. Like the employees at Caterpillar, students will learn through information and media superimposed on top of the task they are trying to master in real time.

Imagine learning chemistry or surgery this way! It's already happening, but this will speed up dramatically over the coming decade and affect every part of human life, always making sure we have the latest knowledge and visualization to help us understand in 3D, which is how our brains think and learn—all with data that's constantly getting better and more detailed. Already, AI is finding cancer in medical scans more accurately than human doctors can. In the future, an exponential learning engine will connect all scanners and doctors together and all doctors utilizing the system will receive the benefits each time the system learns something new.

Can school children be taught by such a method? While we can't see a world where an adult isn't nearby or facilitating learning, we can see many lessons taught via Augmented and Virtual Reality. When we were in school in the 1970s and 1980s, many lessons were taught via film strips or movies. Soon those kinds of lessons will be taught by asking kids to put on a pair of "learning glasses." These glasses will teach everything from history to chemical reactions and the connected exponential learning systems will keep track of every lesson and every student. The adults in the room could then still be notified if someone is falling behind, falling asleep, or goofing off, which is something we still see kids doing in the future.

We've now considered the seven verticals. Let's zoom out to a wider perspective in the next and final section and think about something that we refer to as the "bubbleland."

The "Bubbleland"

We soon will live in a digital ant farm, or, as we put it, the "bubbleland." We came up with the term after watching how autonomous cars see the world. Each has a digital bubble around it, beyond which it cannot see. Humans work the same way, but we don't think of our perception systems that way, sometimes believing that we can even sense the unseen. In the digital world of Spatial Computing, in the case of glasses, robots, virtual beings, and autonomous vehicles, however, their perception systems are limited to what their cameras and 3D sensors can see.

Or are they really limited that way? If you throw millions of such little bubbles onto a city, are there many places that a bubble doesn't touch? No.

The Bubble Network

We see such a city as having an exponentially growing number of exponential learning machines, each with a bubble of what they can sense, all communicating with a central cloud computing system that we call an exponential learning machine. Add a bubble or a new set of glasses or a new autonomous vehicle and this unified system gets more information that it can use to "see" or understand the world we live in better. Add even more and we'll get more services and more utility. It is a new network effect. In previous generations of networks, as more people joined in, the network got more interesting. This is why the web eventually got so complex we needed search engines like Yahoo and Google to keep track of it all.

The new network effect, though, isn't about the information on pages, but it's these information bubbles moving around the real world. One such bubble might have to do with all the information circulating waiting in line at a nightclub. Another might be around someone pumping gas into their car. Another might be around those worshipping at church. Yet another could occur when picking up groceries for tonight's family dinner.

Unified Learning, Shared Experiences

A unified exponential learning system can keep track of all of this, seeing inventory changes at grocery stores, lines at gas stations, activity at nightclubs, keeping track of the latest learning delivered at universities, and much more. Each bubble would be training the system and teaching AIs what to further look for. This unified exponential learning system eventually will turn even hungrier for data and might ask the people wearing the glasses, or the robot car, to move around and gather more data. "Hey, we haven't seen aisle three in a few hours, can you walk down there with your glasses and check out the cookie display?" our glasses might ask soon, maybe even offering a discount on a purchase to incent us to provide more data so that the system would have accurate cookie prices and inventory data to share with everyone on the network.

Soon maps will show these bubbles in real time, or at least the data that they are gathering. While today, when you see an accident on the road, it shows a red line to denote that traffic is backed up, or an icon where the accident is reported, tomorrow, you will see a 3D version of the wreck on the map and you will know the speed of each lane of traffic as reported by these bubbles.

It'll be the same for grocery stores, churches, malls, movie theaters, restaurants, laundromats, National Parks, and more. You might even be able to "dive into" a bubble that is explicitly sharing their digital bubble with the world. Wouldn't you love to do that in someone's bubble who is in the front row of a Lady Gaga concert? We know we would, and we would be happy to share such an experience by telling our glasses "Hey Siri, share this with the world." Other experiences might be more specific "Hey Siri, share this with Grandma." Or, "Hey Siri, share this with other parents at our school."

Soon the 360-degree video cameras that are currently on sale will seem very quaint indeed, as stupid, unconnected, individual data sources. The Spatial Computing glasses of the future, and the autonomous cars and robots, will take the concept a lot further, to where they teach exponential learning systems a lot more about the world as they are walked around, and present viewers with tons of interesting views of the real world, including new digital twins that someone thousands of miles away will be able to move around in, and interact with, and maybe even add to. This bubbleworld of the future is one that is very human, creative, and inevitable.

Pervasive and Proactive Future Assistance

As we've shown here, soon our technology will know we didn't yet put out the garbage or will prepare you for your next meeting in ways you never thought of, not to mention perhaps warning you about a health problem that's coming for you based on your biometric data. Our Tesla cars are already sensing when garbage cans are out, so this day isn't far away, and soon not only Teslas will perform this kind of object and pattern recognition, but so will millions of people wearing new Spatial Computing glasses and little delivery robots rolling around stores and streets.

Next, let's look at a few of the pioneers who are already starting to use these technologies to change everything from transportation to shopping.

11

Spatial Computing World-Makers

In our previous chapters, we covered seven verticals that will be impacted by Spatial Computing. Here, we introduce seven people who we feel will be especially instrumental in making Spatial Computing technologies successful and profitable. Let's meet Raffaella Camera, Dr. Brennan Spiegel, Rob Coneybeer, Ken Bretschneider, John Borthwick, Hugo Swart, and Sebastian Thrun.

The Market Illuminator

Raffaella Camera, Managing Director and Global Head of Innovation and Market Strategy, XR at Accenture Interactive

"Product placement and assortment in a store and on a shelf isn't just guesswork," says Raffaella Camera, Managing Director, Global Head of Innovation and Market Strategy, XR (Extended Reality) at Accenture Interactive.

She sees radical changes coming to retail due to Spatial Computing and is, with her team, already saving consumer products brands and retailers billions of dollars through her research. She is researching eye-tracking, which not only helps in finding better places for products to sit on the shelf, but would also aid a new kind of retail worker, one that has data on their side and uses new Spatial Computing technology to reduce costs. Camera noticed that the old way to design stores and test them out was very expensive.

A lot of older consulting work required building prototype stores, often in a warehouse somewhere. We visited one such store at Sephora, where they had an entire store set up in a San Francisco warehouse. She saw that was expensive because it required executives from each brand to come to a physical location to give feedback on how to improve layouts or do testing with consumers. Instead, she pushed her clients to move to Virtual Reality headsets, which let both customers and all the stakeholders learn more, have earlier input on store layouts, and reduce costs. She told us that this work in VR led to major new insights that they wouldn't have gotten otherwise.

"We were able to prove that there was a high level of correlation between traditional testing and VR," she says, which is a huge return on investment (ROI) of these new technologies. This means that executives at brands can start to trust that results reached by studying customers in VR headsets will match real-world results.

The ROI gets better the more technology a store uses, Camera said her findings showed. She said that as stores have bigger libraries of 3D products and store layouts, they will see additional cost savings because they can redesign stores using existing libraries instead of having to spend a bunch scanning new displays or products.

Her biggest breakthrough, though, may be in the use of next-generation eye-tracking. She says that this field is bringing rafts of new data about how people shop. She is now able to get detailed data about what customers in research situations looked at, what they looked at prior to that, what action were they taking while they were looking at something, and whether they were picking up and turning the product around. How long was that done for? Did they put it in the cart? How did that relate to products prior to that? What she was testing wasn't the typical heat map that shows where people are looking, or hanging out, in a store. "We were inundated with data," she said, while explaining that the data was giving her insights that were impossible to understand at scale before.

This data is leading to changes in everything from product packaging design to how products are grouped together on store shelves.

"We wanted to use technology, and specifically VR, or Virtual Reality, to reinvent how brands gather consumer data and perform research, allowing them to do it faster, more affordably, and at scale," she says, while talking about work she and her team at Accenture did for Kellogg's as it launched a new Pop-Tarts brand. Using that data, they discovered that it was more effective to place the new Pop-Tarts Bites product on lower shelves than on upper shelves. At scale, this could lead to millions of dollars of profit and reduced costs as inventory sits on store shelves for less time.

When we talked with Camera, she walked us through a number of new retail innovations that will soon come to shoppers, including AI that knows where every product is in stores. She sees a world where glasses will navigate shoppers directly to products in the most efficient way possible, but also AR visualizations that make shopping more experiential and fun, all while feeding data back to the retailer and to the brand owners.

She is one of the few, though, who are working with retail brands, helping them think through and design for the changes that are coming in the home as we get radical "virtual stores" that let us walk through virtual showrooms with both AR and VR headsets. Distribution changes are coming with robots and other autonomous vehicles that will make product delivery faster, more consistent, and cheaper, which will also further encourage more people to shop electronically from home. The systems she is working on for the physical stores will someday help robots find and pack products in stores and warehouses too.

When you talk with her, though, her real passion is understanding consumer shopping behavior, and she's most interested in getting more shoppers to use eye sensors that will soon be included in lots of Spatial Computing wearable glasses. These eye sensors will enable her to understand even better how consumer beliefs and behaviors are changing and how packaging should be changed to appropriately grab consumers. She sees huge shifts coming as brands are able to "augment" their products too, and add new digital information onto those packages that will jump onto your glasses as your eyes pass over them, with new kinds of promotional ties and educational experiences, all with the new feedback loop of eye-sensor-tracked consumers giving new data to retailers and brands.

Her work is gaining industry attention, and the project she worked on with Kellogg's won a Lumiere Award for best use of VR for merchandising and retail.

The Pain Reducer

Dr. Brennan Spiegel, Director of Health Services Research at Cedars-Sinai Health System and Professor of Medicine and Public Health at UCLA

Dr. Brennan Spiegel is a true believer that Virtual Reality and 360 Video can be used to manage pain in hospitalized patients. Cognitive behavioral therapy and mindful meditation have been used to lower pain thresholds, along with, of course, opioids.

His belief is backed up by a formal study, which concluded in 2019, and another in 2017, both of which he led and were conducted at the Cedars-Sinai Medical Center. When combined with 360 Video, participants' reported pain relief was significantly greater than that which resulted from the use of conventional pain therapy alone.

For that 2019 study, the 61 participants in the experimental group out of the total test group of 120 used Samsung Gear headsets and software from AppliedVR, a company that produces VR and 360 Video experiences made specifically for medical use. They viewed experiences from a library of 21 possible experiences three times a day for 10 minutes, with additional viewings as needed during pain episodes.

Participants' pain was at least a level three on a scale of zero to 10 when the treatment began. With the 360 Video treatment, for participants reporting pain at seven or above on the pain scale, the average reduction in pain was three levels. And for every 10 years the patient increased in age, an average further reduction of 0.6 on the pain scale was indicated. So, the more pain a participant felt and the older they were, the better the treatment was.

Opioids were still administered, along with the viewing of 360 Videos. Dr. Spiegel believes that "a future study may help answer if (VR) could be an alternative (to opioids)." He hopes that VR can be added not only to treatment with opioids but to any pain management program.

Additionally, in the future, the inclusion of lightly interactive VR experiences in addition to 360 Video is thought to possibly produce an even better result, since interactivity could further engage a patient and make them lose more track of time, taking the focus off of pain further.

According to Dr. Spiegel, a more formal way of looking at the mechanism by which VR and 360 Video could reduce pain has to with "the so-called gate theory of pain... if our mind, our prefrontal cortex is being overwhelmed by pain, what we have to do is introduce another stimulus that is even more compelling." This other stimulus should be of the visual kind, since "the visual cortex accounts for far more than fifty percent of sensory cortex." Dr. Spiegel views this visual stimulus to reduce pain as "a photonic Trojan Horse."

Bolstered by these results, Dr. Spiegel and his team have developed the largest and most widely-documented medical VR program in the world at Cedars-Sinai. About 20 percent of Dr. Spiegel's work time is spent on this medical VR program. Dr. Spiegel has also founded the first international symposium dedicated to medical VR (www.virtualmedicine.health), as well as written a book that will be coming out in October 2020, *VRx: How Virtual Therapeutics Will Revolutionize Medicine*.

Dr. Spiegel thinks that in the future VR and 360 Video therapy could be routinely used for cases of Alzheimer's disease and other kinds of dementia, schizophrenia, anorexia nervosa, and compulsive overeating.

For Alzheimer's disease and other kinds of dementia, as well as for anorexia nervosa and compulsive overeating, the mechanism that could allow VR and 360 Video therapy to work would be related to reinforcement. That is, with these conditions there is a loss of connection with the patient's inner body—the mind and body have become disconnected. The VR and 360 Video experiences would be specially tailored with content that would be re-watched until some kind of connected relief is felt.

For schizophrenia, according to Dr. Spiegel, the way VR therapy could routinely be used has to do with calibrating the alien voice or voices in a patient's head with their own voice in VR until the patient realizes that they could control the alien voice or voices.

"So when they get into Virtual Reality, when they see and hear their 'demons,' the entities are using their voice. And it's actually voiced by the therapist who sits in another room—through a voice that's been put through the computer to sound like their voice. And they can do this over time. Demonstrate to that patient that they can control their own voice, but they have to do it over 12 weeks or so. And eventually they gain providence over that voice. But the voice doesn't go away. The voice becomes a companion, somebody who's actually maybe there to help them out."

In the future, within the next five-to-ten years, Dr. Spiegel believes that there will be a new kind of clinician that he calls the "virtualist." This person will be one who is trained to use VR and 360 Video therapies and technologies within the context of clinical medicine and clinical psychiatry. In this way, the healthcare field will be able to more readily embrace and utilize Spatial Computing for patient wellbeing.

The Investing Visionary

Rob Coneybeer, Managing Director and Co-founder at Shasta Ventures

Rob Coneybeer of Shasta Ventures, an early-stage venture capital firm, has long seen the advantages of building machines that have smarts in them. He was one of the first investors in Nest, which made a thermostat for the home that was connected to a cloud computing service. By doing that, homes became more efficient and let owners control them much more easily, even letting them turn on heat or air conditioning from mobile phones before they got home.

Coneybeer, who has a background in aerospace engineering and is a race car enthusiast, co-founded Shasta Ventures with partners Ravi Mohan and Tod Francis. Shasta currently has more than $1 billion under management, with two-thirds of its portfolio enterprise-related and the rest consumer-related.

Among other investments, Coneybeer has invested in Fetch Robotics, a company that develops robots for logistical and other markets, Airspace Systems, currently the only drone security solution capable of identifying, tracking, and autonomously removing rogue drones from the sky, Starship Technologies, a company developing small self-driving robotic delivery vehicles, and Elroy Air, makers of hybrid-electric autonomous **vertical take-off and landing** aircraft (**VTOL**) for cargo transport.

These four Spatial Computing investments were spotted early by Coneybeer. Shasta invested in Fetch Robotics for their Series A in 2015, and they have continued to invest for their Series B and Series C, which is the latest round. Similarly, Shasta invested in Airspace Systems' Seed Round in 2016, as well as their Series A (latest round), Starship Technologies' Seed Round in 2017, in addition to their Series A (latest round), and Elroy Air's Seed Round in 2017 (still at Seed Stage).

Coneybeer says that, as early as five years ago, there were very few companies that were offering robotics for commercial applications. LIDAR and sensors were just not yet powerful or relatively cheap enough yet to be put into smaller robots. Current companies like Shasta-invested Fetch Robotics and Starship Technologies, though, can take advantage of sensors that enable robots to be tele-operated—that is, supervised from another location by human operators when needed. The software for that is not easy to write, but very useful for the five-to-ten percent of the time when human intervention is needed. That covered differential could make the difference between whether a company will survive or not.

"When you have a system like that, what's beneficial about it is you start to be able to gather statistics and you know that if out of your ten robots on a daily basis there's a path that they use over and over and over again, you can see that you got a problem that you need a human to solve—then you can go ahead and have basically like a scoring algorithm to figure out which problems you solved and then be able to turn them into fully autonomous situations so that the robot can go through and solve those problems on your own because they're encountering them over and over and over again," Coneybeer says.

Coneybeer is most excited about this stage where the interplay between humans and robots is crucial. It is during this time over the next five-to-10 years that neural nets and other algorithms will become more finely tuned after the robot systems have experienced both repetitive and fresh tasks. Companies that take advantage of the need for humans during this time, Coneybeer feels, will be winners.

An example of a technology that's currently being developed where human interplay is a core need is off-road four-wheel-drive autonomous driving, with a team of researchers at the University of Washington leading the effort. Coneybeer adds that some of the best places to find future Spatial Computing technologies and teams are in the research areas at universities such as Carnegie Mellon University and Stanford University, as well as the University of Washington.

Further out, in about ten-to-fifteen years, Coneybeer feels is when we will be able to really get robotic locomotion and manipulation so fine-tuned that "you could have a household robot that can do things like lock up upstairs open doors in your home, and pick things out of the refrigerator and then bring them to you." This kind of robotic virtue related to locomotion and grasping will also be very useful in enterprise situations, such as logistics and manufacturing.

"Advances in perception, driven by Deep Learning, Machine Vision, and inexpensive, high-performance cameras allow robots to safely navigate the real world, escape the manufacturing cages, and closely interact with humans," Coneybeer concludes.

The Immersive Genius

Ken Bretschneider, Founder and CEO of Evermore Park and The Grid, and Co-founder of The Void

In 2012, Ken Bretschneider sold his encryption security company, DigiCert, an encryption security company that had grown to more than 1,000 employees globally. He was on a mission then to develop and open his immersive outdoor 11-acre space, Evermore Park. Before doing that, though, he co-founded the pioneering VR location-based company The Void, short for "The Vision of Infinite Dimensions," in 2014. Evermore Park opened in 2018. In 2019, Bretschneider opened The Grid, an immersive destination and dining space that is located very close to The Void's location in Pleasant Grove, Utah.

Effectively, both The Void and The Grid are more technically sophisticated extensions of what Evermore Park offers — Virtual Reality is core to their business model, while Evermore Park focuses on live actors and does not have any rides, but has three different "seasons." The first is called Lore, which is geared toward Halloween, the second season is Aurora with a Christmas theme, and the third is called Mythos and is filled with magic and dragons.

Regarding the origins of Evermore Park, Bretschneider has said, "It started when I was a little five-year-old kid. I grew up in a really, really bad home situation where my father was very abusive, so it's not all a happy story. But I had (a) wonderful situation happen."

"That was so important for me as a kid—I needed escapism. I had to get out of that environment. It left such a huge impact on my entire life that I kept being drawn to this idea of imagination and creativity, and how it's so important for children and adults alike to be able to explore with their imagination and have an escape for a moment, to do something that's not part of the everyday grind."

Bretschneider had to stop work on Evermore Park for a few years because of its massive monetary and infrastructure development needs. In forming The Void, he could put his artistic and technical abilities to work in the meantime. A few years after its formation, the Walt Disney Company accepted The Void into their 2017 Disney Accelerator program. The initial investment of little more than $100,000, which was added to Bretschneider's own investment into the company, was not the main attraction—it was the support and Hollywood relationships that would prove to be useful, along with Disney's further investments into The Void at later dates.

The Void's first VR location-based experience was one that was commissioned for the new Ghostbusters movie and was called *Ghostbusters: Dimension*. The experience was released in 2016 and had a run at Madame Tussauds' New York location in Times Square. The actual interactive VR experience ran for only about 10 minutes and accommodated four players at a time. The VR headsets for The Void were custom made, along with the batteries needed to power them, and a haptic vest and computer backpack. The Void was the first company that had accomplished a successful VR location-based experience.

Sometime in 2017, Bretschneider decided that he wanted to get back more of his artistic freedom and he distanced himself from the increasingly Disney-operated The Void. He threw himself into getting Evermore Park up and running, which he did in 2018. Almost simultaneously, he started working on getting The Grid up and started, a 100,000-square-foot "experience center, an electronic playground" featuring the second-largest indoor kart race track in the country with vehicles capable of going 60 mph and proprietary VR experiences coming soon—in addition to 4,000 square feet dedicated to The Void experiences, and the One Up Restaurant and Lounge located on a mezzanine level.

According to Bretschneider, other locations for The Grid, including Chicago, Houston, and Seattle, are already on the radar.

Back in 2017, Bretschneider was the first person that spoke to us about using Machine Learning to develop virtual beings for use in VR location-based experiences. He continues to amaze us.

The Synthetics Craftsman

John Borthwick, CEO of Betaworks

John Borthwick sees "synthetic" in the future of Spatial Computing. He's an investor who sees a huge opportunity in using AI to create things we see and interact with. His name for this is "Synthetic Reality," for realities that include virtual beings walking around, and "Synthetic Media," for media, like music or videos that were created by AI with minimal human help.

Borthwick has been passing out $200,000 checks to a variety of companies that fit into this new form of AI-driven media creation and manipulation that he calls "synthetics." He told us he sees synthetics as a new world where there are virtual beings and other media, all created by Machine Learning. Think of them as virtual humans walking around you in either a totally virtual world, or on top of the real world in Augmented Reality forms or, alternately, various devices or combinations of devices and things that look human that perform music and could also bring you radical new art and video styles that weren't possible with just human-created media or forms.

One of his investments, Auxuman, showed us "Yona," a Machine Learning-driven singer-songwriter. Yona makes records in collaboration with human producers, performs live, and appears on social media. On screen, Yona looks like a human singing, but she is anything but human. Every note she sings or has playing in the background, and every action she makes, is created by a series of Machine Learning algorithms running underneath her. In other words, she is closer to a character you might see in a video game, except she has much more talent than a mere scripted character that you might meet in a video game.

Borthwick has great interest in this new field, which includes Lucy, an animated child who interacts with you in VR, built by San Francisco's Fable Studio, and Mica, a humanoid figure that plays games with you inside a Magic Leap headset. Lucy has won a ton of awards at film festivals, and an experience that featured her won a Primetime Emmy for "Outstanding Innovation in Interactive Media." Magic Leap's Mica was first demonstrated at the 2019 **Games Developer Conference (GDC)**, where she sat in a real chair across from humans who waited in line to meet her and then she proceeded to play a puzzle game with the GDC attendees. Magic Leap was careful not to pitch Mica as an assistant, so as not to be construed as a Siri or Alexa competitor. Much would be needed if that were the objective, included some sophisticated Machine Learning tools. As of now, she doesn't even speak.

Borthwick doesn't see these other forms of synthetic characters as competition, but as the beginnings of a new art form that enables many new companies and entrepreneurs. He notes that while some music stars, like the Beatles, were hugely popular, it didn't keep many other performers from getting very rich on stage, and he sees this new world evolving like music, with vast opportunities for entrepreneurs to introduce new capabilities to users, from assistants to entertainers, and sometimes both in the same form.

Your first impression of Yona might cause you to write her off as not being able to compete with humans. We agree she won't win any The Voice TV show singing competitions. Yet. Borthwick takes these criticisms in his stride, and the way that he gently helps us see that these are the future is one of the reasons he's won so many fans.

He says that the point of these early attempts at building synthetic beings isn't to compete with humans, but to make our coming virtual worlds more fun, or open up new opportunities that humans can't be present in. He noted that maybe soon there would be singing competitions with these synthetics and no humans. Since some virtual influencers and performers have already built huge audiences, including some in real life, we understand his point.

Borthwick sees a variety of business models that will potentially drive his investments, everything from licensing to corporations, to presenting them as virtual add-ons in experiences in Spatial Computing glasses, to advertising. He sees lots of business models that most may miss, too. He notes that many retail stores or hotels pay music licensing fees for the "muzak" that they play in the background. The Machine Learning algorithms, like the ones that run underneath Yona, could generate muzak to be played in shopping malls and elevators, and other populated spaces.

Yona wasn't alone in the synthetic stable of start-ups he's invested in. There's Comixify, which uses Machine Learning to turn videos or photos into comics; Deeptrace, which combats AI-synthetized media, known as "deepfakes;" Radical, an AI-powered 3D animation solution that requires no hardware or coding knowledge; and Resemble, which creates much better speech synthesis using Deep Learning, as compared to current technologies; and a few other companies.

Borthwick's start-ups are located inside the multi-story Betaworks offices that he runs in New York's Meatpacking District. He has long built start-ups this way, or guided them, having funded and incubated tons, including GIPHY and Bitly (GIPHY is a search engine for cute graphics that's used by hundreds of millions of people a month, and Bitly is a URL shortener used by many bloggers and social media fans). GIPHY was, as of 2019, still located on one of Betaworks' floors upstairs.

Walking through his offices, which now includes an "open to entrepreneurs" club that he calls Betaworks Studios, you will meet quite a few of the start-ups Borthwick's firm invested in. They get cheap rent here, and even if it wasn't cheap, it's the place to be in New York because of the Studios part of Betaworks, a separate business that is a club in which entrepreneurs from around the region are welcome to hang out at. Here, Borthwick and team throw many business- and technical-related events every week. It is this openness that has put him at the center of New York's growing entrepreneurial community and given him the insights, not to mention the capital, to bring a range of new capabilities to Spatial Computing.

The Chip Innovator

Hugo Swart, VP and GM of XR (VR and AR) at Qualcomm

Literally every smartphone and, soon, every Spatial Computing device, will have Qualcomm technology inside. This company isn't well known by consumers, yet it makes a lot of the chips inside every phone used, which gives it a hugely influential role in the world. Microsoft HoloLens and Nreal headsets use Qualcomm's chips. They also are inside the Oculus Quest VR headsets, among others. Computation, graphics, AI, and wireless chips are its specialty. The company is largely seen as the best example of a "mobile-first" company, having started by building communications devices for trucking fleets. Its competitors, such as Intel and AMD, started by building processors for desktop computers that didn't need to be as small, light, or power efficient as those in mobile devices, and that background has given Qualcomm a unique role in the industry and thrust one of its employees into a very public role: Hugo Swart. He runs the AR and VR efforts for the company, and he's frequently seen keynoting industry conferences explaining its strategy.

In our discussions with Swart, he laid out what makes Qualcomm special: it has evolved making chips for mobile devices from literally the first day it was opened. Their chips, he claims, use less power than competitors and are more flexibly fit into the small form factors that are needed to be worn on people's faces.

In 2019, Qualcomm came out of a legal fight with Apple as a huge winner—its 5G radios will be included inside Apple's 5G iPhones that will be introduced in 2020 and beyond (Apple tried to go with radios from Intel, and was hoping to pay far less for them, but Intel's technology just wasn't as good as Qualcomm's and that forced Apple back to the negotiating table). For that, Qualcomm will receive $9 per phone, and it's taking that money to do new research and development, a good chunk of it on Spatial Computing devices since Swart says that he, and the company, see Spatial Computing as the key use case for getting 5G. Swart is planning for a world where hundreds of millions of users are wearing Spatial Computing glasses to do all the things you are reading about in this book.

He is effusive as he explains how we will live and work in the future. "Soon we will get to the holy grail: a headset that does both Virtual and Augmented Reality," he says. In late 2019 he and Qualcomm laid out an aggressive strategy to bring exactly that to market before 2025, and it announced a new chipset and reference design (which means it has prototypes to show other manufacturers how to build a product that has the chipset inside), the XR2.

The XR2, he says, will enable all sorts of new Spatial Computing devices for people to wear. Along the rim of the devices will be up to seven cameras—two to watch your eyes, one to watch your mouth for help for voice assistants and also avatars that will need to match what you do with your mouth, and four to see the world, both to be able to record it and so that Augmented Reality images could be accurately placed.

Hugo has a background in engineering and started out as a manager in technical marketing in his home country of Brazil, learning the ropes and understanding how regional mobile operators worked with Qualcomm to deploy its technology. That led to a similar role inside Qualcomm. Then he moved into IoT and consumer electronics roles, which led to his current, visible role leading the company's efforts.

This holistic view of Qualcomm pays off because with XR2 it works with different original equipment manufacturers (OEMs) (like Microsoft or Nreal), to build their technology into the very different products that just those two companies are planning. He told us that some of these OEMs might only want a piece of its reference design, which includes separate chips to do graphics, AI, processing, wireless, audio, and other tasks. His pitch is, though, that for best results you'll want to get all of them from Qualcomm. "When we integrate them all together, we can make the whole system run faster," he told us. What he wouldn't discuss is how that changes the bill of materials cost (known in the industry as BOM), but we expect that negotiations over the entire package go better than if you try to get one chip from Qualcomm, another from Intel, and yet another from somewhere else. We'll see how those negotiations go as new products that hit the market at the end of 2020 and beyond have the XR2 chipset inside.

This vantage point that Swart and Qualcomm have brings the best partners in the door, too, most notably Niantic, which as of early 2020 is the number one Augmented Reality company and is behind the Pokémon Go and Harry Potter AR games. It and Qualcomm have announced that it's working on a future headset together, presumably with Niantic's software platform inside, based on the data collected from hundreds of millions of users, and Qualcomm's chips running the headset.

Qualcomm doesn't only do chips, though; they have sizable software teams to make those chips do useful things. For instance, the 835 chipset inside the Oculus Quest has software for the four cameras on the front of that device to do "inside-out VR tracking," which means the headset doesn't need external sensors to work, like previous generations did. We first saw inside-out tracking inside Qualcomm's labs two years before Facebook introduced that device.

Qualcomm, too, is building chips for autonomous cars, drones, robots, and other IoT devices for factories and homes, including medical devices. Increasingly, he says, Spatial Computing will be the way all of those other devices will be controlled.

If Swart's vision is correct (we believe it to be which is why we wrote this book), then who knows how far Swart will rise in stature in our industry over the next decade?

The Future Flyer

Sebastian Thrun, CEO of Kitty Hawk, and Co-founder and President of Udacity

If we were talking to Sebastian Thrun 15 years ago when he was starting his career at Carnegie Mellon and Stanford University, we might write him off as a wild dreamer, telling us about a future of autonomous cars, but today we can no longer dismiss him or his ideas.

Now he is talking to us about flying cars, which he's building as founder of a new startup, Kitty Hawk.

His dreams of the future go far beyond autonomous vehicles or flying cars, though. He sees huge changes to cities and how people live thanks to Spatial Computing, with its new user interfaces on top of both physical and virtual worlds. He sees us talking to something like Alexa or Siri to both order up new transportation and be navigated toward your vehicle.

Back at the beginning of his career, he ran a small experimental team at Stanford University that went on to win the DARPA Grand Challenge, a race through the desert to see if someone could really build a self-driving vehicle. That got the attention of Google's founders, who convinced him and his team of other students doing AI research to join. Today, you see their work in Waymo's self-driving vehicle fleet, which just recently (2019) got approval to drive without humans in a few cities.

Thrun's dreams were born out of tragedy, though. When he was growing up in Germany, a car accident killed a childhood friend, and later another accident claimed the life of a coworker; both were avoidable accidents. He told us that's what drove him to develop autonomous cars.

Now that the idea of autonomous vehicles isn't so futuristic anymore, he's moved on to building other parts of the ecosystem. First, he started Udacity, in part to help finish off autonomous vehicle development. This online education service helps train many developers who then work in the industry, completing his dreams.

Now he is seeing a new problem with all of this—as transportation costs come down, we'll see new congestion near city centers. The costs aren't just economic, either. Already, autonomous vehicles are letting us do more while getting driven around. These give us minutes and sometimes hours of our lives back to do other things.

Either way, we will see humans use transportation a lot more, and for further distances, than ever before, causing more traffic on our roads.

This congestion can also be helped, he says, by using technology that could be an efficient "traffic control" system to perhaps limit the number of cars that are allowed to come toward a city per hour. He told us that you might need to "buy a slot" on the freeway. Leaving at, say, 8:05 a.m. to come into a city like San Francisco might cost more than leaving at 10 a.m., or you might even need to win the lottery to be able to come in at that time at all.

Coming to the rescue of this situation, Thrun's company Kitty Hawk uses an approach aimed at fixing this congestion problem by having vehicles that fly overhead and by using Spatial Computing technology in unique ways to help these electronic flying vehicles navigate the skies safely without a pilot on board. He sees that airspace can support many more passengers than a freeway can, and it'll be cheaper. He mapped out a 100-mile flight for us from Stockton to San Francisco, which today takes two or more hours on the freeway but could be done in about 20 minutes and would cost less than driving a car that far.

Thrun notes that some of these vehicles will be so light and quiet that they will potentially open up new flight paths (they are much quieter than helicopters, so will be accepted closer to homes).

He isn't alone in the belief that autonomous vehicles might increase congestion. Elon Musk, CEO of Tesla, sees this problem coming, too, and has started another company, The Boring Company, to dig tunnels under cities like Los Angeles to enable drivers to get from one side of the city to the other within minutes.

Thrun sees that as impractical. Tunnels are expensive to dig, and you can't dig enough of them quickly enough and in enough directions to really solve the problem. So, he looks to the sky. He sees unlimited transportation real estate there in three dimensions.

The advantages of looking to the air are numerous, he told us. You can – using new Spatial Computing technologies—pack more flying things into "air highways" than ever before. These new vehicles are lighter, which means they are cheaper to operate, and they are quieter, so will be more accepted over residential neighborhoods than, say, helicopters or private jets. Both of these together add up to be game changers, he says.

When we talked with him, we pressed him on some of the many details that will need to get worked out. Governments will need to write new laws. People will need to change their beliefs about whether they need a human in the cockpit and will need to trust electric motors to safely deliver them.

New systems will be needed to ensure that accidents don't happen, and that the new "highways in the air" are effectively used by thousands of flying vehicles. Put all that together and it might scare away most entrepreneurs as too big a challenge.

Thrun's visions aren't done, though. He sees a world where everyone is wearing Spatial Computing glasses that you talk to, or gesture to with hands, or control with your eyes, or all the above. He sees them as providing a new user interface to talk with the transportation system and find a scooter, or a car that can take you further, or even, schedule one of Kitty Hawk's electronic flying vehicles. This dream also lets him revisit the actual design of cities. After all, we won't need as many parking spaces, because we'll have robots rolling around sidewalks bringing us things, and even meeting rooms will change due to these technologies.

It is visionaries like Thrun who are dreaming of this new world and then building the companies to bring these visions to life who will end up dramatically changing human life in ways that 15 years ago seemed incomprehensible. After all, can you imagine seeing hundreds, if not thousands, of autonomous flying vehicles in the sky? One day, we think this will be so.

Spatial Computing Paths

In this chapter, we have presented exemplary Spatial Computing industry people and discussed how we think they will be moving the industry forward in the future. From retail to transportation, it's clear that visionaries are foreseeing huge changes in almost all areas of our lives. With such changes to the very way we live, the ethics surrounding this technology are sure to be significant. In our next and final chapter, we provide guidance on particular ethical issues surrounding Spatial Computing, including issues relating to privacy and security, identity and ownership, and human social good.

12
How Human?

Reaching business nirvana could trigger issues that verge on the unethical. When systems are set up to be hyper-vigilant in order to maximize information gathering and understanding, it is not surprising that boundaries that should not be crossed are. Given that Spatial Computing is in its relative infancy, those boundaries need to be identified. Here, we first provide a framework that will aid in understanding why human beings tend to have cognitive issues with radical new technologies, and then we provide a background on current issues relating to privacy, security, identity, and ownership, and identify their relevance to Spatial Computing. We then proceed to discuss how Spatial Computing business nirvana and human social good could intersect as much as possible.

It does not escape us that in the process of creating and using technologies to aid and entertain, human beings can become slaves to those very technologies, which have the effect of dehumanizing them. Another passage to dehumanization is the effort to reduce too easily to data the characteristics of human individuals and human life for the sole purpose of commerce, rendering humans down to basic tools of utility. When human beings overly view themselves and others as consumption machines and the content of their lives as data points, they become estranged from themselves. An inherent contradiction is that this kind of rationalization is in itself very human. The key to avoid estrangement is to be balanced between our actual human needs and human wants. We have it in our power to manage that balance when it comes to Spatial Computing. Before we can do so, we need to have a good understanding of Spatial Computing technologies, which can only come out of experiencing them.

Transformative Experience

In her book, *Transformative Experience*, Yale philosopher L.A. Paul makes the point that if someone has not experienced something that is hard to imagine due to lack of similar experiences to compare to, then it is very difficult to predict what that experience would be like. The only remedy to this would be to go through the experience.

Opinions about what the experience would be like, versus what the experience is actually like for the person who finally undergoes it, usually do not converge. The connections to Spatial Computing technologies, and how it is difficult to understand them without experiencing them, is the point here. People who have not experienced Virtual Reality and/or Augmented Reality really do not have a good understanding of it, though opinions abound.

Similarly, fully understanding the benefits and utility of Spatial Computing is not possible without actually using Spatial Computing technologies. Many people have issues having to do with digital privacy and are anticipating that there will be many more problems surrounding privacy in the future. They are not wrong about this. Spatial Computing brings with it a whole slew of possible problems here that could be akin to opening up Pandora's Box. However, as we humans become more understanding of what Spatial Computing is good for, we feel that there will be a mediation and balance between individual utility and a person's boundary to digital privacy.

This boundary was severely tested recently, most notably in the Facebook-Cambridge Analytica scandal. We review the scandal in the following section, along with some other examples, in order to show what the current environment is like with regard to digital privacy.

Privacy and Security

Let's now think further about Spatial Computing's impact upon privacy and security. By understanding how the events that follow unfolded, and where the issue regarding privacy really lies, it will be easier to work through how issues regarding privacy and Spatial Computing should be addressed.

On Facebook and Cambridge Analytica

You might have heard about Cambridge Analytica, as many stories broke about it in 2018. There was a huge outcry raised by revelations that it had gathered data from millions of Facebook users, often without those users' knowledge or permission.

It then used that data to build a new kind of Facebook advertising, aimed at manipulating citizens to change their voting behavior. The details tell a cautionary tale as we head into a Spatial Computing world where even more powerful data collection and manipulation of users is possible.

The Facebook-Cambridge Analytica scandal started in June 2014, when a researcher named Aleksandr Kogan developed a personality quiz app for doing psychometric research with Facebook users, called "This Is Your Digital Life," as part of the research that he was doing at the Psychometrics Centre at Cambridge University. That center had been doing a lot of social media research and had created several apps. Those apps had already shown that Facebook users could be manipulated with various content techniques that the lab had developed, and that the data collected from Facebook could show all sorts of sensitive information about people's personalities and political persuasions.

The earlier apps were built by John Rust and his team. The goal of that research, and indeed his entire 40 years spent in the field, was to warn the world about what could be done with that data and the dangers of allowing it to be so freely traded. Rust had warned the University that Kogan's app was taking the research done in the lab further than Rust was comfortable with. Kogan's app slurped up the data from millions of Facebook users, most of whom didn't give approvals to the app for their data to be collected.

Most users didn't know that when you give these apps permission to gather data that the apps get access to your entire network of friends, which Facebook calls "the social graph." Facebook is built around this social graph, which is like a rolodex, but with a lot more things—from photos, posts, and other data—than a simple rolodex would have in it. The app collected the same data on each of your friends, which meant that the database could quickly grow, and it did—to 87 million users by the time it got sold to a new start-up named Cambridge Analytica. Most of those app users had no idea that much of their data now sat in Kogan's databases.

As the developer on this app, Kogan could access data about the users who downloaded it and used it, along with the data of their friends too. "It would go into their entire friend network and pull out all of their friends' data as well," says Christopher Wylie, one of the founders of Cambridge Analytica—now a whistleblower. "The company itself was founded by using Facebook data."

The collection of data on so many people without their knowledge is one thing, but what Cambridge Analytica did with that data was a whole other matter. Kogan learned a whole lot about how to use psychometrics to manipulate voters. Psychometrics is the science of measuring people's mental and psychological traits, strengths, and weaknesses. When he sold the data to Cambridge Analytica, he also helped the company use the user manipulation techniques that the lab had also been studying.

When Kogan's app asked for that data, it saved that information into a private database instead of immediately deleting it. Kogan provided that private database, containing information on about 50 million Facebook users, to the voter-profiling company Cambridge Analytica, which used it to make 30 million psychographic profiles about voters. This was laid out in several articles by the New York Times, the Wall Street Journal, the Guardian, and Robinson Meyer in the Atlantic.

"We would know what kinds of messaging you will be susceptible to and where you're going to consume that. And then how many times you need to touch that to change how you think about something. It is a full-service propaganda machine," Wylie has said.

The Cambridge Analytica scandal showed Facebook had been playing fast and loose with private data, and this saw its stock price drop by $100 billion in value in the space of just one day—at that time about 12 percent of its value—on March 26, 2018 (although it subsequently bounced back). It wasn't the only thing that caused market outrage at Facebook, either, but it was the one that finally got the public to understand that Facebook shared data with more than just itself or other users on the system, and that knowledge dramatically reduced trust in the system and encouraged a new movement.

Since the Cambridge Analytica scandal, the cry "delete Facebook" has been alive on blogs, in media, and on Twitter. People including Cher, Elon Musk, Will Ferrell, WhatsApp cofounder Brian Acton, Rosie O'Donnell, Apple cofounder Steve Wozniak, and tech journalist Walt Mossberg, among others, have announced they have deleted their Facebook accounts and urged others to do the same in Tweets with a #DeleteFacebook hashtag. #DeleteFacebook people often remind you on Tweets, and elsewhere, that Facebook follows you around the internet, building a dossier on you so that it can sell to advertisers using targeting techniques, and that the service watches everything you do to help make its advertising system more efficient. This alone gets some people, like David Heinemeier Hansson, otherwise known as "DHH" on Twitter, to go apoplectic in their urging that Facebook be deleted or be closed down or broken up. In one Tweet in January he wrote, "Every targeted ad is a privacy violation and constitutes the sale of personal data."

In another privacy scandal in 2018, Facebook shared data with other companies like Amazon, Spotify, Netflix, and Bing, giving these companies special access to users' data without anyone else knowing. Why? To get even more data on users so that Facebook's ad targeting system would work even better.

But why does this all cause outrage? In our research, many people really hate being digitally targeted by ads. Many tell us about doing searches for something, like a ski trip, and then ads for skis or four-wheel-drive cars follow you around no matter where you go on the web. Lots of people don't like this kind of targeted advertising, nor do they like that it follows you in a process that the industry calls "retargeting."

It's one thing to have a few corporations following you around as you move around the web, pushing ads in your face. To some that actually might be helpful, if it were something you needed, although invariably the process isn't perfect so you get ads for a car or coffeemaker you just bought, which is both freaky that the system knew you were just showing interest in something like that, and sad because it didn't get it right. However, when similar techniques are used for political manipulation, it brings a whole new level of outrage because the act degrades our democracy and our own part in choosing who we want to represent us.

Then there are a variety of other concerns about Facebook as well, including that it has been built to addict users and take advantage of how their brains work. Salesforce CEO Marc Benioff even said "You can see Facebook is the new cigarettes for our society. It's something that badly needs to be regulated. They're certainly not exactly about truth in advertising. Even they have said that. That's why we're really in a crisis of trust." Academics back up that claim: a study published in November 2019 from Stanford University and New York University even found that quitting Facebook is good for your mental health (http://web.stanford.edu/~gentzkow/research/facebook.pdf).

With Spatial Computing in the offing, especially when it comes to devices we will wear on our eyes that will bring us some mixture of analog and Virtual Reality, these issues become even more amplified. Soon we might see virtual ads on every surface in our lives, and we will have visualizations that can bend what we think of as real, and that present powerful new challenges for the human brain, from potential new addiction problems to inabilities to tell the virtual from the real.

We have done a lot of thinking about privacy when it comes to Spatial Computing, and here are a few of the issues that will come up as we move to living more and more of our lives in some form of digital reality, along with new ways of living, assisted by autonomous vehicles, robots, and synthetic beings.

In the future, it will be possible for big companies and governments to collect a much more complete set of data about you. Where today's systems have to read your comments, follow you around with location-tracking systems, or watch what you like or follow, in our Spatial Computing future these same companies and governments will know a lot about your health. Collecting your heart rate and DNA is just the start. Imagine a set of companies knowing everything you touch, look at, or eat.

And, in the Spatial Computing world, these companies and governments could know a lot more about every social interaction you ever have. Meet someone in the street? It takes note. Go on a date with someone? Play a game? Make a video call? All of this could potentially get tracked in great detail. Eventually the system could deeply know who your business associates, friends, lovers, and infrequently met friends are, your exact activities, and the content of your life.

Furthermore, in the future you will be wearing devices that can present such compelling visuals and audio that present new powerful capabilities. In our other chapters, we discussed how VR is being used to treat a variety of brain ailments, from PTSD to dementia. With such powerful positive capabilities also comes some negative ones. These could be used to manipulate people in a much more complete way than how Cambridge Analytica did with Facebook ads.

There are some choices that we'll have to make over the next decade, as we start to live more of our lives with digital interfaces all around: do we want to have every action we take studied, particularly when we go into stores? Already Amazon Go stores watch literally every step, every touch, every look we make at products. That lets Amazon build powerful new databases about our lifestyles and brand choices that can reveal things about ourselves we didn't even know. Target, the New York Times reported, knew of one young woman's pregnancy before she told her father, based on her buying behavior. Are we ready for other such revelations?

Another choice we'll have to make is associated with advertising. Advertising, at its core, is trying to urge you to take actions you didn't know you wanted to make. "Drink Coke," an ad urges, and does so in compelling ways and at compelling times, like when you are sitting down in a movie theater.

Will we choose systems that have such deep advertising links into every part of our lives? Will there be any control or choice? For instance, instead of seeing a virtual Coke ad at the beginning of a movie, will we have the control to say "please don't show me any more Coke ads, replace them with messages reminding me to drink more water instead, or, don't show me any ad at all"?

Finally, we soon will have virtual transactions on top of both real things ("hey robot, can you bring me a hamburger") and virtual ones, like buying a virtual costume to wear in a virtual world, or a virtual boat ride—something that's already possible in one of the Virtual Reality metaverses we've been in. Whenever we carry out one of these transactions, do we want corporations and governments to know about it? Well, governments will be hard to keep out of these things, but Apple will certainly try to become the main payment processor with Apple Pay. It won't be alone trying to become the main way we buy things.

Of course, we will use systems that do all this stuff, particularly if they provide great utility in return, but as we start to use Spatial Computing glasses and use them to order up all sorts of things, from hamburgers, to music, to new kinds of entertainment, and as we use them to control and visualize a new world with robots and autonomous vehicles, the consequences of giving up our data will be even more discussed, challenged, and questioned.

On the other hand, in the world that COVID-19 brought us, Facebook in April 2019 loosened up its rules and is sharing a new set of location data with researchers. This new information set shows whether people are staying at home and provides a probability that people in one area will come in contact with people in another.

Let's check out another example that shows the power of the data we are constantly generating.

OJ Simpson and Location Data

OJ Simpson was a fugitive from justice on June 17, 1994. The police had an arrest warrant for him, as he was a suspect in the murder of his ex-wife Nicole Brown Simpson and her friend Ron Goldman. On that day, Al Cowlings, OJ Simpson's close friend, was driving his white Ford Bronco on a number of Los Angeles freeways, with OJ Simpson in the passenger seat. Cowlings reportedly made a call to 911, saying that Simpson was armed, with a gun pointed to his own head, demanding that Cowlings drive him to Simpson's estate in Brentwood or Simpson would kill himself. That call was traced to the Santa Ana Freeway. Cowlings made several other calls that were also traced, and police officer Ruth Dixon caught up with them northbound on Interstate 405.

How was his car found? Cell phone tower triangulation. The way cell phones work is they broadcast their location to towers nearby. One to three towers picks up the signal and the system itself tracks each phone and hands it off to new towers or "cells" as its user drives around. This data can't be encrypted, because if it were, the system the way it is currently set up wouldn't be able to effectively work. The triangulation that caught OJ Simpson was accurate enough to focus police attention on a single freeway.

These days, police have even more location data to use, since each smartphone not only uses cell phone triangulation, which isn't very accurate, but has a GPS chip inside that reports its location via services and apps. Apple, for instance, tracks cell phone location for its "Find My iPhone" service, and many mapping apps record your location, as well. Some, like Verizon, even sell real-time data feeds that are discerned from this data to other companies like Google, which uses this data to figure out traffic conditions. While that data is cleaned of personally identifiable information, it could be discerned who is associated with that data later on by piecing together other data about users.

Soon, with Spatial Computing glasses on many people, and autonomous cars and robots rolling around, police will have even more tools to find people, and at least one company, Banjo, is demonstrating how they can find people within seconds without even using personally identifiable information—more on that a little later in this chapter.

Let's get into another example.

Apple and the FBI

It started with a 2015 terrorist shooting in San Bernardino and ended with the FBI filing a lawsuit to get Apple to unlock an iPhone owned by a suspect. Fourteen people were killed during that shooting, and the FBI wanted more information about the shooters and who else they could be connected with.

After the shooting was over, several phones were collected, most of which had been destroyed by the shooters. One that had survived, an iPhone 5C, was studied deeply in an effort to find information about what was behind the killings. Apple was then served with a court order to turn over information from the phone and account of the owner, which it did. Apple worked with the FBI before the lawsuit was filed and helped it uncover a bunch of metadata from encrypted files on the phone, along with what they could get from the cloud account that was associated with the phone.

The FBI, though, soon wanted more. It wanted Apple to unlock the phone itself, which would let the FBI look at all the data and files on the phone. Apple actually did work with the FBI, who tried to get Apple to back up the data and files because backups aren't encrypted, but the officials who were studying the phone had already taken steps to reset the iCloud password. It turns out that if you reset an iCloud password, the only way for a phone to backup is to put in a new password in the phone. However, a new password will not be accepted if passcode protection was enabled by the phone's owner, and this is what happened in this case.

Months later, the FBI filed a lawsuit to attempt to get Apple to unlock the phone or add a backdoor that law enforcement could use to force a phone to unlock and decrypt any encrypted data stored inside. Apple's executives had already met to decide what to do if Apple was ever asked to provide a backdoor. Obviously, Apple wanted to provide any data it could to help catch and stop more terrorist acts and knew that the public might not understand a nuanced argument about backdoors, encryption, and privacy rights, but Apple had decided to hold the line when it came to the phone unlock itself.

Tim Cook, Apple's CEO, ardently argued that civil liberties were at threat with the ask from the FBI, and said about it, "So the act of banning or limiting or putting a back door in—a back door is any vulnerability that if I can get in, that means somebody else can... No one should have a key that turns a billion locks. It shouldn't exist." Cook felt that giving up privacy for security meant exposing "99 percent of good people." The FBI withdrew its case after government officials reported a third party had managed to unlock the iPhone, leaving the case without a clear legal precedent.

This issue will keep coming up, especially when we move more of our computing to Spatial Computing glasses. More of our data will be encrypted and, sometimes, police and other government officials will desperately want to unencrypt that data to catch terrorists, or other criminals. Apple is making the strongest defense of privacy as we move into this new age and it'll be interesting to see if it can keep holding the line.

Today, Apple is facing different demands from the public and the government due to COVID-19 that show its privacy philosophies in a different light. In April 2020, it announced that along with Google, Apple will be adding a tracking system into its iOS operating system that runs inside every modern iPhone. This system will track COVID-19 spread, allowing users to share data through Bluetooth Low Energy transmissions and via approved apps from health organizations. This will allow phones to share lots of data with other phones that are in close proximity with each other. Official apps from public health authorities will get access to this data, and users who download them can report if they've been diagnosed with COVID-19.

This could be a new way for governments to get some new backdoor-like access to mobile phones, and at the time we went to press, it was unclear that these efforts would remain totally voluntary or what would happen to these kinds of efforts and databases in the future. In many places, police were issuing tickets to those at places like parks or beaches, and these apps could be used to prove to police where you live and that you were properly following the social distancing rules in place while the novel coronavirus remains a threat to the health of citizens.

Privacy has long been balanced by security. A parent whose child has been kidnapped would gladly hand over all sorts of personal information in an attempt to get the child back. Sometimes, the privacy ask is too big and doesn't represent enough of a public good to be worth the trade-off, and hopefully these examples have demonstrated some of those decision points. Next, we'll look at identity and ownership, which will back up the trade-offs made in privacy and security.

Identity and Ownership

To have dependable privacy and security, identity and ownership roles need to be defined strongly in tech systems and apps. It's like a building. If you want strong security or high privacy, the identity of everyone who enters that building needs to be known, as well as the ownership rights, or usage rights, for access points in that building. Here we discuss some areas where identity and ownership discussions have changed recently due to the growing use of particular radical new technology.

Blurred Faces on Google Street View

You might have seen a Google Maps car roll by. It has a ball of cameras on top of a car that's being driven around, capturing images and taking other data for its maps and Google Street View. While it's legal to capture images of people in public streets, these new captures have raised a number of new privacy debates. After all, most of our public photography laws were written during a time when capturing images of people required an act of pushing a button on a camera, not driving down the street slurping up everything the camera sees.

Back in 2009, Privacy International's Simon Davies argued that Google should have obtained consent from everyone who is featured in such photos, and so have various other people and governments, including Switzerland's data protection commissioner, Hanspeter Thüer. Most of those arguments have gotten thrown out by courts, or fixed by technology that is much better at blurring out people's faces, along with other identifiable information, like car license plates, which Google has done for its Street View.

In the United States, efforts to get these cameras banned has also been refused because US law allows photography in places where there isn't a clear expectation of privacy. In a world of robots, autonomous cars, and people walking around with Spatial Computing glasses, we are going to see a public street that is mapped out in real time and in great detail.

Already, this is happening because of self-driving vehicles. Zoox, Waymo, Tesla, and others have already shown off new "high-definition maps" that have extremely high precision, with everything imaged down to centimeter level from signs, to potholes, to barriers. As newer cars drive by you, they are also watching you, categorizing you as a pedestrian, bicyclist, runner, and even getting more details like gender and age, which can be used to predict your next likely action. A child is more likely to run quickly into a street than, say, an 80-year-old man would.

Such a car also needs to identify certain people differently than others. Police officers, garbage truck workers, road crews—all will be tracked by cars rolling by. There's a good chance that lots of others will be caught by the cameras on these cars and broadcast to others, too, and it's not clear that their faces will always be blurred. Already we are seeing Teslas capturing other cars on roads and broadcasting their images, along with people walking next to the car, or, worse, criminally damaging the car. This could lead to new privacy fights.

As Spatial Computing glasses get added to the mix, having similar technology to self-driving and mapping vehicles, we'll see new databases being made of people on the streets, leading to new concerns about privacy. At Facebook, they are planning for a day when your glasses will recognize a friend you meet, and will show you things like their last post, or present the opportunity to play a new kind of game with them, too. In February 2020, Facebook bought a new start-up, Scape, which already showed such a multiplayer game you could play with friends in the street. It isn't clear what would happen if someone new walked into the game, especially if someone is broadcasting that game to others on Facebook.

China and Facial Recognition

People who have never been to China have little idea just how much more aggressively China uses technology than other countries. Citizens no longer use credit cards. Everything is purchasable via WeChat; in America, many businesses don't yet accept Apple Pay. In the cities of China, even street vendors take payments via WeChat and no one carries cash anymore. The Chinese government aims to have even rural villages go cashless by the end of 2020. It is with the uses of facial recognition and Artificial Intelligence, though, that the differences in technology usage between China and other countries is even more extreme. While in the United States, Facebook has had facial recognition technology since its $100 million purchase of Face.com in 2012, uses outside of China have been fairly muted, and there's a resistance to facial recognition in many places that simply doesn't exist in China. Cities like San Francisco have even banned its use by governmental agencies.

Within the next 10 to 15 years, though, millions of cameras are forecasted to be moving around the large cities in the world via autonomous vehicles. Some autonomous vehicles, like those from Waymo, have 19 cameras, not to mention other sensors, and during the 2030s, we should see tracking capabilities that will make what's going on in China today seem pretty quaint.

Many Westerners might key in on the human rights abuses that come with China's use of this technology, and these abuses are worth focusing attention on—whether it is its harsh crackdown on ethnic Muslims in its Western region, or its forced hospitalization of people who were tested with an elevated body temperature as the novel coronavirus outbreak started being taken seriously, or the tracking of literally every move of citizens and the building of a social score of each. But it is the range of uses that we are focused on here. Everything from access controls at schools, factories, airports, and other places, to even using facial recognition in soda vending machines to enable quicker transactions.

If you are in China, though, citizens there will likely point out the time in 2018 when technology using facial recognition located a criminal suspect who was attending a concert by pop star Jacky Cheung. The system recognized the suspect, who was identified as only Mr. Ao out of a crowd of 60,000 concertgoers. It is not the only example in China of catching suspects with facial recognition. In 2017, police in Shandong province arrested 25 suspects using a system set up at the Qingdao International Beer Festival.

Hundreds of millions of cameras are used in this facial recognition system throughout China, and the Chinese government forces its citizens to register their face when they pick up their phones, making for easy facial capture and registration. During the novel coronavirus outbreak, new uses came to the public's attention where citizens are tracked via apps on their phones, facial recognition, and other Spatial Computing technology.

One Chinese Deep Learning software company that makes many of the facial recognition systems China uses, Megvii, has filed to go public and has contracts to run cameras in public housing, where its service is used to curb subletting. The company, as of June 2019, had 2,349 employees and was valued at more than $4 billion. Its product does face detection, face comparing, and face searching. It also goes beyond facial recognition, with human body detection, face merging, and photo clustering, where after recognizing faces of photos in an album, photos can be clustered based on faces automatically. It beat Google, Facebook, and Microsoft in tests of image recognition at the International Conference on Computer Vision, with its product Face++, which is the world's largest open source Computer Vision platform. Megvii has an R&D lab in Redmond, Washington, near Microsoft's campus.

With its competitors SenseTime, CloudWalk, and Yitu, Megvii has brought facial recognition even into Chinese classrooms. For instance, China Pharmaceutical University uses facial recognition for everything from students' attendance to monitoring of students' in-class performance. Its use in classrooms is controversial, even inside China, but some people think the system can help prevent dangers, reduce campus bullying, and improve teaching quality. One such system scans classrooms at Hangzhou No. 11 High School and records students' facial expressions, categorizing them as happy, angry, fearful, confused, or upset. It also records student actions such as writing, reading, raising a hand, and sleeping at a desk, even tracking them outside of classrooms—enabling the replacement of ID cards and wallets at the library and canteen.

Facial recognition in China is even being used to catch jaywalkers, but it does have flaws while doing this. In 2018, one such system caught famous Chinese businesswoman Dong Mingzhu (she made first place on Forbes list of the top 100 outstanding businesswomen in China) and put her face on a public screen dedicated to "naming and shaming" jaywalkers caught by the city of Ningbo's facial recognition system. The problem was that she never was there—the system had simply caught an image of her that had appeared on the side of a bus. Similar systems in the city of Shenzhen are also set up to send an automatic notice of a fine, along with visually shaming jaywalkers on large LED screens at intersections, to the caught jaywalker's WeChat, of course, where they can pay the fine right from their phone. How many infractions are there? The South China Morning Post reported that at just one intersection in 2018, there were 13,930 jaywalkers caught by the system in just 10 months.

Issues with Facial Recognition in the US and Europe

Looking backward, we see that China, the United States, and Europe have very different approaches to privacy. This can be seen by traveling to the three. In China, you see a very tech-centric approach literally everywhere, as citizens use WeChat to pay for everything, and on many streets, grids of cameras watch everything. The use of smartphones is heavier in streets and on public transport than you'll see elsewhere, too.

In China, citizens don't have the right to freedom of speech like United States citizens do, and every word posted online is read by either a person or some Machine Learning algorithmic software that decides whether the posts can stay up or not. Behind the scenes, China has blocked most outside web services. Facebook, Google, Twitter, and LinkedIn are usually blocked for citizens there, and it has developed its own versions of each, or in the case of WeChat, a service that really does the same as several of the services in one: shopping, payments, a social network, and a health tracker all in one app. This is backed up in China by extensive use of facial recognition and surveillance tracking. Citizens know they are being tracked literally everywhere, and Machine Learning algorithms even give each citizen a "social score," so if citizens post things that aren't allowed, or perform things that the government doesn't want done, even like jaywalking a street, their social score goes down. If it goes down low enough, they can be blocked from services, or even the ability to use public transit or take domestic or international flights.

Such a set of systems would be impossible to imagine in the United States, and particularly Europe, where the EU has written laws that protect the privacy rights of citizens. Travel through Germany, too, and you see a much higher percentage of people who still read newspapers, rather than the mobile phone usage you see in China, and you can see a different set of attitudes and adoption rates toward technology.

On the other hand, Europe is ahead of the United States in using technology to transact. Apple Pay, and other mobile-based payments, work literally everywhere in Europe, due to Europe's much more ubiquitous adoption of contactless payment systems by even street vendors, taxis, and restaurants. The United States has not seen usage by most of these kinds of vendors yet.

These differences in transactional affordances, in the law, and in penalties, set us up for making some predictions about how much resistance each legal system will have to Spatial Computing devices, which include various forms of smart glasses, along with robots, drones, and vehicles that use Computer Vision, sensors, and AI algorithms for moving, or being moved, around the real world.

We can imagine that a person wearing glasses with several cameras (Qualcomm already has shown a reference design with seven), controlling robots, and self-driving vehicles will be more immediately accepted in China than in Germany, and developers who make the systems that run on each will need to have different systems for different laws. Already, Tesla's autopilot systems turn off features in the EU due to stricter laws than they have in, say, California. We can see one day, coming within a few years, where in Beijing and Shanghai a large percentage of the population will be wearing Spatial Computing devices almost everywhere, yet in Munich or London, we'll see much lighter usage, and much stricter laws for how devices communicate in terms of, say, that they are recording or broadcasting.

We talked with Avi Bar-Zeev, Microsoft HoloLens co-inventor and former senior manager of AR prototyping for Apple, on what the reception might be to people wearing AR glasses in the near future. He believes that there should be an opt-in system for people that is relevant to whether or not someone has the right to take a photo or video of you while you are on a public street. While we don't feel as strongly with him on this point, we do recognize that there are others that probably do.

One privacy law worth digging into, due to the fact that it will impact the way in which Spatial Computing sees adoption over the next decade, is the GDPR, or General Data Protection Regulation, which the EU started using in 2018. The GDPR says that your privacy is a right that will be protected by law, and that corporations and others that collect your data need to do so lawfully, with fairness and transparency. To be compliant with all of this, corporations need to get consent from users, notify them of breaches, let them access their data, let them delete it, (or have the system "forget" them), let them take their data elsewhere or be "portable," and have privacy deeply built into their systems.

Luciano Floridi, Professor of Philosophy and Ethics of Information and Director of the Digital Ethics Lab at the Oxford Internet Institute at the University of Oxford, who has consulted governments on digital privacy, told us that Europeans are adapting very well to GDPR, however, more work needs to be done to make future regulations flexible to allow for continuing European technical innovation.

The United States allowed a far more open system to collecting data, providing very few laws before GDPR when it came to the collecting of, and playing fast and loose with, privacy. This allowed companies like Facebook, Google, Amazon, Netflix, and others to get going and to build massive databases of people's data, from what they buy to what they say online in social networks, to what they watch in the evening on TV. That, in return, enabled the creation of massive new targeted advertising systems, particularly at Google and Facebook, that got built before the GDPR turned on in 2018.

Today we are viewing a new set of challenges to privacy that even the GDPR doesn't protect against, with cars that have neural networks and dozens of cameras and sensors that can slurp up all sorts of information, including whether you put your garbage cans out on the curb or not. Tesla added that capability to its entire fleet in 2019. At the time of writing, Tesla had sold 500,000 cars with this capability, and its network alone has the ability to do a lot more object and, potentially, facial recognition.

We're already seeing facial recognition being adopted, even in the more privacy-conservative Europe. It's being used in shopping malls, supermarkets, airports, and by police who have millions of cameras to monitor. One French city, Nice, even adopted it citywide. This adoption needs to be compared to the legislation that came with GDPR, because GDPR set the tone for other laws in other countries. In the United States, California followed the GDPR with its own set of laws—the California Consumer Privacy Act (CCPA), which is comparatively much more lenient in terms of company fines for privacy infractions.

GDPR and CCPA lay the beginnings of a new regulatory framework that will be needed when it comes to new Spatial Computing technologies. This is true whether we are discussing glasses or various other head-mounted displays with their array of cameras and sensors, or other Spatial Computing technologies, including autonomous vehicles and robots, all of which gather massive amounts of data on our streets, in new virtual metaverses, AR Clouds, and with virtual beings that will interact with us. These earlier laws will still be needed, but with new ones tacked on to cover these new technologies. Necessary laws would cover what can be done with facial, and other identity recognition, and data from new sensors, whether ones that watch our eyes, or 3D sensors that can map out our homes, offices, and other places in great detail.

This gap became apparent as we researched dozens of cases where live facial recognition is used, both in the United States and in Europe, and we picked a few that demonstrate how the technology is being used across each continent. In the United States, we see use cases including police preventing human trafficking. Police departments tend to be big proponents of such technology, both in the United States and in Europe, because of the power of facial recognition to pick faces out of the crowd. Police camera manufacturer Wolfcom has contracts with 1,500 organizations and is pitching body cameras with live facial recognition to them. Competitor Axon, the largest manufacturer of body cameras in the United States, declared in 2019 that it would not put the invasive technology in its hardware, citing "serious ethical concerns." Meanwhile California, Oregon, and New Hampshire have outlawed the use of facial recognition technology in body cams.

This use case won't stay only in police hands for long. Facebook has an internal strategy guide for its future Spatial Computing plans where it has drawings of how friends will recognize others in the street by wearing glasses with cameras on them, and some form of facial recognition plays a big role in its plans to enable new kinds of large-scale games that you can play with others in parks.

For now, however, we wait for these more fun uses of facial recognition and note that it was used to identify someone, later identified as Larry Griffin, who left a package that looked like a bomb in a New York subway in August 2019. His name and photos were sent to the cell phones of every cop in New York and he was arrested in the Bronx the same day and charged with three counts of planting a false bomb.

Facial recognition was also used in a variety of other police or security cases, from identifying the man charged in the deadly shooting at the Capital Gazette's newsroom, to Taylor Swift using facial recognition to identify stalkers. A kiosk, it reported, was set up for fans to view videos of her. Inside the kiosk were cameras that took photos of those fans, then sent the images back to an office in Nashville where the images were cross-referenced with a database of people who had been identified as potential stalkers of the pop star.

Across the Atlantic Ocean, uses are similar. Police at Scotland Yard, the headquarters of London's Metropolitan Police Service, will soon begin using live facial recognition technology in London to help identify criminal suspects. The Metropolitan Police has claimed that 80 percent of people surveyed backed the move, the Guardian news organization reported, rejecting claims that the scheme was a "breathtaking assault on rights." Nearby, in South Wales, police already use live facial recognition, and judges have ruled in favor of the technology.

Another example of the use of facial recognition in Europe is in retail stores. A Budgens supermarket in Aylesbury, Buckinghamshire, UK, had problems with shoplifting. The manager installed a facial recognition system called Facewatch, which warns him if a "subject of interest" walks into the store. If that happens, a manager asks them to leave. The manager there says the technology makes life easier. When he opened his shop, he would have things stolen every day or two, but since he introduced the system it's become less common. Plus, his staff feels safer, he said, especially late at night, which is good for team morale.

Airports around the world are seeing facial recognition systems pop up. One of Europe's busiest airports, Amsterdam's Schiphol, is testing facial recognition boarding. Soon passengers will be able to walk through customs and other security areas without pulling out their passports, thanks to the technology. We've seen similar systems show up in San Francisco, and in Dubai.

Along these lines it is useful to look at a Utah company, Banjo, for evidence of how aggressive the United States could be in its use of Artificial Intelligence, Computer Vision, and huge datasets. Banjo analyzes all sorts of data from the government, including traffic cameras and other cameras. It built an AI system that looks for "anomalies" or things that are unusual. Banjo's marketing promises to alert law enforcement of crimes as they happen. Unlike the Chinese systems that track people as they walk around the streets, Banjo claims they can make these reports within seconds while not infringing on anyone's privacy. Its technology, called "Live Time Intelligence," can supposedly identify and potentially help police solve a bunch of crimes in real time.

We could imagine a Banjo-like system being used by a Google or an Apple, or an upstart like Tesla, to share interesting "patterns" on top of a map. A future system, if it had enough data, could tell you where hot nightclubs are, where rich people get their clothes laundered, and where police are.

Today Banjo does similar stuff to this, but only for government agencies, and usually to help see crimes taking place. Its system does this by ingesting tons of video, audio, and text feeds into the system, and its system has been trained to look for patterns of behavior. Banjo demonstrated how an earlier form of the system could have noticed a mass shooting was happening because of patterns of how people were moving about, sound analysis, and even social media activity from the area. It is a heavy user of video feeds from traffic and security cameras and, in Utah, its home state, it already has contracts with government organizations for access to these feeds, both at a state level–in the case of traffic cameras–and local levels, for security camera access. In July of 2019, it signed a $20.7 million contract with Utah for just this kind of data collection. Banjo's pitch to governments is that the more data that's fed into it, the better its product will work. It also has access to all the 911 calls and systems.

The datasets that Banjo could use are about to get radically larger as car companies add more cameras, along with AI capabilities, to cars, like Tesla already has, and the number of these camera-equipped cars on the road increases. Soon, every few seconds a car will roll by with one of these setups. Ford's CTO, Ken Washington, told us that it is putting such a setup into most of the new Ford Mustang E's that will be sold starting in 2021.

With both Banjo and a similar company, Clearview AI, which does very quick face matching using millions of photos, largely for police purposes also, the thing that bothers many people is how they collect their data.

Banjo, it was revealed, collected data from a variety of apps, made by a company called Pink Unicorn Labs, which was associated with Banjo, but neither that affiliation nor the data capture was disclosed to users. Pink Unicorn Labs' apps asked users to connect them to their social networks.

That act enabled the company to have their systems slurp up data from friends of these users, in much the same way that Cambridge Analytica did. Companies collecting our data without our knowledge, though, might soon be the least of our problems when it comes to our data privacy. Especially in the COVID-19 world that now exists, privacy rules are being thrown out left and right. No longer do you see #DeleteFacebook hashtags on Twitter and other places and governments have halted US data privacy efforts across tech companies. Google and other companies have launched a bunch of new efforts, and even the US Centers for Disease Control and Prevention now have gone Digital with a new system to track the spread of COVID-19 around the United States.

Similar efforts were already done in other countries like Singapore and South Korea. In Singapore the government has a map of the COVID-19 spread that anyone can look up to see if they might be at risk.

As we head into the Spatial Computing age, with AR headsets, autonomous vehicles, and robots capturing and receiving massive amounts of data, with an array of up to 30 cameras and sensors on each, we'll see new capabilities for governments and companies to watch and track us than ever before.

Human Social Good

How do we, as responsible human beings, navigate between protecting our digital privacy and garnering the benefits that could be received by sharing data, both on an individual and wider societal level?

This question cannot be answered in a general way; the actual context in which data is being asked for is extremely relevant to answering it. And then, operationally speaking, it will take some kind of body of peers to enforce what has been decided would be appropriate for human social good.

We spoke with Dan Ariely, James B. Duke Professor of Behavioral Economics at Duke University, about these very issues. The way to think about human decision-making, from his perspective, is that human beings are not rational from a practical and behavioral perspective, but rather irrational, rife with biases and blind spots. Human beings tend to have irrational fears that are then used to make decisions with. Because of this, beneficial opportunities are lost—opportunities that not only could benefit an individual, but rather a whole society.

An example that he used was that when a person visits a doctor with an ailment and the doctor asks that person questions about their health, there is very little worry about answering the doctor's questions, in effect, providing the doctor with data.

Exchange that with having a way to anonymize massive amounts of health data in order to find a cure for a disease and a significant amount of people have a problem with agreeing to provide their health data for this outcome. How is all of this connected to Spatial Computing?

With Spatial Computing, the amount of different kinds of data—from audio to textual to visual—that could be collected is enormous. In the wrong hands, that kind of information could be used in hacks to destroy whole communities and societies. Greedy, unrestrained companies could exploit that data for profit and destroy a person's piece of mind. However, in the right hands for the right purposes, benefits to individuals and societies could truly be vast and transformational.

When we asked the futurist Jason Silva what social project would be at the top of his list with which massive amounts of analyzed data could greatly be addressed, he very quickly answered with, "climate change." Brad Templeton, Futurist-in-chief at Electronic Frontier Foundation and Chair of Networks and Computers at Singularity University, told us that traffic patterns in large cities could be changed enormously for the better if there was some kind of massive organization of and analyses of large amounts of relevant data. But, governments tend to lag when it comes to investing in technology for societal change. The time lag between the wonderful things that are possible to be done at this time and when a very small portion of those things are put in motion to be done is very well known to anyone who has worked in politics and/ or a very large bureaucratic organization.

So, how do we, as human beings, figure out what projects should be addressed with the use of data and then how to get them done? Ariely believes that it is best done by getting the top minds and experts in the relevant disciplines together to serve in societal peer review boards. They would produce recommendations to people as to how they should view company and organizational requests for their data and aid them in their decision-making in this regard. There are many issues that arise, ranging from the organizational to the practical, to how effective advice would be versus legal enforcement. All people, whether they are good with technology or not, will increasingly need to be able to make decisions about what they should do with their data. The true age of personalization is here, and with Spatial Computing it will become even more pronounced and perfected.

Along with Brian Green, Director of Technology Ethics at the Markkula Center for Applied Ethics at Santa Clara University, we foresee that beyond governments and other organizations getting involved in Spatial Computing privacy and ownership issues, religious leaders and religious orders will as well—with the Roman Catholic Church already joining forces in February 2020 with Microsoft and IBM to collaborate on ethical "human-centered" ways of designing AI.

Somewhere in the farther future, when the dignity and rights of human-like robots becomes an issue, human beings can look back to see if the groundwork for Spatial Computing conventions, laws, and opportunities was laid down properly for human social good. It may be that at that time, robots do achieve consciousness as David Chalmers, Professor of Philosophy at New York University, believes they could. We had better start preparing for that possibility now as Spatial Computing grows in sophistication and human usefulness.

Epilogue

In small ways and big ways, our world is about to change. The 2020s are already seeing more change than we've seen in decades, and it is the technology presented here that will drive change at an even faster pace. In a few years, our kids will learn more in a few minutes, wearing Augmented Reality glasses, than many of us learned in an hour in the books and classrooms of old.

Looking at the seven industry verticals we discussed here, there are some commonalities. All benefit from new 3D tools and new ways to work, learn, and live together, thanks to new realities. All will become more efficient, from running a factory, to delivering goods, to getting rides to grandma's house. These changes are profound and needed in order to solve the problems of tomorrow.

There are some major commonalities we are seeing that run, or will run, across all seven industry verticals, which will then extend into the consumer base. The increase in valuing virtual communication and worlds, ultimately reaching a level only previously reserved for the real physical world, is the top commonality. What does it mean to Main Street USA, Germany, China, or India, or indeed anywhere else, beyond that we expect to see many people walking around with some sort of new device on their face? Beyond what we just discussed in this book, as we dug into the changes that seven industries are already seeing due to Spatial Computing?

As the 2020s opened, we saw an explosion in two-dimensional virtual activity, as COVID-19 convinced us all to stay home for months, opening the door to working, educating, entertaining and eating, all at home. As we write these final paragraphs, many physical conferences and other events were being closed down or delayed, with many opting to put on a virtual conference.

In March 2020, we heard that food delivery startups were seeing such explosive growth in usage that they were hiring 20 percent more people every week, and Slack's founder and CEO, among others, shared massive growth numbers, as billions of people around the world discovered how to keep in touch with coworkers, friends, family, and others, via modern tools.

The profound shifts are painful at times, but the move to virtual events leaves us optimistic that more people can get access to the latest education, whether in industry or in new virtual classrooms from universities and other places.

We see this new arc of virtual freedom, which is another commonality continuing to expand, as Spatial Computing is more fully realized within the next three-to-five years with Augmented and Virtual Reality-based objects, assistants, and experiences, and much more. Freedom will come to mean that we will be able to do more, with more people, and do it faster, without being tied down to any particular physical location. Everything from ordering a sandwich to listening to music will change, and radical new capabilities, like designing a new home or building a new machine, will be far easier to do thanks to the 3D tools that will be in front of all of our eyes soon.

If it were only the visuality that is changing due to these new technologies, that would alone be a pretty sizable shift. After all, a few decades ago desktop computers and Windows, or rather, the Graphical User Interface, brought a very sizable shift to the world's tools and what was now possible.

This isn't just a skin-deep revolution, though. Underneath this stunning new 3D-centric world and the augmented layers on top of the existing one, is the third commonality, which includes new kinds of Artificial Intelligence algorithms and systems, Computer Vision, and other systems that fuse dozens, if not hundreds, of sensors and cameras and other information sources, and then process that by looking for patterns that many of us haven't yet dreamed of. As the 2020s open up, we are seeing cars using that technology to recognize everything from stop signs to pedestrians, and witnessing the use of facial recognition technology growing at an exponential rate.

As the 2030s arrive, these systems will recognize minute human patterns, in ways that even futurists are struggling to explain. Sometime in the future, robots based on sophisticated Spatial Computing systems will be able to effectively mimic many human activities, significantly freeing us up to do more meaningful things for ourselves and others.

With Spatial Computing, we have powerful new capabilities to bring a lot of social good to people. Climatologists can explain science to us in more immersive, and thus enlightening, ways that get us to work on our climate and environment. Doctors can predict more accurately, diagnose, and treat cancer and other diseases in new ways, and medical researchers can discover new drugs. Architects and designers can make more useful, beautiful, and efficient products, services, cars, buildings, and other products for us to use.

Spatial Computing's three commonalities of valuing the virtual, providing virtual freedom, and using data to understand our physical world have the capacity of truly changing our world in positive ways. We are very much looking forward to the changes and have appreciated this opportunity to share our knowledge with you.

Index

P

Paccar 295
pain management 250, 251, 328
Panasonic 129
Parkes, Walter 168
Paul, L.A. 342
PayPal 21
PBS 174
Penrose Studios 175, 177
Peterson, Shelley 293
Petrides, Lisa 280
Pfizer xv
Philips 248
Phillips, Everette 193, 197
Pizza Hut 220
point-of-sale (POS) 269
Pokémon Go 17, 47, 57, 105, 130, 255, 336
Pony.ai 88
Porsche Cars North America 314
Positron 171
Precision OS 247
Previsualization 178, 179
privacy xvii, 8, 36, 53, 58, 115, 183, 221,
    259, 281, 305, 317, 339, 341, 342,
    344, 345, 348-350, 353-355, 357-359
PTC 314
PTSD 243, 251, 252, 258, 346
Purdy, Douglas 257

Q

Qualcomm xvii, 34, 43, 45, 50,
115, 131, 134, 311, 335-337, 354

R

Rackspace 59
Radar 80
Radiant Images 153
Radical 206, 334
Rainisto, Roope 316
Raymond Corporation 295
RealWear 215, 289
real-world
    merging, with virtual world 179
Rec Room 37, 162, 165, 294
Re'flekt 57, 319

reminiscent therapy 251
Renault 85
Renouf, Alan 122
Retail Industry 201-233, 238, 272
return on investment (ROI) for VR 326
Reuters 263, 266
Rizzo, Dr. Albert "Skip" 252, 254, 258, 259
Rizzotto, Lucas 163
Robots, see drones and robots
Adams, Robert 303
Rosekind, Mark 79
Russell, Austin 56
Rust, John 341

S

Saatchi, Edward 175, 312
Sag, Anshel 157
Salesforce 277, 345
Samsung 51, 127, 128, 129, 328
SandBox VR 169, 170
Sansar 164
Santa Clara University 359
scalable cloud infrastructure 229
Scape 350
Schell, Jesse 275
Schiphol Airport 356
Scopis 248
Scotland Yard 356
Second Life 164, 270
Seegrid 214
SenseTime 352
SentiAR 248
Sephora 204, 205, 294, 315, 326
Sequoia Capital 89
Shasta Ventures 329
Siemens 189, 191, 196, 199
Simpson, OJ 347
Silva, Jason 359
Simultaneous Location And Mapping
    (SLAM) 17-18, 56-57, 220
Singularity University 96, 247, 359
Sinofsky, Steven 39
Siri 22, 37, 50-54, 64, 69, 97, 104, 108, 145,
    158, 160, 161, 189, 196, 303, 312,
    333, 337
Site Designer 232

Z

Made in the USA
Coppell, TX
26 May 2020